# The World of Music

# The World of Music

David Willoughby

*Eastern New Mexico University*

 Wm. C. Brown Publishers

**Book Team**

Editor *Meredith M. Morgan*
Production Editor *Michelle M. Kiefer*
Designer *Heidi J. Baughman*
Art Editor *Barbara J. Grantham*
Photo Editor *Carol M. Smith*
Permissions Editor *Vicki Krug*
Visuals Processor *Joyce E. Watters*

 **Wm. C. Brown Publishers**

President *G. Franklin Lewis*
Vice President, Publisher *George Wm. Bergquist*
Vice President, Publisher *Thomas E. Doran*
Vice President, Operations and Production *Beverly Kolz*
National Sales Manager *Virginia S. Moffat*
Advertising Manager *Ann M. Knepper*
Marketing Manager *Kathleen Nietzke*
Production Editorial Manager *Colleen A. Yonda*
Production Editorial Manager *Julie A. Kennedy*
Publishing Services Manager *Karen J. Slaght*
Manager of Visuals and Design *Faye M. Schilling*

Cover illustration, part opener illustrations and Study in Sound
illustrations by Lynda Andrus.

The credits section for this book begins on page 367, and is considered
an extension of the copyright page.

Library of Congress Catalog Card Number: 89–60405

ISBN 0–697–05176–5

Printed in the United States of America by Wm. C. Brown Publishers,
2460 Kerper Boulevard, Dubuque, IA 52001

10  9  8  7  6  5  4  3  2  1

# Table of Contents

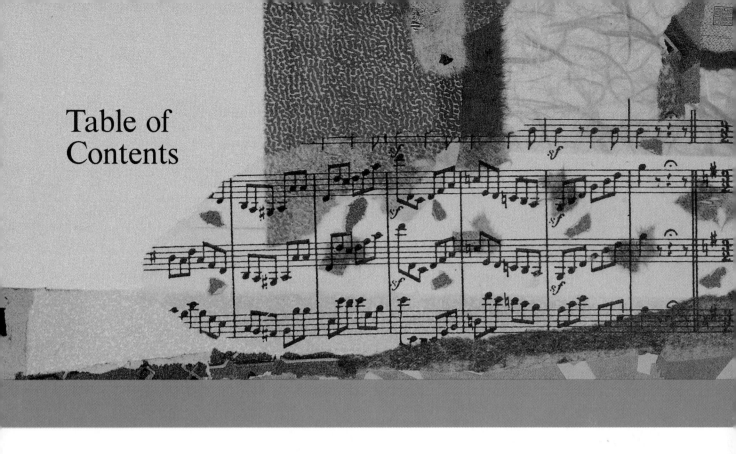

**Chapter 14**
Cultural Factors and
Functions 313

*Ways that music functions in
industry, the media, and the
community*

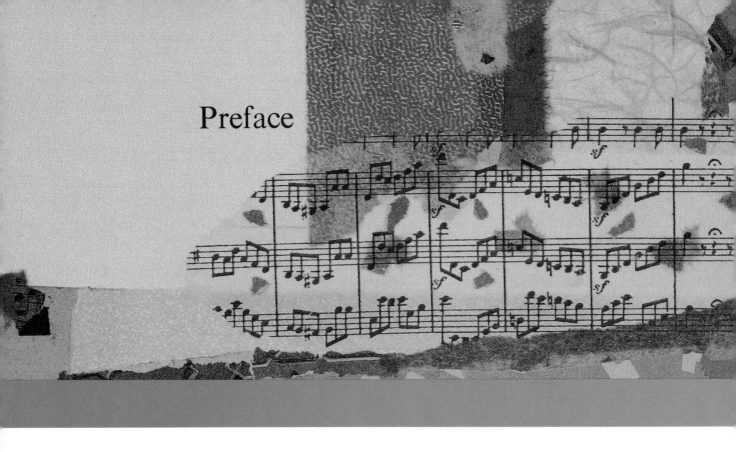

# Preface

This is a "music appreciation" text that goes beyond the traditional limits of repertoire used for music study. *The World of Music* is designed for that growing number of teachers who want to approach the development of listening skills and the study of repertoire through music as it exists in the real world. This text, rather than presenting world music, jazz, and popular music in a few pages at the back of the book, begins with "nonclassical" repertoires. This organization symbolizes that all repertoires are important, differing only in style and function, and all can be used effectively to build an understanding of the nature of music through listening.

The primary unifying strategy for *The World of Music* is the sequential development of listening skills accompanied by an increasingly sophisticated vocabulary for listening. The text does not seek to teach repertoires as much as to use them. It does seek to capture the essence of each repertoire sufficient for students to recognize the different styles, to appreciate their different functions, and to provide a solid foundation for continued learning in areas of special interest. The text, along with the *Resource Manual,* can greatly enhance continued learning on the part of the instructor, for few of us have had formal training in nonclassical repertoires.

In a comprehensive book such as this, there are trade-offs. By giving added attention to nonclassical repertoires, Western European classical music has of necessity been reduced. Again, the goal is to capture the essence of the nature of classical music in its varied styles. All that is sacrificed is the quantity of information.

*The World of Music* is a textbook for introductory music listening courses designed for those not majoring in music. It presumes no prior musical training on the part of the student. Because of the broad scope and introductory level of the material, the text also is ideally suited for introductory music literature courses designed for music majors. It is worth noting, when considering the type of listening skills that this text seeks to develop, that performers and nonperformers have equal advantage. It is assumed that those who enter the course with an extensive performance experience in music typically have not developed skills for perceptive listening to repertoire any more than those who are not performers but who may be active listeners to music.

Two broad, related statements underly the philosophy and approach on which this book is based:

1. The core of the approach leads to the development of listening skills, including the ability to describe and comment on the music heard.
2. Listening skills can be taught through music of any time or place.

**Listening Skills**

The sequential development of substantive listening and descriptive skills is the central purpose of the text. It permeates all but the last chapter. More than the study of specific repertoires, it is the study, through listening, of musical concepts common to nearly all repertoires that ties the chapters together.

Listening guides comprise perhaps a fourth of the text (additional listening examples are included in the *Resource Manual*). Each guide in the Studies in Sound includes the following:

1. Background information
2. Goals for developing listening and descriptive skills
3. The listening guide, an outline of or commentary on the music and its structure and style
4. Reflections on the listening experiences

The musical examples are presented in two categories:

1. The Study in Sound in each of chapters 1–13 includes music from the recordings that accompany the text. Due to the unavailability of certain labels, some of the musical examples discussed in the book may not appear in the record set. This circumstance will be corrected in the second edition of *The World of Music*.
2. The Additional Listening examples in several chapters refer to readily available recordings of music that could not be included in the record set. Particularly in chapters 9–13, they are intended as essential rather than supplementary listening experiences.

The goals for each listening experience have been developed sequentially so that, as students progress, their listening and descriptive skills grow gradually and consistently. The guides are just that; they help lead a listening experience. Since listening can to some extent be subjective, listeners may hear music in a different way than the guide indicates; thus, multiple perceptions may be entirely valid. The reflective comments and questions are presented as an aid to enhanced perception through subsequent listening to the same or new musical examples.

The goals and reflections are meant to be flexible, intended as possibilities, and perhaps point towards a particular curricular direction. Teachers can modify them as desired and, particularly, can have students create their own reflective statements or questions for discussion.

Listening expectations progress from the most obvious concepts to those of greater sophistication. They are rooted in a vocabulary that is not dependent on printed music and that builds as much as possible on prevalent listening habits and capabilities. Expectations are based on several assumptions:

1. The least sophisticated skills are the abilities to recognize pulse and groupings of strong and weak beats (meter) and to count strong beats (bars) as a means of perceiving patterns (phrase structure and form). These skills are presented initially through perhaps the least complicated of all music—traditional folk music.

2. The ability to perceive contrast and repetition and formal structures in uncomplicated music will prepare students well to perceive more sophisticated musical concepts when studying Western European classical music presented later in the book. For example, this preparation includes recognizing simple aaba song forms, twelve-bar blues, and verse/refrain forms in folk, some jazz, and popular music prior to studying more sophisticated principles of style and structure as found in classical music.

3. Because of the extent that music to which every American listens is based on a few familiar chords, students already have an acquaintance with these sounds. Therefore, listening expectations include the ability to be aware of the concept of chord progressions, to recognize chord changes, and to identify the tonic, subdominant, and dominant chords. These expectations, too, begin with simple and clearly sounding progressions in traditional folk and folk-based religious music. This approach also develops the ability to recognize in sound when Western harmonies and chord progressions are not present.

## Repertoire

The choice of repertoire for music study is comprehensive and, hopefully, presented without bias. Such an approach communicates the importance of cultural backgrounds that are not Western European. It also acknowledges the musical validity of using music other than Western European classical music in the curriculum.

The expanded repertoire for music study represented in this text symbolizes several important notions:

1. As the twenty-first century nears, it seems logical to this author that substantive attention should be given to twentieth-century classical and popular music—the *music of our own time.*

2. America is a diverse culture, and curricula should reflect this culture as it is; thus, a strong emphasis should be given to *music of our own nation.*

3. *World music* too often means music of far away, exotic places. It does, but it also can mean music of the native Americans, of American ethnic and immigrant groups, and of Western European-derived repertoires important to our culture, such as Latin American, Hispanic music.

Because of the emphasis on expanded repertoire, choices of inclusion obviously had to be made. The text is organized so chapters, sections, or pieces can be omitted or given emphasis different from the text's to suit individual instructor's needs. In such a case, modifications can be made in the Studies in Sound to retain the sequential development of listening skills.

# Acknowledgments

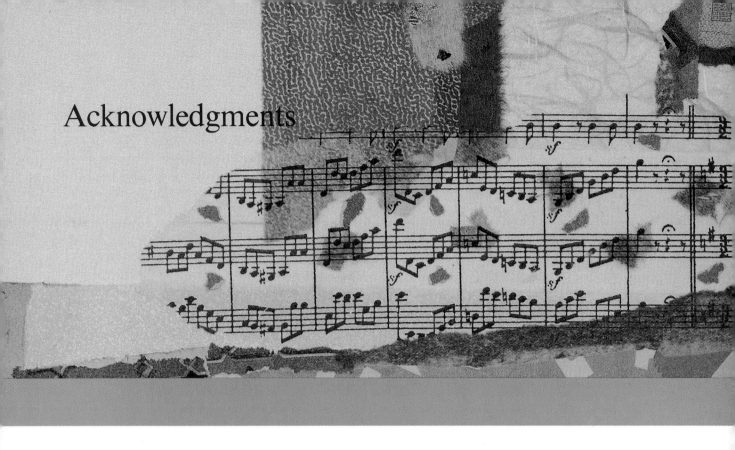

*The World of Music* is an outgrowth of influences from many professional colleagues in music. I wish to acknowledge three individuals who influenced my career direction and professional involvements relevant to the philosophy shaping this text. They are Dr. Donald Shetler of the Eastman School of Music who changed the direction of my professional thinking by rejecting all five possible dissertation topics I presented, by advising me to go to Sibley Library and read about the Contemporary Music Project (CMP), and by suggesting that I come up with one more proposal; Dr. Robert Werner who, as a result of my subsequent dissertation, took a risk and hired me as the Associate Director of the Contemporary Music Project with specific responsibilities in the area of Comprehensive Musicianship; and Dr. Barbara English Maris who, as President of the College Music Society (CMS), launched my continuing responsibilities with the Society's Music in General Studies program. I am grateful for the confidence these individuals had in my capabilities.

Having an abundance of opportunities for observing and participating with outstanding scholar/teachers through CMP Workshops and CMS Institutes significantly shaped my thinking regarding the need and responsibility to encourage a comprehensive approach to the selection of repertoire for music study. Representative of these individuals are Barbara Reeder Lundquist, James Standifer, Robert Trotter, Martin Mailman, and David Ward-Steinman.

Regarding the writing of *The World of Music,* I am very grateful to the Wm. C. Brown Publishers for its willingness to take the leap of faith in producing this text. I particularly wish to acknowledge Karen Speerstra, my original music editor, for having the confidence in my potential as a WCB author; Meredith Morgan, current music editor, who has been most helpful in many ways, especially in motivating me to give that extra effort; and Michelle Kiefer, whose impressive editorial skills helped shape the final copy.

I could not have researched the material without the resources and cooperative personnel at the Golden Library of Eastern New Mexico University.

I benefited greatly from having student secretaries and research assistants, including Ross Roberts, Carmen Medina, and Tracy Gfeller-Lindsay. Tracy deserves a special thanks for her perceptive criticisms and constructive suggestions. Her thoughts significantly helped shape the format of the listening guides.

The contributions of students in music appreciation classes over many years are standard yet critical in the development of these texts. The students in my classes cannot know the extent to which their experiences stimulated innumerable corrections and modifications but also affirmations of strategies and materials being used and, in fact, tested. I shall always be grateful for their tolerance of all the disadvantages and logistical problems associated with a textbook-in-progress: the duplicated pages, reading only from the reserve desk in the library, audio tapes that were not always readily available, the lack of attractive and convenient teaching aids available in a published version, and so on. I have often been amazed and always appreciative that the majority of students stayed with the course in spite of these inconveniences.

Finally, I must express my deepest appreciation to the following reviewers of this text:

James M. Anthony
Towson State University

George Beyer
Cypress College

Katherine Charlton
Mount San Antonio College

Stephen A. Crist
Geneva College

Lucille Field Goodman
Brooklyn College CUNY

Robert V. Howat
Wittenburg University

James A. Keene
Western Illinois University

William L. Kellogg
University of Southern California

Judy Lockhead
Stony Brook SUNY

Alan A. Luhring
University of Colorado

Frank Muller
University of Wisconsin–Parkside

David Pierce
Northern Michigan University

Jerry E. Rife
Rider College

Stephen Slawek
University of Texas–Austin

Donald E. Tyler
Central Florida Community College

Robert Weiss
Southern Illinois University

Their comments and suggestions contributed immensely to the refinements in writing style, philosophical and cultural considerations, and information. In many cases, the most critical reviewers were the most meticulous in their commentary and the most helpful in my refinements of the text. I thank them most sincerely.

# Part I
# Preparation for Listening

Music is a part of all our lives. Some people create it or perform it, but we all listen to it. Music is a part of our experience from childhood through adulthood, as part of games at recess, in the shower with no one listening, in churches and schools, or from a stereo at home or in the car. Many people have become sophisticated in their use of music by learning to play instruments and perhaps even to read music. We see, then, that experiences with music can exist with or without formal training.

The purpose of *The World of Music* is to provide training in listening to music by becoming more knowledgeable about music in general. In order to help

students become better listeners, the text seeks to accomplish the following:

1. Stimulate growth in an understanding of musical context. The text encourages a consideration of the historical background and the social, political, and economic environment of a society that may influence the creation and performance of music.

2. Cultivate an awareness of different repertoires and musical styles. The text includes music representing a variety of cultures.

3. Develop skills in listening to music intelligently. In

preparation for listening, *The World of Music* will examine:

a. In chapter 1, the marvelous variety of music when examined from a global perspective.

b. In chapter 2, the language and nature of music and how we respond to its acoustical and aesthetic qualities.

The study of music from a global perspective can enrich our lives through a deeper understanding of music but also through an increased awareness of music as it relates to various cultural groups within the United States and beyond.

# Chapter 1
# The Infinite Variety of Music

The purpose of this chapter and this book is to gain an awareness of the diversity of this world's music, particularly of the various musics important to large or small groups of people in American society.

Many kinds of music exist in our nation that are derived from many different **cultures** and traditions. Indeed, the roots of American music lie in the music of other cultures and nations, notably of Europe and Africa.

We will begin to concentrate on developing listening skills and will listen to a sampling of the seemingly endless **styles** of music from many parts of the globe. A goal is to acquire a sense of that which exists beyond the limits of our experience.

## A Global Perspective

We live in an increasingly smaller "global village." With advances in worldwide transportation and communication and with increasingly mobile societies, it seems not only appropriate but necessary to develop a **global perspective** of music. With this book, you can gain a sense of the life-styles, traditions, values—and the music—of several nations and cultures throughout the world. You will also gain an awareness of the diversity within our national boundaries that has contributed significantly and beneficially to the cultural richness of our land.

The diversity of musical styles that exist in the United States includes Western European "classical" music (art music) and a number of "popular" musical styles derived largely from Western European ways of making music. Some music is a result of a blending of cultures and traditions. These other styles, including pop, folk, country, rock, jazz, and various ethnic musics, comprise an important part of music in American society. All of these styles constitute "American music."

One premise of this book is that American music in all its magnificent diversity must be a part of the study of music to enable us to recognize how all this music affects our lives.

## The American Mainstream and Ethnic Diversity

Throughout this book, we will discuss the roots and development of a variety of musical styles having the greatest impact on the cultural **mainstream** of American society. The music presented is derived from the cultural norm as well as the diverse cultures from within our society. We will gain a sense of the commonalities and differences among the various musical styles that make up the composite we call "American music."

The first factor that establishes America's cultural norm is the predominance of English (or Anglo-Saxon) settlers in the new land, mostly in the seventeenth and eighteenth centuries. As our society and our government were taking shape, the English culture defined America's politics, religion, and language. All succeeding immigrant groups had to choose between **assimilation** with or isolation from the Anglo-Saxon mainstream.

Those groups that retained the language, customs, or social views of their cultures became what we call **ethnic** minorities. Part of the cultural richness of our nation is derived from its ethnic diversity and its large number of ethnic groups. Immigrant groups may have partially assimilated into the mainstream of our society, retaining the songs, dances, instruments, languages (at least accent and inflection), fashion, food, and life-styles of their native cultures. In many cases, new styles and modes of behavior have been formed by the merging of cultural traditions. For example, jazz evolved, in part, from the merging of the songs and dances of the white Europeans (Anglos), those of mixed French or Spanish heritage who were born in the United States (Creoles), and freed black slaves or their descendants.

The musical mainstream of American society evolved in part because (1) most of the early religious, folk, and popular songs were derived from traditions and styles from the British Isles and mainland Europe; (2) Americans, particularly throughout the

*a.*

*b.*

*c.*

*d.*

*e.*

Guitarists representing five distinct musical styles:
(a) Joan Baez and Bob Dylan, urban folk; (b) John Lee
Hooker, blues; (c) Willie Nelson, country; (d) John
McLaughlin, jazz-rock; (e) Andres Segovia, classical.

nineteenth century, were exposed to European classical music through either visiting or immigrant European artists and musicians; and (3) the Euro-Americans rejected the music of the native Americans as primitive and unworthy. Thus, most of America's popular and classical music is based on the melodic, harmonic, and rhythmic practices of western Europe. The instruments we have traditionally used are for the most part the same or derived from those used in mainland Europe and the British Isles.

## Skills for Listening

Each chapter but the last one includes a Study in Sound that presents representative musical examples, each with a guide to listening, that summarize the material covered in the respective chapter. The first set of examples in each Study in Sound is included on the records and tapes accompanying this text. The Additional Listening guides, in some cases of complete multimovement works, refer to readily available recordings. Collectively, the Studies in Sound provide a rich overview of music's vastness, richness, and diversity.

Begin now to develop your **perceptive listening** skills. Listen with concentration and with a commitment to hear all that there is to hear in the music. Develop a curiosity and a desire to know the cultural **context** of music being heard—why it came to be, what its purpose is, how it serves the people who "use" it, and what you need to know to understand it better. Think about the music and what you are hearing and use words to describe what you hear. Think and write about your reactions to this music and how it is similar or different from music that you already know and enjoy.

Information and a few suggestions presented with each listening guide are included to assist you in your listening experience.

## Prior Musical Skills

These musical examples are all brief samples of much larger bodies of musical repertoire. No prior musical skills are necessary to understand that music exists throughout the world and has existed for many centuries, that people make music a part of their lives for many different reasons, and that musical styles are as varied as the people that make up this land.

No prior musical skills are necessary to listen perceptively and with concentration, interest, and energy. Since you most likely already listen to music, build on the skills you already have. Become acquainted with and use the skills presented in the Study in Sound for chapters 1 and 2. This experience will be good practice in perceptive listening that will serve you well throughout this book as needed skills become more sophisticated.

## Beginning Listening Skills

As the course progresses, in order to develop listening skills sufficient to use Studies in Sound most effectively, you will need, initially, to be aware of certain musical concepts and to determine whether or not they exist in the music. Listen now to the recorded musical examples SS1/1–5 and SS2/1–5 (Study in Sound, chapter 1, nos. 1–5; Study in Sound, chapter 2, nos. 1–5). Collectively, they provide a sense of the magnificent diversity of music. As you listen, respond to the following concepts:

1. Recognize the **pulse** (beat) of the music, if it exists, and the speed with which it moves.
2. Recognize any stronger beats that organize the pulse usually into two-beat or three-beat groupings, often called bars.

*a.*                              *b.*

*c.*                              *d.*

3. Count these groupings (**bars**) and discover that much of this music is organized into **phrases** (cohesive patterns of musical thoughts). Notice that some pieces of music will be comprised of phrases of equal length, in many cases of eight bars each.

4. Sense the **forward energy** within these phrases that moves the music from one point to the next, from the beginning of a phrase to its conclusion.

5. Recognize ends of phrases, that is, when musical thoughts pause or conclude and when thoughts change.

6. Be aware of irregular patterns of pulse, and recognize when the piece does not contain regular musical **patterns.**

Concentrate as you listen, and remember that these first examples are only the beginning of your Study in Sound.

Large and small groups of performers are common in both jazz and classical music: (a) combo jazz, (b) big band, (c) chamber music, (d) symphony orchestra.

## A Study in Sound
*Musical Diversity*

## Example 1

**"Erin-Go-Bragh"**—folk music

A Scotch/Irish narrative ballad

Sung by Ed Kirby

Recorded in Connecticut in 1977

At the time of the recording, Mr. Kirby was a high school principal, singing only for his own enjoyment. He learned this song from his father. It appears in a number of nineteenth-century Scottish song books and in a collection of songs from Nova Scotia.

## Example 2

**"Brittania Blues"**—jazz

Marian McPartland, piano; Jay Leonhart, bass; and Jimmy Madison, drums

This jazz combo features one of America's foremost contemporary jazz musicians, Marian McPartland, a pianist, composer, and author.

## Example 3

**"Pajaro Campana"** (Bell Bird)—popular music

Performed by the Paranas, a Paraguayan pop group that was based in Dallas in the 1970s

Features three guitars and a Paraguayan harp

Recorded in New York in 1976

This piece is a good example of the Latin American style of music. The characteristics that make it sound Latin are found in most styles of music throughout Mexico and Central and South America. The Latin style has permeated much popular, jazz, folk, and classical music of the United States.

## Example 4

"Y'Vorach"—dance music of the Chassidic Jews

Melody played by clarinet, accompanied by small band

Chassidism was a revivalist movement of Jewry that originated in eastern Europe in the eighteenth century. It grew out of the needs of the oppressed and provided a source of joy, optimism, and a feeling of brotherhood that was manifest in their songs and dances.

    Chassidic songs are religious in purpose but derived from folk traditions. The dances are very rhythmic, frequently beginning in slow tempo and working up to an exuberant climax. This example is a more lyrical dance tune, a wordless song.

## Example 5

"Nkende yamuyayu" (The waist of the wild cat)

Africa—music of the Soga people of Uganda

A well-known tune played on a four-holed, V-notched flute made of bamboo

The piece, whose character is energetic, begins with solo flute with the drum entering soon thereafter. The flute melody is of limited range, highly ornamented, and built on one short melodic idea that is constantly repeated but with modifications. In this recording, several men sitting nearby joined in, singing quietly and clapping.

*Discography*

*Ex. 1*   "Erin-Go-Bragh." *Brave Boys: New England Traditions in Folk Music.* New World Records. NW 239. 1:23.

*Ex. 2*   McPartland, Marian. "Brittania Blues." *A Delicate Balance.* Halcyon H 105. 1:15.

*Ex. 3*   The Paranas. "Pajara Campana." Parana Records. 1:45.

*Ex. 4*   "Y'Vorach." *Chassidic Dances.* Tikva Records T-62. 2:15.

*Ex. 5*   "Nkende yamuyayu." *Music of Africa Series, Uganda I.* Kaleidophone KMA 10. 1:08.

*Summary*

What is unfamiliar music to some can be profoundly important music to others. Music exists to serve different purposes—to entertain, to uplift, to stimulate feelings and responses, to enhance certain rituals from a football game to a High Mass.

    These many cultures, traditions, and purposes for creating music produce an infinite variety of music of which we will come to know only a small part.

    People always make judgments about music and develop attitudes, tastes, and preferences. Most have a narrow range of likes, preferring those styles which they know and feel comfortable with. This book will help you build and expand on what you know, will help you understand what is less familiar, and will examine relationships—commonalities and differences—among different musical styles and may broaden your range of musical preferences.

*Terms and
Concepts*

*Cultural diversity*

*A global perspective of music*

*A diversity of musical styles*

*Western European ways of making music*

*The cultural mainstream of American society*

*Ethnic diversity*

*Assimilation*

*Cultural context*

*Perceptive listening*

*Pulse*

*Bars*

*Phrases*

*Forward energy*

*Musical patterns*

# Chapter 2
# Vocabulary for Listening and Understanding

The Studies in Sound in chapters 1 and 2 present selections of music from a cross section of times and places, music created for different purposes, and music in a wide variety of styles.

The goals of chapter 2 and the remainder of the book follow:

1. To continue developing listening skills by intelligently using basic musical concepts and terms in describing music heard
2. To gain an understanding of the structure of music by examining a variety of ways music is organized
3. To learn how sounds are manipulated in a personal way to create a style
4. To be able to recognize stylistic differences, those characteristics that distinguish one piece from another

To achieve these goals, certain musical concepts and terms that make up music—a musical vocabulary—need to be learned and understood.

## The Nature of Music

The nature of music can be examined according to its (1) acoustical characteristics and (2) artistic qualities, that is, its power to communicate feelings and images and our capacity to respond to them and to the music itself.

## Physical Characteristics

### Music Is a Science

The physical characteristics of music involve principles of **acoustics,** physics, mathematics, and engineering. People who are aware of the scientific aspects of music include those interested in the specifications (specs) of stereo components, in sound reinforcement of recording studios and at music concerts, in the creation and performance of electronically or computer generated music, and in the acoustical design of rooms and concert halls.

Acoustics is the science of sound and the physical basis of music (see Appendix A). It is applied to the construction of musical instruments, audio equipment, auditoriums, recording studios, homes, and offices, and to medical technology through sonar (sound) related diagnostics and treatment.

Audio enthusiasts refer to principles of acoustics when discussing such terms as frequency range, echo, graphic equalizers, and signal-to-noise ratios. For example, the quality of audio speakers is measured in part by their frequency response as specified by the range of frequencies they can produce. To produce music, an audiophile will want one speaker, or more commonly a combination of speakers, that will produce the widest frequency response.

Acoustical engineers design recording studios and auditoriums according to acoustical principles, such as resonance and reverberation (echo). For example, determining that a room has good acoustics means that the degree of resonance and reverberation is suited to the purposes of the room. Thus, a facility that is constructed of a considerable amount of porous material will absorb sound waves and create "dead" acoustics. Conversely, a facility constructed of hard, dense material will bounce the sound waves around the room, resulting in "live" or highly resonant acoustics.

### Music Is Sound

Music is an aural phenomenon; we listen and respond to its sounds. Yet, silence is very much a part of music, from short rests to long, dramatic pauses. Many twentieth-century composers of classical music recognize the importance of silence as a compositional technique with its own value rather than merely as a rest from sound.

### Music Moves through Time

Music moves from one moment to the next as do motion pictures. To appreciate music or movies, it is important to remember what happened before and to anticipate what is about to happen. Conversely, photos, paintings, and pottery are static. What is seen one moment will still be there the next moment.

The interior shapes of walls, floors, and ceilings; the use of acoustical panels; and draperies and other absorbent materials all affect the sound heard by the listener.

Much music moves forward with an energy, a momentum, a predictable progression to a clear conclusion, such as the end of a phrase. Other music may move through time with less noticeable forward energy, to the point of seeming static, suspended in time, and without beginning or ending.

Music may be folk art (see chapter 3) or it may be high art, including the creation of great masterpieces of classical music—music of the cultivated tradition. Great music, as with other works of art, can have universal appeal, may be remembered for hundreds of years, and has a degree of substance that challenges the listener and the performer. A musical masterpiece encourages repeated listening, performance, and study. One can explore and find subtleties of expression and depths of meaning. Upon repeated experiences with a work, one will not tire of it and will continue to find new awarenesses and understandings. Such characteristics are not limited to Western European classical music, for a number of other cultures have classical music traditions, their great "masterpieces," their own high art. It can effectively be argued that characteristics of high art music can also be found in Western vernacular music, notably jazz and rock music.

**Cultural, Artistic, and Functional Qualities**

*Music Is an Art*

The creation of great musical masterpieces is very important in Western civilization, although the more common attitude worldwide is to create music for immediate use, not for preservation. Additionally, music from all cultures, as with all the arts, is a reflection of the society in which it was created and, at the same time, helps to shape the future of that society.

Music exists in all nations and among all people and has existed as far back in time as we know about people and their cultures. The musical languages, styles, and functions have differed considerably.

*Music Is a Universal Phenomenon*

People in different cultures value music for different reasons. For example, music will sound different from culture to culture because social groups or societies develop their own tastes about what sounds beautiful in music. They have their own musical traditions. They have different reasons for using music in their communities in such involvements as their religion, their recreation and entertainment, and their public gatherings. They use different instruments and have different ways of creating music; thus, they achieve stylistic differences. They also have different attitudes about performance practices and audience/performer relationships.

However, all cultures have music because of its universal power to stimulate emotional feelings and responses and to convey powerful feelings, moods, images, and associations. Music also provides a means of communication between people who desire common identity and who have common values and aspirations.

## Music Is a Means of Expression

Music is an expressive language, for it can communicate feelings and images and generate **aesthetic** responses, responses that may be culture-specific (not universal). Music can generate such feelings as joy, sorrow, pain, love, merriment, and spiritual exhaltation. It can also stimulate bodily movements, such as foot tapping, yelling or shouting as in certain types of religious expression, and physiological reactions as the skin tingling in response to a special musical moment.

Music can be romantic and sentimental; it can be simple and beautiful; and it can recall special memories and pleasant associations (and probably some that are not so pleasant). Yet, it can be harsh and complex, even noisy, reflecting certain aspects of our modern, technological society.

Music serves many functions. It is a part of ceremony and ritual and something to march and dance to. It affects our moods by entertaining, soothing, enriching, relaxing, uplifting, and helping people escape momentarily from the real world.

Music is able to move the mind, heart, and body in a wide variety of ways. It stimulates responses ranging from excitement to boredom, from love to hate, and from intense involvement to apathetic detachment.

## Music Is a Psychological Phenomenon

Music has the ability to affect and change people's feelings and attitudes. Music is used therapeutically to help disadvantaged people. Many colleges and universities offer degrees in music therapy. Graduates from these programs work in mental health clinics and hospitals, public schools, and in private practice. Among other purposes, music therapists use music to help people of all ages improve their self-esteem, find joy in self-expression, achieve elements of success through music, and find better ways of interacting socially with others.

Music, also, is used functionally in our environment to make people feel good, as in a department store, or to distract from pain or other unpleasant association, as in a dentist's chair. It is used to affect moods whether one desires uplifting and spirited music or quiet, relaxing, or reflective music. Music can be used to improve feelings when alone as may happen in an elevator or when put on hold during a telephone call, and it can also be used to generate feelings of excitement as at a football game.

This is background music and is not music to be listened to attentively and with discrimination. Such music, although it serves an important function in our society, promotes passive listening or nonlistening.

## Music Changes

Music changes as the society it serves changes and because people's needs and tastes change. Music changes because of new or refined instruments and other sound-producing sources and because of new ways of creating music, even with new musical languages. Music also changes because of artists' innate need to grow, to advance in knowledge and understanding, and to stretch the possibilities in performance skills. It most likely has always been this way, but the rate and extent of change have differed throughout history and among various cultures and subcultures.

What is music? Music escapes easy definition, as can be seen from the following statements.

**Definitions of Music**

*"Music is sound that is pleasing to the ear."* If pleasing means pretty or beautiful, then much music is excluded under this definition. Music can be noisy, loud, raucous—anything but pleasing. Music does not have to be beautiful or pleasing to be music, unless one's concept of what is beautiful or pleasing is very broad. This also is an inadequate definition if music that does not sound pleasing to us but may sound pleasing to others is included or if it is to include music that has a larger purpose than to sound pleasing. Such a definition excludes much Western European art music composed in the last seventy-five years as well as much music representative of some non-Western European cultures.

*"Music is sound and silence organized in time."* This definition is to some extent objective and includes all music from any place at any time. It avoids the subjective. Much music so organized can to many people be noisy, weird, displeasing, ugly, and "to my ears, it isn't music!" We, therefore, cannot define music without the subjective factors of taste, judgment, and personal reaction as exemplified in the common expression, "I don't know anything about music, but I know what I like."

*"Music is sound that you want to hear as music."* Sound that is not organized in some fashion typically cannot be called music. Yet the roar of a waterfall, the sound of rain falling on a tent, or the chirping of birds can be "music to my ears." These sounds are not music in the objective sense but as pleasing, perhaps therefore musical, sounds. In fact, the sounds of birds, water, whales, and other sounds of nature have been taped and used in "organized" music.

Conversely, all sorts of drums, cymbals, and gongs; harsh, dissonant harmonies; and abstract, totally unsingable melodies have been organized into music. However, is it really music? As at least one student has asked, "What would prompt a person to write something like that?" A piece of music incorporating sounds that might be perceived as noisy can be music if you want it to be. Even if one does not like a certain style of music, one can respect it, value its creative process, and know its cultural and social context. One can grow from it.

As this exploration of the world of music unfolds, perhaps your sense of what music is and what music is to you will become more clear, more understandable, and perhaps more inclusive of a wide variety of this world's music.

**Music as a Process**

Music is created, performed, and listened to. Without these three functions, music does not exist. However, these functions continually overlap.

When music is notated, a **score** (printed music) contains the composer's symbols that can be transformed into musical sounds. The performer reads and interprets these symbols, transforming them into music that has the power to communicate feelings and images and to generate a variety of responses. When music is **improvised,** it is created, performed, and listened to (by the performer) simultaneously.

For public performers, the audience (listeners) is an important motivating force. Professional performers rely on the economic benefits of a paying audience, but they all value the dynamics of audience/performer interaction—a "full house" and an enthusiastic, supportive audience. However, for most performers the audience may be a small group of friends or family, or perhaps only the performer is the listener. As one dedicated performer has mentioned, "I would still perform music for myself even if no one else listened."

## The Creative Process

The creative process may be simple or sophisticated, whether producing a lullaby or a grand opera. The creator may be a known composer or an unknown creator as is the case for much folk music. Regardless, the process is fundamentally the same—choosing elements of sound and organizing them in some way to achieve a desired result: the creator's own piece of music. It should be noted, however, that music is created by individuals who are part of a culture and who share a particular view with their intended audience. Thus, a creator will choose elements and organize them in ways that are valued by the culture (culture specific).

The process may be spontaneous and immediate or painstakingly deliberate. The music may or may not be notated. The process may be loosely controlled, with the performer given considerable freedom to make creative choices as in jazz improvisation, or it may be tightly controlled with detailed notation and meticulous instructions that the performer is expected to follow exactly as in symphony orchestra music.

## The Performance Process

The performance process is interpretive with the goal of adhering as closely as possible to the intentions of the creator or of deliberately deviating from the creative work. This process, thus, is not without its own creative element, intentional or unintentional. A performer will interpret a piece of music based at times on deliberate choices and at other times on his or her musical instincts. Any pop or jazz singer will perform the notated melody by adding personal interpretations within stylistic limitations. For example, a singer will not interpret "Embraceable You" or "Moonlight in Vermont" in the same way as "I Got Rhythm" or "I Wish That I Could Shimmy Like My Sister Kate." As indicated before, a performer's interpretation brings life to a composer's symbolism (notation) and increases the communicative power of the music.

In a band or orchestra, the conductor is the interpreter. Members of the ensemble must to some degree concede their own perhaps different interpretations to the authority of the conductor.

## The Listening Process

The listening process can be passive as with background music or "homework" music, or active as with going to a concert or listening attentively to a favorite album on your stereo. Active listening requires commitment, energy, and a desire to become involved in a personal and intense way with the music. Active listening is the most important part of developing an appreciation of any type of music.

## Participation in Music

We all participate in music as listeners, many of us as performers, and a few of us as creators.

As performers, we sing the popular tunes of the day. We sing in school and church choirs, play in high school bands and orchestras, and even organize small groups of people to play jazz, rock, or country and western music. Sometimes we play well enough to perform in public and earn money. Sometimes our performing is very private, intended only for ourselves. Only a few of us will develop the skills to read music.

As creators, we may make up a tune for our own private enjoyment. We may have learned to play jazz and create while performing, that is, to improvise. We may have learned enough about a system of notating music and enough about various instruments and voices to compose a written piece of music (score) that someone else can read and perform.

*a.*

*b.*

We may create a jazz or rock piece that is "worked out," that is, arranged in our head (a "head" **arrangement,** meaning not notated) or perhaps limited to a **lead sheet** (melody and chord symbols only). Such music is then put together in rehearsal and performed virtually the same in subsequent renditions.

A few of us create music, many more perform it, but we all listen to it.

People of all ages are involved in the process of music as creators (such as composer T. J. Anderson), performers, or listeners.

## The Elements of Music

The elements of music (pitch, duration, loudness, and tone quality) are derived from the elements of sound described as characteristics of sound waves (frequency, duration, intensity, and waveform). See Appendix A for more information. All other aspects of musical organization, such as rhythm, texture, and form are comprised of combinations of these four elements.

A **sound source** is any vibrating object (instrument, voice, siren, waterfall, train) that produces sympathetic sound waves (waves that generate exactly the same movement in the air or in another object as the waves produced by the sound source). The outer ear (a megaphone in reverse) captures the sound waves and, through the inner ear, converts them into nervous impulses that we perceive as sound.

The *frequency* or rate of speed of sound waves is heard or perceived by us as pitch (the relative highness or lowness of sound). We are aware of the *duration* of a pitch by how long it lasts. The *intensity* or energy that generates the amplitude or height of sound waves determines what we perceive as the relative loudness or softness of the music. The *shape* of a sound wave (waveform) creates the tone quality of the sounds that we hear in music. Additionally, the manner of construction of a sound source affects the waveform and the tone quality. For example, a trumpet is constructed differently than a violin and, consequently, sounds differently.

It is the way these elements are organized that turns mere sound into a piece of music with shape and form.

An oscilloscope trace of a harmonica. This sound has been "sampled" from the natural world and displays the dynamic peaks and troughs that make up the sound.

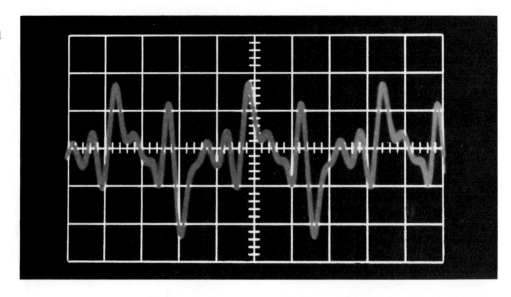

**Pitch (Frequency)**

When we can perceive a single tone, we call it a **pitch.** Most melodies are made of individually recognizable pitches. However, music includes sounds that are less precise. You cannot hum the pitch of a triangle, a cymbal, or a bass drum, yet you can perceive these sounds according to their register (range of frequencies)—a high **register** (a cluster of high frequencies), middle, or low register. The entire **range** of frequencies sounding at once is called white sound or white noise (radio static, the roar of a waterfall). The absence of frequencies is, of course, silence. Noise and silence have become important parts of twentieth-century musical composition.

Notice that we identify pitches as well as these pitch areas (registers) as high or low, not fast or slow (as in the frequency of the vibrations). The faster the frequency, the higher the pitch. The slower the frequency, the lower the pitch.

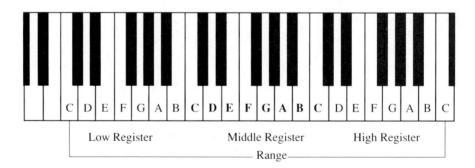

We can also relate pitches visually in a variety of ways according to the construction of the instruments producing them (see Appendix B). On the piano, low pitches are to the left, higher pitches to the right. On the double bass, you move down on the finger board to go higher in pitch, move up to go lower. Also, the high strings are thinner, the low strings thicker. Small drums produce higher frequency clusters, bigger drums lower ones. Likewise, small and thin instruments are higher in pitch range; big and wide instruments are lower. A piccolo is higher in pitch than a flute, a clarinet higher than a bass clarinet, a trumpet higher than a tuba, a short organ pipe higher than a long organ pipe, and so on.

Because music moves through time, all music has sounds that occur horizontally, a sequence of pitches that occur one sound after the other. Adding rhythm (patterns of duration) to pitches can produce a **melody.** We often think of melody as a tune, something that can be easily recognized and remembered, but some music does not have a recognizable melody. The emphasis in the creation of music need not be on a "tune" but on other musical factors, such as rhythm or tone quality. With such music, because we usually listen for a melody or tune, we have to listen differently by tuning in to these other, perhaps more predominant, factors.

In most music that makes use of melodic instruments, the notes chosen by the creator of the music are derived from certain scales or systems of pitch organization, sometimes referred to as pitch vocabularies. These vocabularies are patterns of pitches that help to give cohesion and form to a piece of music. Among the many systems that exist worldwide are major, minor, modal, pentatonic, whole tone, and gapped scales, the Indian *rāgas,* and the twelve-tone serial technique. In some cultures, a system might be associated with extra-musical ideas or images.

The tones commonly chosen for a piece of music are derived from a specific scale. The notes usually are arranged to convey a musical thought, a sequence of pitches with rhythmic durations (melody) that has musical meaning.

In Western music, if most of the tones of a piece are derived from a single scale, it is said to be **diatonic.** Frequently, notes are added that are not part of the scale to add interest and color. If many nonscale tones are added, it obscures the tonality and creates an unstable feeling. This music is said to be **chromatic.**

The distance in pitch between two tones of a melody is known as a melodic **interval.** For example, the two tones comprising the interval of an **octave** span eight different diatonic pitches (the first and last tones of a major or minor scale). They have the same pitch quality or, in Western notated music, the same pitch names. An interval of a fifth spans five tones, a third spans three tones, a seventh spans seven tones, and so forth. Figure 2.1 can help clarify melodic intervals.

A melody having mostly consecutive melodic intervals of the second is said to be **conjunct.** The melody moves stepwise, has a flat contour or melodic shape, and may sound "tuneful" or singable. If a melody includes many larger intervals, commonly called skips, it is said to be **disjunct.** This type of melody has a jagged or angular contour and may not sound like a "tune." Most of the world's vocal and folk music features conjunct melodies.

*Horizontal Organization (Melody)*

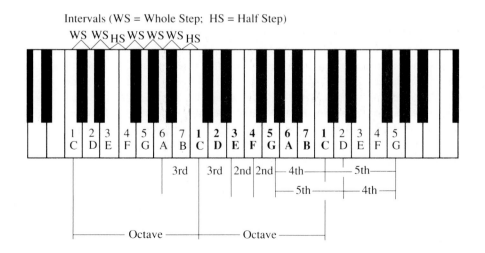

Intervals (WS = Whole Step; HS = Half Step)

Figure 2.1
Intervals and octaves.

**Figure 2.2**
Devised and conventional
notation for "Erin-Go-
Bragh."

Listen again to SS1/1 and follow the devised or the conventional notation in figure 2.2. Trace the approximation of tone relationships and melodic shape (contour) as shown.

## Vertical Organization (Harmony)

When music is organized vertically, pitches are heard simultaneously. We hear two simultaneous sounds as a harmonic interval and, in Western music, three or more simultaneous sounds may be perceived as a **chord.**

The system of using chords in Western European art music and most of America's folk and popular music is known as **harmony.** Most of the music that we know is based on rather simple harmonies and harmonic (chord) progressions (movement from one chord to the next), but not all music is based on this tradition. Some music does not use simple chord progressions or any harmonic system. The emphasis may be on a different and sometimes more complex system of using vertical sonorities (simultaneous sounds).

The four most common chords are built on thirds (see fig. 2.3). The **tonic** or "one chord" is built on the first tone of the major or minor scale—the root of the chord. The root of the **dominant** or "five chord" is the fifth scale tone. The dominant seventh or "five-seven chord" is the fifth but with the seventh tone above the root added to the chord. The **subdominant** chord is built on the fourth scale degree.

Three or more adjacent tones (no tones in between) sounding simultaneously are called **tone clusters.** In some modern piano music, many simultaneous, adjacent tones can be sounded by depressing the keys with the fist or forearm.

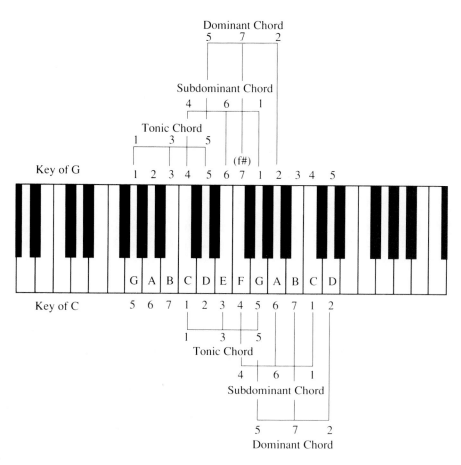

a.

**Figure 2.3**
(a) The primary chords (tonic, subdominant, and dominant) shown in relation to two major keys as visualized on a piano keyboard, (b) the notation of the primary chords shown in relation to two keys, (c) the structure of the primary chords shown in relation to the pitches (scale degrees) of any major or minor scale (the first scale degree is tonic; the fifth scale degree is the dominant).

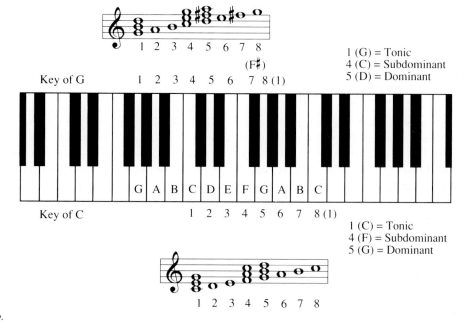

b.

Figure 2.3
*Continued*

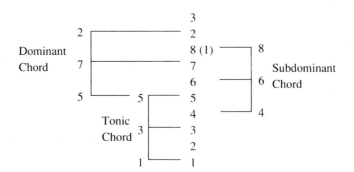

c.

Most music incorporates simultaneous sounds. A chant and an unaccompanied folk song or lullaby are examples of music that would not have chords or sounds that are organized vertically.

Listen to SS2/1 and 2 for conventional tonic/subdominant/dominant chord progressions, and listen to SS2/4 for music that is not based on Western harmonic practices.

*Tonality*

A number of systems of pitch organization will be mentioned in later chapters, but for now it will be sufficient to examine **tonality,** which is the application in Western music of the major/minor tonal system and specific **scales.** This tonal system has formed the basis of most Western music since the late seventeenth century. The concept of tonal center and the organization of pitches is derived from both melodic and harmonic pitch patterns and structure. In Western European music, the starting and ending tones of the scales as they are used in a piece of music become the tonal center (the home tone; the tonic). These are the points at which, in part, musical movement or forward energy ends. Shifting from one key (tonal center) to another is called **modulation** and is a common procedure in all but very short, simple pieces of music. To hear modulation in music, listen to SS1/4 and use the following guide. Notice that the tonic key plus three different keys are involved. Recognize the moment when these keys change (when the music modulates).

### Shifting key centers (SS 1/4)

| *Phrases* | *Bars* | | | | | | | |
|---|---|---|---|---|---|---|---|---|
| | 1 | 2 | 3 | 4 | 5 | 6 | 7 | 8 |
| Tonic Key (minor) | | | | | | | | Modulation |
| First New Key (major) | | | | | | | | Modulation |
| Tonic Key (minor) | | | | | | | | Modulation |
| First New Key (major) | | | | | | | | Modulation |
| Second New Key (minor) | | | | | | | | Modulation |
| Third New Key (major) | (trumpet) | | | | | | | |
| Second New Key (minor) | | | | | | | | Modulation |

| Phrases | Bars | | | | | | | |
|---------|------|---|---|---|---|---|---|---|
| | 1 | 2 | 3 | 4 | 5 | 6 | 7 | 8 |
| Third New Key (major) | | | | | | | | Modulation |
| Second New Key (minor) | | | | | | | | Modulation |
| Third New Key (major) | | | | Ends with modulation to second new key | | | | |

**Duration (Time)**

Music moves through time. It continues from one moment to the next. You cannot hear a piece all at once (as you can see most paintings). You listen to it as it moves through time, remembering what went before and anticipating what is to come. You can visualize short pieces of music in their totality in printed form as in sheet music, but this is not music, only symbols of music. It is music only when the symbols are transformed into sound by a performer.

We can perceive music on various levels of **duration:** the length of an entire piece of music, the length of each section (as each movement of a symphony or each chorus of a jazz tune), the length of a phrase or musical thought, and the length of each individual tone.

A piece of music may last one minute or one hour. A sound event (a single tone, a short melodic fragment, a phrase) can be short or long. An eight-bar phrase typically lasts longer than a four-bar phrase. However, this is not always so; it depends upon each phrase's respective rates of speed (tempos). A slow four-bar phrase can last longer than a fast eight-bar phrase just as, in Western notated music, a short tone (such as a quarter note) in slow tempo could last longer than a long tone (such as a half note) at a brisk tempo. For example, four bars of "Silent Night" take as long to sing as sixteen bars of "Jingle Bells," depending on the notation of the meter and tempo.

**Rhythm**

The manner in which various durations are given to pitches (note values) creates **rhythm.** Rhythm can be regular or irregular, simple or complex, floating or driving. However, rhythmic activity is not merely a mechanical arrangement of pitches and note values. Combinations or patterns of durations can generate a rhythmic feel, an energy, a vitality that create one of the most powerful aesthetic forces in the arts—the rhythmic impulse. Music having a strong rhythmic impulse stimulates us to dance, march, and tap our feet.

*Tempo, Pulse,*
*Meter,*
*Syncopation*

The **tempo** of music is the rate of speed described as fast/slow or speeding up/slowing down. To describe tempos or changes of tempo, musicians use terms such as *allegro* (fast), *andante* (moderate tempo), *largo* (slow), *accelerando* (get faster), *ritardando* (get slower), and *rubato* (a flexible pulse, interpreting music in a highly expressive manner).

Most of the music we listen to has a pulse or a steady beat, the "heartbeat" of the music. The pulse is usually organized into groups of two or three beats (metric groupings), creating **meter.** By stressing (accenting) every other beat, we have duple meter (STRONG, weak, STRONG, weak). By grouping the beats into patterns of three, we have triple meter (STRONG, weak, weak, STRONG, weak, weak). To see this another way, duple meter is 1 2/1 2/1 2 or 1 2 3 4/1 2 3 4. Four beats is a multiple of 2; thus, it is duple meter. Triple meter is 1 2 3/1 2 3.

Some music has no pulse (nonmetric), a weak pulse, or an irregular pulse. Some music has a clear pulse, but the strong beats occur in different patterns. We call this mixed meter, STRONG, weak, STRONG, weak, weak, STRONG, weak, or

1 2/1 2 3/1 2.

These shifts of accent may occur irregularly or may create regular patterns of shifting accents:

1 2 1 2 1 2 3/1 2 1 2 1 2 3/1 2 1 2 1 2 3.

Placing accents on weak beats or weak parts of beats produces **syncopation.** For example: weak, STRONG, weak, weak; weak, STRONG, weak, weak, or

1 2 3 4/1 2 3 4.

Syncopation takes place on the second beat of each group (bar or measure in notated music). The following is another example:

1 + 2 + 3 + 4 + /1 + 2 + 3 + 4 +.

Syncopation occurs on the second half of the second beat and on the first half of the fourth beat of each bar.

*Bars (Measures),*
*Phrases*

As was previously indicated, each metric group constitutes a measure or bar. In much music, a group of measures can constitute a phrase. Common groupings are known as an eight-bar phrase, a twelve-bar blues tune, or a thirty-two bar chorus. Bars are perceived from the awareness of strong metric beats; the number of "downbeats" (the first beat of each bar) equals the number of bars. In twelve-bar blues, for example, one can typically count twelve downbeats to each phrase or chorus (listen to SS1/2 for a twelve-bar blues).

Listen to SS2/3–5 and concentrate on their rhythmic characteristics.

**Loudness**
**(Intensity)**

The degree of **loudness** or softness of music varies with the degree of intensity or energy expended in producing the sound. The degree of intensity creates variance in the amplitude or height of the sound waves. See Appendix A for more information about the physical properties of sound: the speed, duration, height, and shape of sound waves. The greater the intensity, the louder the sound; less intensity generates a softer sound.

In music, **dynamics** refers to the loudness level: *forte* (loud), *piano* (soft), *mezzo piano* (medium soft), *crescendo* (gradually get louder), *decrescendo* (gradually get softer). An **accent** is achieved by increasing the intensity (increased stress, emphasis) on a single note or chord. One might think that the larger the number of musicians performing, the greater the loudness, but this is not necessarily so. For example, it is quite possible for a group of twenty musicians to perform as softly as a group of four.

In audio technology, we have volume controls that can adjust loudness levels. We turn up the volume or turn it down or off. Intensity (volume of sound or sound energy) is measured in decibels. The greater the intensity, the higher the decibel level and the greater the loudness.

All sound-producing devices possess their own distinctive **tone quality** or **timbre** (tam′-bur). A flute sounds different than a clarinet; a man usually sounds different than a woman; a koto sounds different than a sitār just as a guitar sounds different than a banjo; and a snare drum sounds different than a tom-tom.

**Tone Quality (Timbre): Instrument Classification**

Learn to recognize the sounds of various instruments and voices because they are relatively consistent in quality. The reason for this consistency lies in the acoustical construction of the devices, whether naturally made as in the human voice or manufactured as in musical instruments.

Instruments are generally classified according to the way their tones are produced, according to their characteristic timbre. See Appendix C for more information. We have brass instruments, stringed instruments (usually thought of as those of the violin family), woodwinds, and percussion. These classifications are useful as related to our bands and orchestras but are not sufficient when including a large number of instruments used in other cultures.

A classification that would include instruments from all parts of the world follows:

1. *Chordophones.* Instruments involving strings in their method of tone production, whether bowed or plucked.
2. *Aerophones.* Instruments that are blown and involve enclosed columns of air, such as the clarinet or trumpet, and those that act on the principle of the free reed, such as the accordian.
3. *Idiophones.* Instruments made of elastic metal or wood that are struck, shaken, plucked, or rubbed.
4. *Membranophones.* Instruments that are struck, mostly drums, in which a stretched skin or plastic drum head is the sound-producing agent.
5. *Electrophones.* Instruments in which the acoustical vibrations are produced by electric contrivances.

The elements of music (pitch, duration, loudness, and timbre) always work together in a piece of music. As you listen to any music and the musical examples presented later in this chapter in particular, practice recognizing the following musical elements, using your growing musical vocabulary to describe what you hear:

**Interaction of the Elements**

1. Highs and lows of pitches and how they change and are combined
2. The relative durations of pitches and how they are organized
3. The dynamic levels as related to the relative loudness of the music and how they change
4. Tone qualities of different sources of sounds (voices or instruments)
5. Pulse, meter (duple, triple), measures (bars), phrases

To continue efforts to understand the music, we will consider other ways creators of music use abstract sounds to develop a piece and create a style that communicates the intentions of the composer and that evokes intended or desired responses in the listener. The purpose is to increase understanding of how the creative process works in music.

**To Create a Style: Musical Concepts**

## Unity and Variety

If music had no variety, it would produce an intolerable sameness. If it had no unity (nothing but variety, always moving on to something different), it would produce music that rambles. Both circumstances would be, for most people, boring and unsatisfying. Establishing familiarity helps listeners feel comfortable with a piece of music.

Most, but not all, Western music incorporates some aspects of departure and return. A departure suggests a musical idea that is different from that which has already been presented—a point of **contrast.** A return is either an exact or modified repeat of the original idea.

Another factor that gives unity to a piece of music is the **repetition,** exact or modified, of a short musical pattern. The repetition can be rhythmic, melodic, harmonic, or any combination of the three. It can be the repetition of a melodic pattern a step lower (**sequence**), or it can be a constantly repeated pattern that provides a foundation for the melody (**ostinato**).

## Tension and Release

In traditional Western music, an increase in harmonic or rhythmic complexity, an increase in the dynamic level (loudness), a rise in the pitch area of the melody, a change of key or tonal center, or an increase in the thickness or density of sound all can provide musical **tension.** Tension typically needs **resolution** (release of tension) to make the listener relate comfortably to the music. Just as constant variety would seem uncomfortable, so would constant tension.

A release from tension is accomplished by returning from the complex to the simple, from the high to the low, from the loud to the soft, from the less comfortable to the comfortable sounds as we perceive them.

One kind of tension is **dissonance.** Dissonance, like other forms of tension, traditionally requires resolution—a release of tension, a move from the unstable dissonance or tension to a more stable or consonant sound. **Consonance** is caused by intervals or chords that create repose, resolution, and comfort rather than tension. Often, tension and dissonance, in particular, are stronger in the middle of phrases with repose or release of tension at the end.

## Forward Energy

Much music in American society is intrinsically drawn forward from one point to the next, from the beginning of a phrase to the end, sometimes from one tone or one chord to the next. This forward energy is derived from a rise in tension followed by its release. It arises from an unstable feeling that drives the music forward to points of relative stability as at the end of a phrase. Forward energy often is generated by the melodies and harmonic progressions of traditional Western music. Certain tones or chords in sequence generate this energy; other notes, chords, or musical structures may not. A composer may choose to avoid forward energy. This music may be described as static, floating, or lacking in the tendency to progress.

## Texture

In one sense, the **texture** of music may be described as thick and full as in a band or symphony orchestra or thin and transparent as in a string quartet or jazz combo. This relates to the number of simultaneously sounded lines. Likewise, piano music with six or eight tones sounding simultaneously will produce a thicker, more complex texture than piano music using two or three tones at a time.

In another sense, texture refers to the manner in which the horizontal pitch sequences are organized. A single, melodic line without any other horizontal or vertical sounds is described as having a monophonic texture (one sound). Chant and unaccompanied solo singing fall into this category.

More than one melody sounding at the same time, having equal emphasis but not necessarily starting and stopping at the same time, is known as polyphonic music (multiple sounds). A word commonly used to describe this compositional technique is counterpoint (music having a contrapuntal texture).

When one melody is predominant (in the foreground) and is supported by a harmonic or chordal accompaniment (in the background), this music is known to have a homophonic texture. Almost all our popular, folk, and more recent religious music fall into this category.

Much music incorporates combinations of textures. Music that has a polyphonic texture may also incorporate homophonic texture. It is a matter of which texture predominates.

Listen to SS1/1 and SS8/1 for examples of monophonic texture; SS4/4, SS8/2, and SS9/3 for polyphonic texture; and SS2/1–3 (among many others) for homophonic texture. To identify other stylistic concepts just presented (contrast, consonance, etc.), listen to SS2/1–5 after studying the next section on form and melodic growth.

## Genres and Forms

A **genre** is a type of music, a category, such as a symphony, hymn, ballad, march, or opera. A **form** is the shape or structure of a piece, a pattern of organization described, for example, as aba or aaba. Patterns of departures and returns, contrasts and repetitions, and key relationships (schemes of modulations and returns to the tonic key) are determining factors in establishing the form of a piece of music.

Forms can be perceived at various levels, from the form of a complete four-movement symphony to the form of a familiar hymn or a popular song. Small forms can be perceived within large forms. For example, one can describe the structure of the first section of the first movement of a symphony as well as the overall scheme of its various movements.

Virtually all genres and forms of music change and evolve. They are both a reflection of existing practices and a flexible model for the work of future creators of music.

### Generic Forms

Forms that are "generic," that is, common in many musical styles, include two-part or **binary** (ab) and three-part or **ternary** (aba) forms with *a* meaning the statement of the first musical idea or phrase (the first part or the first section) and *b* meaning a contrasting part or section (a departure from the opening statement). A second contrasting part would then be identified as the *c* section. Other forms relate to specific styles from specific times and places.

### Specific Forms

The thirty-two-bar **song form** (aaba) is found in nearly all styles derived from Western European musical traditions: art songs, religious music, folk songs, and both old and current jazz and popular tunes.

In many American popular songs and religious music, a **verse/chorus** or verse/refrain form can easily be found. Typically, the text varies in each repetition of the verse (a musical narrative) but is repeated with each return of the chorus or refrain (usually more tuneful and memorable than the verse).

The **twelve-bar blues** is a form used in a style of American folk song called the blues but is also used in virtually every style of jazz and popular music. Typically, the twelve bars are divided into three four-bar segments utilizing a specific set of chord progressions.

Among the forms we find in Western European art music are the sonata-allegro form, the minuet and trio, the rondo, and the theme and variations. We will return to a study of these forms in later chapters.

**Melodic Growth
and Character**

To conclude this development of a working vocabulary for listening, we will look again at melody, its components and its characteristics. Melody is that part of music most listeners can understand, remember, and "tune in to."

In most of the music of Western culture, the melody does not exist in isolation from other musical factors, such as harmony, timbre, and texture. If you listened only to the melody of a piece of music without the support of these other musical elements, you would find it a very different piece of music and probably would not find it nearly as satisfying. Again, it is all these elements interacting and working together that make a piece of music cohesive, satisfying, and memorable.

Typically, a melody is comprised of phrases, complete or relatively complete musical thoughts. Phrases end when the music generates points of repose—at points of release of tension, of forward energy, and of harmonic, melodic, and rhythmic rest. These points are called **cadences.** Some cadences give a feeling of temporarily stopping, with an awareness that musical movement will continue. Other cadences convey a strong feeling of finality, as at the end of a piece of music.

A melody or a phrase often begins with a **motive,** the smallest group of notes that has an identifiable character, from three or four notes to a couple of bars. It may be the basis of the music that is to follow. A motive is not necessarily melodic; it may be harmonic or rhythmic. Most likely, it will incorporate a combination of musical elements.

Music evolves; it develops and grows. A motive often is the basis for this further development and growth. It is usually repeated, perhaps exactly, but more often it is modified. Generally, contrast occurs when a new motive is introduced and the character of the music changes.

As noted before, instability is a desired attribute in music, for it contributes to tension, dissonance, and other characteristics that provide variety in music. This variety is generated by departures or elements of musical contrast that set up returns to music that is more familiar, comfortable, and satisfying. A modulation, or change of key, creates a degree of instability that is satisfied when the music returns to the original key.

Listeners seldom are aware of these intricacies and subtleties of compositional technique. However, these are the factors that generate listeners' psychological and aesthetic responses to music and determine in what ways and to what extent a piece of music communicates.

To bring these words and concepts from abstractions to a living, working part of your vocabulary, identify them as they function in any music you listen to. Continue to increase your awareness of and your ability to describe what is happening in the music. In the following Study in Sound, listen for ways composers organize musical elements and, particularly, to various ways the following musical concepts are applied:

**Application
of Concepts**

1. Melodic, harmonic, and rhythmic characteristics
2. Diatonic and chromatic melodies
3. Shifts in tonality (modulation)
4. Points of contrast and unity (departure and return)
5. Repetition and patterns of repetition, such as sequence and ostinato
6. Tension and release
7. Consonance and dissonance
8. Forward energy and repose (phrases and cadences)
9. Texture
10. Form
11. Motives and the ways they contribute to the growth and development
    of the music

**A Study in Sound**
*Vocabulary for Listening*

## Example 1

**"Little Ole You"**—Jim Reeves

A country style—the early years of the Nashville Sound

Recorded in 1962

A blend of traditional country and popular urban approaches to performance

### *Goals:*

Recognize and identify pulse, downbeats, meter, and tempo.

Distinguish between melody (foreground) and accompaniment (background).

Recognize the sound of tonic.

*Guide:* The melody is the more prominent line (the foreground); it is heard in the voice or the highest pitched instrumental line. The accompaniment (the background) provides a supportive role and is performed on a number of instruments. Identify the sounds of the various instruments.

The pulse should be counted in a moderately fast four (a moderately fast tempo), but note that the music also has a strong two-beat feeling. When counting, emphasize the strong beats, each one indicating the beginning of a bar:

1 2 3 4/1 2 3 4/1 2 3 4 . . .

The music begins on the second beat of the bar. Each of the following numbers denotes a four-beat bar (duple meter).

```
---1---2---3---4---                          Introduction
   1---2---3---4---5---6---7---8---          It's a great big . . .
   1---2---3---4---5---6---7---8---          And lucky me . . .
   1---2---3---4---5---6---7---8---          Little ole you . . .
   1---2---3---4---5---6---7---8---          It's a fast life . . .
   1---2---3---4---5---6---7---8---          In the middle of . . .
   1---2---3---4---                          Instrumental interlude
   1---2---3---4---5---6---7---8---          Little ole you . . .
   1---2---3---4---5---6---7---8---          It's a fast life . . .
   1---2---3---4---5---6---7---8---          In the middle of . . .
   1---2---3---4---                          In this great big . . .
```

*Verse*
*It's a great big world full of little surprises*
*Theres's a lot of pretty girls in all kinds of shapes and sizes*
*And lucky me, although my chances are few*
*In this great big world I found little ole you.*

*Chorus*
*Little ole you, no bigger than a minute*
*It's hard to believe this big world had you in it.*

*Verse*
*It's a fast life and everybody's lookin' so busy*
*There's so much to do it almost makes me dizzy*
*In the middle of it all you appeared right out of the blue*
*In this great big world I found little ole you.*

*Chorus*
*(repeated)*

**Reflections:** Notice how the pulse is steady and falls into regular patterns of strong and weak beats (meter). The strong beats are represented by numbers, the weak beats by dashes. Each group of four pulses represents one bar. There are eight bars to each line of the lyrics (the poetry), with the exception of the last line. Each line represents one phrase. Be aware of the predominantly diatonic melody.

Listen carefully to the accompaniment as well as to the melody. Distinguish the sounds of different instruments.

# Example 2

**"Someone to Watch Over Me"**—1920s-style American popular music (Tin Pan Alley)

Music by George Gershwin; lyrics by Ira Gershwin

George Gershwin, piano

Recorded at a private party in New York City in 1926

## Goals:

Identify meter, count bars (downbeats), and recognize phrases.

Recognize stepwise motion in the melody.

Identify contrasting and repeating sections.

Be aware of rhythmic and melodic patterns.

**Guide:** "Someone to Watch Over Me" is in duple meter. Count four beats to the bar at a moderately fast tempo. It can also be felt in a moderately slow two-beat pattern.

```
1---2---3---4---5---6---              Introduction
1---2---3---4---5---6---7---8---      Main melody—first time
1---2---3---4---5---6---7---8---      Main melody—second time
1---2---3---4---5---6---7---8---      Contrasting section
1---2---3---4---5---6---7---8---      Main melody—third time
1---2---3---4---5---6---7---8---      Main melody—fourth time
```

***Reflections:*** Notice that the phrases after the introduction are of equal length (eight bars) and that the end of each phrase has a sense of finality and closure. Be aware that phrases or sections of music might be repeated exactly but that many times they are repeated with modifications while retaining the traits that make them identifiable.

Notice the musical energy that gives a regularly recurring rise and fall feeling, culminating when the music seems to have arrived at points of rest (the ends of phrases).

The melody can be described as tuneful and singable, having a lilting, easy swing to it—the feeling of dance. It is constructed primarily with a step-wise motion. This tune may sound old fashioned now but did not when it was written. Tastes have changed.

# Example 3

**String Quartet, Op. 33, No. 2 "The Joke"**

II—Scherzo (excerpt)

Composed in 1791 by Franz Joseph Haydn

Western European classical chamber music

String Quartet: two violins, viola, cello

The number of this quartet, Op. 33, No. 2, refers to the second composition of a group of works catalogued as Op. 33. Opus means *work,* or in this case, it means the 33rd in a series of works published by Haydn (see chapter 10).

"The Joke" is a nickname for this piece. It was derived supposedly from the fact that Haydn put some extensive pauses (rests or silences) near the end of the quartet in order to catch people off guard who may have been talking while the music was playing.

This excerpt is from the second of four movements of the quartet. It is labeled Scherzo (a fast, dancelike style).

## Goals:

Recognize the beginnings of phrases and the points of rest (cadences) where forward energy subsides (ends of phrases).

Recognize foreground (melody) and background (accompaniment or supportive harmony).

Recognize conjunct (stepwise) melody.

***Guide:*** The music is in triple meter; it can be felt and counted in a fast three:

<u>1</u> 2 3/<u>1</u> 2 3

or a moderately slow one:

<u>1</u>--/<u>1</u>--

In either case, the phrases begin on the third beat of the bar (with a pickup). The following numbers coincide with each down beat; thus, they will guide you in counting the bars. As you listen, count the numbers making sure they match the music's strong beats.

```
1--2--3--4--5--6--7--8--9--10--    First phrase
1--2--3--4--5--6--7--8--9--10--    First phrase repeated
1--2--3--4--5--6--7--8--9--10--    Contrasting phrase—
                                     notice descending
                                     pattern
1--2--3--4--                       Transition
1--2--3--4--5--6--7--8--9--10--    First phrase repeated
1--2--3--4--5--6--7--8--9--10--    Contrasting phrase
                                     repeated
1--2--3--4--                       Transition
1--2--3--4--5--6--7--8--9--10--    First phrase repeated
```

*Reflections:* A four-bar passage occurs after each contrasting phrase that serves as a transition back to the first phrase. These transitions do not constitute self-contained musical thoughts; thus, they cannot be considered phrases.

Be aware of the complete musical thoughts (phrases). They are separated at points that musical energy comes to a rest (cadences). Identify when the music returns to tonic. Listen for changes in thought (a different melody, a different instrument playing the melody, or anything that seems to be in contrast to what preceded it). Remember the original melody and listen for when it changes and when it returns to its original character.

Notice that virtually all of the notes of the melody fall within a single major or minor scale (a diatonic melody). Notice, also, that the stepwise melody creates a relatively smooth and flat contour (melodic shape). It does not contain many wide skips.

# Example 4

**"Rokudan No Shirabe"** (two excerpts)—Japanese classical music—music for koto

Composed by Yatsuhashi Kengyo (1613–1685)

## Goals:

Contrast stepwise melodic motion with pitches connected by sliding motion (glissando).

Compare and contrast the sound (timbre) of the koto with those of familiar plucked instruments such as the guitar.

Recognize the positive aspects of irregular pulse, nonmetric music, and imbalanced or unclear phrases.

*Guide:* The beginning can be felt in a moderately slow, two-beat meter. The second excerpt is in a little quicker tempo; the tempo slows, the activity lessens, and, after a descending glissando, ends on a single tone. The music flows with few perceivable cadences or phrase groups.

*Reflections:* A distinguishing characteristic of this piece, and of Japanese music in general, is the oriental, gapped scale. This music is characterized by the melodic interval that is wider than normally found in the Western major or minor scale. Slides and ornaments are common and integral to this style of performance.

# Example 5

*Billy the Kid* (excerpt)—American classical music

Composed by Aaron Copland

This example, an excerpt from an orchestral version of music to Copland's ballet of the same name, is derived from the Western European concert music tradition. It is American music in one sense because the composer is American. It is American in another sense because the story and many of the tunes Copland uses in this ballet are derived from the songs and traditions of the American people and from American folk traditions.

## Goals:

Recognize and describe texture, timbre, and dynamics.

Recognize patterns in the music as it develops, particularly patterns in the treatments of meter, repeated musical ideas, and contrast.

Be aware of rhythmic vitality and identify ways it is achieved.

Distinguish between the sound of a solo instrument and of a group of instruments.

*Guide:* Be aware of the density of instrumentation; describe the sound of one or a few instruments as having thin texture and of many instruments as having thick texture.

Listen for contrasting sections and changes of tempo (speed), range (high or low pitch areas), and musical thoughts (phrases).

*Reflections:* The folklike melodies, usually presented only in fragments, are often passed from instrument to instrument. Begin to identify the instruments from their sounds.

Describe the meter and rhythm. Can you tap your foot to the music? Is there a regular beat? Is it danceable music or does much of it have only the "feel" of music to be danced to?

*Discography*

**Ex. 1**   Reeves, Jim. "Little Ole You." *Country Music in the Modern Era 1940s–1970s.* New World Records. NW 207. 2:08.

**Ex. 2**   Gershwin, George, and Ira Gershwin. "Someone to Watch Over Me." . . . *And then we wrote . . . (American Composers and Lyricists Sing, Play, and Conduct Their Own Songs).* New World Records. NW 272. 1:20.

**Ex. 3**   Haydn, Franz Joseph. String Quartet, Op. 33, No. 2 (II). Vox SCBX-556. 1:04.

**Ex. 4**   "Rokudan No Shirabe." *Japanese Music for Koto and Shakuhachi.* Toshiba Records Th 7002. 3:35.

**Ex. 5**   Copland, Aaron. *Billy the Kid.* Columbia ML 5157. 3:30.

*Summary*

This chapter has helped you develop your listening skills to a higher level of perception. You have acquired the beginnings of a musical vocabulary for listening. You have learned words that symbolize musical concepts, which are those illusive, subjective style characteristics that happen in the music to make it communicate and to which we respond.

More importantly, you have worked with these words and concepts in thinking about and describing the music you have listened to.

You have considered what music is, how it is put together, what makes some music different from other music, and what is basic in music and common to all musical styles.

*Terms and Concepts*

*The nature of music*
*The physical basis of music*
*Artistic qualities*
*Musical processes*
*The elements of music*
*The interaction of musical elements*
*Musical style*
*Musical structure (form)*

# Part II
# Listening to Vernacular Music

Classical music in America is art music, a part of high culture. It is in a language and context that many Americans do not relate to, and therefore, do not appreciate and include in their daily experience. Many do not understand the music itself and do not feel comfortable with the environment in which it is usually found, such as concert halls and opera houses.

Not all music is part of high culture. Music is an integral part of our environment at all levels of society, is created in a language that the common people understand, and exists for all of us. It is music in the vernacular,

in the language of the people, and includes folk music, some religious music, commercial (popular) music, certain types of jazz, and much music outside of the Western European heritage.

Part II, "Vernacular Music" (chapters 3–5), gives an overview of the many "musics" that are important to some Americans, to some ethnic groups, to those in particular geographical areas, or to groups of Americans ranging from large groups to small groups with specialized listening preferences. People in rural areas may have different listening preferences than those living in major metropolitan areas. People

in the southwest may have different listening preferences than those living in New England. Older people may have different listening preferences than younger people.

Chapter 3 presents traditional folk songs, fiddlin' tunes, blues, and ballads. It also discusses elements of traditional American religious music: gospel music, hymns, and spiritual songs. Jazz is discussed in chapter 4 both as a vernacular music and as sophisticated art music. Chapter 5 discusses music of Tin Pan Alley, country music, black popular music, rock, and their roles in our society.

# Chapter 3
# Traditional Folk and Religious Music

This chapter is about folk music and music closely related to folk traditions: ballads, lyric songs, country dances, blues, gospel music, and certain other forms of religious expression important to the development of American culture. White and black American, Protestant religious music is emphasized not to convey that music from other traditions did not exist or were not important but because of the dominant and profound impact the various styles of Protestant music have had on American culture. In fact, music from two other traditions is covered elsewhere in the book: the religious music of the Jewish people is presented in chapter 7 as part of world music, and the liturgical music of the Roman Catholic church is covered in chapter 8 as part of Western European classical music.

## Folk Music

Folk music is close to the souls of many Americans and has influenced much music around us today. It is a living, ever-changing music. Authentic folk music is understood by the community of participants—singers, players, dancers, listeners—within a cultural group. The music reflects the spirit and personality of the people who produce it, use it, and value it. It is music that grows spontaneously out of the lives of the people and conveys in song their joys and sorrows, relationships and romances, and events and circumstances that are important to them.

In American society, the predominant folk music originally was the songs of British-based white people in New England (the Anglo-Americans) and of the African-based black people in the rural south (the Afro-Americans). As the British immigrants moved westward and southward and as the black slaves were freed and they and their descendants moved north, their respective folk music influenced that of the other. From these cross-cultural influences, new musical styles and practices developed, combining desired traits from both black and white cultures.

Folk music is an **art music** but referred to commonly as **folk art** as distinguished from high art. When we speak of art music, we generally refer to classical music. We define art music as music that is formal, sophisticated, urban, and appreciated by an educated elite—a cultivated tradition based largely on notated music. Folk music, on the other hand, can be considered informal, aesthetically and musically unsophisticated, and preserved and transmitted by means that require learning songs from memory rather than from notated, printed music. Thus, we can think of folk music as a body of repertoire comprised of traditional songs and dances derived from an **oral tradition.** However, in some cultures that have a high art or a classical music (examples would be India and Japan), oral tradition is the primary means of the preservation and dissemination of their music.

## Oral Tradition

Traditional songs are learned by hearing and memorizing. They most likely have gone through many changes as they were sung father to son, uncle to nephew, grandmother to granddaughter, neighbor to neighbor—through generations and sometimes centuries. For example, 243 variants in the folk song, "Barbara Allen," have been identified. This is an outgrowth of an oral, rather than a notated, tradition. The notion of how texts change has been illustrated in Abrahams and Foss' book, *Anglo-American Folksong Style,* in which the authors provide a series of versions of a line, "Save rosemary and thyme." It is presumed that subsequent singers misunderstood the words in the memory process or did not know the meaning of these herbs.

*Save rosemary and thyme.*
*Rosemary in time.*
*Every rose grows merry in time.*
*Rose de Marion Time.*
*Rozz marrow and time.*
*May every rose bloom merry in time.*
*Let every rose grow merry and fine.*
*Every leaf grows many a time.*
*Sing Ivy leaf, Sweet William and thyme.*
*Every rose grows bonny in time.*
*Every globe grows merry in time.*
*Green grows the merry antine.*
*Whilst every grove rings with a merry antine.*
*So sav'ry was said, come marry in time.*

Also, compare the three versions of texts of "Barbara Allen" (SS3/4).

Songs that are not accepted by the community will soon be forgotten or will change. As the memory process proceeds from community to community and through time, those songs that do survive may be changed to such an extent that they bear little resemblance to the original version. In fact, the original version may not be known. Songs change because of inaccurate memorization, a misunderstanding of a word or meaning in the text, or simply forgetting lines and creating new lines on the spot. Songs also change because singers may want to improve them, to add their own personal interpretation, or to adapt them to suit the tastes of the community. Changes in songs are an accepted and valued part of the process of oral tradition. The changes may weaken a song, but more likely they give it a new life or make it more meaningful to a community.

Folk music typically is not created by professional composers and lyricists; the creators are usually unknown. It is true, however, that commercial popular songs or other songs in recorded form may appeal to a traditional folksinger. Thus, the memory process begins whereby a composed song may enter into oral tradition.

The songs are preserved by oral tradition within the communities and cultural groups, but folklorists have collected, classified, transcribed, and published traditional folk songs and preserved them in printed editions. Important folk-song collectors were Francis James Child who published 305 traditional English ballads, known as the "Child ballads," and Cecil Sharp, who recorded and published over a thousand English folk songs he discovered being sung in the southern Appalachian states upon his visit there in 1916. Listen to "Barbara Allen" (SS3/4), a Child ballad, and follow the notation in figure 3.1; the notation is only approximate. Numerous notated versions of this melody are included in Child's collection.

**Figure 3.1**
Notation for one version of the Child ballad "Barbara Allen." "Barbry Ellen" written by John Jacob Niles.

An amphitheater. A relaxing summer evening enjoying folk music.

**Field Recordings**

Collectors such as Cecil Sharp, John and Alan Lomax, and Charles Seeger have preserved traditional songs through **field recordings.** These recordings were made where the people were: in their kitchens, living rooms, or community gathering places. Such recordings were not made in the acoustically controlled environments of professional recording studios.

Commercial recording companies also went into the field as early as the 1920s to record traditional songs and instrumental music as the popularity of this music became more widespread. The availability of these recordings contributed to the growing popularity of folk music. Because of these scholarly and commercial efforts, traditional folk music is better understood and is preserved for the benefit of future generations.

**Types of Folk Music**

Scholars have determined that folk music in general possesses broad, common characteristics but with considerable national, regional, and community variation. What are the types of folk songs? Where do people sing these songs? What generalizations can be made about the musical characteristics of this music: the melody, scale, rhythm, tempo, tone quality, texture, and form? What are the relationships between music and words? The following discussion will provide information that can help you understand the musical characteristics of much American folk music.

The broad genres of American traditional folk music include the following:

1. *Narrative ballads (story songs).* These songs originally came from New England, having been brought to America in the seventeenth, eighteenth, and nineteenth centuries by immigrants from the British Isles, particularly Scotland and Ireland. A ballad singer is a storyteller. The story has a beginning, a middle, and an end and may convey a romantic and sentimental mood or heroic action. Occasionally, dialogue between two characters in the story is inserted. A narrative **ballad** may have many stanzas,* each frequently comprised of four lines of poetry with a consistent rhyme scheme. The music is **strophic** (the same music for each stanza regardless of the meaning and mood of the text). Listen to SS3/1 and 4.

*In this text, stanza and verse are used interchangeably.

2. *Lyric songs.* These are songs other than narrative ballads, including love songs, ceremonial songs, and folk hymns, among many other types, that were derived from English folk music from New England. These songs convey emotional content and mood in a more private context than a ballad. Action and drama are minimal, the text content is wide ranging, and musical forms and poetic structure are diverse. Here is an example of a love song whose stanzas are related only through the imagery of the "Little Sparrow":

1. *Come all ye maids and pretty fair maidens,*
   *Take warning how that you love young men;*
   *They're like the bright star in a summer's morning,*
   *First appear and then are gone.*

2. *It's once I had a own true lover,*
   *Indeed I really thought he was my own;*
   *Straight way he went and courted another*
   *And left me here to weep and moan.*

3. *I wish I was a little sparrow,*
   *Or some of those birds that fly so high;*
   *It's after my true love that I would follow,*
   *And when he talked I would be nigh.*

4. *When he was talking to some other,*
   *A-telling her of many those fine things;*
   *It's on his bosom I would flutter*
   *With my little tender wings.*

5. *But now I ain't no little sparrow,*
   *Nor none of those birds that fly so high;*
   *I'll go home full of grief and sorrow*
   *And sing and pass the time by.*

The most popular folk song genre is the ballad with most songs falling in between the extremes of the narrative ballad and the lyric song.

3. *Blues.* African-based music of black Americans led to the **blues,** a style of music that was to exert considerable influence on jazz, rhythm and blues, soul, rock, and other forms of more recent American popular music. People specialize as blues singers; they "sing the blues." It is one of the most powerful means of musical communication. The feeling is mournful and melancholy (although not all blues are sad songs).

Blues has several connotations: it refers to a three-line poetic stanza, a twelve-bar musical structure, a scale, and a feeling. The first line of poetry is usually repeated. This is followed by a contrasting third line (aab form). The poetry reflects most frequently the element of mistreatment, derived from the injustice and misery of an oppressed people or the loss of a lover or a loved one.

*I got a brownskin woman, she's alright with me.*
*I got a brownskin woman, she's alright with me.*
*Got the finest woman that a man most ever seen.*

*Lord, I can't stay here, and my lover gone.*
*Lord, I can't stay here, and my lover gone.*
*Sometimes I wonder, my brownskin she won't come home.*

Work songs can make labor a bit more tolerable.

The music reflects the poetic structure, with four bars of music to each of the three lines of poetry, thus, the "twelve-bar blues." Additionally, through time, this structure has evolved into a regular pattern of chords—a consistent chord progression. It is significant that the blues is discussed or at least referred to in chapters 3, 4, 5, and 13 of this text, reflecting its role in American folk, jazz, popular, and classical music.

The blues scale is created by alterations to the major scale. Usually, the third or seventh scale tone is lowered slightly creating the "blue notes." In addition, blues performers "bend" the tones (a slight lowering of the pitch followed by a return to the original), or they slide into or out of the pitches to enhance their moaning, mournful, "bluesy" quality. All these alterations by a masterful blues singer help create the feel of the blues.

Listen to SS3/5.

4. *Work songs.* These are songs of both black and white Americans and include sea chanties, railroad songs, and lumber songs. They are rhythmic, often incorporating a call and response technique, and are sung to a beat compatible with the beat of the oar, sledge hammer, or axe.

5. *Children's songs.* These songs, such as lullabies and game songs, are usually short, simple, and functional. They are easily remembered and extremely varied in type and style.

6. *Broadside ballads.* These ballads are "folk songs" composed by professional songwriters. They flourished during the eighteenth and nineteenth centuries in Western Europe and the United States. A broadside ballad was a song published on one large sheet of paper called a broadside. It was sold widely and cheaply and was considered one of the popular songs of the day. Hundreds of British and American broadsides were published.

# The Proteſtant-FLAYL :
*A tory thing*

## An Excellent New SONG.

To the Tune of, *Lacy's Maggot* ; Or, *The Hobby-Horſe.*

*14ᵗʰ. Juно. 1682*

*144*

**[ 1 ]**

Liſten a while, and I'll tell you a Tale
Of a New Device of a *Proteſtant Flayl,*
With a *Thump, Thump, Thump, a Thump,
Thump, a Thump, Thump.*
This *FLAYL* it was made of the fineſt wood,
Well lin'd with Lead, and notable good,
For ſplitting of Bones, and ſhedding the Bloud
Of all that withſtood,
*With a Thump, Thump,* &c.

**[ 2 ]**

This *Flayl* was invented to thraſh the Brain,
And leave behind not the weight of a grain,
*With a Thump,* &c.
At the handle-end there hung a *Weight,*
That carried within unavoidable Fate,
To take the Monarch a rap in the Pate,
And go vern the State,
*With a Thump,* &c.

**[ 3 ]**

It took its Degree in *Oxford*-Town,
And with the Carpenter went down,
*With a Thump,* &c.
If any durſt his Might oppoſe,
He had you cloſe, in ſpight of your Noſe,
To carry on clever the *Good Old Cauſe,*
And down with the Laws,
*With a Thump,* &c.

**[ 4 ]**

With this they threatened to fore-ſtall
The Church, and give the Biſhops a Mawl
*With a Thump,* &c.
If *King* and *Lords* would not ſubmit
To the *Joyner's* wit whiles the *Houſe* did ſit,
If this in the right place did hit,
The Cauſe it would ſplit,
*With a Thump,* &c.

**[ 5 ]**

Two handfuls of Death, with a Thong hung
By a Zealot who hang'd himſelf at laſt,
*With a Thump,* &c.    *Stephen Colledge.*
With a moving head both ſtiff and ſtout,
Found by the *Proteſtant Joyner* out,
To have at the King & the Laws t'other bout,
And turn them both out,
*With a Thump,* &c.

**[ 6 ]**

Inviſibly 'twou'd deal his Blows,
All to maintain the *Good Old Cauſe,*
*With a Thump,* &c.
VVou'd *Liberty* and *Freedom* bring
To every thing except the King,
At *Monarchy* it had a fling,
And took its ſwing,
*VVith a Thump,* &c.

**[ 7 ]**

This *Flayl* was made of the Neweſt Faſhion,
To heal the Breaches of the Nation,
*With a Thump,* &c.
If *Faction* any difference bred,
T'wou'd ſplit the Cauſe in the very Head,
Till *Monarchy* reel'd, and *Loyalty* bled,
And were knock'd in the Head,
*With a Thump,* &c.

**[ 8 ]**

VVhen any Strife was in the State,
This *Flayl* wou'd end the whole Debate,
*With a Thump,* &c.
'Gainſt *Arbitrary Power* of *State,*
And *Popery* which the *Zealous* hate,
It wou'd give them ſuch a Rap on the Pate,
They muſt yield to their Fate,
*With a Thump,* &c.

**[ 9 ]**

It had a thouſand Vertues more,
And had a Salve for every Sore,
*With a Thump,* &c.
VVith this they thought to have maintain'd,
The *Loyal* Tribe, and *Royaliſts* braind:
But the *Joyner* was hang'd, and the *Flayl* was
And the Conqueſt Regain'd,    [Arraign'd
*With a Thump,* &c.

**[ 10 ]**

May *Tony* and all our Enemies, *ô Shaftsbury.*
Meet with no better fate then his,
*With a Thump,* &c.
May *Charles* ſtill Live to rule the State,
And *York* whom all *Diſſenters* hate,
To be reveng'd upon their Pate,
By timely fate,
*With a Thump, Thump, Thump a Thump,
Thump, a Thump, Thump.*

*LONDON*: Printed for *A. Banks,* MDCLXXXII.

a.

b.

(a) Rural folk music,
(b) modern rhythm and
blues.

Sometimes only the words were published, perhaps with instructions to sing them to a well-known tune. The broadside ballad was a narrative, retelling accounts of current historical events and functioning somewhat as a newspaper among illiterate populations.

The origin of many folk songs has been traced to broadsides. Thus, we see a case where songs originally written down were eventually passed on by word of mouth; thus, they became part of the oral tradition we associate with traditional folk songs. It could be argued that the modern counterparts of the broadside are the urban, commercial folk songs of the 1960s and 1970s. The songs of Woody Guthrie, Pete Seeger, Bob Dylan, Joan Baez, the Kingston Trio, and others are examples of this movement. Many of these commercial folk songs were intended to achieve popular success and to make political statements in urging improvements in our society. They adopted some of the characteristics of traditional folk music.

7. *Dance Music.* Dancing was and continues to be an important part of the lives of Americans of all backgrounds; thus, instrumental dance music plays a vital part in traditional folk music. The fiddle has been the primary melody instrument in virtually all instrumental folk dance traditions. **Fiddle tunes** for dancing have been arranged for a variety of instrumentations, notably string bands. The string band in the nineteenth century featured fiddle and banjo; the guitar became popular only in the twentieth century. Most of the songs are sung with accompaniment, usually guitar, fiddle, or a small instrumental group.

Listen to SS3/3.

Folk music is primarily a vocal genre with easily singable melodies; chromaticism is rare. Regularity, balance, and predictability are common and are important aids in the memory process. The verse form (with stanzas) is most common, although many verse and refrain forms can be found. The refrain follows each stanza with words repeated each time (listen to SS3/8). The verse carries the action forward, and the refrain stimulates a greater emotional involvement.

Modern protest songs. Pete Seeger, Jackson Browne, and John Hall at an antinuclear rally in 1978.

The voices of folksingers bear little resemblance to the voices of singers who have been formally trained. Compared with singers with classical vocal training, folksingers generally tend to produce a more earthy, unsophisticated sound. Many of them sing in a relatively imprecise manner, conveying a desired spontaneity in their performance. The vowel sounds, the pronunciation of words, the sliding into or out of pitches, and the flexibility of the rhythm combine to create a distinctively "country" singing style. Likewise, the vocal quality of other types of folksingers, from whatever race, region, or nation, reflects the same simplicity, lack of formal training, and down-to-earth quality of the southern folksinger. Charles Wolfe, a native of the Ozarks, has described the traditional folksinger as follows:

> The folk of rural America used their voices in wonderfully inventive ways. They hollered in the fields and sang work songs on their boats; they made their way through long, lonesome ballads; they taught their children with rhymes and chants and entertained them with nonsense songs, imitations, and bizarre mouth sounds; they listened to the music of auctioneers and street cries and square dance callers; and they celebrated their God with all manner of joyful noise.

## Religious Music

This part of chapter 3 emphasizes the religious music that developed from American folk culture as well as from European notated traditions. American religious music, like folk music, also can be examined from both Anglo- and Afro-American traditions. We identify these musical styles as black gospel music, including spirituals, and white gospel music, including psalm tunes, hymns, spiritual songs, and anthems.

White gospel music was originally influenced, as was Anglo-folk music, by the hymns and songs of the British. As people moved south and west from New England, their religious music took on a distinctive, folklike character that separated it stylistically from the more formal British music. Black gospel music was derived largely from the musical expressions of freed slaves and their descendants in the deep south combined with the British-influenced hymns and songs that became "Americanized" as they moved into the South from New England.

Through the listening examples, we will be able to observe both commonalities and dramatic differences among these musical styles, particularly the "modern" American religious music—that of the last 100 years.

## Psalm Singing

America was settled in the early 1600s by English, Dutch, and French immigrants, but the English Pilgrims and Puritans who first settled in Massachusetts provided the most significant musical contributions. Both groups fled religious persecution and desired to establish colonies where they could practice their religion in freedom. Part of the practice of these early immigrants included the unaccompanied singing of metered and rhymed versions of the Psalms. Two widely divergent styles of **psalm singing** emerged during this nation's first 100 years: a European, refined style found among the more urban and the more musically literate populace and a less-sophisticated, folk-like style found among the rural populations and the less musically educated.

The refined style involved singing hymns in harmony and from printed music. It was part of music's notated tradition and required singers to be able to read music. The folk style which became more popular included the technique of congregational singing known as lining out. This style, still a common practice in some rural regions, became part of music's oral tradition and led to the creation of a body of traditional folk hymns.

Psalm singing has had a profound effect on the development of American religious music. It was preferred over the liturgical music of the Roman Catholic church and over Lutheran chorales because of the aversion of these English immigrants to state religion and ecclesiastical power.

## *Psalters*

The Puritans and the Pilgrims both used English **psalters,** that is, hymn books that provided settings of the psalms to be sung in worship. The Pilgrims used the Henry Ainsworth's psalter, *The Book of Psalms: Englished both in Prose and Metre* published in 1612. This book included thirty-nine different melodies, one of which was Old Hundredth, commonly known today as the Doxology. The Puritans favored the psalter by Sternhold and Hopkins, published in several editions that included, in its third edition of 1553, fifty-one psalm settings but no hymn tunes. For the music, they used a published collection of ninety-seven four-part harmonizations of psalm tunes composed by leading English composers of the day. It was compiled and published in 1621 by Thomas Ravenscroft.

In 1556, a version of the Sternhold and Hopkins psalter with music was published. A version published in 1562 contained all 150 psalms and became the standard hymn book for all American Protestants and for many in England. More than 600 editions appeared from the first in 1562 to the last in 1828. The first American psalter was published in 1640 in Cambridge, Massachusetts. Printed on a press that had been brought from England, it was the first book of any kind published in British North America. It was known as the *Bay Psalm Book* and included no music. Seventy American editions were published through 1773, eighteen editions in England, and twenty-two editions in Scotland. The first edition with music appeared in 1698.

## *Lining Out*

The music in the psalters did not benefit those, particularly in the rural areas, who could not read music. To sing the hymns, those in the congregation would use a combination of their own memory and the leading of someone with a powerful voice. The leader would sing one line at a time with the congregation singing it back; thus, a hymn was sung by lining it out. **Lining out** was not a new idea. It had its beginnings in England and Scotland.

As with most music derived from oral tradition when memory rather than notation perpetuates the music, consistency and accuracy in lining out were not assured or necessarily desired. Local variations developed, fragments of one tune would find their way into others, and the number of tunes in common usage diminished.

Lining out created a style of singing common to the folk tradition that included florid lines and vocal embellishments (slides, turns, note bending, and other ways of ornamenting the melody) sung by various members of the congregation. People, in effect, changed the melodies according to their own musical tastes and abilities. Without strong direction, singers tended to sing songs in their own way at tempos that accommodated the slowest singers. The leader, in singing each line, interrupted the flow of the congregational singing and contributed to slow tempos.

Listen to SS3/7.

**Singing Schools**

Psalm singing began with notated music, but the oral tradition had taken over. By the early eighteenth century, a state of dissatisfaction with the state of psalm singing had emerged, particularly in New England. Essays were written and sermons preached decrying this folk style and the practice of lining out. It was felt that the "proper" tradition of psalm singing had been lost. They urged a return to singing from musical notation. This led to the establishment of **singing schools.**

In eighteenth-century America, religious life took on dual functions: in addition to a place for worship, the church functioned as the town meeting place, the center of community life, both sacred and secular. Conversely, psalm singing took place in homes, taverns, and out-of-doors as well as in churches. Also, in some cases, psalm or hymn tunes and secular folk tunes became closely related or interchangeable. Therefore, it was logical to have an important need of the church met by a community activity not affiliated with any particular denomination, and that activity was the singing school.

In New England around 1720, a few ministers decided to do something to improve the "deplorable" state of psalm singing. The singing school was created to get people to sing together "decently" and with "some semblance of art." More specifically, the participants, many of whom were teenagers and young adults, would come together for an evening or in some cases two or three days to learn to read music and to learn more hymn tunes. The leader was usually an itinerant "singing master." The young people also came to make friends and to have a good time.

The need for improved singing grew from the church, but as with the church, the singing schools indeed met social needs of the community as well. They met not only in churches but also in schools, homes, and other meeting halls.

The identification of church music was with the performer rather than the listener. The ideal was to participate in singing, not to listen or be sung to. How the music sounded to a nonparticipant was of little importance. The performing experience through congregational singing allowed the congregation to be active participants in worship.

The singing school tradition continues today in certain rural areas of the south and southwest. Its greatest impact was threefold: (1) raising the general level of musical literacy, (2) greatly expanding the repertoire of music available, and (3) encouraging the development of native composers.

**William Billings**

In order to read music, singing school participants bought tune books. They wanted new tunes—tunes composed and printed in America. As singing schools increased in number and spread geographically throughout the colonies and into the south and southwest, the demand for tune books increased. In 1770, William Billings published his *New England Psalm Singer*. Its success stimulated a great outburst of American musical creativity. It was an ideal situation for those inclined to compose music. They could write music for which there was a clear demand and appreciation for their product.

**Figure 3.2**

A fuging tune. One of the most popular of the fuging tunes. It was published in a collection called *The Easy Instructor* (1802), which was printed in shape notes (also called buckwheat notation). The Library of Congress.

Sherburne
DANIEL READ

Example 66

One of the most popular of the fuging tunes. It was published in a collection called *The Easy Instructor* (1802), which was printed in *shape notes* (also called *buckwheat notation*). (Courtesy of the Library of Congress.)

Collections of Billings' music that followed the *New England Psalm Singer* were the *Singing Master's Assistant* (1778), *Music in Miniature* (1779), *Psalm Singer's Amusement* (1781), and *Continental Harmony* (1794). This last collection included a number of anthems, which are extended and difficult sacred pieces intended for trained singers. The earlier collections, however, included "plain tunes" or hymns. These pieces are tunes in simple, homophonic settings that have four-part harmony with diatonic lines, and are homorhythmic (each part moving with the same rhythm). These settings are sometimes said to be in "familiar style," a style common to most hymns.

Some of Billings' settings were **fuging tunes,** a style of hymn writing that was popular in England and achieved some measure of popularity in America. A fuging tune is typically a four-part hymn with a short middle "fuging" section in which each part enters at a different time, starting one after the other as shown in figure 3.2. Each part has a similar rhythm, frequently has similar melodic characteristics, and enters "in imitation" of the preceding part.

Listen to SS3/6.

## The Fasola and Shape-Note Systems

In Boston in 1721, John Tufts published the first music textbook in America. It was called *Introduction to the Singing of Psalm-Tunes* and included an experiment to help people read music. Instead of placing ordinary notes on the staff, he substituted the initial letters of four syllables—fa, sol, la, and mi—which were part of a system known as the **fasola system** then in wide use in Great Britain. Each syllable represented a different pitch. A full scale would use the syllables as follows:

| 1 | 2 | 3 | 4 | 5 | 6 | 7 | 8 |
|----|-----|-----|-----|-----|-----|-----|-----|
| fa | sol | la | fa | sol | la | mi | fa |

The purpose of using these syllables was to aid in the immediate identification of scale degrees. In learning to read music, such as at singing schools, people would learn a hymn tune using these syllables before adding the words. However, Tufts' system was only moderately successful.

**Plate 1**

Edward Hicks. *The Peaceable Kingdom,* circa 1840–
1845. Oil on canvas, 45.8″ × 61.2″. The Brooklyn
Museum, 40.340. Dick S. Ramsay Fund.

**Plate 2**

Georgia O'Keeffe. *Cow's Skull: Red, White, and Blue.*
Oil on canvas, 39⅞″ × 35⅞″. The Metropolitan Museum
of Art, The Alfred Stieglitz Collection, 1952. (52.203)
Copyright © 1984/88. By the Metropolitan Museum of
Art.

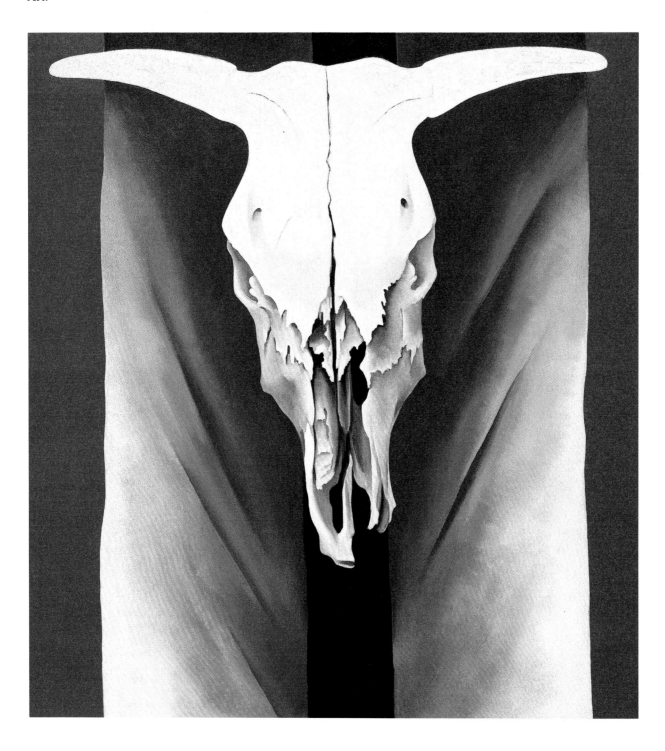

**Plate 3**

Edward Hopper. *Early Sunday Morning,* 1930. Oil on
canvas, 35″ × 60″. Collection of Whitney Museum of
American Art. Purchased with funds from Gertrude
Vanderbilt Whitney. 31.426.

**Plate 4**

Andrew Wyeth. *Christina's World,* 1948. Tempera on
gesso panel, 32¼″ × 47¾″. A well-known painting by
the conservative, contemporary American painter.
Wyeth's favorite subjects are country scenes around his
home in Chadd's Ford, Pennsylvania, and in Maine.
Collection, The Museum of Modern Art, New York,
Purchase.

Ziegfeld Follies song, "A Pretty Girl is Like a Melody,"
had words and music by Irving Berlin and a cover design
by Henry Clive. This song became the theme song for all
subsequent Follies.

"The Easy Winners," one of Scott Joplins' earliest and best rags. Published by John Stark, St. Louis, 1901.

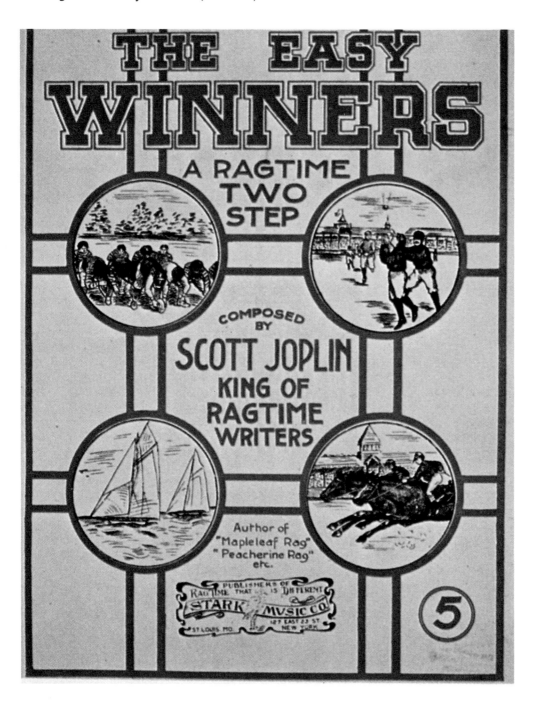

Figure 3.3
Shape-note scales. Fasola and doremi, the four-shape and seven-shape methods.

Figure 3.4
A hymn from the oldest known shape-note book, *The Easy Instructor*. The melody is the familiar Doxology on second staff from the bottom. From White Spirituals in the Southern Uplands, by George Jackson Pullen. First published by the University of North Carolina Press in 1933.

*The Easy Instructor,* a publication appearing in 1801, introduced a **shape-note system** whereby each pitch of a hymn tune was notated on a staff, but each notehead had a distinctive shape that represented a specific pitch of a scale as shown in figures 3.3 and 3.4. A triangular notehead represented fa, a round one sol, a square one la, and a diamond-shaped one mi. This system utilized standard notation rhythmically but added this graphic, quickly comprehensible system (the distinctively shaped noteheads) for recognizing and singing the correct scale degrees. *The Easy Instructor* was published in Philadelphia and, along with other shape-note hymn books that soon followed, contained hymns and anthems by New England composers, usually including some pieces by William Billings. These books were used in the singing schools that were organized throughout the South, thus spreading the shape-note system. However, new collections that appeared in the next several decades contained pieces that were different than those of New England.

These new collections included three- and four-part hymn settings of melodies that resembled the oral-tradition ballads, songs, and fiddle tunes of the South. The "composers" were presumably arrangers of indigenous folk melodies. They, in effect, captured in notation hundreds of these traditional melodies, arranged them as "folk hymns," and published them in shape-note hymn books. The best known of these hymn books that contained folk hymns were *The Southern Harmony* (1835) and *The Sacred Harp* (1844). Both collections were used widely in singing schools, church congregations, social meetings, and conventions. Conventions and all day "sings" were organized around these hymn books, such as those sponsored by the United Sacred Harp Musical Association, the Chattahoochee Musical Convention, and the Southern Musical Convention.

The singing school was the chief medium of dissemination of shape-note music, and to this day, annual sings are held in various parts of the rural South. The shape-note tradition remains one of southern, rural America. Many of the hymns sung today in

Protestant America, such as "Nearer, My God to Thee," "Rock of Ages," and "Sweet By and By," were written by urban composers and later became incorporated in the shape-note repertoire.

Listen to SS3/6.

**Isaac Watts**

During the seventeenth and eighteenth centuries, psalm singing was the prevalent style of congregational singing. Writers created metrical and rhymed versions of the psalms to sing to composed psalm tunes. The most successful and effective writer was Isaac Watts who created psalm settings and religious poetry. He was convinced that singing only psalms was too restrictive and, in 1707, published his *Hymns and Spiritual Songs,* a collection of poems reflecting current religious attitudes. Watts' poetry stimulated a new kind of hymn, one not dependent on the psalms. Vivid imagery, simplicity, and emotional intensity characterized his poetry. For two centuries, its appeal has ranged from the urban New Englander to the Anglo and the American black populations of the rural South and West. His words and sentiments were able to catch the mood of religious passion and fervor that had been sweeping the country since the Great Awakening in the mid-eighteenth century, a time that saw denominations, including large ones, such as the Presbyterians, Methodists, and Baptists, introduce mass public religious rallies conducted by evangelists who, as Charles Hamm describes it, "through impassioned oratory, roused people to emotional heights causing them to embrace or reembrace Christianity, spontaneously and publicly."

**Gospel Music**

The term **gospel music** is used to describe that extensive body of evangelical hymns and songs used at camp meetings, revival services, and churches. Gospel music came into being during the second phase of the Great Awakening in the early nineteenth century when itinerant preachers and evangelists stimulated a remarkable revival of religion.

**The Revival Meeting**

The Great Awakening spread quickly throughout the South as preachers traveled and conducted mass meetings to spread the gospel among blacks and whites in order to win converts to Christianity. These public religious rallies or revival services were often held nightly for one or two weeks. The momentum for promoting Christianity through the great revival services continued to build throughout the nineteenth century, and they became religious, social, and recreational events. The evangelists used impassioned oratory to arouse people's emotions and to cause them to commit or recommit themselves to the Christian faith. The preachers understood very well the role of congregational singing in stimulating the emotions of a crowd.

In the second half of the nineteenth century and into the twentieth century the emphasis shifted from rural to urban settings. Great temporary buildings called tabernacles were built to house the revival meetings. Preachers were paired with song leaders who conducted congregational hymn singing and sang special spiritual songs. The most famous evangelists were Dwight Moody and his song leader, Ira Sankey; Billy Sunday and his song leader, Homer Rodeheaver; and Billy Graham and his song leader, George Beverly Shea (as of this writing Graham is still active with his song leader, Cliff Barrows). The Billy Graham Crusades continue to be urban and international and make extensive use of the media, particularly radio and television.

The modern counterpart of the music of the revival movement is the music that plays an integral part in the programs (services) of television's "televangelists." These are highly professional media productions with music that incorporates many elements from popular and rock musical styles. This music has led to a genre of commercial

An early Methodist camp meeting.

popular music now known as contemporary gospel or Christian rock. The purposes of the TV "revival meetings" and the "old-time religion" are the same: to "win souls to Christ" and to use music to help make it happen.

## Urban Reform

The music sung at revivals and camp meetings in the early decades of the second Great Awakening was most often from the oral tradition, folk repertoire. Familiar songs were adapted to religious poetry. In the middle of the nineteenth century, an urban reform movement sought to improve hymns and congregational singing. The result was a tremendous number of hymns composed and published in collections. Many hymns sung in American churches today came from these collections. Lowell Mason composed, adapted, and arranged hymns and published more than twenty collections; his *Carmina Sacra* alone sold half a million copies. Thomas Hastings composed 600 hymn texts, more than a thousand hymn tunes, and fifty collections of music. William Bradbury published more than fifty collections, one of which sold over 250,000 copies.

A dramatic divergence of taste emerged in the last half of the nineteenth century, evidenced by the various hymn collections or hymn books: the "highbrow" and the "lowbrow." The urban churches wanted highbrow music that was more liturgical and European and that would combine psalm tunes and music from classical composers with the more traditional folk hymns. The rural churches and Pentecostal or holiness denominations and sects preferred a lowbrow, popular type of song, such as the camp meeting spiritual and the hymns used at revival meetings. (See figs. 3.5 and 3.6.)

## Black Gospel

The infusion of ragtime, blues, and jazz into the religious musical expression of black Americans in the early twentieth century created black gospel music. It became a style that comfortably merged sacred and secular influences. This music combines passionate religious feelings with effective showmanship. The more popular black gospel music grew out of the Church of God in Christ and other holiness or "sanctified" churches. These churches functioned as folk theatres, community centers, houses of worship, and "homelands of the soul." Centers of black gospel music in the early to mid-twentieth century were Philadelphia and Chicago.

## Amazing Grace! How Sweet the Sound

John Newton, 1725-1807

AMAZING GRACE C.M.
Early American Melody
Arr. by Edwin O. Excell, 1851-1921

**Figure 3.5**

An early American folk melody of unknown origin. It appeared in the South during the nineteenth century in many of the oblong tune books under such names as "New Britain," "Redemption," "Harmony Grove," "Symphony," and "Solon." The earliest known collection containing it (found by George Pullen Jackson) is the *Virginia Harmony* printed in 1831 in Winchester, Virginia and compiled by James P. Carrell and David S. Clayton (Lebanon, Virginia). This arrangement by E. O. Excell, a Chicago gospel-songbook publisher, was included in his *Make His Praise Glorious,* 1900, no. 235.

## To God Be the Glory

Fanny J. Crosby, 1820-1915

TO GOD BE THE GLORY 11.11.11.11. with Refrain

Willam H. Doane, 1832-1915

**Figure 3.6**

From a collection of Sunday School songs of 1875. This gospel song became immensely popular during the Billy Graham crusades in Great Britain in 1954. It has since become widely known throughout America.

**Figure 3.6**
*Continued*

Black gospel music.

Modern gospel texts typically are about black suffering, are ghetto influenced, and are about surviving from day to day. The songs are about poverty, segregation, unemployment, sickness, and broken families—about depression, betrayal, and isolation. They sing of dreams of "mansions o'er the hilltop," "vacations in heaven," and other visions of a better day.

Black gospel is emotional, vocal, physical, theatrical, and musically skillful, and it stimulates enthusiastic physical and emotional response by the audience. The sound of black gospel is the dominant vocal influence in contemporary popular soul music and helped provide the rhythmic and theatrical impulse of rock music. Its appeal transcends sectarian boundaries. The style includes shouts, moans, and melancholy slurs (influenced by the hymn texts of Dr. Watts). The music has syncopation, rhythmic vitality, and blue notes. Singers decorate, embellish, and vary the music in all sorts of ways. They frequently exhibit wide vocal range and perform intricate melodic and rhythmic patterns with remarkable dexterity. A hard-driving energy is typical. The style frequently incorporates interplay between a leader and respondents who may be the choir, the congregation, or both.

Among the most successful black gospel singers are women. Compared with men, women are considered equal or superior performers and innovators. The best known female artists are Roberta Martin, Rosetta Tharpe, Clara Ward, Mahalia Jackson, and Aretha Franklin. The best known males are Thomas A. Dorsey, James Cleveland, Sam Cooke, and Little Richard.

White gospel music is that sung by the white evangelists, song leaders, and congregations at camp meetings and revivals. Much of this music has stylistic similarities to country and western music. Black gospel music grew out of the black congregations, had its origins in black folk music but became the music of professionals, and has stylistic similarities to modern soul music or black popular music (see chapter 5).

The Study in Sound will provide additional information about American gospel music along with examples of various types of religious musical expressions found in American society.

**A Study in Sound**
*Folk and Religious Music*

# Example 1

**"Erin-Go-Bragh"**—Scotch/Irish folk music

A narrative ballad sung by Ed Kirby

Recorded in Connecticut in 1977

At the time of the recording, Mr. Kirby was a high school principal, singing only for his own enjoyment. He learned this song from his father. It appears in a number of nineteenth-century Scottish song books and in a collection of songs from Nova Scotia.

## Goals:

Recognize strophic form.

Identify monophonic texture.

Identify meter, phrases, and types of cadences.

Recognize the pickup and the tag.

**Guide:** The piece is in triple meter (three-beat) and counted in a slow tempo, one beat to the bar. It is in strophic form (music repeated for each stanza of poetry). The texture is monophonic (single line melody with no accompaniment or supportive harmony). Rather than beginning on the first beat of the bar (downbeat), each phrase begins with a pickup.

```
Stanzas
    1    -1--2--3--4--5--6--7--8-    In London one day . . .
         -1--2--3--4--5--6--7--8-    And lookin' me over . . .
    2    -1--2--3--4--5--6--7--8-    Will the big black . . .
         -1--2--3--4--5--6--7--8-    And I silenced his . . .
    3    -1--2--3--4--5--6--7--8-    Well they all . . .
         -1--2--3--4--5--6--7--8-    We'll lock 'em in . . .
    4    -1--2--3--4--5--6--7--8-    The devil you'll . . .
         -1--2--3--4--5--6--7--8-    And me mother's . . .
    5    -1--2--3--4--5--6--7--8-    Well the lickin' . . .
         -1--2--3--4--5--6--7--8-    As we lathered . . .
Tag      -1--2--3--4-                And we showed' em . . .
```

*Reflections:* Notice that (1) the music to each stanza is the same; (2) each stanza is comprised of two phrases; (3) the cadence at the end of the first phrase of each stanza generates an expectation of the music continuing (an open cadence); and (4) the cadence at the end of the second phrase of each stanza has a strong sense of finality (a closed cadence).

Why does it seem more appropriate to count one rather than three beats to the bar?

Describe what happens to the tempo during the tag.

# Example 2

**"Endearing Young Charms"**— Ozark mountain music

By the Leatherwoods from Mountain View, Arkansas

From the album, Third Time Charm

The instrumentation of the Leatherwoods is fiddle, guitar, mandolin, dulcimer, autoharp, and spoons. The melody is a traditional Irish tune.

## Goals:

Identify the sounds of traditional folk instruments such as the fiddle, dulcimer, and autoharp.

Recognize contrasting and repeated phrases.

Recognize foreground and various background lines, particularly the colorful, supportive harmonies.

*Guide:* Triple meter; count in a moderately fast three. The numbers denote strong beats (bars) and the dashes, weak beats. The music starts on the third beat (pickup).

```
Verse
    1    -1--2--3--4--5--6--7--8-
         -1--2--3--4--5--6--7--8-    Repeat
         -1--2--3--4--5--6--7--8-    Contrast
         -1--2--3--4--5--6--7--8-    Repeat of first
                                     phrase
    2    -1--2--3--4--5--6--7--8-    Bass added
         -1--2--3--4--5--6--7--8-    Repeat
         -1--2--3--4--5--6--7--8-    Contrast
         -1--2--3--4--5--6--7--8-    Repeat of first
                                     phrase
```

```
3        -1--2--3--4--5--6--7--8-
         -1--2--3--4--5--6--7--8-     Repeat
         -1--2--3--4--5--6--7--8-     Contrast
         -1--2--3--4--5--6--7--8-     Repeat of first
                                      phrase
```

***Reflections:*** Notice the intricate texture created by multiple plucked instruments.

Notice that each phrase has a one-beat pickup but is balanced by having one less beat in the eighth bar (still eight bars of three beats each).

Be aware of the underlying harmonies and chord changes; notice any patterns.

# Example 3

**"Knit Stockings"**—fiddle tune

Played by Wilfred Guillette, fiddle, and Maurice Campbell, piano

Recorded in Vermont in 1965

Fiddle tunes such as this were brought to this country by French-Canadian fiddlers who crossed the border to work in lumber mills or on the farms of northern New England. The foot tapping you hear is common among French-Canadian fiddlers; it provides their own rhythm section. Guillette, a carpenter by trade, learned this tune from another fiddler in Island Pond, Vermont.

## Goals:

Identify the sound of the fiddle (violin).

Recognize the internal patterns of phrases.

Identify the patterns of contrast and repetition of phrases by letter names.

***Guide:*** The music is in duple meter and performed two beats to the bar at a moderately fast tempo. It begins with one slow beat for an introduction. The bass starts on the second bar.

```
a      1-2-3-4-5-6-7-8-     First phrase
b      1-2-3-4-5-6-7-8-     Contrasting phrase
a      1-2-3-4-5-6-7-8-     Repeat of first phrase
a      1-2-3-4-              Partial repeat of first phrase
b      1-2-3-4-5-6-7-8-     Repeat of contrasting phrase
a      1-2-3-4-5-6-7-8-     Repeat of first phrase
b      1-2-3-4-5-6-7-8-     Repeat of contrasting phrase
a      1-2-3-4-5-6-7-8-     Repeat of first phrase
Tag
```

***Reflections:*** All but one of the phrases are comprised of eight bars. Each of the eight-bar phrases are comprised of two four-bar fragments, providing additional symmetry and balance to the music.

The formal structure of a piece of music is derived from its patterns of contrast and repetition of phrases or sections. The structure of this piece as indicated by the letter names above can be described as an abaababa form and charted as follows:

```
    a       b       a       a       b       a       b       a    Tag
  4 + 4   4 + 4   4 + 4     4     4 + 4   4 + 4   4 + 4   4 + 4
```

The purpose for describing music in this way is to help listeners keep track of patterns of contrast and repetition, particularly for developing the memory. As a piece of music unfolds, it is important to remember the character and style of the first phrase or primary section and how any subsequent phrases or sections relate, whether they are repeated, modified, or contrasted.

# Example 4

**"Barbary Allen"**— two versions of oral tradition folk music from the rural South

"Barbary Allen" is the best known, most durable, and most widely sung of the Child ballads. It may be one of the most popular and long-lived songs learned through oral tradition. Hundreds of versions have been documented. Originally, it was a Scottish song traced as far back as 1666.

The first version is sung by Jean Ritchie, one of the best known traditional singers in America. She is the youngest of a family of thirteen, a family known as The Singing Ritchies of Kentucky. This rendition represents a typical southern white singing style from the Kentucky mountains.

The second version is sung by J. B. Cornett from Masons Creek (Middle Fork), Kentucky. Identify ways in which it is similar or different from the previous version.

### Goals:

Recognize a common folk style of singing and compare with other familiar singing styles.

Recognize minor variations and personal interpretations in the melody.

***Guide for both versions:*** The music has a flexible pulse and imprecise meter. The tempo is moderately slow. Refer to notation on page 41 (fig. 3.1).

The first example includes three of twelve stanzas; the second example, two stanzas. The texts for each version plus a third version follow for the purpose of comparison. Text for first version:

> *All in the merry month of May*
> *When the green buds they were swellin'*
> *Young William Green on his death bed lay*
> *For the love of Barbary Allen.*
>
> *He sent his servant to the town*
> *To the place where she was dwellin'*
> *Sayin', Master's sick and he sends for you*
> *If your name be Barbary Allen.*
>
> *So slow-lie, slow-lie she got up*
> *And slow-lie she came a-nigh him*
> *And all she said when she got there*
> *"Young man, I believe you're dyin'."*

Text for second version:

> *It was away 'bout martin time*
> *When the green buds they were swelling*
> *And sad Johnny Green of the West country*
> *Fell in love with Barbry Allen.*

*He sent his name down to the town*
*To the place where she was dwelling*
*Said Hark—and come to your master dear*
*But give me Barbry Allen.*

Text for third version without musical example:

*Oh, don't you remember the month in May,*
*When golden flowers were blooming?*
*Sweet William on his death bed lay,*
*For the love of Barbary Allen.*

*He sent his neighbor down to the town,*
*And sent him [to] her dwelling;*
*"Oh, better never will I be,*
*Till I get Barbary Allen."*

*So slowly she got up her bed,*
*And slowly she went to him,*
*And all she said when she got there,*
*"Young man, I think you're a-dying."*

*Reflections:* Describe the singing style, particularly the ornamentation, and compare it with popular singing or other familiar singing styles.

Recognize the different flavor of the music. Its sound is derived from a modal scale, a sound that is different from that derived from a major or minor scale.

# Example 5

**"Violin Blues"—** black folk music—the blues

The Johnson Boys (guitar, vocals, violin, and mandolin)

Recorded in Memphis, Tennessee in 1928

This "string band" probably played on the Mississippi riverboats and in rural communities along the Mississippi delta. String bands sometimes added a one-string bass or a jug to play the primary bass notes. In the latter case, they were sometimes called jug bands.

## Goals:

Recognize twelve-bar phrases.

Identify characteristics of the blues.

Recognize pitch bending, slides, and "blue notes."

*Guide:* Count the pulse in a moderate four. The melody begins with a pickup. The instrumental introduction contains four bars and each verse, twelve bars.

Intro.
Verses

| | |
|---|---|
| 1 | Violin lead |
| 2 | Vocal lead |
| 3 | Vocal lead |
| 4 | Violin lead |
| 5 | Violin lead (higher octave) |
| 6 | Violin lead (tremolo)—fade |

*Reflections:* Notice the regularity with which the chords change. Listen for chord changes on bars 5, 7, 9, and 11 in each verse. The patterns of change are constant. Recognize these changes and become aware of chord qualities and the nature of chord progression (the tendency for one chord to move to another, forward energy).

Describe the singing quality and style; compare and contrast with the singing in previous examples.

Describe deviations from the basic melody (the performer's personal interpretation), both violin and vocal.

Recognize the higher pitch area in the fifth verse when the violinist shifted the melody up to a higher octave. In the sixth verse, the tremolo is the fast bowing of the violinist that creates a melody of fast, repeated notes.

# Example 6

**"Sherburne"**—an early American fuging tune composed by Daniel Read

This hymn is an example of a fuging tune from the early New England period. It was published in *The Sacred Harp,* a collection of four-part settings of folk hymns first published in 1844. This rendition was recorded in 1959 in a country church in northern Alabama at a weekend meeting of the Alabama Sacred Harp Convention.

## *Goals:*

Recognize polyphonic texture.

Recognize the strophic form.

Recognize the four-part, chordal, hymn style.

Describe the meter and rhythm.

*Guide:* The meter can be felt in a two-beat at a moderate tempo. The first time through, the participants utilize the "fasola" style of reading the shape notes. After singing the syllables, they use the hymn text. The phrase structure with the hymn text is the same as with the "fasola." Refer to notation on page 52 (fig. 3.2).

The first phrase is chordal style homophonic texture. The remaining phrases are in polyphonic texture except at the cadences at the sixth bar of the third and fifth phrases.

```
1-2-3-4-5-              While Shepherds Watched Their Flocks . .
1-2-3-4-5-6-7-8-        The Angel of the Lord . . .
1-2-3-4-5-6-7-          The Angel of the Lord . . .
1-2-3-4-5-6-7-8-        The Angel of the Lord . . .
1-2-3-4-5-6-7-          The Angel of the Lord . . .
```

*Reflections:* The singers make no attempts to "pretty up their voices"; they sing at full volume at a quick tempo. One hears no embellishments or ornamentations.

The rhythm can be described as steady and straightforward. Notice the four-part vertical structures (harmony) common in hymn singing, but in the second phrase of each verse, the treatment of both harmony and rhythm changes. At first, each vocal part (soprano, alto, tenor, and bass voices) moves rhythmically at the same time. At the sixth bar, the music shifts texture. Each voice then moves separately, one in imitation of the other (polyphonic texture); thus, each vocal line has the melody (like a round) with melodic fragments passed around from voice to voice.

# Example 7

**"Amazing Grace"**—two versions: a four-part hymn and a setting that illustrates lining out

The first version was sung by the Harp of Heritage Singers, a group organized under the auspices of the Harmony Plains Singing School of Cone, Texas. It was recorded at the New Salem Primitive Baptist Church, Floydada, Texas, around 1975. The music was compiled and conducted by Dr. R. Paul Drummond. The tune of this hymn is "Harmony Grove," found in the *Virginia Harmony* hymn book of 1836.

The second version was sung in the lined-out manner by the congregation of the Old Regular Baptist Church of Jeff, Kentucky. This church is in eastern Kentucky near the home of Jean Ritchie, a famous singer of traditional southern songs. She sang with the congregation on this recording.

### Goals:

Recognize the two styles of hymn singing: the familiar four-part setting and the less familiar lining-out technique.

Describe the two singing styles in terms of vocal quality and interpretation.

**Guide:** The two stanzas of the hymn text for both versions follow:

> *Amazing grace! how sweet the sound,*
> *That saved a wretch like me!*
> *I once was lost, but now am found,*
> *Was blind, but now I see.*
>
> *'Twas grace that taught my heart to fear,*
> *And grace my fears relieved.*
> *How precious did that grace appear*
> *The hour I first believed!*

The first version presents the two stanzas in a straightforward setting in which all voices move with the same rhythm. The emphasis is on the melody and the harmony.

In the second version, the leader sings each line of the hymn followed by the congregation singing the same text but to a melodic phrase different from the leader's. The response, rhythmically quite free, is slower than the leader's phrase.

**Reflections:** The first rendition is musically refined with no embellishment or ornamentation. In the lined-out version, the congregation sings in unison and embellishes the melodic line. A classical choral blend of voices and a refined musical style are not sought after musical attributes by those whose traditions include lined-out hymn singing.

# Example 8

**"If the Light Has Gone Out in Your Soul"**—holiness spiritual

Sung by Ernest Phibbs and His Holiness Singers

Recorded in Bristol, Tennessee in 1928

Three vocals; two fiddles; and piano, banjo, guitar, and mandolin

The holiness spiritual featured instrumental accompaniment, hand-clapping, and foot-stomping. It was part of the religious practice that encouraged leaping, rolling, jerking, dancing, and other expressions of religious ecstasy that were found in the Pentecostal or holiness groups.

The blacks of the sanctified churches originally were part of this same tradition and helped shape its musical style.

### Goals:

Recognize energetic rhythm with afterbeats.

Identify verse/refrain form.

Be aware of chord changes and chord qualities.

Recognize the sound of closed cadences.

**Guide:** Identify specific chords by name and by the Roman numerals: I is the tonic chord, the chord of stability and finality; V is the dominant, a chord of movement and instability; and IV is the subdominant, a chord whose energy tends to move to the dominant, sometimes to the tonic. Learn the sounds of these chords, where they occur in the music, and what they contribute to the music.

Count in a moderately fast duple meter. The pattern for each of the three stanzas is as follows:

```
Verse      - 1 - 2 - 3 - 4 - 5 - 6 - 7 - 8
             I               V       I
           - 1 - 2 - 3 - 4 - 5 - 6 - 7 - 8      (closed cadence)
             I       IV      I   V   I
Refrain    - 1 - 2 - 3 - 4 - 5 - 6 - 7 - 8
             I               V       I
           - 1 - 2 - 3 - 4 - 5 - 6 - 7 - 8      (closed cadence)
             I       IV      I   V   I
```

**Reflections:** Like many examples of religious music, this example features the repetition-filled, verse/refrain form. The music is rhythmically energetic, the chord progression is clear and consistent, and the singing style is distinctively country.

How is the refrain different from the verse?

Recognize that the three chords (tonic, dominant, subdominant) possess certain qualities when used in certain ways; learn these chord qualities.

Notice that the closed cadences provide a strong sense of finality to a phrase.

The text focuses on sin and death and appeals to the convert to "feel in his heart the dark dread of a life without the redeeming light of salvation."

*When the sun of your life has gone down,*
*And the clouds in the west turn to gold;*
*Oh how sad when the year's end has come,*
*If the light has gone out in your soul.*

*Chorus*

*Oh just think how in death you must feel,*
*With the light growing dim in your soul,*
*Oh how lone it would be, oh how sad,*
*If the light has gone out in your soul.*

*When you come to the end of the way,*
*And life's story for you has been told;*
*Oh how sad all the years will appear,*
*If the light has gone out in your soul.*

*Chorus*

*When the chilly winds of death around you steal,*
*And the clouds hang around black as coal;*
*What a dread in your life you will feel,*
*If the light has gone out in your soul.*

*Chorus*

*Oh I mean to live for God while I'm here,*
*Soul and body by Jesus controlled;*
*When I come to the end of the way,*
*With the light burning bright in my soul.*

*Chorus*

# Example 9

**"What a Friend We Have in Jesus"—**

A traditional hymn in the black gospel style

Aretha Franklin, vocal

James Cleveland, piano

The Southern California Community Choir,

James Cleveland, director

With organ, guitar, bass, drums, and congas; the celesta (the tinkly, music boxlike sound) heard near the end is played by Aretha

Recorded at the Temple Missionary Baptist Church in Los Angeles in 1972

This is black gospel music for mass appreciation. Aretha, who sang gospel music in her church since she was ten years old, was influenced by Sam Cooke who left gospel music for the world of popular music.

The role of the choir director is important. He or she directs the music and the energies and emotions of the choir and congregation.

## Goals:

Describe the black gospel music style.

Define ritard and hold.

Recognize patterns of chord changes.

Recognize the sounds of both open and closed cadences.

*Guide:* To review, the Roman numerals identify chords: I is tonic, IV is subdominant, and V is dominant. In this guide, an "x" refers to a chord other than the I, IV, or V. Again, listen to the chord qualities and how they function in the music.

The tempo is a moderately slow four beat.

```
Bars    1---  2---  3---  4---  5---  6---  7--   8---  9---  10---
Intro. I---  x-V-  I-IV  I-V-                                (instrumental)
   a    I          IV          I     x     x     V          (open)
   a    I          IV          I     x  V  I IV  I          (closed)
   a    I          IV          I     x     x     V          (open)
   a    I          IV          I     x  V  I IV  I          (closed)
   b    V          I           IV    x  x  x     V          (open)
   a    I          IV          I     x  V  I IV  I          (closed)
   b    V          I           IV    x  x  x     V          (open)
   a    I          IV
        I--IV I--IV I--IV I--IV I--IV I--IV I--IV I--IV
        I--IV I--IV I--IV I--IV I---   x-V-  I-IV- I---     (ritard/hold)
   b    V          I           IV    x  x  x     V          (piano/celesta/
                                                             humming)
                                                            (open)
   a    I          IV                                       (piano/words)
        I--IV I--IV I--IV I--IV I--IV I--IV I--IV I--IV x-V- I-IV-I---
                                                            (builds to climax)
                                                            (ritard/hold)
```

*Reflections:* A phrase that ends "open" has a feeling of continuance. A "closed" cadence ends with a greater sense of finality.

Notice that the underlying pulse at times is divided into groupings of three notes.

*Discography*

**Ex. 1**   "Erin-Go-Bragh." Brave Boys: New England Traditions in Folk Music. New World Records. NW 239. 1:23.

**Ex. 2**   Leatherwoods. "Endearing Young Charms." *Third Time Charm.* Dulcimer Shop, Mountainview, Arkansas. 2:30.

**Ex. 3**   Guillette, Wilfred, and Maurice Campbell. *Brave Boys: New England Traditions in Folk Music.* "Knit Stockings." New World Records. NW 239. 1:00.

**Ex. 4**   Ritchie, Jean. "Barbary Allen." *British Traditional Ballads.* Vol. I Folkways FA 2301. 1:05.
Cornett, J. B. "Barbary Allen." *Mountain Music of Kentucky.* Folkways FA 2317. :26.

**Ex. 5**   The Johnson Boys. "Violin Blues." *Let's Get Loose: Folk and Popular Blues Styles form the Beginnings to the Early 1940s.* New World Records. NW 290. 2:25.

**Ex. 6**   Read, Daniel. "Sherburne." *White Spirituals from the Sacred Harp.* New World Records. NW 205. 1:33.

**Ex. 7**   "Amazing Grace." *Harp of Heritage.* Musical Heritage Society 912131M. :52.
"Amazing Grace." Folkways FA 2317. 1:57.

*Ex. 8*    Ernest Phipps and His Holiness Singers. "If the Light Has Gone Out of Your Soul." *Oh, My Little Darling: Folk Songs and Types.* New World Records. NW 245. 2:00.

*Ex. 9*    Franklin, Aretha. "What a Friend We Have in Jesus." *Amazing Grace.* Atlantic SD2-906. 6:30.

*Summary*

The study of traditional American folk and religious music has provided two important benefits: (1) insight into America's history through understanding the musical styles that have been an important part of the lives of many Americans, and (2) a continued study of those musical characteristics and techniques that contribute to the development of listening skills as preparation for more complicated music in subsequent chapters.

By now, you should have developed a higher level of musical perception, such as the ability to recognize meters and phrases; to count the number of bars in phrases to perceive form; to recognize cadences and their open/closed characteristics; and to hear when chords change and, hopefully, to identify the primary triads (tonics, dominants, and subdominants).

The section on religious music is based on generalizations about the common practice of millions of church-going Americans from the beginnings of our nation to the present. Music has been important in the churches and to their parishioners. It is music that continues today, both in style and substance. Some practices have not changed in the past one hundred years. Others have adapted to recent changes in taste and style and to advances in audio technology, electronic music, and television.

As with all of American culture, particularly its folk music, American religious music is rooted in the traditions and styles of the Europeans. The story of America's folk and religious music is in its development and evolution as it moved from the northeastern cities to the rural south and west and merged with folk music and sometimes with music of other cultures, particularly African-based music.

*Terms and Concepts*

*Cross-cultural influences: Anglo- and Afro-Americans*

*High art*

*Folk art*

*Psalm singing*

*Gospel music*

*Hymn books*

*Oral tradition: preservation and dissemination*

*Field recordings*

*Folk song genres*

*Folk song characteristics*

*Strophic*

*Blue notes*

*Fiddle tunes*

*String bands*

*Psalm singing: refined style, folk style*

*Psalter*

*Lining out*
*Singing schools*
*Fuging tunes*
*Fasola system*
*Shape-note system*
*Gospel music*

# Chapter 4
# Jazz in America

Jazz is a twentieth-century American phenomenon whose artists and styles are now recognized worldwide. It includes widely divergent styles ranging from entertainment music to art music. Jazz is ever-changing and defies simple definition.

The role of jazz in society has changed. The image of the jazz musician as a cigarette-puffing, alcohol-drinking, drug-using misfit who talks and dresses strangely applies to only a few of the great jazz artists. Others have lived long and productive lives whose artistry has been honored by American presidents and other heads of state. Some have been awarded honorary doctorates by leading universities.

Within the scope of this course, we will attempt to gain some understanding and awareness of the following:

1. How jazz fits into American society
2. The cultural factors that contributed to its creation as an art form
3. Its common instruments and their sounds
4. What jazz is in musical terms
5. The major artists that contributed to the development of jazz
6. The various jazz styles

## The Jazz Context

The image of the jazz musician as societal misfit was created, at least in part, by the fact that jazz began in the seedy bars and nightclubs of the worst parts of the cities. These bars and clubs were the places where jazz musicians were able to obtain employment. Musicians have always been mobile, willing to play wherever they could get jobs or could improve their performing careers.

Jazz has come a long way. Today it is international and has a strong following in such places as Europe, Scandinavia, Japan, Africa, South America, and Canada. It is performed and listened to everywhere. Not only is it heard in bars and nightclubs but also in the finest hotels, on college campuses, in concert halls, and even in churches. Jazz has become an accepted part of the curriculum in schools and colleges. Entire courses are devoted to the study of jazz, and music students in many schools can pursue degrees in jazz. The National Association of Jazz Educators was organized to further the study and performance of jazz in our educational system. Jazz ensembles are offered for academic credit in American colleges and universities, and most high schools have "stage bands."

Jazz has been to a large extent a black art form—created by blacks and performed by blacks. Most importantly, the major innovations in the history of jazz development were contributed by black artists. Among them were Jelly Roll Morton, Louis Armstrong, Fletcher Henderson, Duke Ellington, Count Basie, Coleman Hawkins, Lester Young, Charlie Parker, Dizzie Gillespie, Miles Davis, the Modern Jazz Quartet, Ornette Coleman, and John Coltrane. Among the successful white jazz artists were Benny Goodman, Stan Getz, Gerry Mulligan, Stan Kenton, and Dave Brubeck.

Women who have achieved distinction as jazz musicians have done so as singers or occasionally as pianists. Many of the successful pianists, such as Lil Hardin Armstrong, Mary Lou Williams, Marian McPartland, and Toshiko Akiyoshi have been influential in other ways, as composers or arrangers, as leaders of jazz groups, or as writers and teachers.

Jazz is one of the most unique forms to emerge from American culture. It is an art that reflects a blending of the traditions and cultural values of the diverse peoples that comprise our society. Jazz essentially resulted from the blending of songs, dances, and musical instincts and preferences of people of African and European heritage, particularly France and Spain.

Jazz is part of the very large, very complex entertainment industry. It began in the early days of radio and recordings. Recordings brought jazz music to the attention of the public. It also brought the music of jazz musicians to their colleagues, an invaluable way to share, to learn, to grow, and to influence other musicians and, indeed, the future course of jazz. Jazz musicians make records to sell, to become popular, but not at the expense of the integrity of their art. Jazz polls do exist, and jazz pieces occasionally show up on the music charts, but jazz is much more.

Jazz aspires to do more than entertain, and the great jazz musicians continually strive for greater forms of expression, sometimes in very sophisticated forms and styles. For these reasons, it has never, other than during the Swing era, achieved mass popularity. Jazz is not considered "pop" music or music created for the sole purpose of entertaining and is for many musicians considered a genuine form of art music. The great artists possess a high level of musicianship, a sense of what jazz is and of its powers to communicate feelings, and a desire to share their art with others.

For virtually every statement that is intended to describe jazz, exceptions can be made:          **The Jazz Style**

1. "To be jazz, the music must **swing**." Some jazz music does not swing.
2. "To be jazz, the music must be improvised." Improvisation is at the heart of jazz, but much jazz music is not improvised. Also, improvisation is not unique to jazz. It exists in classical music, black gospel music, and in music of many foreign cultures.
3. "To be jazz, the melodies must be syncopated." Virtually all jazz has a considerable emphasis placed on syncopated rhythms. Also, syncopation is found in other styles of music.
4. "To be jazz, the music has to be played on certain 'jazz' instruments." Some instruments such as the saxophones (saxes), trumpets, trombones, drums, bass, and piano are characteristically jazz instruments when they are played a certain way in a certain context. However, they are all used to play other styles of music, such as a band, orchestra, popular, musical theatre, religious music, and so forth. Conversely, jazz music also is played on flute, tuba, organ, harp, and other nontraditional jazz instruments.

Listen to popular songs, hymns, folk songs, marches or any pieces that you know do          **The Swinging**
not fall into the category called jazz. Do they swing? Listen to pieces that you know          **Style**
are jazz, including almost all the pieces used for the Study in Sound accompanying this chapter. Observe the differences and identify those factors that make the music swing.

Swing is a manner of performance, perhaps more of a feel than a precise, analytical musical technique that is easily describable. At the risk of being too simplistic, swing is the product of a combination of the following:

1. Music is played rhythmically in a way that creates heightened energy and vitality. Repeated, evenly spaced rhythms are rare in jazz. The more common swing rhythm is comprised of syncopated long/short figures, symbolized in a most elemental way by the following patterns (each number represents a beat):

```
Evenly spaced          1   +   2   +   3   +   4   +   1
pattern
Long/short pattern     1      +2      +3      +4      +1
Syncopated, long/      >               >       >       >
short patterns with    1      +2      +3      +4      +1
accents
```

2. A unique combination of time keeping and syncopation. The drummer may keep time with the bass drum and a cymbal while giving emphasis to off-beat accents with the snare drum or another cymbal. In accompanying a soloist, the bass player often keeps time by playing a note on each beat (known as **walking bass**) while the pianist plays syncopated chords at irregular intervals of time providing rhythmic energy and vitality (known as **comping**). This rhythmic energy is also generated in big band jazz by **riffs.** These are short, syncopated patterns usually written for specific groups of instruments. They provide punctuated background material while another section or a soloist is playing the melody or improvising. Occasionally an entire chorus will be comprised of riffs without a recognizable melody.

3. Melodies that are not played as written. A jazz musician will always interpret a melody to make it swing. This person will vary the rhythm, slide into or out of pitches, shift the accents, bend the pitches, add notes, and do whatever feels right to give a tune the feel of jazz, to make it swing.

4. A **vibrato** that is consistent with the jazz style. The "shaking" or "wobbling" of particularly the sustained tones in a melody is essential to the jazz style. It is frequently a slow, wide vibrato, sometimes a combination of straight tone followed by vibrato. Compare the vibrato of singer Ella Fitzgerald in SS4/7, or that of any jazz singer, with opera singers. Compare the clarinet vibrato of Benny Goodman in SS4/5 with any classical clarinet soloist. Compare the vibrato of Miles Davis' trumpet playing in SS4/2a with that of trumpet players in bands, orchestras, or brass quintets.

5. Instruments played in ways somewhat unique to jazz. For example, in jazz, the drummer plays a trap set having a variety of percussion instruments—snare drum, tom toms, several different cymbals, bass drum—whereas in a band or orchestra these instruments are played by different musicians. In jazz, the bass player usually plucks the strings rather than using a bow as is most common in an orchestra. In jazz, the trumpet or trombone player frequently will use mutes to alter the quality of the sound, which is less common in band and orchestral playing, and the instruments are used in numbers and in combinations different from those found in bands or orchestras.

## Improvisation

Simply put, to improvise music is to compose at the same time as performing, to make it up as you go along. It is a fundamental characteristic of jazz and is important in every jazz style. Improvisation does not convey total freedom; it is not totally playing whatever you feel like playing. In all jazz styles, there is structure on which to base the creative improvisation. In some styles, the structure is quite clear and controlling. In others, the control or guideline is minimal. A structure might be an eight-bar phrase of a thirty-two-bar chorus; it might be a specific chord progression that underlies a popular tune or a twelve-bar blues tune; or it might be the meter that the improvisor adheres to.

Listen to SS4/8 and 9.

In fact, the ability to swing and the ability to improvise often set apart the jazz musician from other musicians. Many of the best classically trained musicians do not possess these skills, and they have been known to envy the improvisatory skills of the jazz musician. A classically trained musician who does not possess jazz skills will play a jazz piece in a square, unswinging manner. The "feel" of jazz is lacking.

The stylistic differences in improvisation will emerge in the Study in Sound section of this chapter.

The development of jazz has provided what may be called standard jazz instruments and instrumentation, acknowledging that many exceptions exist. We will consider **big band jazz,** from ten players on up, usually around fifteen players (approximately), and **combo jazz,** from one to nine players.

Groups of instruments are known as **sections:** the rhythm section (piano, bass and drums), the brass section (trumpets and trombones), and the sax section (two alto saxophones, two tenors, and one baritone). Big bands usually will carry three or four trumpets and three or four trombones, on occasion French horns or a tuba, a guitar, and often a featured singer. Probably the most basic instrumental group is the rhythm section: piano, bass, and drums. The rhythm section is basic to both combo and big band jazz and frequently functions as a self-contained jazz combo. The guitar is sometimes included in the rhythm section, although it frequently functions also as a solo instrument.

A common jazz combo adds one or more solo (**lead**) instruments to the rhythm section: trumpet and tenor or alto sax are most common (listen to SS4/8), sometimes trombone, clarinet, vibraphone (vibes), flute, soprano sax, or baritone sax. In modern jazz, groups often add a percussionist to play a variety of such instruments as bongos, claves, castanets, or other instruments to add color and vitality to the rhythm. The conventional piano has shifted to the electric piano, synthesizer, and **MIDI** technology or a combination of electric and nonelectric (acoustic) keyboard instruments. The electric organ occasionally is used. The label has shifted from piano to keyboards to reflect this versatile, electronic technology. The acoustic (stand-up/nonelectric) bass has for the most part given way to the electric bass (bass guitar). The influence of electrified rock is evident in modern jazz.

To fully appreciate the sounds of jazz, learn to recognize the sounds of the instruments and to differentiate sections, instruments, and styles.

Listen to SS4/5 and 6.

## The Beginnings of Jazz

Just as society in the United States is the product of many cultures and influences, so is jazz. It represents the merging of cultures and musical styles in certain aspects and the retaining of the distinctiveness of ethnic characteristics in other ways.

### The Roots of Jazz

In the late nineteenth and early twentieth centuries, Americans, both black and white, were singing and dancing to "jazzy" music. The roots of jazz, thus, were in the existing music of Americans of the North and of the South and can be found in the following types of music:

1. *Popular songs.* The syncopated melodies of the minstrel songs, cakewalks, vaudeville songs and dances (listen to SS5/1 and 2), and the dance orchestras of New York City and other emerging centers of popular music were part of notated songs that had considerable rhythmic vitality. They all possessed a syncopated melody with a strongly pulsating accompaniment. The music was diatonic, written largely in major keys, and based mostly on the tonic, dominant, and subdominant triads. (Refer to the section on early popular music presented in chapter 5.)
2. *Blues songs.* Blues as such is not jazz. It is part of the oral tradition of folk music (see chapter 3). Blues songs (listen to SS3/5) were the expressions of the oppressed blacks of the deep South and were derived from the shouts and work songs of the slaves and their descendants. They were

Scott Joplin has had
many of his piano rags
published and recorded.

originally sung by black men accompanying themselves on guitar or
other simple accompanying instrument (country blues). When blues
moved to the city, it was performed often by women singers accompanied
by a jazz, dixieland-type ensemble (urban blues). The most famous jazz/
blues singers include Ma Rainey, Bessie Smith, Billie Holiday, Ella
Fitzgerald, Sarah Vaughan, Jimmy Rushing, Joe Turner, Billy Eckstine,
and Joe Williams all of whom were black Americans.

Blues evolved into specific forms: the aab form of the poetry and the
twelve-bar blues form of the music. The twelve-bar blues form is found
in all styles of jazz (listen to SS4/9) and in much popular music
including rock. It forms the basis of boogie woogie, rhythm and blues,
and early rock and roll (rockabilly).

3. *Ragtime.* **Ragtime** (listen to SS4/1) became a notated form of popular
music originally for solo piano. It developed in the St. Louis area, and its
most popular creator and performer was Scott Joplin. (Joplin,
incidentally, aspired to be a great composer of classical music; his opera,
*Treemonisha,* was premiered in Atlanta in 1972.) Through performances
by various traveling musicians and the sale of popular ragtime pieces,
ragtime arrived in New Orleans and other southern cities. It was
arranged for an instrumentation derived from the popular black brass
bands (see No. 4). In its piano form, ragtime led to stride piano and the
artistry of a series of great pianists: Fats Waller, Earl Hines, Art Tatum,
Erroll Garner, and Oscar Peterson all of whom were black Americans.

4. **Brass bands.** Brass bands of New Orleans and other southern cities were associated with private black lodges, social clubs, and fraternal organizations who employed black musicians to play for dances, parties, parades, and especially funerals. A typical instrumentation of these groups included clarinet, trombone, cornet, banjo, tuba, and drum. The first jazz pieces were arranged for a similar instrumentation.

5. **Gospel music.** The early gospel music, particularly of the rural and nonliterate blacks, combined the shouts and moans of black blues with exciting rhythms, high energy, religious fervor, theatrical presentations, and religious texts. This style developed through the nineteenth century and exists today, having gained popular acceptance by both black and white people. (Refer to chapters 3 and 5 for other references to gospel music.)

Listen to SS3/9.

The George Williams Brass Band in New Orleans.

The Preservation Hall Jazz Band continues to keep the early jazz tradition alive.

## The Merging of Cultures and Styles

The blacks of the deep South were of African heritage and were deprived of significant formal educational opportunities. The whites and those of mixed blood (the Creoles in Louisiana) were educated in Western European traditions. The mingling of people from these two disparate heritages (African and European) was the most pervasive factor that enabled jazz to happen. This interaction contributed significantly to developing their music into an art that, other than perhaps the minstrel song, was to become the most uniquely American art form.

The most famous mingling of cultures took place in the mid-nineteenth century in New Orleans in Congo Square on Sunday evenings when people of the different races and backgrounds shared their traditional songs and dances. They created new music, forms, and expressions, some of which became jazz. It happened in New Orleans more than in any other southern city because of its cosmopolitan environment and its comparatively liberal social attitudes.

American society in the second half of the nineteenth and the first half of the twentieth century was becoming more mobile. Transportation was becoming more readily available, enabling people to move easily from city to city. It allowed rural people to move into the cities and immigrants to arrive from many different countries. The increasing mobility provided opportunities for an intermingling of cultures as people gathered and shared their songs and dances. It was increasingly easy for music and culture to be interchanged and, likewise, for jazzy music, such as the syncopated, highly rhythmic music described earlier, to become widely accepted.

The music industry (the composing of songs to sell and to become popular) was emerging. The style of popular music created in New York City incorporated many of the elements that were to become part of jazz, particularly the syncopation and the strong rhythmic pulse. Musical instruments were inexpensive and readily available, particularly through mail-order houses such as Sears, Roebuck, & Co.

The desire for musicians to entertain and for the public to be entertained seemed increasingly compatible with music having jazzy characteristics. Jazz music became established in New Orleans when artists began to emerge, particularly in the second decade of the twentieth century, artists such as Jelly Roll Morton, King Oliver, Sidney Bechet, and Louis Armstrong.

**New Orleans Jazz**

New Orleans jazz was performed mostly in a section of the city known as Storeyville. It included bars, nightclubs, and brothels that hired jazz musicians for entertainment and for dancing. In 1917, Storeyville was closed down as part of urban reform. With that closing went opportunities for employment by aspiring jazz musicians, but jazz musicians have to perform. They left New Orleans, some traveling on boats up the Mississippi River; many ultimately settled in Los Angeles, New York, and particularly Chicago.

The most notable recording artists to come out of New Orleans are Jelly Roll Morton, piano; Freddie Keppard, cornet; Kid Ory, trombone; King Oliver, cornet; Johnny St. Cyr, banjo; Louis Armstrong, cornet; Lil Hardin, piano; Baby Dodds, drums; Johnny Dodds, clarinet; Nick LaRocca, clarinet; and Sidney Bechet, clarinet. Nick LaRocca, the only white person among those listed, headed a white jazz group from New Orleans that later became known as the Original Dixieland Jazz Band. This group made the first recording of jazz music in 1917 in New York City. King Oliver hired the best New Orleans musicians for his Creole Jazz Band. Kid Ory, after moving to Chicago, headed the first black jazz group to be recorded, but later recordings of Oliver's Creole Jazz Band are said to be the best documentations of New Orleans black combo jazz.

**Two Artists**

Jelly Roll Morton left New Orleans in 1907 to pursue a career as a jazz pianist, composer, arranger, recording artist, and entertainer. Virtually all the New Orleans jazz was learned from the head (worked out among the musicians, not from notated music); thus, Morton's compositions and arrangements paved the way for a more sophisticated, rehearsed jazz that was read from notation and was to be commonplace in the 1930s. He, perhaps more than any other musician, successfully combined solo improvisation in a composed piece without losing the spirit of New Orleans jazz.

Louis Armstrong (listen to SS4/4) became the giant among all the New Orleans musicians, pursuing an illustrious career as a trumpet player, singer, and entertainer well into the 1960s. His primary influences were from his recordings made in Chicago in the 1920s with his Hot Five and his Hot Seven combos. They not only educated the public about New Orleans jazz but established a model for Armstrong's greatest contributions to the development of jazz, which were the following:

1. The possibility of the jazz musician as a solo artist by demonstrating innovative, extended jazz improvisations—more than in a two-bar break.
2. The possibility of solo jazz singing, particularly improvised singing as an instrumentalist improvises—a style known as **scat singing.**

Louis Armstrong playing the trumpet with his ever present handkerchief.

**Chronology of Styles**

The history of jazz style generally begins with New Orleans jazz. Since most of the outstanding New Orleans musicians by 1920 had moved elsewhere, particularly to Chicago, and no recordings were made of New Orleans jazz in New Orleans, we rely on recordings made in Chicago by these transplanted artists to learn about this first popular style of jazz known as Dixieland.

**Dixieland**

**Dixieland** (listen to SS4/4) emerged in Chicago in the 1920s. It became the first widely popular jazz style. It has sustained popularity to this day, with dixieland groups existing in many cities. The 1920s were exuberant years—the flapper, the Charleston, prohibition, the beginnings of radio and recordings, and the great Tin Pan Alley popular music and Broadway music of Gershwin, Kern, Porter, and Berlin—until the crash of 1929 and the Great Depression.

The New Orleans and the Chicago styles actually are quite similar:

1. Both have a high energy and rhythmic vitality.
2. Both have a rhythm section of piano, bass, and drums. (Again, there are many exceptions—sometimes tuba or no bass at all, sometimes no drums, and sometimes no piano but with banjo or guitar.)
3. Both styles have solo instruments of clarinet, trumpet (or cornet), and trombone (not many exceptions).
4. Both styles have arrangements that are not notated but worked out in rehearsal or, in time, are played according to traditional practices.

5. Both styles employ polyphonic group improvisation among the solo instruments according to the following rather strict, conventional practices.
   a. Musicians create melodic lines that fall within the chords dictated by the melody.
   b. The trumpet plays the lead, the clarinet an obligato (a higher, decorative part), and the trombone a lower melodic line derived from the main chord tones.
   c. All parts move in independent lines but interact with each other.
6. The rhythm section fulfills a timekeeping role. Sometimes the performers put equal emphasis on each beat. Other times they may stress the first and third beats or the second and fourth beats. The piano (or banjo or guitar) plays block chords in the same manner; none of them performs soloistic functions.
7. The music has occasional **breaks** (stop time). All musicians stop except for a soloist who improvises for two bars. This usually happens at the end of a phrase.
8. Musicians use **fills** to provide movement while the rhythm of a pattern or phrase stops. Fills provide embellishment between phrases.

## Stride and Boogie Woogie

Because of the Depression, the hiring of jazz groups declined, and the craving for jazz was in large measure fulfilled by hiring solo pianists. Ragtime, a notated popular music (page 76), evolved into the improvised, more energetic stride piano style. This style also featured the strongly rhythmic, walking (striding) left hand and the syncopated right-hand melody, but it typically was improvised and more upbeat than ragtime. **Boogie woogie** was the twelve-bar blues form combined with a unique style of piano playing featuring a constantly repeated left-hand ostinato pattern moving through the blues chord progression with energetic right-hand patterns that varied with each twelve-bar repetition.

## Swing

The Swing era of the 1930s and early 1940s was the only style of jazz that earned the popularity of the masses. It was the popular music of the day, placing many jazz tunes on The Hit Parade (equivalent to the top-forty charts). As Americans rebounded from the Great Depression, they wanted to be entertained, to dance, and to pay to achieve these ends. It was a great era for popular music, jazz, jazz musicians, radio, and the recording industry.

The Swing era also emerged from the need of jazz artists to fulfill their need to explore, innovate, and apply a higher standard of musicianship and jazz sense than was available to them through the relatively confining style of dixieland. It essentially was the era of big bands and for dancing to jazz music. Many of the tunes were Tin Pan Alley-type popular songs arranged for big bands in a popular, easily accessible manner.

In the late 1920s, a number of musicians became interested in creating arrangements (now called **charts**) of jazz for larger ensembles. To perform this music successfully required performers to read music, to play with precision with other musicians, and to improvise in the context of notated music. The most important arrangers of early big band jazz pieces were Fletcher Henderson, a New York sweet swing leader; Don Redman, who played with the Henderson group and then became influential in Kansas City jazz; and Duke Ellington, who became one of the most durable and successful of all jazz composers, arrangers, and big band leaders.

Listen to SS4/6 and 7.

a.                                                             b.

(a) Billie Holiday's unique singing style derived from her own deep feelings and experiences, (b) Ella Fitzgerald has proven that both popular and jazz singing can be merged with good musicianship and taste.

Jazz in the Swing era fell into three categories:

1. *Sweet swing.* This jazz was intended strictly for entertainment, dancing, and easy listening. Some would not call this music jazz, because improvisation was minimal as was the feel of the jazz swing. These were dance bands, society bands, or syncopated dance orchestras. They actually had existed for several decades, the most prominent being the dance bands of James Reese Europe in the late teens, Paul Whiteman in the 1920s, Glenn Miller in the 1930s, Guy Lombardo from the 1940s through the 1970s, and Lawrence Welk in recent decades. The fact is that these bands, particularly Paul Whiteman's, frequently employed some of the best jazz musicians available.

2. *Hot swing or big band jazz.* This jazz served the more serious jazz composer, arranger, and performer. It included more musically sophisticated charts, expected more extended improvised solos, and was more demanding musically than sweet swing. The recording industry was flourishing, but the long-play recordings had not yet come into existence. Most compositions and arrangements were limited to three minutes, the length of one side of a record. This greatly restricted the possibilities for extended improvisations by the leading jazz artists.

   Big band jazz was geared more to a listening than to a dancing audience. It has sometimes been called concert jazz. Among the best and most durable of the big bands were those of Duke Ellington and Count

Duke Ellington at a
concert in Paris in 1967.

Basie. Other prominent bands included those of Woody Herman, Stan
Kenton, and, in recent years, Thad Jones/Mel Lewis, Toshiko Akiyoshi/
Lew Tabackin, Maynard Ferguson, and Buddy Rich.
Listen to SS4/6.

3. *The jazz of Benny Goodman, the King of Swing.* Goodman's music is
   embodied in hot jazz, gentle swing, and combo jazz. He is probably the
   best known of all jazz musicians. He has received the highest honors
   from his peers and from governments. A Hollywood movie about his life
   received wide exposure. Books and articles have been written about him.
   He did more than any other to bring respectability to jazz and to bring
   visibility to the racial integration of jazz musicians and of jazz
   audiences. He has performed as a clarinet soloist with major symphony
   orchestras. His combo jazz foreshadowed the Bebop era, providing
   opportunities for such musicians as Teddy Wilson, Lionel Hampton, and
   Charlie Christian to develop their improvisatory skills.
   Listen to SS4/5.

Three major factors growing out of both economic and musical necessities created **bebop**
(listen to SS4/8):

**Bebop (Bop)**

1. Many jazz musicians wanted to find new ways of playing the same chords,
   to find imaginative and unexpected chords to "work around," and to
   interpret a melody in a new way. However, notated swing arrangements
   with the common three-minute restriction of the 78 rpm recordings gave
   little opportunity for the serious jazz musician to engage in creative
   exploration. Combo jazz, common to bebop, would allow greater
   opportunities for more substantial, extended jazz improvisation.

(a) Fats Waller. Stride pianist, composer, entertainer; (b) Thelonius Monk. Bop, pianist, composer, innovator; (c) Dave Brubeck on piano with Gerry Mulligan on baritone sax, cool jazz; (d) Herbie Hancock. Jazz/fusion composer, entertainer on keyboards.

*a.*

*b.*

*c.*

*d.*

2. People partied and danced at night; therefore, jazz musicians worked at night. When they were working, they played the style the audience and thus the employer wanted or needed. Too often the required style did not allow experimentation and creative exploration. After-hours **jam sessions** resulted, often lasting all night. It was at these sessions that exploration could take place, and it was at these sessions that bebop was born.

3. By the 1940s, big band swing music was declining in popularity, and because of World War II, people were not as available for dancing and entertainment. Musicians were also not as available. Gas was rationed,

Dizzie Gillespie.

restricting possibilities for travel, and, of course, many men had gone to war. The response to these circumstances was in part a return to combo jazz and the creation of the bebop style.

Bebop began in the early 1940s in New York City. Dizzie Gillespie, trumpet; Thelonious Monk, piano; Kenny Clark, drums; and others gathered to explore new musical possibilities and to satisfy their own unfulfilled musical instincts. The search for a new style did not solidify until a jazz musician arrived in New York on his way from Kansas City. His name was Charlie Parker. Parker's skills of improvisation and musical instincts led to a clarification and synthesis of the bebop style.

The roots of bebop date to the late 1930s in the solo improvisations of tenor sax players Coleman Hawkins, Johnny Hodges, and Lester Young; trumpet player, Roy Eldridge; vibes player, Lionel Hampton; and guitarist, Charlie Christian. All of these artists, through their recordings and live performances, influenced those who became the leaders of bebop jazz. Other important bebop musicians include Max Roach, perhaps the most outstanding bop drummer; Sonny Rollins, tenor sax; Mary Lou Williams, piano; and Bud Powell, piano.

Bebop is a cerebral, intellectual jazz. It is complex, intensive, and often very fast. The emphasis is on unusual harmonic, melodic, and rhythmic treatments of a song and on the performers' virtuosity on their instrument. The song often was a popular song of the day, but it was not unusual for the underlying chords and the title of the song to be all that would remain. The melody of the song often was obscure or not present at all, and improvisations were based on harmonic progressions rather than on melodic patterns.

The thirty-two-bar, aaba song form was common. The following is a model of what a bebop piece might be like:

The first phrase (a) would begin with the full ensemble, the lead instruments in a unique duet, often in unison.

The second phrase (a) repeats.

The third phrase (b) provides contrast usually with an improvised solo.

The fourth phrase (a) returns to the original theme. Several solo choruses
follow.

The sax may play a full chorus or more. The trumpet player will play one or more
choruses, and the pianist will do likewise. The bass and drummer may share a chorus;
and the piece will end with a return to the ensemble chorus as at the beginning.

Bebop is combo jazz. The standard instrumentation consists of two solo lead instruments and a rhythm section of piano, bass, and drums. The leads most commonly
are tenor or alto sax and trumpet but can also be trombone, vibraphone (vibes), flute,
or guitar.

## Cool, Hard Bop, and Fusion

Because bop was complex and sophisticated, it has never achieved widespread popularity in the public sector or among jazz musicians. Immediately, musicians began to
explore alternatives. Since the 1940s, many styles and influential artists have emerged.
This period (the 1950s and the 1960s) can only be described as a period of diversity
in jazz music.

Three important jazz styles emerged:

1. *Cool jazz.* It began with Lester Young in the late 1930s and was given
   impetus by Miles Davis, a bebop trumpet player, in an album called *The
   Birth of the Cool* (1949). It was an attempt to apply musically
   sophisticated ideas in a more relaxed, softer, more accessible manner
   than bebop. Cool jazz is typified in the music of early Miles Davis, the
   Modern Jazz Quartet, Dave Brubeck, Gerry Mulligan, Stan Getz, Chet
   Baker, Lenny Tristano, and Lee Konitz.
   Listen to SS4/2a.
2. *Hard bop.* This is perhaps a catch-all name for the music of those musicians
   who attempted to maintain the principles of bop but in a way that would
   not alienate the listening public. One version was to return to jazz roots,
   with harmonic and rhythmic simplicity but a strong beat, sometimes
   called funk. Many jazz musicians continued to experiment with new
   styles and techniques. Two of the most outstanding experimentalists were
   (1) Ornette Coleman, alto sax, who explored free-form jazz, a style that
   is almost pure improvisation without adherence to predetermined chord
   structures or melodic motives, and (2) John Coltrane, tenor and soprano
   sax, whose tone quality and approach to improvisation have influenced
   countless other jazz musicians.
   Listen to SS4/2b.
3. *Fusion.* Many current artists synthesize the jazz style with pop, classical, or
   rock styles (crossover) creating a new jazz genre that is referred to as
   fusion jazz. Keyboards, bass, drums, guitar, synthesizers, computers,
   MIDI **samplers,** and other electronic technology permeate virtually all of
   modern jazz. Again, diversity is a major characteristic of this music,
   although without question, the impact of rock and electronic instruments
   is significant. In fact, in some styles of modern jazz, it is sometimes
   difficult to identify jazz in the traditional sense. Its style—in fact, the
   definition of jazz—is changing.
   Listen to SS4/10 and 11.

Marian McPartland.
Contemporary jazz
pianist, educator, and
spokesperson for women
in jazz.

Toshiko Akiyoshi. Contemporary big band leader, composer/arranger, and pianist.

*a.*

*b.*

(a) Pat Metheny illustrating the application of computer technology to fusion jazz, (b) sophisticated music software.

**A Study in Sound**
*Jazz*

## Example 1

**"Sugar Cane"**—ragtime

Composed by Scott Joplin (1868–1917)

From the album, *The Red Back Book*

The New England Conservatory Ragtime Ensemble,

Gunther Schuller, Conductor

Recorded in 1973

*The Red Back Book,* originally published in 1918, was a collection of popular ragtime pieces arranged for a combination of instruments. The publisher of this book was John Stark, who also published Joplin's "Maple Leaf Rag," the piece that was to make Joplin famous.

Although ragtime was essentially a piano genre, instrumental rags were common. This rare, authentic instrumentation from *The Red Back Book,* which follows, was used for this recording:

| | |
|---|---|
| Trumpet | First violin |
| Clarinet | Second violin |
| Trombone | Viola |
| Flute and piccolo | Cello |
| Tuba | Bass |
| Drums | Piano |

### Goals:

Identify the ragtime style with emphasis on rhythm, syncopation, tempo, phrases, and form.

Identify various instruments from their sounds.

**Guide:** This piece is in duple meter and can best be felt with a strong, two-beat pulse at a moderately slow tempo. It begins with a pickup.

| First chorus | a | 16 bars | Full ensemble | |
| Second chorus | a | 16 bars | Full ensemble | Repeat of first chorus |
| Third chorus | b | 16 bars | Clarinet lead | Drum afterbeats |

| Fourth chorus | b | 16 bars | Violin lead | Trombone countermelody |
| Fifth chorus | a | 16 bars | Full ensemble | Repeat of first chorus |

*Reflections:* Notice that each chorus (each sixteen-bar phrase group) can be subdivided into two eight-bar groupings (antecedent phrase with open cadence followed by the consequent phrase with closed cadence). Each phrase can further be broken down into identifiable four-bar musical ideas (motives).

The drum afterbeats (often called offbeats) are heard in both the third and the fourth choruses. Counting each bar in a fast four, the afterbeats occur on two and four, the weak beats. Afterbeats are a type of syncopation. Recognize other syncopated patterns in the music. What does syncopation contribute to the sense of rhythm?

Recognize the several sequential patterns (repetition of musical ideas at a higher or lower pitch level).

A countermelody is a secondary melody accompanying the main melody. In the fourth chorus, it is the trombone playing against (counter to) the violin lead.

# Example 2

"**Summertime**"—from *Porgy and Bess*—two versions

Composed by George Gershwin

The two versions are presented to illustrate different approaches to jazz interpretation and style. Two giants of jazz, Miles Davis and John Coltrane, give their personal treatment of one familiar tune.

The first version, featuring Miles Davis, is an example of cool jazz. It was recorded in New York City in 1958. The music, arranged and conducted by Gil Evans, was written for a large and unusual instrumentation, as follows:

Nineteen pieces: four trumpets, four trombones, three French horns, one tuba, one alto sax, two flutes, one bass clarinet, string bass, drums, and featured soloist Miles Davis, trumpet and fluegelhorn

The second version of "Summertime" by John Coltrane reflects his unique post-bebop style. It is combo rather than big band jazz. This version is performed by John Coltrane, tenor sax; McCoy Tyner, piano; Steve Davis, bass; and Elvin Jones, drums.

## *Goals:*

Contrast the jazz styles in the two versions.

Recognize ostinato, walking bass, and vibrato.

Identify muted trumpet and other instruments.

Distinguish between interpreting a melody in a jazz style and jazz improvisation.

*Guide* to the first version: Count this piece in a moderate four; no introduction. It starts with a pickup.

| a | 8 bars | Ostinato in background; open cadence |
| a | 8 bars | Repeat of the "a" phrase but ends with closed cadence |
| b | 8 bars | Contrasting phrase ending with open cadence on seventh bar |
| a | 16 bars | Solo improvisation; open cadence on fifteenth bar |
| Fade | | |

*Reflections:* Describe Davis' inventive interpretation on muted trumpet. To what extent and in how many ways does he deviate from the established melody? Be aware of his use of vibrato, the role of the drums and cymbals, and the bass line.

Notice the ostinato pattern in the background. It is a series of block chords played mostly by woodwinds, sometimes with flutes predominating. Observe the subtle variations to the usually ascending line.

Describe the energy level and the mood of this music, and describe your reaction to it.

*Guide* to the second version: Count in a moderately fast four, no introduction.

First Chorus

| a | 8 bars | Open cadence on seventh bar |
| a | 8 bars | Closed cadence on seventh bar |
| b | 6 bars | Free sounding interlude |
| a | 8 bars | Return |
| a | 8 bars | |
| b | 6 bars | Interlude ends with break (stopped time) on the fifth bar |
| | | Same structure as first chorus; elaborate improvisation |

Second chorus

| a | 8 bars | |
| a | 8 bars | Fade |

*Reflections:* Notice the importance of the bass in clarifying the pulse in each of the *a* phrases. The bass is syncopated and irregular in the first four bars then shifts to walking bass beginning in each fifth bar.

Describe the mood and style of this music. One could describe it as searching music and find that it deserves repeated listening. Notice how much (or how little) the familiar tune is heard.

Describe ways in which the drummer and the pianist add rhythmic accents and punctuations.

# Example 3

"Stardust"—two versions of this popular standard

Music by Hoagy Carmichael

The first version was sung as a ballad. It was recorded in 1942 with Carmichael singing, whistling (not in this excerpt), and playing the piano. Joining Carmichael are Art Bernstein, bass, and Spike Jones, drums.

The second version, arranged by Neal Hefti as a jazz tune for trumpet lead, strings, and rhythm section with guitar, featured the influential Clifford Brown on trumpet. Max Roach, drums, was the most famous of the sidemen. The recording was made in 1955.

## Goals:

Recognize the jazz style in a slow ballad.

Be aware of vibrato and its contribution to the jazz style.

Describe the impact of backup strings in a jazz piece.

Differentiate the styles of the two featured performers.

Identify two-beat and four-beat bass.

*Guide* for both versions: The meter is duple, counted four beats to the bar. Of the four eight-bar phrases, each of the first three end on open cadences; the fourth phrase, of course, is closed. The tune starts with a three-beat pickup. The highest note is the downbeat of the first full bar.

The first version is moderately fast. The second version is moderately slow. The strings enter on the second beat of the third bar, and the bass begins on the downbeat of the fourth bar.

*Reflections:* In what ways are these examples jazz, and in what ways are they not jazz? Is one example more jazz than the other? If so, why?

In listening to the bass line, differentiate between two-beat (the bass is played on beats one and three of each bar) and four-beat (walking bass, played on each beat of the bar).

# Example 4

**"Hotter Than That"**—dixieland

Composed by Lillian Hardin Armstrong

Louis Armstrong and His Hot Five

Recorded in Chicago in 1927

Combo jazz: Louis Armstrong, cornet and vocal; Kid Ory, trombone; Johnny Dodds, clarinet; Lil Hardin Armstrong, piano; Johnny St. Cyr, banjo; and Lonnie Johnson, guitar

## Goals:

Recognize syncopation, breaks, and scat singing.

Identify the dixieland style.

Identify instruments from their sounds.

Describe group improvisation.

Describe the relationship between improvisation and structure.

*Guide:* Count in a fast four or a slow two.

| | | |
|---|---|---|
| Intro. | 8 bars | Full ensemble; group improvisation |
| First chorus | 32 bars | Solo improvisation, cornet<br>First break, cornet;<br>Second break, clarinet |
| Second chorus | 32 bars | Solo improvisation, clarinet<br>First break, clarinet<br>Second break, vocal |
| Third chorus | 32 bars | Solo improvisation, vocal (scat singing).<br>First break, vocal<br>Second break extended; vocal and guitar dialogue |
| Interlude | 4 bars | Piano |

| Fourth chorus | 16 bars | Solo improvisation, muted trombone; cornet break. |
| | 20 bars | Group improvisation, cornet lead, includes stopped time patterns; guitar break; brief cornet and guitar dialogue, the guitar having "the last word" with the final, unresolved chord. |

**Reflections:** Be aware of the group improvisation among the cornet, clarinet, and trombone in the introduction and the final chorus. Recognize the two-bar breaks and the improvised dialogues between both the voice and guitar and the voice and trumpet. Describe the vocal improvisation known as scat singing.

# Example 5

**"Body and Soul"**—combo jazz from the swing era

Benny Goodman, clarinet; Teddy Wilson, piano; Gene Krupa, drums

Recorded in 1935 in New York City

## Goals:

Distinguish between the jazz interpretation of a melody and jazz improvisation.

Identify the bridge in the thirty-two bar chorus (aaba form).

Recognize the sound of a clarinet.

Be aware of the timekeeping role of the drums.

Describe how this music differs from dixieland.

**Guide:** Each chorus is thirty-two bars and is comprised of four eight-bar phrases. It is in aaba form. Count in four at a moderate tempo.

a     Clarinet lead—a jazz interpretation of a standard tune.
a     Clarinet lead repeated
b     Piano lead—contrasting phrase (bridge); improvisation based on harmonic movement (chord progression)
a     Clarinet lead repeated

**Reflections:** The *b* section of the aaba form (the contrasting phrase) is known as the bridge.

With the clarinet lead, the melody is always recognizable although Goodman embellishes it with slides, pitch bending, and added tones. Notice any variations in his interpretation.

Notice the clarinet vibrato and also how much Goodman, rather than placing tones precisely on each beat, will play "around the beat," providing a mild syncopation. This is an important part of interpreting jazz and in generating and creating the swing feeling.

Wilson comps when Goodman takes the lead. He adds background chords and rhythmic punctuation, reinforces the harmonic movement (chord progressions), and adds activity when the melody decreases (adding fill). The drummer keeps strict time throughout.

When Wilson takes the lead in the *b* section, the melody is not recognizable. His piano style, more elaborate and complex than Goodman's interpretation, uses wide-ranging scale passages and arpeggios whose notes are compatible with chords suggested by the tune.

# Example 6

**"Harlem Air Shaft"**—big band jazz

Duke Ellington and His Orchestra

Composed by Duke Ellington

Recorded in New York City in 1940

## *Goals:*

Recognize the style of big band jazz.

Describe the instrumentation by sections and by specific instruments.

Identify the sounds of sections and specific instruments.

Recognize the form of the thirty-two-bar chorus, including the bridge.

*Guide:* Count in a moderately fast four.

Intro.—twelve bars

|  | *a (8 bars)* | *a (8 bars)* | *b (8 bars)* | *a (8 bars)* |
|---|---|---|---|---|
| First chorus 32 bars | Muted trumpets in two-bar segments—saxes in background | Repeat | Saxes answered by trombone with plunger mute—two-bar segments | Repeat of first phrase |
| Second chorus 32 bars | Saxes—(rhythmic break seems irregular but pulse is constant) followed by trumpet solo—four bars | Repeat | Saxes with trumpet | Repeat of first phrase |
| Third chorus 32 bars | Trombones with clarinet solo improvisation—two-bar segments | Repeat | Brass riffs with clarinet solo improvisation | Repeat of first phrase |
| Fourth chorus 34 bars | Soft—high bass—repeated short riff patterns—muted trumpet solo | Repeat | Brass riffs—upward sweeps in clarinet | Big brass riffs to end, with two-bar tag |

*Reflections:* Listen for the driving beat and a high degree of rhythmic energy. Identify the walking bass and the sounds of the saxes, trombones, trumpets, and trumpet and trombone solos.

Notice that few extended melodies exist. The piece is based on many short, repeated patterns called riffs. Pick out these patterns and follow them, and see how they are modified. Identify the instruments playing them. Notice the two-bar breaks in the second chorus. The underlying rhythm stops while the melody instruments continue, creating a seemingly uncertain pulse.

# Example 7

**"You'd Be So Nice To Come Home To"**

Composed by Cole Porter

Ella Fitzgerald, vocal

Recorded in France in 1964

With Roy Eldridge, trumpet, and rhythm section: piano, bass, and drums

Ella Fitzgerald is considered one of the best and most successful jazz singers of all time. More than just a singer, she is a musician. She sings with excellent control of her voice, pitch, rhythm, and phrasing.

## *Goals:*

Recognize comping.

Observe one person's jazz interpretation of a song.

Recognize vocal improvisation.

Recognize musical dialogue.

*Guide:* Count in a moderately fast four.

| Intro. | 10 bars | Two-beat pickup; muted trumpet |
|---|---|---|
| a | 16 bars | Open cadence |
| a | 16 bars | Closed cadence |
| Interlude | 4 bars | Muted trumpet and vocal dialogue |
| b | 12 bars | Vocal; improvisation (scat singing); open cadence |
| Interlude | 4 bars | Muted trumpet and vocal dialogue |
| b | 12 bars | Closed cadence |
| a | 16 bars | Imaginative interpretation of the melody; open cadence |
| a | 18 bars | Highest energy in first eight bars; closed cadence with two-bar extension |
| Ending | 18 bars | Muted trumpet; more sustained line; less rhythmic activity in voice; hold on last bar. |

*Reflections:* Antecedent/consequent pairs comprise each sixteen-bar phrase group. Listen for repeated or similar patterns throughout.

Consider the importance of the piano comping in support of the singer.

The piece is mostly in a minor key. Be aware of the distinctive sound of minor as compared with major tonality.

Observe Fitzgerald's sense of style, particularly her rhythm, the frequency with which she sings around the beat, either slightly ahead or slightly behind, constantly shifting accents, and frequently adding notes and syncopations to give the music a swing feeling.

# Example 8

"**KoKo**"—bebop style performed by the people who invented bebop

Music by Charlie Parker

Performed by Charlie Parker and His Re-Boppers

Recorded in New York City in 1945

Combo jazz: Charlie Parker, alto sax; Dizzy Gillespie, trumpet and piano; Curly Russell, bass; and Max Roach, drums

Bebop jazz typically is highly energetic, fast, complex, virtuosic, and often derived from the chords of popular songs of the day. Occasionally, musicians compose original bebop pieces such as "KoKo." It is a musician's jazz and appeals to those who appreciate sophisticated jazz.

Some authorities consider Charlie Parker to be the greatest of all jazz improvisors. He is featured here in an extended improvised solo. Notice that there is no piano player other than Gillespie. He comps during Parker's solos and plays trumpet at the beginning and at the end.

### Goals:

Recognize the bebop style and form.

Recognize the sound of the alto sax.

### Guide: Count in a very fast four (or a moderate two).

| First chorus | 32 bars | Ensemble chorus |
|---|---|---|
| a | 8 | Trumpet and sax sometimes in harmony, sometimes in unison |
| a | 8 | Muted trumpet |
| b | 8 | Alto sax |
| a | 8 | Full combo |
| Second chorus | 32 bars | Sax solo improvisation |
| Third chorus | 32 bars | Sax solo improvisation |
| Fourth chorus | 32 bars | Sax solo improvisation |
| Fifth chorus | 32 bars | Sax solo improvisation |
| Sixth chorus | 28 bars | Drum solo improvisation |
| Seventh chorus | 28 bars | Ensemble chorus |
| a | 8 | Full combo |
| a | 8 | Muted trumpet |
| b | 8 | Alto sax |
| a | 4 | Full combo |

### Reflections: Typically, the first and last choruses of a bebop piece are performed by the full combo. Be aware of the extent that the two leads (in this case, sax and trumpet) perform in harmony or in unison.

# Example 9

**"Brittania Blues"** (excerpt)—combo jazz

Composed by Marian McPartland

Marian McPartland, piano; Jay Leonhart, bass; and Jimmy Madison, drums

Recorded in the 1970s

Marian McPartland is one of the most important contemporary jazz pianists and an articulate spokesperson for jazz.

### Goals:

Recognize the twelve-bar blues form in a jazz setting.

Recognize walking bass, drum functions other than timekeeping, and a complex style of piano playing.

### Guide: Count in a moderately fast four.

| Intro. | 12 bars | Bass and drums |
|---|---|---|
| First chorus | 12 bars | Piano presents the main blues tune |
| Second chorus | 12 bars | Piano improvisation on the blues tune |
| Third chorus | 12 bars | Piano improvisation |
| Fourth chorus | 12 bars | Piano improvisation |

***Reflections:*** Notice the walking bass and the rhythmic accents and punctuations in the drums. Notice the interaction of the right and left hands of the piano playing (high and low): the right hand plays mostly single note, melodic patterns, the left hand plays mostly accents and punctuations.

Does this piece adhere to the twelve-bar blues structure? Without a text, to what extent does it convey the feel of the blues?

# Example 10

**"Kathelin Gray"**—modern jazz

Composed by Pat Metheny and Ornette Coleman

Performed by Pat Metheny, guitar and guitar synthesizer; Ornette Coleman, alto saxophone and violin; Charlie Haden, bass; Jack DeJohnette, drums; and Denardo Coleman, drums and percussion

Recorded in 1985

Since the early 1960s, Ornette Coleman has contributed significantly to the development of jazz as an improvisor and as a composer. He is a musical innovator, identified mostly with free jazz. Free jazz involves improvising without predetermined chord structure or other external means of influencing how one improvises, such as traditional scales or form.

Pat Metheny is one of the most popular jazz guitarists of the 1980s. His music falls in the jazz-rock/fusion category. Metheny has moved into the arena of electronic jazz, having experimented with a guitar-driven synthesizer heard in this excerpt.

## Goals:

Recognize stylistic elements in modern jazz.

Describe the interplay of the lead musicians when playing a duet (how they relate to each other musically) and how the lead or leads interact with the rhythm section.

Describe the organization of meter and phrase groups.

Describe ways in which the main melodic idea (motive) is used.

***Guide:*** Although the pulse is slow and uneven, one can perceive metric organization (mostly duple meter) in much of this excerpt. The following chart is an approximation of the structure.

| | | |
|---|---|---|
| First phrase | -1-2-3-4-/5-6-7--/8------------14 | Open cadence |
| Second phrase | -1-2-3-4--/5-6-7--/8-----------14 | Repeat of motive; closed cadence |
| Third phrase | 1-2-3-4-5-6- | Ascending motive; sequence |
| Fourth phrase | 1-2-3-4-5-6- | Descending motive |
| Fifth phrase | 1-2-3-4-/5-6-7--/8--------12 | Repetition of first motive |

***Reflections:*** Observe the sequential patterns in the third and fourth phrases. Discuss the timbres of the guitar and the interplay of Coleman and Metheny in their duets, particularly as to whether they do or do not play in unison. What role does the drummer play?

Describe your aesthetic response to this music. Construct an alternative chart for this excerpt that communicates how you hear the music.

# Example 11

**"Jungle Book"**—modern jazz (jazz-rock/fusion)

Performed by Weather Report:

Josef Zawinul: vocal, piano, guitar, clay drum, tamboura, tac piano, kalimba, maracas, and organ

Don Ashworth: ocarinas and woodwinds

Isacoff: tabla and finger cymbals

Dom Um Romao: triangle, tambourine, and cabassa

Recorded in 1974

Weather Report, headed by Joe Zawinul, keyboards, and Wayne Shorter, saxophonist, has been an important and unique jazz group from the early 1970s through the mid-1980s. Both Zawinul and Shorter came out of the bop tradition to create a group that would stress group improvisation, minimize solo improvisation, and use a wide variety of tone colors, exotic rhythms, and unusual instruments. They encourage an expanded role of the rhythm section to do more than provide rhythmic support for a soloist.

"Jungle Book" may be considered an example of jazz-rock or fusion jazz, but perhaps it would be more appropriate to refrain from labeling it and simply to call it a unique musical style that crosses over and synthesizes several styles.

## Goals:

Recognize a fusion style of jazz.

Be aware of new sounds and differing timbres.

Be aware of layers of sound.

**Guide:** The introduction is the initial, high pitched, sustained sound with no pulse or metric feeling. This piece represents a continuous evolution of sounds and patterns with certain identifiable rhythmic and melodic motives that emerge and recede as the piece unfolds. One could describe the music as monothematic because there is no distinct, contrasting section.

**Reflections:** Describe patterns of contrast and repetition, unifying factors such as melodic or rhythmic motives, organization of themes and phrases, shifting metric feeling, and changes of tempo and rhythmic activity.

Listen for the various layers of sound such as foreground/background material, high/middle/low pitch areas, and melodic/harmonic/rhythmic sounds. Be aware of the shifting prominence of the percussion.

Discuss the relationship of this music to jazz. To what extent does it swing? Is it improvised or notated? In what ways does it use traditional jazz instruments and techniques?

Describe the various timbres, particularly those that are new or unfamiliar. What is the function of the vocals in this music? Discuss implications of the mixing of cultures and styles in a piece of music.

After studying chapters 5 and 6 on world music, it may be beneficial to return to this piece. Discuss what musical aspects in it derive from Western culture and from other cultures.

*Ex. 1*   Joplin, Scott. "Sugar Cane." *Red Back Book*. The New England Conservatory Ragtime Ensemble. Conducted by Gunter Schuller. Angel S-36060. 1:47.

*Ex. 2*   Davis, Miles. "Summertime." Smithsonian Collection of Classical Jazz. 1:30.
Coltrane, John. "Summertime." *My Favorite Things*. Atlantic SD-1361. 2:15.

*Ex. 3*   Carmichael, Hoagy. "Stardust." *. . . and then we wrote . . . (American Composers and Lyricists Sing, Play, and Conduct Their Own Songs)*. New World Records. NW 272. 2:20.

*Ex. 4*   Armstrong, Louis. "Hotter than That." Smithsonian Collection of Classical Jazz. 2:57.

*Ex. 5*   Goodman, Benny. "Body and Soul." Smithsonian Collection of Classical Jazz. 1:18.

*Ex. 6*   Ellington, Duke. "Harlem Air Shaft." Smithsonian Collection of Classical Jazz. 1:35.

*Ex. 7*   Porter, Cole. "You'd Be So Nice To Come Home To." Smithsonian Collection of Classical Jazz. 2:48.

*Ex. 8*   Parker, Charlie. "KoKo." *Bebop*. New World Records. NW 271. 2:53.

*Ex. 9*   McPartland, Marian. "Brittania Blues." *A Delicate Balance*. Halcyon H 105. 1:15.

*Ex. 10*   Coleman, Ornette, and Pat Metheny. "Kathelin Gray." *Song X*. Geffen 9 24096-2. 2:03.

*Ex. 11*   Weather Report. "Jungle Book." *Mysterious Traveller*. Columbia CK 32494. 7:20.

*Discography*

This chapter on jazz attempted to get you started in knowing, appreciating, and respecting the literature, heritage, people, and sounds of jazz.

Jazz is a broad and complex topic. One can generalize about a style and immediately find exceptions. For example, you learn that Miles Davis is a bebop musician, then find him an influential cool jazz artist, and later discover him active in fusion and electronic jazz. Max Roach was presented as one of the best of bop drummers, but you find him on many of the cool jazz recordings. You will find cool jazz, bebop, and other styles all in the same piece. The big band jazz of Stan Kenton, for example, frequently has elements of bebop, cool, and swing all in one arrangement. Many of the great artists defy classification, because they continue to grow and change.

*Summary*

*The changing cultural contexts of jazz*
*The evolving musical styles of jazz*
*Jazz as an art form*
*Jazz as popular music*
*Combo jazz/big band jazz*
*The giants of jazz*

*Terms and Concepts*

# Chapter 5
# The Roots of Popular Music

Included in this chapter on American popular music is a study of the major contemporary styles of pop, rock, and country and their historical backgrounds, trends and influences that shaped them, and representative artists that made them important parts of American popular culture. The purposes are to help you know more about musical styles with which you may be very familiar and, again, to use relatively simple music to sharpen your listening skills, your musical vocabulary, and your awareness of the elements of music.

## The Definition and Scope of Popular Music

One goal of this study is to learn those common characteristics that make a piece qualify in the "popular" category, as opposed to jazz, classical, or folk music which may be popular but to smaller groups of people or to specialized audiences. A second goal is to perceive and articulate those factors that distinguish one popular style from another. What makes a country tune different from a "pop" or Tin Pan Alley tune? What makes rock music different from rhythm and blues, and rhythm and blues from blues, or late rock from early rock?

You will hear and learn about music that has mass appeal. Its appeal is cross-cultural and transcends regional, ethnic, economic, political, and educational boundaries. It is music that is consumed (that is, bought) by the largest number of people, and may be said to have the widest appeal. This is vernacular, not high art, music. It speaks directly to the people in ways that people can respond directly, both musically and emotionally. It should be noted, however, that many rock musicians have explored jazz and classical music, having helped to shape this music in the 1970s and beyond.

Popular songs typically are easy to listen to, and their sounds are easily recognizable (listen to SS5/3,6,9,10). Many popular melodies are simple and tuneful, mostly diatonic and singable, and based on tonic, dominant, and subdominant chords. The music usually has a strong beat and regular meter, rhythmic patterns, and phrases. Popular music by definition is not as challenging or as complex as classical music. It is visceral, foot-tapping, emotional, and immediately understandable music. Much popular music is permeated with the possibility of extramusical associations: the personality of the performers, the social activity that is always part of a live concert, relationships to our social/economic/political history, and memories of friendships and romance. It is or has been well known, if not a specific piece then at least its style. If it is not well known now, it may have been at an earlier time in our history. Popular tastes change, sometimes rather quickly.

In American society, today's popular music began in the second half of the nineteenth century with songs from minstrel shows, then in the early part of the twentieth century incorporated Tin Pan Alley songs and songs from vaudeville, Broadway musicals, and film. Hillbilly expanded from a regional music to a nationally popular genre that included western swing, bluegrass, and the Nashville sound. Black popular music, including rhythm and blues, gospel, soul, and the Motown sound, is now enjoyed by both black and white Americans. Rock and roll became rock: folk rock, acid rock, punk rock, Christian rock, pop rock, heavy metal, new wave, new age, and "whatever emerges next year." Currently, crossover music, that is, those songs incorporating characteristics of two or more styles, is popular.

Popular music is an integral part of the music industry. It relies on marketing, advertising, distribution, and sales strategies to manipulate taste and to create and promote hits and star performers. Popular music styles change rapidly as tastes change but are consistent in their overall character. For example, a country and western song may be popular for a few months, but the style of country and western can usually be recognized as distinct from rock, swing, old-time Tin Pan Alley, or modern MOR (middle-of-the-road—adult contemporary, soft rock, or pop rock). For another example, a swing band arrangement of a pop tune may have been popular only in the 1930s, but the basic character and form of that song may have been consistent and consistently popular throughout subsequent years.

The popularity of songs is measurable and has been regularly measured for decades: the number of times a song was played on a jukebox or on the radio (**airplay**) and the sales figures of records and tapes. Before recordings, popularity was measured by the sale of sheet music. Popularity has been reported to the public by means of The Hit Parade, the long-running radio show of the 1930s and 1940s, and *Billboard* magazine that still provides weekly **charts** of sales (that is, popularity) in a variety of categories, such as rock, jazz, rhythm and blues, and country.

Sheet music is a printed song arranged for voice and usually piano accompaniment. Contemplate the impact of the shift from printed music to recordings. To learn a song from sheet music, one has to perform it by singing it or by accompanying the singer. Therefore, the consumer is musically an active participant. With recordings and radio, one need only listen to know and appreciate a popular song. Thus, the listener musically is a passive participant. Although people occasionally learn to sing a song from listening to it on the radio or from a recording, one can wonder what impact generations of essentially passive listening has had on our ability to listen actively and intently to music.

The general public is subject to musical fads, rapidly changing tastes, and manipulation by the media and the music industry. Thus, songs typically do not stay popular for a long time. Popular songs come and go, frequently in a matter of months. Only a few sustain popularity through decades and generations. These songs become **standards.**

Listen to SS2/2 and 4/3.

## The Roots of American Popular Music

Because popular music by nature is ever-changing, it would be more productive to concentrate on the roots of American popular music—the events, artists, and styles that have created the music we listen to today. The purpose for studying particular artists is to consider their contributions to and their influence in shaping American popular music. We will try to determine the extent to which an artist was innovative, influenced other artists, and helped shape the future of popular music. This is difficult to judge in a short time. Sometimes it takes decades to gain sufficient perspective to assess the significance of an artist.

## The Colonial Period

Popular music did not flourish in the early years of our nation. Moral and religious scruples, some manifested as laws, prohibited "entertainment" music, particularly music for the stage. Religious music and concert art music were acceptable. After the Revolutionary War, many of these strictures were relaxed and entertainment music became commonplace.

By the early part of the nineteenth century, Americans improved their ability to read music and play the piano, and they could afford to buy sheet music. The earliest popular songs were composed for amateurs to sing and enjoy in their homes for small groups of family and friends. Songs that colonial Americans enjoyed were mostly imported from Europe and the British Isles and included melodies from European operas fitted with English texts, settings of traditional Scottish and Irish airs, German art songs, and simplified arrangements of vocal solos composed for professional singers. A typical popular song was strophic. It was set in a relatively low vocal range with a simple piano accompaniment. The music was usually diatonic, in a major key, and relied upon the three primary I, IV, and V chords.

## THE TURN OF THE TUNE
### TRAVELLER PLAYING THE ARKANSAS TRAVELLER

SQUATTER — WHY STRANGER I'VE BEEN TRYING FOUR YEARS TO GIT THE TURN OF THAT TUNE — COME RIGHT IN — JOHNNY TAKE THE HORSE AND FEED HIM — WIFE GIT UP THE BEST CORN CAKES YOU CAN MAKE — SALLY MAKE UP THE BEST BED — HE CAN PLAY THE TURN OF THAT TUNE — COME RIGHT IN AND PLAY IT ALL THROUGH STRANGER - YOU KIN LODGE WITH US A MONTH FREE OF CHARGE.

Through the middle nineteenth century, music in
America had its own distinctive character.

The first person known to have written songs for voice and piano in America was Francis Hopkinson, a signer of the Declaration of Independence and the first Secretary of the Navy.

Some examples of early American popular songs follow:

"The Blue Bells of Scotland"—traditional Scottish air

"Auld Lang Syne" and "Coming through the Rye"—traditional Scottish airs with texts by Robert Burns

"Ave Maria" and "Serenade"—composed by Franz Schubert

"Home Sweet Home"—text by Sir Henry Bishop. This song sold 100,000 copies in 1832, its first year, and several million by the end of the nineteenth century.

"The Last Rose of Summer" and "Believe Me If All Those Endearing Young Charms"—traditional Irish tunes with texts by Thomas Moore

**The First "American" Songs**

Through the middle of the nineteenth century, American popular music took on a more diverse character. Songs influenced by British music and European opera continued, but others began developing a distinctively American character.

*Henry Russell*

Henry Russell was the next important songwriter. He was born in England, came to America to enhance his performing and composing career, and concertized widely. His songs and his singing of them were intended to be appealing to many different types of people and to elicit emotional responses from large audiences. He had a sense of what type of song would be popular for that time. Although his songs were influenced by European opera, he was able to infuse them with an American spirit that helped shape the course of popular songwriting. He influenced others, notably the greatest of all nineteenth-century composers of American songs, Stephen Foster. Russell's most famous song is "Woodman, Spare That Tree."

*Stephen Foster*

Stephen Foster was, like Russell, a trained musician who was knowledgeable of the art music of the day. Both wanted to "speak to the American people in song." No composer achieved the success of providing songs that became a shared experience by so many Americans as did Stephen Foster. His songs include minstrel songs, plantation songs, and sentimental and dramatic songs. In his later minstrel songs, Foster began offering an image of blacks as human beings who experience pain, sorrow, and love. Many of his songs have become identified with American culture to an extent that they almost seem to be a part of the American folk song tradition.

Examples of Stephen Foster songs follow:

"Old Folks at Home" (Way Down upon the Swanee River)

"Oh! Susanna"

"My Old Kentucky Home"

"Old Black Joe"

"Jeannie with the Light Brown Hair"

"Come Where My Love Lies Dreaming"

"Beautiful Dreamer"

*The Rallying and Protest Songs*

These songs comprise another genre to emerge in the mid-nineteenth century. They were songs openly associated with social or political causes such as temperance, abolition, antislavery, women's suffrage, antiwar, and political campaigns. The most popular of these songs were tuned to the pulse of the people, to the moods of the masses.

Examples of rallying songs follow:

"John Brown's Body"
"Battle Hymn of the Republic"
"Dixie"
"Rally 'Round the Flag"
"When This Cruel War Is Over"—This song expressed the emotions of
    millions of Americans who bought copies in 1863.
"Little Brown Jug"—a temperance song
"I'll Take You Home Again Kathleen"—another temperance song
"Grandfather's Clock"

Rallying and protest songs became an integral part of American popular music, particularly as seen through the music of Woody Guthrie in the 1930s and 1940s and of his successors in the urban folk song movement of the 1960s: Bob Dylan, Pete Seeger, and others.

## The Minstrel Song

The **minstrel song** was the first distinctively American music genre. It was a product of rural American folk traditions and emerging urban composed music. Typically, it was lively, syncopated, and often humorous. These songs were written by white Americans for white Americans. They were sung by white Americans in black face (white faces painted black); and they portrayed black Americans as comical and illiterate. This portrayal had little to do with the realities of black culture, but the songs became an important part of American popular music. Two of the most famous of early minstrel entertainers were "Daddy" Rice, who capitalized on Jim Crow routines, and Dan Emmett, one of the earliest composers of minstrel songs who wrote "Dixie" and "Old Dan Tucker."

## The Minstrel Show

By the middle of the nineteenth century, minstrel songs were popular both in America and Europe, partly because of the success of traveling minstrel troupes such as the Virginia Minstrels, with Dan Emmett, formed in New York in 1843, and the Christy Minstrels, also formed in New York in the 1840s. Their success paved the way for hundreds of successors and imitators. It was a logical step to take the popular minstrel songs and dances performed by troupes and individual entertainers and put them in a sequence of acts on stage; thus, the minstrel show was created. Hundreds of shows were produced in the late 1800s in America and Europe.

The music for minstrel shows was drawn from traditional folk material, popular songs of the day, songs from Italian opera, and songs newly composed for the show. These shows also included comic dialogue, dances, acrobats, black face songs, and instrumental pieces. Since plots in minstrel shows were minimal, the music was incidental to and did not necessarily enhance any dramatic action that may be present. Ironically, the black face minstrel shows were so popular that blacks themselves began writing and performing them. The first black song writer of note was James Bland who wrote "Carry Me Back to Old Virginny" and "Oh, Dem Golden Slippers." Black minstrel shows began in 1865 in Georgia with the Georgia Minstrels. The style and content were essentially the same as white minstrel shows.

## Tin Pan Alley

The 1890s through the 1950s saw the greatest period of song writing in the history of American popular music—the **Tin Pan Alley** tradition. Its most productive years were the 1920s and the 1930s. From Tin Pan Alley have come our pop tunes, standards, most beloved songs—songs for amusement, entertainment, and escape. The period of Tin Pan Alley in the history of American popular music ended with the beginnings of rock and roll and the shift of the center of song writing and publishing to Nashville.

Tin Pan Alley symbolizes three aspects of popular music:

1. A street in New York City where virtually every publisher of popular music in the early part of this century was located. The term was coined because of the sounds of the cheap upright pianos that each publisher maintained in its salesroom for customers to try out a song.

2. That part of the music industry that was devoted to the sale of popular songs. In the early years, the primary medium of publication was sheet music; thus, the industry stimulated the sale of pianos, player pianos, and piano rolls. Beginning with the 1920s, the industry promoted the sale of radios, phonographs, and recordings. Publishers assessed the public's taste and proceeded to write and publish more of the same. They maintained their own composers, frequently called hacks, who ground out the songs daily. Most of these songs were forgotten shortly after they were published.

3. It came to refer to the type of song written during these decades (listen to SS5/1,2,3,4). Typically, it meant a song in verse/chorus form with the chorus usually comprised of thirty-two bars with four equal phrases. The chorus had the more memorable lyrics and melody. The lyrics of a Tin Pan Alley song dealt with personal emotions. They were sentimental, unsophisticated, unreflective of the real world, and romantic. Tin Pan Alley songs were performed in vaudeville, the Ziegfeld Follies and other revues, Broadway musicals, films, and nightclubs, on radio and recordings, and by big band jazz and swing bands and their singers. The most durable and popular of American songs are the Tin Pan Alley standards.

Tin Pan Alley, despite its widespread use of hacks, had a way of encouraging genius among America's popular composers, lyricists, and performers. Among the best of the composers who flourished in the Tin Pan Alley tradition were Jerome Kern, Cole Porter, George Gershwin, Irving Berlin, and Richard Rodgers. Among the outstanding performers of this period were Al Jolson, Eddie Cantor, Rudy Vallee, Kate Smith, Paul Whiteman, and Bing Crosby.

Three styles of music—ragtime, blues, and swing (discussed more fully in chapters 3 and 4)—became extremely popular among both black and white Americans. The music industry (that is, Tin Pan Alley) exploited these styles by producing hundreds of rag songs and blues songs, calling them rags and blues whether or not they really were.

**Vaudeville**

**Vaudeville,** centered in New York City, replaced the minstrel show in popularity. It was a variety show. With the minstrels, the entire troupe was usually on stage. Vaudeville included a sequence of unrelated acts: singers (not usually black face), dancers, comedians, jugglers, child performers, trained animals, and dramatic sketches. Its more sophisticated counterpart on Broadway was the revue. These variety shows were known at different times as follies, scandals, or vanities. The most famous was the Ziegfeld Follies, produced from 1907 through 1932.

Listen to SS5/2.

A World War I comedy song popularized by Sophie Tucker and Eddie Canter in 1919. It was used by Eubie Blake and Noble Sissle in "Shuffle Along" (1921).

Old hit of the all-black show "Shuffle Along" (1921), was used as the campaign song for Truman in 1948.

Irving Berlin rehearsing
with Ethel Merman
before the opening of
"Call Me Madame."

Tin Pan Alley songs were the essential element of vaudeville and included sentimental popular songs, some black face minstrel songs, and racial or ethnic dialect songs. Vaudeville songs represented a new direction in American popular music. It introduced songs that dealt with contemporary city life in what was still a basically rural, agrarian society.

## Musicals

The American musical, the best of which has been produced on Broadway, includes songs, staging, and drama. In contrast to minstrel and vaudeville shows, it is a unified piece with dramatic flow; it is a musical play. Musicals were created by song writers of great genius such as Kern, Gershwin, Porter, and Berlin. Although centered in New York, the American musical reached the entire country.

The first important composer of Broadway musicals was George M. Cohan who was also the lyricist for his productions. His *Little Johnnie Jones* was produced in 1904 and included the song, "Give My Regards to Broadway." Cohan, of Irish heritage, used popular, patriotic airs such as "Yankee Doodle" and "Dixie." His own song, "You're a Grand Old Flag" is from his 1906 production, *George Washington, Jr.* The best Tin Pan Alley composers wrote Broadway musicals: George Gershwin with *Girl Crazy, Strike Up the Band, Lady Be Good* ("Fascinating Rhythm" and the "The Man I Love"), and *Porgy and Bess* ("Summertime"); Cole Porter, *Anything Goes;* Jerome Kern, *Roberta* and *Showboat* ("Ol' Man River"); Irving Berlin, *Annie Get Your Gun* ("There's No Business Like Show Business"); and Richard Rodgers, *Oklahoma* and *Carousel* ("If I Loved You").

**Film**

*The Jazz Singer,* the first commercial movie with a synchronized sound track, was made in 1927. In the decade that followed, composers, arrangers, singers, dancers, and producers headed for Hollywood. The early movie musicals used large orchestras, lavish sets and costumes, large casts, and expensive stars. They provided marvelous opportunities for talented artists.

These movies were entertaining spectacles. They presented an unreal world of glittering sophistication, the carefree world of show people, exotic travel, and the make-believe world of childhood. They brought escape from the hardships of the Great Depression and projected things that were not available to most Americans. People who were deprived of any luxury wanted to be entertained by seeing excesses of it. Movie-goers were aware of the luxurious life-styles of the rich and famous and of the extravagant incomes of movie stars. They didn't seem to mind; no one protested this imbalance in our society. Seeing these unreal experiences and situations somehow made their lives a bit more bearable.

Many songs from these movies became very popular. They took people's minds off their troubles. The lyrics do not convey how people lived as much as their reactions to the way they lived. Again, the Tin Pan Alley composers became important creators of film music from which many of their most successful songs came. Also, many of the successful popular singers pursued successful careers in film, such performers as Al Jolson, Bing Crosby, Doris Day, and Frank Sinatra.

**Radio and Recordings**

The media (meaning network radio and the production and national marketing, advertising, and sales of recordings) changed the face of the music industry. It created the "hit" song, determined what songs produced profits for the creators and producers, and developed a way to report the hits—the Lucky Strike Hit Parade and later the charts of *Billboard* magazine and other polls of the industry. To a large extent, it determined who would be the "stars" of popular song, what Americans would listen to, and in effect, what their tastes in popular music would be. Tin Pan Alley stars, such as Rudy Vallee, Bing Crosby, and Kate Smith, achieved great success as radio artists.

Copyright laws were made effective through litigation. There was a resulting increase in awareness and understanding of these laws, and the establishment of performance rights agencies, such as the American Society of Composers, Authors, and Publishers (ASCAP) and Broadcast Music, Incorporated (BMI). These agencies developed methods of monitoring the sales of recordings and performances on radio, on jukeboxes, and at live concerts. Then they were able to make appropriate payments to copyright holders, usually the composers, lyricists, and their publishers.

The first radio station was established in Pittsburgh in 1920, the first commercial sponsorship in 1922, and the first network radio in 1926. By 1929, 40 percent of American families owned radios. Radio, thus, became a powerful medium for selling popular music. Network radio in the 1920s exposed those in the rural south and southwest to the urban music of the northeast. In time, this influence caused a shift in taste from the British-influenced folk songs and ballads to commercial hillbilly. WSB in Atlanta was established in 1922 and broadcast hillbilly music—singers, fiddlers, and string bands. WLS in Chicago established The National Barn dance, and WSM in Nashville started the Grand Ole Opry.

In the 1920s, the commercial record companies recognized the financial benefit of doing field recordings (see chapter 3) of the folk songs and dances of various immigrant groups, the blues of black singers, and white rural folk songs, ballads, and dances. These companies, while realizing commercial gain by selling the recordings back to these specialized audiences, also preserved a diverse folk repertoire, created an invaluable musical resource of American culture, and transformed many traditional folk singers into professional recording artists. The most popular jazz bands or swing bands achieved national exposure from touring and, particularly, from network radio broadcasts from hotel ballrooms, dance halls, and nightclubs. This made them prime targets for Tin Pan Alley song pluggers. Publishers marketed (plugged) their songs through the big swing bands, particularly those who featured vocalists such as Ella Fitzgerald, Frank Sinatra, Peggy Lee, the Andrews Sisters, and others whose acceptance of a song would virtually guarantee its commercial success.

With modern advances in the manufacture of recording equipment, particularly microphones, audio engineers have been able to easily balance the sound of a solo singer with the sounds of a big band or a full theatre or studio orchestra.

In time, singers felt hampered by the inflexible pulse of swing. They valued the intimate and personal lyrics of their songs and craved to add freedom and interpretation of personal feeling to their performances. This crooning, melodramatic, personal style was not conducive to dance music, lost its rhythmic vitality and spark, and led to the decline in popularity of Tin Pan Alley songs in the 1950s, as the new, vibrant music of Fats Domino, Little Richard, Chuck Berry, Buddy Holly, and Elvis Presley rose to take its place.

## Country Music

In chapter 3, we heard fiddle tunes, string band music, songs and ballads, and voices with a nasal twang. That was country music derived from oral tradition. It was the folk music of the rural south.

Country music in this chapter refers to the song writing, record producing, and making of "stars" of a popular style of music having a close kinship and a common ancestry with southern folk music. It is a regional music made national. The music includes hillbilly, or old-time country songs, western swing and cowboy songs, bluegrass, and the "Nashville sound."

## Hillbilly

Originally, **hillbilly** (listen to SS5/5) was used to describe in a deprecating way the "culturally and musically inferior" songs of the poor, white, rural, uneducated southerner. This music was a product of the rural South. However, in the second quarter of this century, hillbilly records were sold widely, and hillbilly music was broadcast from Atlanta, Chicago, Nashville, and many other cities. The popularity of hillbilly music as measured by record sales may have represented an image of an older and simpler America, an alternative to jazz and the popular dance music of the 1920s, and a yearning for the good old songs of the nineteenth century. Hillbilly music was projected as wholesome, down-to-earth, family-style entertainment.

Hillbilly songs are variants of British ballads, camp meetings songs and hymns, and popular, sentimental songs of the late nineteenth century. They represent a merging of rural and urban influences and a conflict between maintaining rugged simplicity and a desire to be accepted by middle-class, urban America. The songs were simple and direct, reflective of the values, aspirations, and fears of the rural, Protestant South. Hillbilly singing projected sincerity, deep human emotions, and real situations related to love, death, and religion. The singers preserved regional accents and dialect, the familiar twang and nasal vocal quality, and the slides and ornamentation of much southern, mountain music.

The 1920s saw a tremendous national effort by commercial record companies to record music by blues, jazz, gospel, folk, Tin Pan Alley, vaudeville, and hillbilly performers. Radio created additional demand for performers. The first hillbilly recording artists were Uncle Dave Macon, the Carter Family, and Jimmy Rodgers.

## Western Swing and Cowboy Songs

Western music is an extension of hillbilly. Singers from the South along with many others headed west in search of greater opportunity, taking with them their religion and their songs. The gulf widened between hillbilly and its folk roots. Western hillbilly dealt with loneliness and infidelity rather than religion, sentiment, and nostalgia. Some western music was performed on the piano in small-town saloons and was called honky tonk.

By the 1930s, the movie industry began making westerns that romanticized the "wild west" and produced a vast quantity of cowboy songs. Gene Autry, Tex Ritter, and Roy Rogers were the most famous of the singing cowboys. Their most famous songs, such as "Tumbling Tumbleweed," "Cool Water," "The Last Roundup," "Back in the Saddle Again," "The Yellow Rose of Texas," "Deep in the Heart of Texas," "Don't Fence Me In," and "I'm an Old Cowhand" were newly composed, many by Tin Pan Alley composers.

A brand of western music that used a larger instrumental ensemble including saxes, brass, and a standard jazz rhythm section of piano, bass, and drums is **western swing.** The most influential exponent of western swing was Bob Wills who, with his Texas Playboys, flourished in Tulsa from 1934–1942. By 1938, Wills was using fourteen musicians and virtually a swing band instrumentation plus fiddle and Hawaiian steel guitar. He popularized his music through radio broadcasts, recordings, dances, and personal appearances throughout the southwest.

## The Nashville Sound

In 1925, radio station WSM in Nashville started a hillbilly program that was in time to become the Grand Old Opry. In 1938, Roy Acuff was engaged as a regular performer; he achieved national success. His prominence in part was responsible for the Opry's new prominence, one attracting national interest. All the great country artists have appeared on the Grand Ole Opry, some as regulars for years and even decades; they include Bill Monroe, Ernest Tubb, Eddy Arnold, Hank Williams, Kitty Wells, Loretta Lynn, and Dolly Parton.

As hillbilly music became commercialized, such instruments as the Hawaiian steel guitar, bass fiddle, and electric guitar were added. Brass and woodwind instruments, drums, and backup singers ultimately were added, as well as small or even large string sections that included violins and cellos. Arrangements of country tunes became more elaborate, sophisticated, and urban. The roots of country music as found in the folk tradition were becoming increasingly obscure.

The New York record companies were aware of the emerging nationalization of country music. Many opened studios in Nashville to be close to the stars of country music. They began producing records and attracting song writers. Chet Atkins, a talented and successful guitarist, singer, and songwriter, was employed as RCA's recording director in Nashville. He was a prime force in the innovations that took place in response to the popularity of rock and roll in the 1950s. The charge was to create a product that would have the widest possible appeal, yet would preserve as much as possible the traditional attributes of country music.

As the music industry in Nashville grew, a new sound began to emerge that was achieved in highly sophisticated recording studios. The characteristic sound featured a large instrumentation, frequently excluded the hillbilly sounds of the fiddle and the steel guitar, and included background singers. It was hillbilly made popular—the **Nashville sound.** Nashville now symbolizes the full-scale commercialization of country music. It reigns as the recording capital of the industry, and some would say the entertainment capital of the world.

Bill Monroe and his Bluegrass Band at the Nightstage in Boston, Mass.

## Bluegrass

In hillbilly music, a typical song accompaniment might have included guitar, banjo, and fiddle. With its commercialization and the addition of the Hawaiian steel guitar and electronic instruments, **bluegrass** was developed as a return to the style of the old-time songs and dances. Its purpose was not to again become regional and culturally isolated but to facilitate the transition from a rural folk music to a part of the national popular culture. It is mountain music that originally was the music of Appalachian ethnic groups and is now an internationally popular style of country music. Bluegrass music includes story songs, part singing, fiddle tunes, and religious music. However, it was taken to the cities, parks, nightclubs, college campuses, and bluegrass festivals. The typical instrumentation of a bluegrass group includes the acoustic guitar, fiddle, mandolin, bass fiddle, and five-string banjo—no electric guitars.

Listen to SS5/7.

As with ragtime and blues, styles that became extremely popular, bluegrass was exploited by the industry in order to sell more records. They added bluegrass to the title or description of the music whether or not the music was, in reality, consistent with the style that was created by bluegrass pioneers. The pioneer of the style to be known as bluegrass was Bill Monroe who in 1945 headed a group called the Bluegrass Boys; thus, the name of the style was created. Lester Flatt and Earl Scruggs split away from Monroe in 1948 and formed a bluegrass group called the Foggy Mountain Boys. Many other groups soon followed as its popularity spread.

Hank Williams.

Elvis Presley.

Emmylou Harris.

Barbara Mandrell.

Black music is music performed by black Americans that is intended primarily for black audiences. It includes gospel, rhythm and blues, and soul.

**Black Music**

Seldom, however, does music fit neatly into categories and definitions. Any music conceived to "rise on the charts" has to have a wide enough appeal to sell a sufficient number of records to declare it a hit, a status intensely desired by artists of popular music. Thus, some black music is intentionally "watered down," that is, commercialized so those unfamiliar with the style would have a better chance of appreciating the music. This is particularly true of some gospel music and definitely true of a style of black music produced in Detroit in the 1960s known as the Motown sound.

Modern black gospel music (listen to SS3/9) represents the urbanization of the spirituals and hymns sung in rural churches and at camp meetings (see chapter 3). It is the sacred counterpart of the blues. The leading proponent of modern black gospel was Thomas A. Dorsey, a blues pianist, promoter, organizer, and manager. The modern superstar of black gospel was Mahalia Jackson who died in 1972. Her fabulous national popularity began after joining forces with Dorsey in the early 1940s.

**Gospel**

The country blues is typified by the old black man from the South singing the blues songs while accompanying himself on the guitar. The urban or classic blues were originally sung by women, such as Ma Rainey and Bessie Smith, with accompaniment by an instrumental jazz ensemble. Later urban blues singers who also sang jazz or jazz-styled popular music included Billie Holiday, Ella Fitzgerald, Sarah Vaughan, and their male counterparts, Billy Eckstine, Joe Williams, Joe Turner, and Jimmy Rushing.

**Rhythm and Blues**

**Rhythm and blues** (R & B) describes blues singing with boogie woogie-style piano accompaniment (see chapter 4) and electric guitar. It resulted from the migration of blacks to the cities, primarily to Memphis and Chicago. R & B, which flourished during the 1940s and early 1950s, was black, ghetto music intended for black audiences. *Billboard* published R & B charts from 1949 through 1969.

Country blues singers who could adapt to the city music and the electrified sound became a part of the R & B tradition. The most notable of these were Lightning Hopkins, John Lee Hooker, Howlin' Wolf, T-Bone Walker, and Muddy Waters. These were older blues men, some from the Mississippi delta, who didn't find fame until they moved to Memphis or Chicago. Walker used electric guitar as early as 1935, developed the single-string technique of guitar playing, and took the blues to the west coast where he achieved a considerable popularity.

The most famous of R & B artists was B. B. King, also a bluesman from the Mississippi delta who moved to Memphis. Part of his phenomenal success was due to his popularity among the British rock musicians of the 1960s. Other R & B musicians of the 1950s were Fats Domino, Little Richard, and Chuck Berry. It was their music that was found by a teenage, white audience who liked the freedom, expressiveness, and sensuality of the black music.

Berry Gordy was a songwriter from Detroit who founded his own record production company, Motown Records. At first, he drew talent exclusively from the black population of Detroit. He had an instinct for making black music widely popular among both black and white populations. He stressed arrangements in a style derived more from the black gospel than of blues or jazz traditions. He exerted firm control over the recordings and produced a stylistic consistency known as the **Motown sound.**

**The Motown Sound**

Motown recordings with their studio-produced sounds climbed to the top of R & B charts and of the white pop charts. The most common recording artists were singing groups with featured soloists: Gladys Knight and the Pips, Diana Ross and the Supremes, Smokey Robinson and the Miracles, and Martha and the Vandellas. A more

Rhythm and blues as well as rock generates enthusiastic audience response, especially when the performer is B. B. King.

recent Motown superstar is Stevie Wonder. Success brought increasing commercialization to the Motown sound. Blacks began to feel that the music was too commercial, having a heavily diluted pop sound. The artists began to perform more and more for white audiences, and the backup instrumentation began to look and sound more like a symphony orchestra. The Motown sound, or black pop, had moved away from the black music and the black audience that earned it its original recognition and success.

## Soul

**Soul** was an extension of R & B and, in fact, was popularized by previous R & B singers. In 1969, *Billboard* shifted its R & B chart to soul as its label for black popular music. Soul music came to symbolize any black music of the 1970s no matter how "pure" or how commercial. The pure sound was intended only for black audiences with singing styles derived from blues and jazz as well as black gospel. Soul became the black music for black audiences that Motown no longer served. It represented a communication and sharing of strong emotions and of a wide spectrum of life's experiences among blacks. It was the music of the ghettos and the militants within the Black Power movement and was identifiable with and a product of the black experience in the United States.

Soul was the music of northern-born former Motown blacks and of southern-born former Memphis blacks. It was the music of Ray Charles, Otis Redding, Aretha Franklin, Ike and Tina Turner, and its superstar, James Brown.

**Plate 6**

Benny Goodman at a jam session.

**Plate 7**

Combo jazz in a nightclub setting.

Dionne Warwick, pop singer.

**Plate 8b**

Ray Charles and Gladys Knight in concert.

**Plate 9**

Mexican dancers create a fiesta atmosphere.

**Plate 10**

Japanese bugaku at Hachimangu Shrine.

Little Richard, an early rock and roll superstar of the 1950s.

World War II pretty much stopped the dancing craze of the 1930s. In its place, popular music by the early 1950s, particularly among white Americans, consisted of sentimental ballads and trivial novelty songs. The black popular music was jazz, blues, and rhythm and blues, and country and western was just emerging as a national popular music market.

**Rock**

Rock music, originally called **rock and roll,** began in the mid-1950s. It was essentially an underground, antiestablishment, and protest music. Yet, it was a commercial product, soon to become a powerhouse of the recording industry. The older generation (the "establishment" of the 1950s) believed that this music was a fad and would not contribute anything substantial to our musical culture. A significant factor contributing to this feeling was the fact that the rock phenomenon grew out of an American youth culture that rejected the traditional attitudes and values of contemporary society. Rock was more than the music. It had a kinship with folk art in its spontaneous, immediate, and direct communication. It was art unseparated from life. The music and lyrics reflected a segment of the culture, politics, morality, and taste of society.

From its beginnings, rock performers and their audiences were interracial and international. Rock was an umbrella for young people (the teenyboppers) providing common symbols, language, and dress codes for white and black people alike.

Rock appealed to urban and rural people; the wealthy, middle class, and poor people; and especially the rebellious young people. Rock was music all young people could dance to.

James Brown.

Fats Domino.

**The Roots of Rock**

Rock was an amalgamation of several styles and influences, but it was primarily a melding of rhythm and blues and country and western music—a merging of black and white traditions.

Most radio stations, catering to white audiences, did not play songs performed or written by blacks. Concerts typically were still segregated. However, this was an age of the landmark 1954 civil rights legislation and a time of intense national awareness of racial issues, particularly of those relating to segregation and integration.

White Americans discovered that R & B was music that could be danced to, and they enjoyed listening and dancing to this music. They began recording R & B songs previously recorded by blacks and found that these sold considerably better, but they lost the earthy quality of the originals. These versions were refined, watered down, and more acceptable to white consumers than the original R & B arrangements.

Since many of the R & B artists were from the South, and a number of country artists had rubbed elbows with southern blacks, it was no surprise that country performers were attracted to rock and roll music. The resulting form often has been called **rockabilly.**

Rock and roll cannot be traced to a single song or a single artist. Significant contributions were made by Bill Haley and the Comets, Chuck Berry, Little Richard (listen to SS5/10), and Elvis Presley through their popular hits of the 1950s. "Rock Around the Clock" was the first rock and roll song to climb to the top of the pop charts, symbolizing the powerful popularity of rock and roll. Through television as well as recordings and personal appearances, Elvis Presley became a superstar of popular music to an unprecedented degree. He was explosive in eliciting frenzied responses from his audiences. He then retreated into more conventional, conservative styles that appealed to a wider market.

**The Establishment**

Mainstream white popular music (the conservative, Tin Pan Alley-type music) was controlled by several major recording companies: the major labels (Decca, Columbia, RCA, etc.) were the establishment. All the early rock and roll hits were produced by the much smaller independent labels. The popularity of their songs made the establishment sit up and take notice.

At first, this new teenage music was discredited by the establishment. When this tactic did not succeed in redirecting aesthetic tastes, the major labels countered with more watered down versions of R & B songs sung by white pop stars, such as Pat Boone and the old crooners, Bing Crosby, Frank Sinatra, and Perry Como. They then "manufactured" the teenage idols: Fabian, Bobby Avalon, Ricky Nelson, Bobby Rydell, and others. Their music was white, urban, and only remotely related to R & B. It dealt almost solely with teenage romance. The music of these teen idols was given considerable exposure on the "Ed Sullivan Show" and, most importantly, on Dick Clark's "American Bandstand," a show that unquestionably was a powerful force in taming the popularity of the controversial rock and roll and making it acceptable to the establishment.

The establishment won out. Rock and roll diminished in popularity at the end of the 1950s—until February 8, 1964, when the Beatles appeared on the "Ed Sullivan Show." The "British Invasion" began.

**The British Invasion**

Liverpool, England, was a seaport city with a large population of working-class people who supported hundreds of local musical groups. Sailors having been to America brought home rhythm and blues and rock and roll records. This music influenced these local musicians to the extent that it sustained popularity in England after it waned in

The British invasion.

the states. Local favorites were the Everly Brothers, Buddy Holly, Chuck Berry, and Little Richard. The most durable and influential groups coming from England were the Beatles, the Rolling Stones, the Who, and Pink Floyd.

In 1967, the Beatles' album, *Sgt. Pepper's Lonely Hearts Club Band,* was the first one with music clearly and completely in the new rock style to climb to the top of the pop charts. The album became known to virtually everyone interested in popular music. For many, this album was their first exposure to a style of popular music now simply called rock. It became more than dance music. It was music for listening, and it was respected as "legitimate music" by many educated musicians. This album signaled a new age in American popular music.

The music of the Beatles and other British groups (listen to SS5/11) served mostly urban white people. It did not achieve popularity among the black and country and western audiences. Thus, in bringing new life to popular music, it did not recapture the cross-cultural feature of early rock and roll.

## Recent Styles

Modern styles of rock music result from advanced electronic technology, including sound amplification, studio manipulation of sound, synthesizers, MIDI applications, sampling, studio mixing, a wide range of instruments, and flexible and varied forms. Performances stress both audio and visual impacts. Performers stress unique if not bizarre dress and on-stage behavior.

An outdoor rock concert.

Rock opened an age of the study of popular culture by scholars, authors, and writers of theses and dissertations. It opened an expansion that included a diversity of styles including folk rock, art rock, heavy metal, southern rock, punk rock, jazz rock, and new wave.

Recent popular music also includes the following:

1. The urban folk song movement of the 1960s stimulated by the music of the Weavers; Pete Seeger; Bob Dylan; the Kingston Trio; Peter, Paul and Mary; and Joan Baez.
2. The Tin Pan Alley tradition of popular song continuing through such singers as Andy Williams, Tony Bennett, Frank Sinatra, and Barbra Streisand.
3. Funk and Disco styles of the 1970s.
4. Crossover artists with hits on more than one chart.

How does one categorize the multifaceted talents of Frank Zappa and the Mothers of Invention, Ray Charles, Stevie Wonder, Jimi Hendrix, Janis Joplin, the Beach Boys, Joni Mitchell, Elton John, and Bruce Springsteen? The list of great artists of American popular music could go on and on, and it will.

# A Study in Sound
## *American Popular Music*

## Example 1

**"How 'Ya Gonna Keep 'Em Down on the Farm (after They've Seen Paree)"**—

Tin Pan Alley; from *Shuffle Along,* a Broadway musical produced in 1921

Eubie Blake, composer; Noble Sissle, lyricist

*Shuffle Along* was written, performed, produced, and directed by black artists. Its music represents a synthesis of ragtime and operetta that featured jazz dancing.

"How 'Ya Gonna Keep 'Em Down on the Farm" (originally written by Walter Donaldson, composer; Sam Lewis and Joe Young, lyricists) represents the syncopated tunes first popularized in the minstrel shows. Noble Sissle sang this song for this recording made in 1919. The band was the military group organized by James Reese Europe in World War I, his "Hell Fighters" band.

### *Goals:*

Recognize an early American popular music style reminiscent of the nineteenth-century minstrel song style.

Be aware of syncopated patterns and their contribution to the sense of rhythm.

Identify the sound of the slide trombone.

***Guide:*** Count the piece in a moderately fast two-beat.

| Intro. | 14 bars (4 + 4 + 6) | Instrumental |
|--------|---------------------|--------------|
| Chorus | Five 8-bar phrases | Vocal; ascending trombone slide—pickup to bars one and five of fourth phrase |
| Chorus | Five 8-bar phrases | Instrumental; ascending trombone slide—pickup to bars one and five of fourth phrase |

***Reflections:*** Describe the vocal quality and compare it with singing styles heard previously. Identify and sing various syncopated motives heard throughout. Compare musical characteristics of this example with those of current popular music.

# Example 2

**"Shaking the Blues Away"**—Tin Pan Alley; vaudeville

From the Ziegfeld Follies, 1927

Composed by Irving Berlin

Sung by Ruth Etting

## *Goals:*

Recognize a style representing vaudeville, one of the great eras in American popular music.

Identify patterns of contrast and repetition.

Recognize the standard Tin Pan Alley verse/chorus song form.

*Guide:* A  First section; count in a moderately fast four or slow two.

| | | |
|---|---|---|
| Intro. | 8-bars | Piano |
| Verse | Two 8-bar phrases | Vocal |
| Chorus | Four 8-bar phrases | Vocal |

B  Second section; based on a familiar spiritual; count with a slower pulse.

| | | |
|---|---|---|
| First phrase | 16 bars (4 + 6 + 6) | |
| Second phrase | 17 bars (4 + 6+ 6+ 1) | Tempo increases at end of the phrase; a one-bar transition back to the first section is added (piano only) |

A  First section (return—fade)

*Reflections:* In the verse, do the phrases repeat or contrast? In the chorus, identify the form. Listen for repetition within each phrase. Does syncopation play a big part in this style?

# Example 3

**"Someone to Watch Over Me"**—1920s-style American popular music (Tin Pan Alley)

Music by George Gershwin and lyrics by Ira Gershwin

(Listen to SS2/2 and see page 32.)

# Example 4

**"Stardust"**—one of the most popular and durable of the standards

Music by Hoagy Carmichael and lyrics by Mitchell Parish

(Listen to SS4/3 and see page 91.)

# Example 5

**"There's Poison in Your Heart"**—hillbilly

Kitty Wells

Recorded in 1955

Kitty Wells, the "Queen of Country Music" in the 1950s, was the first female country superstar. She became a member of the Grand Old Opry in 1952.

A partial text of this song is provided to illustrate a typical imagery or theme used in hillbilly music.

*Your lips are as sweet as honey
but there's poison in your heart.*

## *Goals:*

Identify chords and recognize their function in this music.
Describe the hillbilly style of singing.

*Guide:* Count in a moderate four; each phrase begins with a pickup.

| | 1--- | 2--- | 3--- | 4--- | 5--- | 6--- | 7--- | 8--- | |
|---|---|---|---|---|---|---|---|---|---|
| Intro. | I--- | I--- | I-V- | I--- | | | | | Instrumental; two beats added in fourth bar |
| First verse | I | | IV | I | I | | V | | Vocal |
| | I | | IV | I | I | | V | I | One bar added |
| Interlude | I | | IV | I | I | | I V | I | Instrumental; one bar added (violin, four; guitar, five) |

Second verse (fade)

*Reflections:* Identify the open and closed cadences, and recognize the antecedent/consequent phrase structure. Discuss the modern counterparts, if any, of hillbilly music. To what extent is hillbilly music popular today?

# Example 6

**"Little Ole You"**—early Nashville sound

Jim Reeves

(Listen to SS2/1 and see page 31).

# Example 7

**"Blue Ridge Cabin Home"**—bluegrass

Performed by Flatt and Scruggs and the Foggy Mountain Boys

An authentic bluegrass recording made in 1955 in Nashville

Instrumentation: two vocals, fiddle, guitar, banjo, mandolin, dobro (acoustic guitar with a metal resonator that is played on the lap, Hawaiian-style), and bass

*Goals:*

Identify the typical, original bluegrass style.

Identify chords and recognize chord progression.

Differentiate the sounds of the plucked, stringed instruments.

*Guide:* Count in a moderately fast two. The phrase pattern and chord structure that follows is repeated throughout with the exception of a bar added at the end of the introduction and fiddle chorus.

|                        | 1 - 2 - 3 - 4 - 5 - 6 - 7 - 8 - |     |     |     |           |
|------------------------|------|------|------|------|-----------|
| Intro. (two times)     | I    | IV   | V    | I    | Extra bar |
| Vocal (four times)     | I    | IV   | V    | I    |           |
| Fiddle (two times)     | I    | IV   | V    | I    | Extra bar |
| Vocal (four times)     | I    | IV   | V    | I    |           |
| Guitar (two times)     | I    | IV   | V    | I    | Fade      |

*Reflections:* During the last chorus, notice the pitch bending, slides into pitches, and "blue notes" played on the guitar.

Notice the off-beats, the change in texture in each vocal chorus, and the antecedent/consequent phrase groups.

# Example 8

**"What a Friend We Have in Jesus"**—black gospel

Aretha Franklin, vocal

James Cleveland, piano

The Southern California Community Choir, James Cleveland, director

(Listen to SS3/9, and see page 67.)

# Example 9

**"Paying the Cost to Be the Boss"**—rhythm and blues (R & B)

B. B. King, vocal and guitar

Rhythm and blues is black popular music. It preceded and influenced the beginnings of rock and roll, led to the category of soul on the popular music charts, and eventually replaced soul as the predominant style of black popular music.

*Goals:*

Describe the rhythm and blues style.

Identify the twelve-bar blues form, and recognize the deviations from the standard form.

Recognize the chord progression and the chord qualities. Identify the chords and any variants of the standard blues progression.

*Guide:* Twelve-bar blues form (sixteen bars in third and fifth choruses)

| Chorus | 1 | 2 | 3 | 4 | 5 | 6 | 7 | 8 | 9 | 10 | 11 | 12 | |
|---|---|---|---|---|---|---|---|---|---|---|---|---|---|
| 1 | I | IV | I | | IV | | I | | V | IV | I | V | Instrumental |
| 2 | I | IV | I | | IV | | I | | V | IV | I | V | Vocal |
| 3 | I | | | | IV | | I | | V | IV | I | V | Vocal (first four bars repeated) |
| 4 | I | IV | I | | IV | | I | | V | IV | I | V | Instrumental |
| 5 | I | | | | IV | | I | | V | IV | I | I | Vocal (first four bars repeated); with tag |

*Reflections:* In this song, notice the following variations of the twelve-bar blues:

1. The tenth bar of each pattern moves to the subdominant (IV), a common variation of the standard progression (I --- IV - I - V - I -).

2. In the third and last choruses, the first four bars on the tonic chord are repeated, making these choruses sixteen bars.

3. The chords for the second and twelfth bars of each chorus vary.

Be aware of a big-band instrumentation, and notice the hard electric guitar sound. Notice the underlying triplets in the piano (triple subdivisions of the pulse), any ostinato patterns, and the embellishments and liberties taken with the melody.

Describe the differences between R & B and country blues and between R & B and jazz.

# Example 10

**"Good Golly, Miss Molly"**—1950s rock and roll

Performed by Little Richard

Recorded in 1958

Little Richard is one of the most influential of early rock musicians.

Notice, as in previous pieces, the frequent repetition of phrases that give conciseness, cohesion, and identity to the piece. Notice also the regularly repeated high notes in the piano.

This is a twelve-bar blues. The text in typical blues form is aab (second line a repeat of the first; third line different).

## *Goals:*

Recognize the twelve-bar blues form.

Recognize breaks, riffs, and boogie woogie patterns.

## *Guide:*

Chorus

| | |
|---|---|
| 1 | Piano—boogie woogie pattern |
| 2 | Verse |
| 3 | Repeat of verse |
| 4 | First 4 bars—"break" or "stop time" (rhythmic activity in accompaniment stops—a common jazz technique; notice the extra two beats). |

Last 8 bars—the second and third lines of the verse

5 10 bars—verse with big band jazz accompaniment, riffs, and tag (riffs are the repeated brass and wind chords on the second and third beats of bars three through ten).

*Reflections:* Describe any relationships of this music to jazz.

What musical characteristics make this music different from hillbilly? from rhythm and blues? from Tin Pan Alley music?

How is this music different from current popular music? How have tastes changed since the late 1950s?

# Example 11

**"Revolution"**—1960s British rock

The Beatles

A 1968 release; the flip side to one of the Beatle's most popular singles, "Hey Jude"

The Beatles were a rock group that in the mid-1960s took this country by storm, changed the shape of American popular music, and was the source of a wealth of great songs, some of which have now become standards. They influenced American society with their appearance, their presentation, and their music. To many Americans, their music was loud, raucous, and a passing fad. To many others, it communicated something direct and important that caused this British rock group to become probably the most successful rock group of all time in terms of record sales, fame, and influence.

*Goals:*

Describe the timbre produced by electronically enhanced guitar playing.

Recognize differences in styles of rock and early rock and roll, rock and Tin Pan Alley or country and western, and rock and rhythm and blues.

Be aware of layers of sound: percussion, vocals, guitars, bass ostinatos, etc.

*Guide:* Count in a moderately fast four.

```
Intro.     1---2---3---4---                          Instrumental
Vocal      1---2---3---4-(+2)-5---6---               Main theme
Chorus     1---2---3---4-(+2)-5---6---
           1---2---3---4-(+2)-5---                   Contrast
           1---2---3---4-(+2)-5---6---7---8---
Vocal      1---2---3---4-(+2)-5---6---               Main theme
Chorus     1---2---3---4-(+2)-5---6---
           1---2---3---4-(+2)-5---                   Contrast
           1---2---3---4-(+2)-5---6---7---8-(+2)-
Interlude  1---2---3---4---    5---6---7---8---       Instrumental
Vocal      1---2---3---4-(+2)-5---6---               Main theme
Chorus     1---2---3---4-(+2)-5---6---
           1---2---3---4-(+2)-5---                   Contrast
           1---2---3---4---    5---6---7---8---
           1---2---3---4---    5---6---7---8---       Hold last beat
```

*Reflections:* Notice the breaks in the third phrase of each vocal chorus, the drum triplets in the fifth bar of those phrases, and the additional repeated phrase in the last chorus.

In the contrasting phrases, notice the two-bar phrase segments, the boogie woogie patterns (ostinato bass), and the influence of rhythm and blues, particularly through the chord progressions.

Compare the sound and style of Little Richard with the Beatles only ten years later. Contemplate the changes in style and taste in popular music in that decade (1958–1968).

*Discography*

**Ex. 1**  Blake, Eubie. "How Ya Gonna Keep 'Em Down on the Farm (after They've Seen Paree)." *Sissle and Blake's Shuffle Along.* New World Records. NW 260. 1:22.

**Ex. 2**  Berlin, Irving. "Shaking Away the Blues." *The Vintage Irving Berlin.* New World Records. NW 238. 2:20.

**Ex. 3**  Gershwin, George, and Ira Gershwin. "Someone to Watch Over Me." *. . . and then we wrote . . . (American Composers and Lyricists Sing. Play, and Conduct Their Own Songs).* New World Records. NW 272. 1:20.

**Ex. 4**  Carmichael, Hoagy. "Stardust." *. . . and then we wrote . . . (American Composers and Lyricists Sing, Play, and Conduct Their Own Songs).* New World Records. NW 272. 2:20.

**Ex. 5**  Wells, Kitty. "There's Poison in Your Heart." *Country Music in the Modern Era 1940s–1970s.* New World Records. NW 207. 1:10.

**Ex. 6**  Reeves, Jim. "Little Ole You." *Country Music in the Modern Era 1940s–1970s.* New World Records. NW 207. 2:08.

**Ex. 7**  Flatt and Scruggs. "Blue Ridge Cabin Home." *"Hills and Home: Thirty Years of Bluegrass."* New World Records. NW 225. 1:50.

**Ex. 8**  Franklin, Aretha. "What a Friend We Have in Jesus." *Amazing Grace.* Atlantic SC2-906. 6:30.

**Ex. 9**  King, B. B. "Paying the Cost to Be the Boss." *Electric B. B./His Best.* MCA Records MCA 27007. 2:29.

**Ex. 10**  Little Richard. "Good Golly, Miss Molly." *Rock Music.* Opus Musicum OM225-27. 1:37.

**Ex. 11**  The Beatles. "Revolution." *Hey, Jude.* Capitol SW 385. 3:21.

*Summary*

The rationale for the study of American popular music focuses on three factors: (1) its musical development, (2) its social implications, and (3) its economic impact. We are all affected in one way or another by our relationship to popular music.

Popular music has developed in clear stages and this growth has been recorded in the literature of music. For these reasons, one can approach the study of vernacular music (music other than art music) with a scholarly perspective.

It is the nature of popular music to change with a relatively high degree of rapidity as the tastes of the masses change rapidly. Yet we can examine the roots of important styles and trends that have contributed to current popular music. We have attempted in this chapter to explore these styles, influences, and artists that represent the beginnings and other important stages of various popular styles in music, from the minstrel song, to Tin Pan Alley, to country and western, to several manifestations of black popular music, and rock.

*Terms and Concepts*

*Popular culture*

*Mass appeal*

*The music industry*

*The manipulation of taste*

*Airplay*

*Charts*

*Standards*

*The evolving musical styles of popular music*

*The giants of American popular music—creators and performers*

*Media*

*Modern technology*

# Part III
# Listening to World Music

Chapters 6 and 7 will present a sampling of perhaps unfamiliar music from both Western and non-Western cultures. Non-Western musical sounds and structures may be quite different from the more familiar ones found in Western European-American music. Chapter 6 includes music from the Western Hemisphere, including music of the native Americans and music from Canada, Mexico, South America, and the Caribbean region.

Of great importance is the attempt to understand ways music exists in various cultures and, in doing so, to better understand music from our own culture. We will attempt to build bridges to other cultures by finding commonalities and ways to appreciate our musical differences.

To provide basic information and musical examples from a few of this worlds' cultures that may or may not be derived from Western European traditions is to acknowledge the following:

1. Music plays an important role in developed and undeveloped societies throughout the world.

2. Music in other cultures can have a tradition, a history, and a value in society as profound and as substantial as our own. Such music may be as involved, cultivated, elite, and intellectually well-founded as Western art music.

3. Music exists in cultures for a wide variety of reasons, frequently for reasons that are not common to our own experience.

4. Any culture or nation has subcultures and regional variations; thus, its music would reflect these variations. Stylistic diversity is not unique to American music.

5. Music in other cultures may sound quite unfamiliar to our Western ears, yet it can be as valued in those cultures as in our own.

6. People in different parts of the world have different likes and dislikes as to the elements of musical style that they can relate to and enjoy—the kinds of melodies, harmonies, rhythms, forms, textures, and instruments and instrumental combinations.

7. The performance practices of musicians may vary. Music is performed in different settings and for different reasons. Such differences include the dress of musicians, types of performance sites, and audience behavior.

Our taste in music—the kinds of music we like and respond favorably to, the music that communicates to us, the music that is important to us—has been shaped by our environment from our birth. This is true for all people from whatever nation or region of the world. This conditioning creates biases that sometimes make it difficult to respond with empathy to unfamiliar music and make us uncomfortable when confronted with the unknown. Music we know can delight us, but that which is based on different musical systems and performed in seemingly strange contexts can

sounding the same or like disorganized noise. Many students are prone to say such music sounds weird.

We need to strive to listen to world music, as well as music of all unfamiliar styles, in the context of those who create, perform, and consume the music. We need to listen to music of other cultures on its own terms and not from a Western point of view. On the other hand, it will help us to remember that Western music, having familiar sounds and performance contexts to us, may all sound the same and seem uncomfortable and weird to listeners from other

# Chapter 6
# World Music
## *The Western Hemisphere*

Bridges to other cultures do not necessarily span great distances. A bridge can be crossed by sampling the music of the native Americans. It is ironic that *native* American music is often treated more as music of a world culture rather than one type of American music. Certainly an important justification for this is that its traditions, its functions in society, and the sounds and structures of its music are sufficiently different from any other "American" music. Bridges can also be crossed within our own national boundaries by considering the music of the immigrants to the United States who brought with them and retained the songs and dances of their native lands (see chapter 7).

## Music in Culture

To study music of other cultures as well as our own can involve merely analyzing the music or describing it in musical terms. The problem with this approach is that our language is not universal. It is geared to Western European musical concepts and cannot describe equally well all the musics of the world. To study music in culture suggests much more than describing music. To study music of other cultures as well as our own can include considering the context of music in a society, music as it relates to human behavior, and the general attitudes of a people about their music.

The scholars who study music in culture are known as **ethnomusicologists.** They do the research, write about the music of a culture, and teach others about that culture's music. They live for a period of time in the countries or regions where these "world musics" are produced. They record the music, talk to the people who make the music, and find out why and in what ways it is created, performed, and listened to. They try to understand the music as those from whose culture it comes understand it. To study music in culture applies not only to musics of faraway places but also to cultures within the Western Hemisphere and our own national boundaries.

## Social Aspects

The research by ethnomusicologists seeks to learn about community musicians, asking such questions as who creates? who performs? who listens? Scholars try to determine what the life of a musician is really like and what this person's status is in the community: whether highly respected or more like a servant, whether professional or amateur, and whether formally schooled or unschooled. They also discover ways in which the musician acquires and develops skills.

This research produces information about a community's ideas about music, how music ties into its belief system, and how it relates to the fabric of the society that it serves. Researchers consider if music is intended for immediate consumption or preserved in some way for future generations. They explore how a group of people perceive music in relation to nature and to society.

Ethnomusicologists observe the community's musical preferences. Do the people consider music to be beautiful, or is that even a concern? What are considered to be pleasing, satisfying sounds? Is there "good" and "bad" music in the society? Is there a popular music and a classical music? In addition, ethnomusicologists ask where music is performed, how musicians dress when they perform, and on what occasions music is performed, whether for rituals, entertainment, concerts, ceremonies, sports, dance, drama, or religion. They examine the performer/audience relationship—what the "audience" does during a presentation and whether the nonperformers are active or inactive, quiet or noisy, attentive or inattentive.

Ethnomusicologists study a society and its music to determine its common musical styles, genres, forms, and the recorded history and theory of its music. They also try to discover what can be learned about the culture from the texts of its songs, what the music sounds like, and what language problems emerge in describing the music. They find ways to describe the creative process and the use of melody, the tonal framework, the rhythmic organization, and the timbral preferences. These scholars determine how the music is learned, how it is taught, how it is passed from one generation to the next, and whether the music is notated, that is, from a high culture, or transmitted exclusively by oral tradition (by example, imitation, and memory) as from a primitive or oral culture.

The ethnomusicologist will discover the tangible things used in the community to produce music: instruments, equipment, printed music, or recordings. They also study to what extent the technological and urban, perhaps Western, influence is evident: mass media, sound reinforcement, concert ensembles and performances, functional harmony, professional musicians, the music industry.

**Musical Aspects**

Ethnomusicologists will observe the extent to which a society is affected by outside political, economic, and cultural factors. They study to what extent its people accept or accommodate outside influences and make them a part of their culture and to what extent they reject or conquer them and preserve the purity of their culture. The process by which a culture assimilates or adapts to the characteristics and practices of other cultures is **acculturation** or the blending of cultures.

Cultures change, sometimes rapidly, sometimes imperceptibly. In this modern, technological age, however, it is unlikely that there are many cultures that have not been affected by outside influences, accepted some of these influences, and changed their cultural behaviors and practices somewhat rapidly in this century.

The ethnomusicologists have taught us much about music of non-Western cultures, subcultures of American society, and Western-influenced cultures found in other parts of the world. They have taught us to be global in our perspective, not ethnocentric or interested only in our own culture and our own music. Finally, music is part of culture, but it also resides outside of culture, reflecting and commenting on it. We learn much about a culture or a subculture from its arts: its songs, dances, and other expressions that depict or suggest feelings, attitudes, and events important to a society.

**Acculturation**

A verbal panorama of music in the cultures of a small selection of nations and regions is presented. This is done not so much to share the specifics of a particular culture but collectively to gain impressions and insights into the nature of musics outside of our own culture and experience.

When we speak of American music, we tend to think of music from the continental United States and not music from other countries of North America, Central or South America, or the Caribbean, all of which geographically are part of "the Americas." We do not typically include the music of the native Americans for reasons to be discussed in the next section. Before we consider music of more distant countries, we hope to gain a sense of some of the music and musical traditions and influences found within the Americas. We will focus first on the music of the aboriginal Americans (the native Americans) and the traditions and character of the music of American countries and regions outside of the United States.

## Music of the Americas

Native American
dancers in characteristic
costumes.

## Native American Music

The indigenous music of the Americas is that of the Indians: the native Americans, the native Canadians, the native Mexicans. Reasons that we typically do not include their musics under the genre of American music include the following. Native American music is

1. From a culture essentially different from any European-based culture, perhaps having more in common with oriental music.
2. Essentially different from any European-based music, both vocally and instrumentally.
3. Essentially different in function and in aesthetic qualities.
4. To a large extent ignored by Europeans and Americans, while many native Americans ignored European-based music.
5. Of little consequence in the development of music in American society, particularly when contrasted with European music or music from Africa.

Indian cultures were nonliterate and had no recorded history. Any knowledge of their music has come from anthropological and archaeological findings, stories told by "the old people," and ethnologists who began studying Indian cultures in the mid-nineteenth century. Through annihilation and acculturation, most of the old songs have been lost.

Each tribe had its own culture, language, and music. Even among tribes living in close proximity, minimal cultural interaction and exchange took place. The result was long-term cultural isolation and minimal acculturation. Likewise with their music, broad characteristics and patterns can be generalized, but upon close scrutiny, a tremendous diversity exists in native American music.

Aboriginal cultures of Mexico and the Latin American countries came under the influence of Europeans, particularly the Spanish, much earlier than their northern counterparts. These groups have more thoroughly adopted the cultural behaviors, traditions, and language of their "invaders." Because the Latin American Indian culture has been more assimilated, less is known of the original music of these cultures than of the music of the more segregated aboriginal cultures of the United States and Canada.

*Style and Context*

The aboriginal cultures, in contrast to the European, have viewed music as an essential part of life. Their music, consisting primarily of songs and dances, was designed to achieve some purpose, such as good health, a successful hunt, victory in war, needed rain, or contact with the spirit world. Music usually was associated with rituals, but sometimes their songs and dances were purely for entertainment. They were transmitted by oral rather than notated tradition.

Music was composed, sometimes deliberately as a "composer" would create music. These songs mostly were for recreation rather than religion or ritual. Similar songs frequently were borrowed from other tribes or even from Christians. Other songs were received in dreams or visions as if they were received directly from the spirits.

The music was not intended to be listened to alone as a concert or recording, abstracted from its function. It might be said that the music should not exist out of its original and intended context. Many songs were valued for their power and were "owned" by individuals who would protect the power of the songs by not performing them except under special, often ceremonial, circumstances.

The words to a song may have told a story, expressed a prayer or a wish, or described an emotion. Sometimes the words carried no meaning as words but were intended only as vocal sounds known as **vocables.** In some songs, these vocables, through the total experience of the ritual or dance, conveyed a meaning or a mood. They sometimes appeared in recognizable, perhaps quite intricate, patterns that native listeners identified with particular songs or kinds of songs. Some songs combined meaningful words with vocables, and some vocables never may have had any meaning, or their meanings were obscure or long-forgotten.

Instrumental music by itself was seldom performed, and melody instruments were rare. The most common instruments were drums of all shapes and sizes, rattles, and sometimes tambourines or bells and other percussion instruments. Drums were played with a single drum stick. A unique drum in construction but common in use was the water drum, prevalent throughout all of the Americas. Drums were made of clay, iron, wood, or aluminum. The heads were buckskin, chamois, or rubber. Drum patterns were usually very simple, maintaining a steady four-beat pattern. The drums never were played alone as in African music. The most common wind instrument was the vertical flute, whistle, or, in some cultures, the panpipes. The flute was seldom used in religious ceremony. It was more often used to accompany love songs.

The songs encompassed a small range, only occasionally more than an octave. Many were based on scales that approximated the European major scale. Although they often encompassed only a few tones, the most common was the **pentatonic** (five-tone) **scale.** Songs were made up of short phrases with considerable repetition or sometimes a subtle variation. The singing was intense, earthy, and harsh, sometimes in a high-pitched voice, and included ornamentation, slides, shouts, and animal calls. There was no harmony, only the single line melody with percussion accompaniment. Melodies were often quite rhythmic and supported by the timekeeping of the drums. Virtually all aboriginal songs accompanied dancing. In ceremonies, musicians and dancers usually were dressed in elaborate costumes with feathers, makeup, and sticks or other hand-held objects.

New Mexico, Santa
Clara Pueblo Indians
performing on their
drums.

## Assimilation and Preservation

The pressures and the attractions of the "white man's" world have led many native Americans to reject their own culture and enter the mainstream of American life. In recent years, however, there seems to be an increased awareness among native Americans of the importance of their culture and the necessity of preserving it.

Although many ceremonies and rituals remain private within the Indian community, the most popular attempts to preserve the Indian culture today lie in the annual intertribal ceremonies and pow-wows to which the public is invited. These festive activities take place on reservations and in cities maintaining large native American populations. The interest is more in preserving their culture as a whole rather than specific tribal characteristics and behaviors. The ritual and the supernatural are largely gone, but the dancing and entertainment songs thrive. These public ceremonies include songs and dances, colorful costumes, and concessions to sell food and gifts. The public is encouraged to attend. The performers include professional musicians making the pow-wow circuit. Recording and sound reinforcing equipment are used.

Considering the extent to which native Americans have been assimilated into American society, their music has not merged with or influenced European music, probably because of its radically different style and function. The native Americans, however, have accepted the popular music of America, but their own music remains separate. Native Americans listen to rock and country music. They have formed their own performing groups and have made recordings in both rock and country styles. A few radio stations in the Southwest regularly program for the native American population, playing tribal music, Western popular music, and religious music.

Indigenous American music still exists even though most of the old songs and dances and the old traditions have long since died. Native Americans seem to be truly multicultural, keeping some of their own behaviors and adopting other European/American behaviors.

Canadian Voyageurs developed a substantial folk song tradition singing about their adventures. Etching by Rudolf Cronall.

## Folk and Classical Music of Canada

As with most of the American nations, Canada has been transformed from a wilderness into a modern civilization. Its culture and its music, other than that of its aborigines, are based on European models, mostly French and the British. Dating to the early 1600s, the first permanent colonies were settled by immigrants from northern France. They were farmers and laborers who apparently loved to sing and dance. The result was the identification of more than 9,000 French/Canadian folk songs. As is true with all folk music, these were songs that they could perform without elaborate planning, rehearsal, or special facilities. They were largely unaccompanied songs. There were multiple texts for any one melody and multiple melodies for any one text. There was no "correct" version.

An interesting societal group of Canadians was the voyageurs. They were French/Canadians, often of Canadian Indian ancestry, who transported goods and passengers for large fur-trading companies. They paddled canoes on the rivers and lakes, traveled far into the interior, hunted and fished for their food, and slept under their canoes. They developed a substantial folk song tradition singing about their adventures and their romantic visions of frontier life.

The British influence, too, was significant. The immigrants from England, Scotland, and Ireland brought their ballads, folk songs, reels, and jigs. It was a common practice in the nineteenth century to compose new folk songs or set "Canadian" words to old tunes. Folk songs have been collected and published since the mid-nineteenth century. The Child Ballads, discussed in chapter 3, were known in Canada. Canada's popular music has been its folk ballads and songs, then parlor songs, and then acculturated modern popular music as in the United States and many other places in the world.

The classical music of Canada is based on the Western European art music tradition. It includes organ and choir music for church services, chamber music, and concert music for bands, orchestras, and choirs. Since 1945, there has been a great increase in the creation, performance, and teaching—and awareness—of music consciously reflecting nationalistic aspects of Canadian life: its people, culture, emotions, and history.

Canadians also have been active in jazz and in experimental, avant-garde, and electronic music composition. Among its most successful composers are Healey Willan, John Weinzweig, John Beckwith, R. Murray Schafer, and Barbara Pentland.

## Music of South America and the Caribbean

The influences and characteristics of music in South America and the Caribbean include the following:

1. *Mestizo* folk music
2. Popular and folk music styles derived from Spanish and, in some cases, African practices
3. Instruments commonly used in popular and folk music
4. Church and missionary influences
5. Establishment of music schools and conservatories
6. European models of art music
7. Beginnings of nationalistic practices in art music

## The Mestizo People

The folk and popular (vernacular) music of Latin America is derived mainly from the traditions of the **mestizo** people, those natives of mixed Indian and Spanish blood (in Brazil, the mestizos have mixed Indian and Portuguese blood). The mestizo music exists throughout most of South America. It is Latin America's predominant indigenous music, the music of its natives. This music often was derived from the combination of Spanish tunes and words with native dances. Other vernacular music is derived from those people having African/Hispanic heritage. The Afro-music, largely dance based, exists in the Caribbean islands, such as Cuba, Puerto Rico, and Trinidad and in some parts of South America.

Several South American Indian groups, such as the Incas of Peru, had high social and political organization and apparently had strong musical traditions. However, very little pure Indian music exists today. Only a few Indian groups are relatively untainted by European traditions.

The Spanish and the African mestizos either (1) learned the songs of the white people and adapted them to their own way of performing music, (2) learned white ways of performing music and adapted them to their own songs, or (3) learned the songs of the whites and superimposed their native performance practices on them. From whatever combination of influences, frequently the original song or the source of a song became obscure or unknown as its subsequent versions became altered, a circumstance common in oral tradition folk music.

## Musical Instruments

Native Latin Americans became proficient at playing and making musical instruments. The following instruments were widely used throughout the region:

1. *Wind instruments (Aerophones)*
   Reed flutes, ocarinas, panpipes, *quenas* (vertical or end-blown flutes), clay or conch-shell trumpets
2. *Percussion instruments (Idiophones or membranophones)*
   Rattles, rasps, drums of all sorts, claves, castanets, guiros, maracas, marimbas, xylophones, and steel drums
3. *Stringed instruments (Chordophones)*
   Violins, *charangos* and *jaranas* (little guitars) and *guitarrones* (bass guitars), lutes, and harps

Tahuantinsuyo, an Andean folk ensemble.

Brazilian Indians of the Yawalapiti Tribe take part in the flute dance called the "urua" during the sacred ceremony Kuarup to honor the dead.

*Folk Songs and Dances*

Much Latin American music is foot-tapping, finger-snapping music. It typically has a strong pulse and metric feeling and is frequently associated with dancing: the rumba, samba, fandango, reggae, salsa, *gato, bailes, huapango, jarabe,* and *joropo.* Given regional and stylistic variations, a number of generalizations of Latin American folk and popular music can be made:

1. Melodies and harmonies are European in style with prevalent tonic and dominant harmonies.
2. Music is simple and repetitive; differing, simple lines when combined can create a more complex texture.
3. Chromaticism is uncommon.
4. The melodies encompass a limited range; a countermelody paralleling the melody at an interval of a third or a sixth is common.
5. Improvisation and freedom of melodic and rhythmic interpretation as in jazz are virtually nonexistent in Indian/Hispanic music but common in Afro-Hispanic music.
6. Phrases tend to be clear and regular.
7. Tonalities for the most part are major or minor, often both in the same song (the most common type of modulation).
8. The rhythm is regular, syncopated, and percussive, particularly in Afro-music.
9. The music is metric, often having pulses or bars with alternate divisions of twos and threes; for example:

Constant pulse with shifting divisions in twos and threes
1 + 2 +/1 + + 2 + + /1 + 2 + /1 + + 2 + +

or

Shifting speed of pulse with constant divisions in twos
1 + 2 +/1 + 2 + 3 + /1 + 2 + /1 + 2 + 3 +

Many of the dances are songs having instrumental accompaniments. Other songs (*cancions* or *sons*) include narrative ballads or story songs, *rancheros* (cowboy songs), and lyrical love songs (*romances* and *corridos*) and their religious counterparts (*villancicos* and *alabados*). The call and response technique is common as is the verse (stanza) and refrain form. The stanza is sung by soloist and the refrain by more than one singer. The familiar **mariachi** band adds trumpets and sometimes a trombone or clarinets to a common ensemble that includes violins, guitars, a folk harp, a *jarana* (small guitar), and a *guitarron* (bass guitar).

*Church Influence*

From the early sixteenth century, the musical life of the natives was dominated by the Catholic church. The missionaries taught receptive Indians Gregorian chant and Renaissance polyphonic church music (see chapter 8). The Indians were ready and rapid learners and were adept at making and playing musical instruments. They participated in church activities and possessed a keen aptitude for imitating and assimilating European cultural traits.

The cathedral was the center of public life in the community. Indians were employed as church musicians but seldom for the more prestigious and better paying positions of chapelmaster (choir director) or organist. Cathedral musicians, including Indians and mestizos, became composers and performers of religious art music and of secular art concert music as well. They created songs of praise for religious fiestas and processions—in Latin and later in the vernacular—and, by the nineteenth century, musical plays, opera, chamber music, and salon music for piano.

Mexican ensemble of folk instruments (a popular mariachi).

A village orchestra from Oazaca, Mexico.

*Music Education*    In the sixteenth and seventeenth centuries, certain elite Indian groups, such as the Aztecs and the Incas, were given special educational opportunities. For blacks, the owners of sugar plantations in some cases accepted responsibility for the formalized education of their black slaves. However, during the first half of the nineteenth century, the development of artistic activity was enhanced by the organization of private and government run music schools and conservatories. These schools trained native musicians in European musical literature and performance practice. They learned to sing opera, but the local opera companies engaged illustrious European singers and conductors, depriving native talent from important artistic development and opportunity.

*Concert Art Music*    A few of the schools and professional symphony orchestras, however, did encourage native composition of concert art music by providing opportunities for performances of their works. By the early twentieth century, Latin American composers were being recognized nationally and even internationally. They composed music based on European models, such as symphonies and string quartets, but they also composed nationalistic music derived from native songs and dances and from native folk lore and legend (see next section). The most illustrious of these composers are Heitor Villa-Lobos from Brazil, Alberto Ginastera from Argentina, and Carlos Chavez from Mexico.

As mentioned, the "classical" Latin American music reflected European models, including Latin polyphony of the sixteenth century; the arias, cantatas, and Italian opera of the seventeenth and early eighteenth centuries; homophonic instrumental music of the symphony orchestras and chamber groups of the late eighteenth and early nineteenth centuries; and orchestral and piano music of the nineteenth century.

Native composers were in abundance during the nineteenth century composing opera and light musical theatre songs and piano music, all reflecting European practices. The most popular piano music became known as **salon music.** These were short, simple pieces published as sheet music. They were often based on dance songs, such as the tango, habanera, and the conga. The contradance was a common type of salon music in Latin America.

*Nationalism*    **Nationalistic music** possesses definable national characteristics. It is concert art music in which composers incorporate elements that reflect or characterize the following:

1. The folk and popular traditions of their nation
2. The cultural characteristics of the people of the nation rather than of people universally
3. The history, tales, and legends of the nation
4. The glories and triumphs of the nation and its people

Composers have been influenced, for example, by the *gaucho* guitarists of Argentina and their folk dances, particularly the *gato.* The "Indianist" approach to nationalistic composition utilizes native Indian melodies and rhythms. Another approach incorporates native instruments and rhythms, an example being the use of the claves, guiro, or bongos in an orchestra piece based on Cuban dances. Composers of nationalistic music will at times quote directly from a nation's folk literature or will compose in a manner only reflective of the moods or rhythms of this music.

The early missionaries who came to Mexico tried to suppress native Indian culture and considered any original Mexican music good only if it conformed to European ideals.

## Folk and Classical Music of Mexico

The indigenous music of Mexico, like most of the Americas, is that of the Indian cultures. In Mexico, the great civilizations of the Mayan and Aztec Indians and their descendents are the most important.

In the early 1500s, the Spaniards under Cortes conquered the Aztec nation, which by then encompassed most of what we know now as Mexico. Unfortunately, they destroyed much of the tangible artifacts that would have provided much information and insight into the Aztec culture. As in most of Latin America, the Spanish missionaries that followed converted Indians to Christianity; many realized the value of music in the task of conversion. The missionaries tried to suppress the Indian culture and taught the finest of European art music, developing Indian choirs to sing in the churches.

The classical music tradition, again like the rest of Latin America, was an outgrowth of the postconquest, Spanish-influenced culture which from the fifteenth century stressed the European art/religious music of Gregorian chant and Renaissance liturgical polyphony with Latin texts (see chapter 8). To the conquerors and the missionaries, any original Mexican music was considered good only if it conformed to European ideals.

For the first two hundred years of Spanish domination, Mexico developed no roots for its own classical music tradition. The level of its musical vitality reflected the vitality of the Spanish culture. By the beginning of the nineteenth century, this vitality had declined; Mexico's musical life was in a depressed state. It had not developed music schools of a caliber to prepare world-class musicians or to maintain a high standard of musical achievement. Its standards of composition had declined, as had its performance standards. Europeans continued to obtain the prestigious positions, discouraging native talent. Even in the mid-nineteenth century, the person appointed to organize the faculty of the first government-supported conservatory of music was Giovanni Bottesini, the famed Italian double bass artist who was living in Mexico at the time.

The revolution in the early nineteenth century, which resulted in the Spanish being expelled, put Mexico on its own. José Mariano Elizaga became the first important native composer and music educator in the new republic. He believed, in order for the Mexican musical life to be successful, that the general level of public musical sensitivity must be raised, and this could best be done through the formal study of music and superior music teaching. Elizaga's contributions were his writing of two textbooks on music, establishing a house to publish music textbooks, and founding a conservatory of music. His energetic efforts did much to advance the cause of music in Mexico.

The classical musical life in the nineteenth century was dominated by opera and salon music. The people generally seemed to like music, and it was considered a worthy vocation. The piano became a universal household instrument.

Little interest was shown in the composition or performance of chamber music or symphonies except perhaps in Mexico City, but Mexicans had a mania for opera, particularly Italian operas sung in Italian. The "stars" were Italians, again siphoning off resources not available to native Mexicans. The conservatories focused their curricula on preparing people to sing in operas, to accompany operas, and to write operas.

Salon music—polkas, valses, schottishes, mazurkas, marches, boleros, and paso-dobles—was composed in large quantities by many Mexican composers. One of the most popular tunes from the 1951 film, *The Great Caruso,* was from Mexican salon music. It was a set of waltzes by a full blooded Otomi Indian by the name of Jurentino Rosas. The title of the song in the movie was "The Loveliest Night of the Year."

Classical composers of the twentieth century began to extol the virtues of indigenous music and incorporated native Mexican melodies in their music wherever possible. Three of the more well-known pieces are Luis Sandi's "Yaqui Music," "Musica Yaqui," by Manuel Ponce, and "Sinfonia India" by Carlos Chavez. The three best known Mexican composers of this century are Silvestre Revueltas, Manuel Ponce, and Carlos Chavez. Of these, Chavez stands out as the outstanding Mexican musician—composer, conductor, pianist, scholar, administrator, and international music personality. He has conducted the New York Philharmonic Orchestra, served as Director of the Conservatorio Nacional in Mexico City, and had his own compositions performed in New York and Boston. As conductor of the Orquesta Sinfonica de Mexico, he regularly programmed works by Mexican composers and frequently gave opportunities to native Mexican artists to perform. The achievement of Carlos Chavez has not only been a Mexican achievement but an achievement of the first order of the entire New World.

**A Study
in Sound**
*World Music of
the Western
Hemisphere*

# Example 1

**"Rabbit Dance"**—native American music—Indians of the northern plains

Recorded in 1975

This type of dance is one of the few in which men and women are allowed to dance together. It is a social dance and a time for merriment.

## Goals:

Recognize textures, vocal qualities, timbres and other musical characteristics in native American music.

Describe the musical relationship of the singing and the drum.

*Guide:* This dance is in three easily distinguishable parts (Indian words, then English, then Indian). The melody is similar in each part.

Listen carefully to the second part. The words are in English and are as follows:

*Hey, sweetheart, I always think of you,
I wonder if you are alone tonight,
I wonder if you are thinking of me.*

*Reflections:* Notice the wild-sounding intensity with which these Indians sing and the pulsating effect they achieve with their voices. Notice, also, that the singing and the drums are usually not in exact synchronization.

The English words in the second section match the character of the sounds of the Indian words. The rhythms, pitches, and tonal qualities are very similar. You may merely hear the English words as a continuation of the Indian words.

# Example 2

**"Butterfly Dance"** (excerpt)—native American music of the San Juan Pueblo, New Mexico

Recorded on Easter Sunday in 1975

The Butterfly Dance is associated with warfare, for the butterfly (considered a symbol of elusiveness, of always getting away, of just escaping in the nick of time) has qualities desired in a warrior.

This musical example, the opening of a set of nine songs performed for the Butterfly Dance, calls the participants to get in position for the dance. The instruments used are a double-headed cylindrical rawhide drum played by the lead singer and a set of bells worn behind the knee of the male dancer.

## Goals:

Describe typical textures, rhythms, and instruments in native American music, particularly in this musical example.

Discuss the functions of native American music.

Discuss the vocal quality and compare with other familiar singing styles.

*Guide:* Count according to the drum beats and follow the phrases and patterns. The slash (/) represents a change in the phrasing or other shift in pattern; the dash (-) represents a short pause in the movement of the drum beat. A double slash (//) represents a pause (hold) at a phrase ending.

```
1    2  3
1    2  3   4/  5-  6    7   8   9   10
1    2  3   4   5   6    7
1    2  3   4   5   6    7                    Sequence
1    2  3   4   5   6//                       Sequence
1    2  3//
1    2  3   4   5   6    7/  8   9   10
1-   2  3   4   5   6//
1    2  3   4   5   6/   7   8
1-   2  3   4   5   6
1    2  3/  4   5   6
1    2  3/  4   5                             Fast/slow
1    2  3/  4   5   6    7                     Fast/slow
1    2  3-  4-  5   6    7   8/  9//
1    2  3   4   5   6/   7   8
1-   2  3   4//
```

*Reflection:* The chorus sings in unison with loud, full voices in the low range. Notice the use of vocables.

Describe the vocal range, phrasing, form, and rhythmic aspects of this music, particularly as related to pulse and meter and to the relationship between voice and drum.

The sequence refers to a motive repeated from the previous line at a lower pitch.

# Example 3

**"Corn Dance"**—native American music of the Seneca Indians

Recorded at the Allegany reservation in New York in 1975.

The Corn Dance emphasizes the agricultural concerns of the eastern tribes. A cycle of six sections comprises the complete dance. Only the first three sections are presented here. The dance features a complex interplay of leader, chorus, hand rattles, and bells. The instruments used are a cylindrical wooden water drum, steer horn hand rattles, metal ankle bells, and a rawhide double-headed frame drum.

## Goals:

Describe the differing musical characteristics of each of the three dances.

Differentiate among the instrumental timbres.

**Guide:** The dance begins in a free, declamatory style. It features both solo and group singing and the constant shaking of rattles. A "yo ho" passage signals the end of each section.

The more rhythmic, second dance has a stronger pulse, a feeling of duple meter, and identifiable motives that are repeated, usually with modification.

The rhythmic activity slows down, and the "yo ho" declamation with the shaking of the rattles signals the beginning of the third dance.

**Reflections:** This musical example combines both unison and responsorial singing. The melody of the first dance is based on a four-note, minor-sounding scale. The second dance shifts to a major-sounding, five-note (pentatonic) scale. The third dance also is based on a "major" pentatonic scale. Differentiate between the major and minor qualities.

# Example 4

**"Klondike!"**—music of Canada

Sung by Phil Thomas with Phil Thomas, banjo; Barry Hall, guitar; and Stanley Triggs, mouth organ

Recorded in Vancouver, Canada, in 1962

This folk song is a reworking of a London journalist's humorous verses on the Klondike's goldrush of 1897–1898. Phil Thomas learned it from Charles Cates of North Vancouver who learned it from his father.

## Goals:

Recognize verse and refrain form.

Identify chords and recognize chord changes.

**Guide:** The song is in triple meter; count it in one slow beat to the bar; it starts with a pickup.

```
                 1   2   3   4   5   6   7   8
First verse—     I       V       V       I           Open cadence
  solo           I       V       V       I           Closed cadence
Refrain—         I       IV      V       I
  chorus         I       V       V       I
                 I       V       V       I           One extra bar
Second verse (same structure as above)
Refrain (same structure as above)
Instrumental interlude (sixteen bars)
Refrain (same structure as above)
```

**Reflections:** Notice the simplicity of melody, harmony, and rhythm, yet a certain vitality. The melody is mainly stepwise and diatonic.

# Example 5

**"La Llorona"** (The Weeping Woman)—Mexican folk song

Sung and played by Suni Paz

Recorded in New York in 1979

"La Llorona," derived from Aztec mythology, is a figure who comes out at night, clad in white, sobbing and shrieking as she looks for her children. Since anyone who looks at her dies, her appearance is considered a bad omen. Many versions of this song exist.

    This piece is a solo with guitar accompaniment and is sung in Spanish.

## *Goals:*

Observe the relationship of the solo voice and the guitar accompaniment.

Be aware of chord progressions and identify the sounds of the I, IV, and V chords.

Differentiate between the major and minor sounds.

Recognize the parallel motion between the voice parts in the duets.

*Guide:* The piece is in triple meter and can be counted in a moderate one. Capitalized Roman numerals symbolize major chords; lower case Roman numerals symbolize minor chords; an "x" denotes chords other than I, IV, and V. Each line of chords represents a phrase, and there are four phrases to each of the six verses. Notice that many of the phrases are set as a vocal duet.

```
1    2    3    4    5    6    7    8    9    10
V--  V--  i--  i--  i--  i--                        Guitar intro.
i--  i--  iv--iv--i--  i--  V--  V--
i--  i--  iv--iv--i--  i--  V--  V--
i--  i--  x--  x--  x--  x--  V--  V--
i--  i--  x--  x--  x--  x--  V--  V--  V--  V--
V--  V--  i--  i--  i--  i--  i--                   Ending phrase
                                                   Hold on second
                                                   bar
```

*Reflections:* The meter can also easily be perceived in duple meter with a triple sub-division of each pulse. The two possibilities are illustrated by the following diagram

```
1 2 3 1 2 3 1 2 3 1 2 3
1 - - 2 - - 1 - - 2 - -
```

# Example 6

**"El Muchacho Alegre"**—mariachi music (Tex/Mex border music)

Performed by Los Norteños—vocal duet with mariachi band

Recorded probably in south Texas in the late 1940s.

This *cancion* or song is an example of a Mexican-American musical style. It developed in southern Texas and northern Mexico around the turn of the twentieth century and was popular among the Mexican laborers involved with the crops that were raised and harvested along the Rio Grande valley.

## Goals:

Recognize the parallel lines of the vocal duet (melody and countermelody).

Identify the differences in metric feeling, phrase organization, and clarity of chord progressions between the vocal and instrumental choruses.

Recognize the short transitional passages.

*Guide:* Count in a moderately fast two.

```
Instrumental chorus
Transition
First stanza─vocal
Instrumental chorus
Transition
Second stanza─vocal
Instrumental chorus
Transition
Third stanza─vocal
Instrumental chorus
Transition
Fourth stanza─vocal
Instrumental chorus
```

*Reflections:* The chords are mostly tonic, subdominant, and dominant (I, IV, V). Notice the parallel lines in the vocal duet created by a countermelody at the consonant intervals of thirds and sixths.

The stanzas (vocal) are comprised of tonic/dominant chord changes and have an imprecise metric feeling. The choruses (instrumental) have regular phrases, a clear duple meter, and easily definable chord progressions. The instrumental choruses other than the final one are followed by short transitional passages to the next stanza.


# Example 7

**"Collaguas"**—South American Indian music

An illustration of aboriginal music of the Andes: an Aymara Indian dance from Peru

Instruments: harp, *charango,* and drums

In the first section, the unusual-sounding harmony is played on the *charango,* a mandolin-type instrument. The music begins as though from a distance, getting louder as it seems to approach.

## Goals:

Recognize crescendo.

Count irregular groupings of pulses.

Recognize chord symbols and an abb phrase structure.

*Guide:* In the first section, count at a moderately slow tempo; notice the irregular groupings. It starts on the downbeat. The long crescendo is in the first section. The shout announces each dance.

```
First section 1 - 2 - 3 - 4 - -
              1 - 2 - 3 - 4 - -
              1 - - 2 - 3 -
              1 - - 2 - 3 - 4 - - 5 - 6 -
              1 - 2 - 3 - 4 - -
              1 - 2 - 3 - 4 - -
              1 - - 2 - 3 -
              1 - - 2 - 3 - 4 - - 5 - 6 - Shout!
      Dance 1 - 2 - 3 - 4 - 5 - 6 - 7 - 8 - Faster tempo
      a       I   IV  V   I   I   IV  V   I
      b       I   I   I   V   I   I   V   I
      b       I   I   I   V   I   I   V   I Shout!
                                  (Dance is repeated twice)
```

***Reflections:*** Discuss differences of musical characteristics between the first section and the dance.

# Example 8

**"Pajaro Campana"** (Bell Bird)—Latin American pop music (Paraguay)

Performed by the Paranas

Recorded in New York in 1976

The Paranas was a Paraguayan pop group based in Dallas in the 1970s. This example featured three guitars and a Paraguayan harp. "Pajaro Campana" is a good example of those musical characteristics that contribute to making music sound Latin.

## *Goals:*

Recognize rhythmic and melodic ostinato patterns.

Be aware of duple and triple subdivisions of the pulse and a "three-against-two" feeling in the music.

Identify the harp timbre.

Be aware of layers of sound and their function as foreground or background material.

***Guide:*** The piece is in duple meter. After the introduction, count in a moderately fast four.

The introduction starts with a very slow pulse, gradually getting faster. Counting in two, each note represents one count until the downbeat of the sixth bar where it shifts to "double time" (the rhythmic activity is twice as fast). It reaches the ongoing tempo of the piece one beat later, at the beginning of the first phrase.

Be aware of the three layers of sound. The melody in the high pitch range is played on the harp. Listen for the continual variations with each new eight-bar phrase. The guitars can be heard strumming on each beat in the middle pitch range. The bass has its own distinct pattern in giving a rhythmic and harmonic foundation to the music.

```
                                  1 2 3 4 5 6 7 8
        Intro.            6 bars  x x x x x x
        First phrase      8 bars  V V I I V V I I
        (same structure
        for all remaining
        phrases)
```

***Reflections:*** Notice in the background material the regular ostinato pattern in the bass guitar and the regular on-the-beat guitar strumming in the middle range.

Observe the shifting subdivisions of the pulse between twos and threes. Against a a bass line that is felt in a subdivision of two, the rhythm of the melody (foreground material) incorporates many triplets (a triple subdivision of the beat). This juxtaposition sets up a three-against-two feeling. Notice that triplets occasionally span two beats, giving a more pronounced three-against-two feeling. Furthermore, the harp melody frequently goes back and forth between duple and triple subdivisions. The following chart illustrates these triple/duple patterns. Recognize them in this example as in virtually any example of Latin American music.

```
Pulse
Subdivision   1   +   2   +   3   +   4   +   1   +   2   +   3   +   4   +
of two
Subdivision   1  + +  2  + +  3  + +  4  + +  1  + +  2  + +  3  + +  4  + +
of three
Two-beat      1       +       +   2       +       +   1       +       +   2       +       +
triplet
```

# Example 9

**"High Life"**—steel band music of the Caribbean

Performed by the Westland Steel Band

Steel bands play contemporary music combining Latin, French, and African elements. It is music of the common people. Hundreds of them exist in the Caribbean area, mostly in Trinidad. They also exist in England, Australia, the Orient, and the United States.

The instruments used in steel bands are idiophones made out of metal oil barrels. The bottom of the barrels are heated and shaped in segments of different sizes and depths, generating the different pitches. The drums come in soprano, alto, tenor, and bass sizes. The number of pitches for each drum ranges from two on the biggest drum to as many as thirty-two on the highest (smallest) drum. A gourd filled with seeds, providing a rattle effect, is the only nonmetal instrument typically used in a traditional steel band.

***Goals:***

Recognize ostinato.

Identify the sounds of open and closed cadences, and recognize antecedent (open) and consequent (closed) phrase groups.

Recognize the rhythmic and harmonic foundations.

***Guide:*** This piece is built on a long series of repetitions of a short, syncopated two-bar pattern (ostinato).

The structure is determined by a pattern of antecedent phrases with open cadences and consequent phrases with closed cadences. Each letter (o=open; c=closed) represents a four-bar phrase. The piece is in duple meter; count in a moderately fast two.

```
Intro.
1     o  o  c  c
2     o  o  c  c
3     o  o  o  o  c  c
4     o  o  c  c
5     o  o  o  c  c  c  c
6     o  o  c  c
7     o  o  c  c
8     o  o  c  c
9     o  o  c  c
Tag
```

*Reflections:* The phrase groups are mostly regular, some ending with open cadences in a descending melodic pattern and others with closed cadences in an ascending pattern. Notice two phrases that have short extensions.

The bass ostinato is constant throughout, providing rhythmic and harmonic foundation. Inner voices provide sustained, harmonic support.

*Discography*

**Ex. 1**   "Rabbit Dance." *Songs of Earth, Fire, and Water: Music of the American Indian.* New World Records. NW 246. 1:30.

**Ex. 2**   "Butterfly Dance." *Songs of Earth, Fire, and Water: Music of the American Indian.* New World Records. NW 246. 1:30.

**Ex. 3**   "Corn Dance." *Songs and Dances of the Eastern Indians from Medicine Spring.* New World Records. NW 337. 2:25.

**Ex. 4**   "Klondike!" *Where the Fraser River Flows and Other Songs of the Pacific Northwest.* Vol. 1. Skookumchuck Records SR 7001. 1:28.

**Ex. 5**   Paz, Suni. "La Llorona." *The Sky of My Childhood—Folk Songs of Latin America.* Folkways FW 8875. 3:50.

**Ex. 6**   Los Nortenos. "El Muchacho Alegra." *Texas-Mexican Border Music.* Vol. 1. Folklyric 9003. 3:10.

**Ex. 7**   "Collaguas." *Music of Peru.* Folkways FE 4415. 2:25.

**Ex. 8**   The Paranas. "Pajara Campana." Parana Records. 1:45.

**Ex. 9**   Westland Steel Band. "High Life." *The Sound of the Sun.* Nonesuch H-72016. 2:55.

*Summary*

Much of what we call *world music* exists close to home, within the United States and throughout the Western Hemisphere. We call it world music because it is unfamiliar repertoire to most American citizens and is out of the mainstream of American music, yet it represents a part of the heritage of our neighbors. Chapter 7 will present world music from beyond the Americas, including the music of India, Japan, and Africa.

World music, too, is considered that which is based on non-Western European traditions. Native American music, for example, is based on compositional techniques, aesthetic values, and performance practices different from European-based music, but Latin American music is based on European scales, tonalities, harmonic progressions, form, and other aspects of musical language.

*Bridges to other cultures*
*Performance practices*
*Music in other cultures*
*Music in context*
*Ethnomusicologist*
*Acculturation*
*Aboriginal cultures*
*Indigenous music*
*Ceremonial music*
*Water drum*
*Pentatonic scale*
*Mestizo*
*Latin American instruments*
*Latin American songs and dances*
*Nationalistic music*
*Salon music*

# Chapter 7
# World Music
## *Beyond the Americas*

An Indonesian gamelan
orchestra with dancers.

World music typically refers to those styles that are centered in parts of the world other than western Europe and the Americas and that are derived from cultures and traditions other than our own. It is the music of Asia, Africa, Indonesia, Polynesia, and other exotic places. We sometimes refer to it as "non-Western" music (perhaps the "non-Western" people refer to our music as "non-Eastern"). However, world music is not necessarily far away, for non-Western music and Western music that is influenced by non-Western cultures exist within the United States. We have already pointed out that the music of the native Americans is indigenous to American culture yet is indeed foreign to most of us and is treated as a world music.

We are looking at this world's music with a special emphasis on its impact on America's music. As with American society in general, American music is a product of the merging of cultures and musical styles from all parts of the globe. American music is, in fact, a result of cross-cultural influences from the contributions of millions of immigrants.

A folk trio from
Azerbayan, USSR.

Cross-cultural influences on American music have further affected the creative work of composers who have studied the music of these cultures. Some American jazz and classical musicians have, of course, used books and recordings in their inquiry into music of other cultures. However, many others have visited and studied with musicians from these world cultures, particularly India and Africa. In fact, many musicians from these and other countries teach their music in the United States where a growing number of colleges and universities offer courses and native performance experiences in specific world musics, making the study of other cultures easily accessible.

This chapter focuses on American immigrant music from Russia and Eastern Europe, the traditional music of the Jewish people, and characteristic music of India, Japan, and Africa. At the same time, we shall learn of the distinctive features of these repertoires that make these musics sound different than "our own" music. Those interested in the further study of world music might consider studying the music of China, the Mediterranean countries, or the islands of Java or Bali (Indonesia) that have a rich tradition of gamelan orchestra music that is becoming increasingly well known in the United States.

## Music of Russia and Eastern Europe

Through the centuries, the eastern European countries, through war and conquest, have come under the influence of different nations having differing cultures. Their cultural roots include ancient Greece, Islamic nations, the orient, and western Europe. Their musical roots lie in the chants of the Byzantine church, the pentatonic modes of Mongolia, the complex rhythms of Arabian and other Hindu musics, and the musical language of western Europe. This cultural mix resulted in a great diversity of styles, with each country having its own rich cultural heritage. Yet among these nations, one finds a commonality of musical styles, of techniques of composition, and of types of folk repertoire. A greater diversity in musical styles exists in eastern Europe than can be found among the western European nations.

## Musical Characteristics

In all these countries, including Russia, the Western European concert art music tradition flourishes, along with some of the world's foremost composers:

Russia: Tchaikovsky, Rimsky-Korsakov, Prokofiev
Hungary: Bartók
Czechoslavakia: Dvořák
Poland: Chopin

A Ukranian bandura
ensemble.

Eastern European folk melodies are derived from a variety of scales, some based on the familiar Western European major and minor scales and some involving other regular patterns of pitches, such as the pentatonic (five-tone) scale. Usually, the vocal range of the songs is relatively small. The melodic and rhythmic qualities of the folk songs are strongly influenced by the stress, length, and pattern of the words. The musical structure is determined by the structure of the text.

The lyrical songs tend to reflect the peasant, agrarian society, conveying emotions, love, the beauties of nature, the horrors of war, and the pangs of poverty. The narrative songs are based on epic poetry and are usually longer than British narrative ballads.

The main character may be a national hero having many adventures in war and love. Songs that reflect the social and political conditions of the people must fall within the state-approved ideological goals.

Whereas the aaba song form is common in western Europe, the abba form is more common in eastern Europe. The *b* section is often the same tune as found in the *a* section but transposed to a different key, rather than providing a contrasting melody or mood.

Instrumental music is common either as dances or as accompaniments to songs. The bagpipe, double recorder, and hammered dulcimer have been common folk instruments. More modern instruments include the accordian, fiddle, and several types of flutes.

Many composers of concert art music have studied the folk songs and dances of their region and incorporated them directly or indirectly in their music. The two most important Eastern European composers, Bartók and Kodály from Hungary, contributed much of what is known about Hungarian and Rumanian folk music through their published folk collections. We also know to some extent the spirit of these folk repertoires from state-produced folk orchestras and choruses who have come to the United States to perform and whose recordings are available in this country.

## Immigrant Music

During the nineteenth and early twentieth centuries, over 35 million Europeans emigrated to the United States. They at first came from England, then Ireland, Germany, and the Scandinavian countries, then Italy, Poland, and the Balkan and other eastern European countries.

Today, these journeys may take from a few hours to no more than a day. Then, such a trip may have taken up to three months, accompanied by considerable hardship.

These immigrants left their families and friends behind; they would not return. Their departures were decisive and permanent and were the result of individual family decisions. There was no organized exodus, no grand plan. These courageous people were not seeking adventure. They were desperate peasants, craftsmen, and artisans who lost their jobs in societies being transformed from agrarian to industrialized economies.

Desiring to get to the wide open spaces in the land of opportunity, most of these people could not afford to get past the cities where they landed. Thus, rural Europeans became urban Americans. They became isolated in a society of strangers. They cherished the coherant and stable traditional culture of their homeland and expressed their nostalgia through their folk tales, songs, and dances. They often retained their native language, cooking, and customs.

By the late nineteenth century, the recording industry had developed, and its executives became very much aware of the profit potential in providing recordings in foreign languages to sell to these immigrants. By the 1890s, recordings of folk music were available in Hebrew, Polish, Czech, Spanish, and many other languages. These recordings supplemented memories of the homeland. They reinforced the worth of retaining old languages and customs in the new land.

The performers, at first, were trained artists recorded in Europe using sophisticated arrangements, which robbed the peasant and village music of its original flavor. It didn't answer the need for the "real" folk music. The peasants brought with them a taste for the rougher music and the singing of the fields and mountains, which did not find acceptance in the sophisticated cities.

These immigrants became acculturated in their new communities. They came to enjoy new singers and instrumental groups. They learned new songs. Then, the recording companies found an answer to providing a more acceptable folk music; it was in the music of the black and white people from the deep south who migrated north. It was the blues, jazz, and the music of the white, rural people that became known as hillbilly music. This was music with fiddlers, rough-voiced singers, village orchestras, and other representations of authentic folk styles. The importation of urbanized folk music from eastern Europe and other countries came to a halt as these immigrants took on new tastes, new loyalties, and new traditions.

## Music of the Jewish People

For hundreds of years, the Jewish people have been spread throughout the world without a homeland, until 1948 with the creation of the state of Israel. Jews have settled in over 100 countries, from a few hundred of them living in the Philippines to millions of them making the United States their homeland.

Wherever the Jews have gone, they absorbed much of the culture of their host land but retained their religious traditions and practices. They remained religiously separated and held on to many of the old styles and forms of Jewish religious music.

Modern Jewish music is a result of the Jews' commitment to adapt, to compromise, to assimilate while at the same time retaining their ethnic values and traditions. This balancing of ethnic preservation and acculturation has resulted in considerable cross-influence between Jewish traditions and other cultures.

What would the music of the United States be without the contributions of the Jewish people who emigrated to America within the last 100 years? For example, all of the following Jewish composers have contributed immeasurably to American music during this century: Cole Porter, Irving Berlin, George Gershwin, Aaron Copland, and Leonard Bernstein. Their music was Jewish because they were Jews, but their music was also American. One cannot deny their success in capturing the American spirit in their music and in helping shape what is considered characteristically American music.

The many Jews from diverse cultures throughout the world who returned to Israel brought with them the music and art of their native land, creating a cultural and musical richness in Israel. They came from the Jewish communities (ghettos) of Europe, Russia, the Near East, and India, bringing their unique musics with them.

Jewish music is comprised of liturgical music, religious poems, secular songs, music from the Islamic traditions, and the new Jewish music from the modern state of Israel.

The liturgical music places emphasis on prayers and invocations and is transmitted by oral tradition. The music is **melismatic,** that is, having several notes of the melody for a single syllable of text. The result of a melisma is a fast-moving melody to a slow-moving text. The songs are known as cantillations and are sung by a cantor. They may be sung unaccompanied, with organ, or with instrumental accompaniment.

The nonliturgical religious music typically includes religious poetry set to music borrowed from the secular folk traditions, particularly from Europe and the Near East. Jewish religious poems have considerably more variety than those from the liturgical repertoire.

The secular songs of the Jews, usually accompanied, reflect the life and times in the land of their origin. The songs may be borrowed from the Gentile tradition or may be specific songs brought with them from their native ghettos.

The common instruments used in Jewish music reflect the acculturation of styles. Tambourines and block flutes or *halils* are derived from the Near East, guitars and accordians from Europe. Among the ancient instruments, the one that has been retained in the culture, at least for ritualistic purposes, is the *shofar* or ram's horn.

The scales or modes on which songs are based are Near Eastern, but European or Russian harmonies are superimposed on them. Western harmonic tendencies in secular music have crept into the religious music.

What is it that makes music sound Jewish? One might ask what makes jazz music sound like jazz, or what gives hillbilly its characteristic sound, or what distinguishes bluegrass from the blues. What is it in Jewish music that is shared by Jews from such different regions and backgrounds as Yemen (Yemenite Jews), Spain or Portugal (Sephardic Jews), Germany (Ashkenazic Jews), India (Cochin Jews), the black Jews from America, and the Orthodox, Conservative, or Reform Jews from throughout the world? What does the Jew consider to be Jewish music?

It may be the musical materials, the background of the composer, or the context in which the music was created and performed. It may be the text, language, or content of the songs. Most likely it is that unexplainable mix of factors that speaks to a group of people, that communicates to the very soul of these people in ways that would not be shared as personally or as deeply by others.

## Music of India

India brings to mind the river Ganges, the snowcapped Himalayas, and the Taj Mahal; Bombay, Kashmir, and Calcutta; and yoga, gurus, and Sanskrit. The predominant religions are Hinduism and Islam. It is a country of dense population, extreme wealth, and extreme poverty. It is also a country of diverse geography, peoples, religions, and musics. Important names with which Americans are familiar include Mahatma Gandhi and Ravi Shankar, and familiar words that relate to its music include the *sitār* and the *rāga*.

India is more than a distant, exotic land. Americans have imported from India textiles, cloths, vases, tables, and lamps. Particularly since the 1960s, we have been influenced by India's religion and philosophy. Many have benefited from yoga, transcendental meditation, and perhaps even the messages of the Hare Krishnas. We have learned of India's music from visits by accomplished artists, such as Ravi Shankar, and from increasingly large numbers of Americans who have studied Indian music in India and returned to teach others.

India's music is comprised of tribal music, music for dance and film, music for religion and ritual, and both classical and folk music traditions. Like most cultures, it has its work songs, music for festive occasions, and devotional songs for religious ceremonies and personal devotion. The folk, popular, and ceremonial repertoires are as varied as the peoples of India. Its music, both folk and classical, as its entire social structure, is in some way based on or related to a religious philosophy, whether Hindu, Islam, or another.

The best known music of India, music that has been researched, recorded, and reported most widely, is classical music. The art music of India is based on ancient traditions, is associated with great artists, is founded on a long-standing theoretical system of music, and has been written about by Indian scholars for centuries. For these reasons, we shall concentrate our study of the music of India on its great classical music tradition.

## The Classical Music Tradition

The classical music of India has been studied and passed down for many centuries. It is a music of the patrons, the upper class. It was performed by and for this elite class. Prior to India's independence from the British Commonwealth in 1948, the center of musical performance and study was in the courts of the upper class. Since then, the cities and towns of democratic India have become the musical centers.

The musical styles since the thirteenth century have been identified according to differing practices found in the north, known as Hindustani music, and in the south, known as Karnatic music. Different style characteristics and instrumental preferences, as well as many common characteristics, can be identified. Our purpose, for the most part, will be to look at those factors that are common to all of India.

That which underlies all Indian classical music is its aesthetic basis (*rasa*). It is not just the music but the power of the music to convey thoughts, feelings, moods, and images. Indians value the relationship of their music to nature, to religious or philosophical beliefs, and to temporal elements—the stages of life, the seasons of the year, or the times of the day.

The music is akin to chamber rather than orchestral music. Whereas the Western listener is accustomed to sitting quietly and absorbing the sounds of a symphony orchestra or a string quartet, the Indian audience will listen quite actively and audibly to from three to five musicians sitting on a floor, as likely in a home as in a concert hall.

The Indian ensemble most likely will consist of a solo instrumentalist who will play a plucked stringed instrument, such as the sitār. Often a second stringed instrument serves in an accompaniment role, and there is the "keeper of the drone," a drummer, and sometimes a solo singer.

## The Musical Elements

The classical music of India essentially is a highly developed melodic music. It is primarily improvisatory. Precomposed songs are learned from memory; notated music exists but is not valued or adhered to as in Western music. The common type of classical piece is based on a system of organizing music by means of an established melodic pattern known as a **rāga** and a rhythmic pattern known as a **tāla.** The level of artistic achievement is determined by the musician's ability to develop the melodic pattern or rāga to its fullest extent and to explore all the rhythmic intricacies implied in the tāla. A student with a musical gift becomes a disciple of a guru (master teacher) and learns rāgas and precomposed pieces through imitation and practice. The disciple must not only master the broad repertoire of rāgas and tālas but must learn performance mannerisms (ornamentation) and also how to feel and think about the music.

The *rāga* represents the basic means by which the melodic or pitch aspects of Indian classical music are determined. Western music is based on scales (a system of pitch organization), usually in a major or a minor key. A rāga is a sequence of ascending and descending pitches similar to a scale, but it conveys much more. It can be thought of more as a melodic shape than an abstract pitch structure. The rāga can convey certain melodic patterns, pitch registers conceptualized as high, middle, or low, and ornamentations that make a particular rāga immediatly recognizable. It communicates to the performers and to the audience the mood and aesthetic character of the rāga.

The performer uses the pitches, the sequence of pitches, the melodic patterns, the mood, the symbol, and the meaning of the rāga to develop an extended improvisation. The best musicians are able to improvise rāga performances based on an internalized set of rules that guide the choice of melodic figures, overall structure, and style of the music. The improvised sections are alternated with less freely improvised sections that may be based on a precomposed melody or song.

The *tāla* represents the basic means of organizing the temporal or durational aspects of Indian classical music, the rhythm and meter. It dictates to a performer the complete pattern or cycle of counts as well as the recurring subdivision within the cycle. For example, a tāla may be sixteen counts in length and have an internal subdivision of $4 + 4 + 4 + 4$, or it may have fourteen counts with a subdivision of $5 + 2 + 3 + 4$. Two or more tāla cycles may comprise a phrase. The drummer learns to improvise using a set of drum strokes and rhythmic patterns that subdivide the on-going pulse of the tāla. The drummer learns to improvise sections that pull against the tāla creating tension, then returns to patterns that correspond to the tāla, creating a release of tension.

Harmony in the sense of chords and chord progressions is not a valued part of the music of India. Simultaneous sounds are the result of the interaction of the melodic, plucked instruments and the sounds of other instruments or voices rather than a conscious effort to use vertical sonorities (harmony) as ends in themselves.

Ravi Shankar, India's best known sitār player.

In Hindustani India, the most common plucked instrument is the *sitār*. It is the lead or solo instrument in a performance. Two important accompanying instruments are the *tablā,* a pair of drums struck by both hands, and the *tamburā,* a stringed instrument on which the drone is played. The drone effect results from the constantly repeated, trancelike tones played only on the open strings that help to establish the main notes of the rāga.

Among many variations of forms and genres of Indian music, one example will serve to illustrate essential differences between performances of Indian and Western European music. Just as a symphony, string quartet, or a piano sonata is comprised of movements or sections, so too is a typical Hindustani instrumental rāga.

A rāga performance, which can last thirty minutes or longer, begins with the lead instrument (sitār player) performing a slow, rhythmically free, improvised statement of the rāga in which the musician reveals its main characteristics. This section is known as *alap*. A second section (*jor*) provides increased and more repetitive rhythmic activity accompanied by the constant drone. A third section (*jhālā*) builds in speed and rhythmic intensity in anticipation of the next section. The final section is the *gat*. It

**Performance**

A tablā drummer from
India.

A classic Indian
ensemble of the tablā,
tamburā, and the sitār.

firmly establishes the tāla and is devoted to extended improvisation and interaction between the lead and the percussion and other accompanists. The structure of both the tāla and the rāga are employed in an increasingly fast, intricate, and complex style. In rāga performance, there is always a delicate balance between exciting virtuosic display and sensitive musicality.

Music of Japan

Scanning the published list of musical events in modern Tokyo for virtually any week of the year, one finds an abundance of concerts appealing to a wide range of tastes—concerts by symphony orchestras and string quartets, by jazz and rock groups, and by blues and bluegrass musicians. The performers at these concerts may be Americans or Europeans on tour, or they may be Japanese who grew up playing and listening to Western musical styles.

For more than 100 years, the Japanese school system, including university music schools and conservatories, has been teaching the Japanese the music of Bach and Beethoven and the Western aesthetic values in music, including the following:

1. Thick textures as found in orchestras, bands, choirs, and big band jazz.
2. Harmonies and chord progressions that give music a forward movement.
3. Major and minor tonalities with emphasis on the tonic and dominant sonorities.
4. Desire for dramatic changes within a composition—melodic contrasts, modulations to new keys, differing timbres.

We will soon see that these Western values are not very applicable to traditional Japanese music, which is different in style and requires a different way of listening.

In modern Japan, traditional Japanese music is performed in concert halls, theaters, the courtyards and gardens of shrines and temples, and indoors where the illusion of natural settings is achieved by screens painted with scenes of nature, such as trees, flowers, and ponds. Japanese music is inextricably entwined with visual and dramatic effects. It is often part of theatrical productions that include dance, costumes, acting, colorful staging, poetry, and stylized movements. This is why Japanese music should be seen as well as heard, and a recording, offering only a one-dimensional impression, does not convey the total experience. As with Western music, performances of songs and instrumental pieces from theatrical productions find their way into concert halls for more people to enjoy. Many of these visual and dramatic effects become part of these concert performances.

Japanese music exists side by side in modern Japan with music from Western European culture. It may be accurate to say, however, that many Japanese have not learned to appreciate their traditional music any more than many Americans have learned to appreciate Appalachian folk music, country blues, bebop, or the music of Charles Ives and Aaron Copland—our traditional or uniquely American music. Yet several factors have enabled the Japanese to preserve the essence of themselves and their culture. These factors include reverence for family and ancestors and an ethnic solidarity that has kept traditional Japanese culture viable despite the ever-changing, technological, Western-influenced world.

The Musical Tradition

The musical history of many great civilizations can be traced from religious chants and songs, including the music of India (Hinduism and Vedic chants), modern Western music (Christianity and Gregorian chants), and the music of Japan (the chants of the Shinto and Buddhist religions).

Chinese musicians. A wall painting from the cave of Tung-Chuang in the province of Kan-su from the time of the T'ang dynasty.

To carry these parallels a step further, the roots of Western music are found in the theories and practices of ancient Greek civilization and, by extension, in the music of the Catholic church as developed in the first several centuries, A.D. The roots of Japanese music lie in the ancient Chinese civilization through the music of Buddhism, brought into Japan during the Nara period (553–794 A.D.), about the same time that the music of the Catholic church was emerging.

Japanese music, as is true of Western music, developed through the centuries into a number of different historical periods having a variety of musical styles and genres. Such developments are, of course, affected in large measure by the political, economic, and cultural factors of the society. Two political periods affecting the evolution of Japanese music and culture are of particular importance:

1. The Edo period (1615–1868) was a period of isolation, of minimal contact with the outside world. It produced its own native artistic resources without extensive outside influence. The current instruments, styles, and performance practices of traditional Japanese music solidified during this period.

2. The Meiji period (1868–1912) was a period when Western culture inundated the land. It was a time during which the modernization of Japan took place, although contemporary life in Japan is to a large extent a result of post-World War II reconstruction based on the American model. Emphasis on composers was minimal until this period. The great music and musical developments of the eighteenth and nineteenth centuries in Japanese music are comparable in scope and influence to the great works of the master composers of the same period of time in the history of Western music (see chapters 10 and 11). The social status of musicians in general, as in the West, began to rise in the twentieth century.

Traditional music existed in its own little world, because the public schools and teacher training institutions stressed Western music, being taught by those who acquired skills in the musical centers of Europe and America. Children in schools heard only Western instruments and Western children's songs, and they were taught to sing harmonized choruses rather than monophonic traditional music. It was not until the 1950s that traditional Japanese music was included in school curricula.

Japan is a land of many islands, a factor that has produced distinctive, regional folk traditions and musical styles. Allowing for regional differences, Japanese folk music has certain common practices and characteristics: a propensity for theatricals and festivals; visual effects from elaborate costumes and grotesque masks; a high, tight-throated, nasal vocal quality; and a melismatic melodic style with typical accompaniments of handclapping, drums, and flutes.

**Musical Styles and Performance Practice**

The Japanese value a distinct chamber music quality wherein all parts are heard separately rather than merged, as in orchestral music. A public performance will involve from one to three musicians, except for the larger *nagauta* ensemble associated with *kabuki* theatre (see page 168). Traditional music is typically performed in traditional dress and in cross-legged seated position.

One listens for the skill and beauty with which a musician manipulates traditional materials rather than exploring new ideas. This is in contrast to the Western tendency towards experimentation and evolution rather than preservation of styles. The Japanese musician exercises restraint and control and strives to communicate the emotions of the subject rather than of his or her own. The musician values refinement rather than expansion of his or her limited tonal and instrumental resources. The Japanese musician opts to perfect a few meaningful musical ideas rather than explore a wide range of sonic possibilities. He or she strives for a maximum effect from minimal resources.

Most Japanese music is learned by memory, from the minds of master teachers known as *sensai*. Notational systems exist but are sometimes quite vague and still need the interpretation of the teachers.

A summary of musical characteristics include the following:

1. Narrow range of dynamics
2. Predominantly monophonic texture
3. Pentatonic scale commonly used with ornaments that provide minute deviations from the melody
4. Harmony nonexistent except incidentally
5. Rhythmically regular, not driving, but often quite free

Nagauta musicians are on stage in a Kabuki theater.

6. Timbre varied and unblending but not striking; emphasis on delicate
   nuances
7. Main values on melody and timbre
8. Improvisation uncommon

Several important styles have been selected as representative of the Japanese musical tradition. Japan's first instrumental music genre is the court music of ancient Japan known as *gagaku*. Music for theatre is represented by the *kabuki* tradition. Music for *koto, shakuhachi,* and *shamisen* will be discussed as will music composed for these instruments individually and in combinations.

## Gagaku

**Gagaku,** the oldest documented orchestral music in the world, was performed in the Japanese imperial courts that flourished from the ninth through the eleventh centuries. It was a form of courtly entertainment that was a total theatrical experience, including dance, masks, and visual effects. It was music reserved for the elite, the scholars, and the curious.

Musically, gagaku was static, comprised of blocks of sound that had little forward movement. Its primary instruments were the *hichiriki,* a double reed, oboe-like instrument, and the *sho,* a mouth organ having seventeen small pipes. Some gagaku music was purely instrumental; other types accompanied dancing. Gagaku music of both types is performed today.

## Kabuki

**Kabuki** theatre grew out of the noh tradition and also flourished outside the imperial household. It is a medium that still has wide appeal. It is a melodrama that includes colorful dancing, an on-stage music ensemble known as the *nagauta* which provides the basic accompaniment, and narrative *gidayu* songs sung on-stage with shamisen accompaniment. Kabuki theatre also has an off-stage music ensemble known as the used for noise, sound effects, signals, and music not covered by the musicians on-stage.

Shakuhachi player.

The nagauta is the basic genre, the mainstay of kabuki music. It has developed its own concert life independent of the kabuki theatre. It is analogous to a song with orchestral accompaniment. The orchestra in this case is comprised of about a dozen musicians: three drums, a flute, several shamisen players, and singers. The nagauta emerged from combining the lyricism of shorter songs with the sustaining power of longer, narrative music.

*Koto, Shakuhachi, Shamisen*

The **koto** is a thirteen-stringed zither-like instrument. Japanese learn to play this instrument from venerable masters called *kengyō* (translated maestro), many of whom are blind musician/teachers. An accomplished koto player will use slides, scrapes, struck strings, and other techniques to produce ornaments and microtones typical of traditional Japanese music. The koto is the genteel instrument of Japan much as the parlor piano was in nineteenth-century America. The presence of this instrument in a Japanese home symbolizes good breeding and an artistic upbringing.

A **shakuhachi** is an end-blown flute whose ancestor is the bamboo flute of ancient Japan. Ornaments and other deviations from the melody played on the shakuhachi are common. The shakuhachi is used frequently in combination with koto music. Flute-type instruments in general have universal appeal and are found in virtually all cultures. The **shamisen** is a three-stringed plucked chordophone used by entertainers and amateurs. It is basic to Edo period songs and theatre music and is played as an accompaniment instrument for much folk repertoire.

The shamisen, shakuhachi, and koto comprise a common chamber music trio known as *sankyoku*. The musicians concentrate on the minute and delicate shadings and timbres that each of them can bring to the melodic line.

Koto and a shamisen.

## Music of Africa

Africa is a huge, complex continent where over 200 different languages are spoken. Its musical diversity reflects the diversity of its people and the influences from cultures outside of Africa. It is the land of the exotic Mediterranean countries in the north whose cultures are influenced by the Islamic and Arabic traditions: Algeria, Morocco, Libya, Tunisia, Egypt, and other countries north of the Sahara. The classical, popular, and folk music of North Africa, derived more from oriental music, is so distinct from the rest of Africa that scholars do not include it as indigenous African music.

This chapter focuses on the land of black Africa south of the Sahara. It is the music of this region that produces indigenous African music—the music of Nigeria and Ghana; of the Congo and Zaire; of Kenya, Uganda, and Tanzania; and of Rhodesia (Zimbabwe), Southwest Africa (Namibia), and the Republic of South Africa. The values and aesthetics of the traditional cultures and the life-styles of the people in this region are changing rapidly. The people are being pulled between adapting to the impact of Western culture and preserving the essential uniqueness of their traditional culture.

## Music in Context

Music plays a significant role in the lives of most Africans, perhaps more than for Westerners. Africans participate. Their music is not for an audience who sits quietly and listens, whereas Westerners generally are spectators or listeners rather than producers.

In the West, a greater distinction exists between the performers and audience than in Africa. Music in Africa may be performed in an open area with people all around rather than on a stage with an audience separated from the performers. Africans may sing, play, dance, and compose. They may be trained and have the reputation of possessing knowledge, skill, and command of particular musical techniques.

African music, typically, is created to include more than music. An expression may include props, costumes, dancing, sculpture, crafts, and drama—all further enhancing possibilities for participation. Music is an outlet for social interaction and the sharing

Guinea Bissau-Bijagos people in a tribal dance.

of community attitudes. It enhances social activities, is performed for amusement, or communicates important messages and feelings. Music may be used for signals, or it may be a tribute to an individual, an offering to a deity, or a service to a potentate.

Music is created for specific purposes, and it is seldom performed out of context. For example, a religious song is performed only for a religious occasion; a work song is performed only in the context of the work that it relates to; or dance music is performed only for dancing, not for listening.

Songs are used for expressions of a wide variety of thoughts and dramatic action. They are part of the storytelling tradition that propogates the legends and history of the people. They are associated with ceremonies celebrating birth, puberty, marriage, and death as well as hunts, war, work, or secret societies. Their purposes may be to enhance a religious service, educate children, aid in therapy, describe current events, provide amusement, or express social protest against a chieftain, a tax collector, or a relative.

Traditional music still occupies a position of great importance in the cultures of black Africa, and it is an art in which nearly all Africans participate. While African youth are tending to reject traditional ways in favor of the Western influence found in the urban environment, their current music reveals a considerable crossover among traditional African music, African popular music, and Afro-American popular music.

## The Instruments

Africans without question use an enormous variety of musical instruments, the most common type being percussion. Instrumental music plays an important role in their musical life, a role perhaps as important as that of vocal music. Common instruments include drums and rattles of all sizes and shapes, one-string bowed fiddles, musical

African musicians.

bows, xylophones, mbiras (kalimbas, sansas, thumb pianos), natural trumpets, and flutes. In some cases, drums have specific purposes and are not used for any other reason. Different drums may be associated with funerals, with gods, or with a chief.

Instruments are used to accompany singing, although rhythmic handclapping may be used to accompany some vocal groups. Instruments are used in ensembles, either drum ensembles or groups comprised of instruments of different families. Performing groups may be spontaneous or organized, and they may be attached to occupational organizations, special households, or royal courts. They will range in size from two or three musicians to large drum orchestras numbering in the hundreds; however, small groups are the most common.

The idiophones (an instrument whose basic material of construction is its sound producing agent) include rattles, metal or wooden bells and gongs, shells, log drums, clay pot drums, xylophones, and mbiras. The mbira, also known by many other names, has from eight to thirty "keys" or metal reeds that are plucked by both thumbs. The length of each reed determines its pitch, and its resonator typically is a box with sound holes, although sometimes a gourd is attached.

The sizes and shapes of membranophones (drums with stretched skin heads) are innumerable. They may have a skin at both ends. If the drum is covered with skin only at one end, the other end may be open or closed. They may be played with sticks, hands, or a combination. A common technique involves using an intricate manipulation and

The Rakamba Phepares are celebrating the coronation of their queen.

alternation of fingers, thumb, and the heel of the hand in striking the head. Among the most important instruments in Africa are the master drums, which are used to lead ensembles and to signal important events.

The chordophones (stringed instruments) are comprised of lute-, zither-, harp-, and fiddle-type instruments. Here, too, the shapes and sizes are innumerable, and the number of strings and the tunings for each instrument vary greatly. Most stringed instruments are plucked rather than bowed, accommodating the African tendency toward strong rhythmic articulation.

The aerophones (wind instruments) include natural horns or trumpets that are made of wood, ivory, or animal horn, usually having no finger holes or valves. This category also includes both vertical and horizontal flutes and reed instruments.

## The Musical Style

Rhythm is the heart of African music. It is more highly developed than melody or harmony, and it is more highly developed than rhythm in the music of many other cultures (India, a notable exception). Compared with African rhythmic textures, the most common Western sense of rhythm seems simple and straightforward. In fact, rhythm in African music will often sound extremely complex to Western ears as though a number of unrelated things are going on simultaneously.

African music usually is performed by drum ensembles, although solo singing is common and is often accompanied by drums or other folklike instruments. Singing quality tends to be earthy, melodies have limited range, and harmonic progressions are not important in traditional African music but are important in the considerable quantity of popular and folk styles influenced by Western music.

*Rhythm*

The strong rhythmic articulation in African music appears not only in drums and other percussion instruments but in the strings, winds, and voices. Very little African music is smooth and connected; in most music, individual tones are attacked strongly. As was mentioned earlier, stringed instruments are plucked more often than bowed, further enhancing the percussion quality.

A rhythmic structure or pattern with regular beats and syncopation are common, although Africans do not necessarily tap their feet to "keep the beat"; they follow patterns or a "time-line" determined by the master drummer. Such patterns are not based on duple or triple meters as in Western music but on extended numbers of beats, such as eight or twelve. Much African music combines simultaneous lines of different rhythmic patterns in a context where the beats of the different instruments may not always coincide, resulting in cross rhythms or polyrhythms and an irregular rhythmic feeling. For example, it is quite possible that three musicians playing three independent lines may be playing in three separate patterns. African musicians have a high level of ability to maintain these polyrhythms for extended periods of time in the context of complex and changing rhythmic activity. This enables both performers and listeners to enjoy elaborations and variations without straying from established beats or patterns.

*Other Musical Aspects*

African music usually is fast moving and makes frequent use of ostinato. The scales on which melodies are based are often pentatonic or diatonic as in Western music or at least similar to these scales (they may sound "out-of-tune" to Western ears). Improvisation is common but mostly in the context of varying a phrase or a rhythmic pattern each time it is repeated.

The texture is frequently polyphonic, each voice typically using different material because of the nature of the instruments (a voice may have a different melodic line than a flute).

In vocal music, melodies reflect the rhythm and contour of speech. Some melodies will sound comfortable to us, particularly those similar to Western diatonic keys. Other songs will test our openness because of a singer's tendency to apply a variety of vocal tone colors: raucous tones, growls, tense singing, yodeling, or imitations of animal sounds. Occasionally lowered thirds and sevenths will be heard, conveying some of the qualities that we have come to know in American music as blue notes.

African music largely depends on short units incorporating antiphonal or responsorial techniques. Short phrases are repeated or alternated systematically. Solo music is common, but the most characteristic music is that performed by small groups, with emphasis on the rhythmic interplay and tonal coloring of the various musical lines. Rhythm and timbre predominate.

Harmony is incidental in traditional African music. When it exists, it is the result of sounds occurring simultaneously that were intended for purposes other than harmonic effects. Harmony is important, however, in African music that combines native traditions with influences from the Western world.

Traditional African music is not notated. Notation is not felt to be needed, neither for preserving music nor for teaching it. Music, typically, is preserved by memory. It is learned by rote—from oral tradition, but their learning by memory does not result in music that is disorganized or lacks structure.

**Western Influences**

Black African cultures are affected by urbanization, the media, transistor radios, Christianity, and Western-style education.

The hundreds of distinct African tribes have not sought to maintain mutually exclusive traditions, nor have they sought agreement with others as to musical style, instrument construction and tuning, or any aspect of musical practice. They have developed a network of overlapping practices that share common features, structures, functions, and performance contexts. People from some tribes have traveled extensively. As communications and mobility improved, the considerable cultural interaction that took place resulted in the borrowing and adapting of cultural materials, including music.

Through the influences of European settlers, Africans of European orientation, and Christian churches and schools that were established by Western missionaries, further changes in society took place. The Christians did not accept Africa's indigenous music, perceiving drums to be pagan and not suitable for Christian worship. Instead, they emphasized Western hymns, art music, instruments, and performance practices. Current practice, however, reveals a developing tolerance for including traditional African musical styles and instruments in the Christian churches.

In time, those exposed to Western cultural practices influenced the development of music in Africa. Adjustments were made. African composers created choral music in the Western classical style. African popular songs were fashioned in Western styles while retaining some African elements. Western harmonic practices and Western instruments, notably the guitar, became commonplace. These outside influences brought native Africans new ways of viewing their world, new tastes in music, new performer/audience relationships, and new ways of appreciating music performed in new contexts. Changes in music reflected the changes in society, and new songs reflected these changes, bringing an expansion of repertoire to traditional African music. The new repertoire reflected a receptiveness to outside influences, notably those of Western cultures.

**A Study in Sound**
*World Music beyond the Americas*

# Example 1

**"Malenky Barabanshtchik"** (The Little Drummer Boy) (excerpt)—immigrant music

A Russian, Cossack folk dance

Performed by the Krestyanskyj Orkestr
(a Russian ensemble)

Recorded by Russian immigrants in New York City in 1927.

This ensemble includes lead fiddle, two accompanying fiddles, bass, percussion, and bass saxophone.

*Goals:*

Identify patterns of contrast and repetition.

Recognize a vamp.

Identify form.

Be aware of shift to minor mode.

*Guide:* Count in a fast two.

| | | |
|---|---|---|
| Vamp | 4 bars | |
| a | 8 bars (4 + 4) | |
| b | 8 bars (4 + 4) | A contrasting key |
| a | 8 bars (4 + 4) | A return to the original key |
| b | 8 bars (4 + 4) | The same contrasting key |
| a | 8 bars (4 + 4) | A return |
| a | 8 bars (4 + 4) | Repeat |
| c | 8 bars (4 + 4) | Shift to a minor key; fade |

*Reflections:* The vamp is introductory material usually based on a simple harmonic pattern derived from the tonic chord.

This folk dance is a medley of tunes in contrasting pitch areas (higher or lower sounds). Notice when the changes occur. There are many repetitive sounds; listen for changes in the percussion.

# Example 2

**"Oberek Pulawiak"** (Oberek from Pulawy) (excerpt)—Immigrant music

A Polish dance

Performed by the J. Baczkowskiego Orkiestra

Recorded in Chicago in 1928

The *oberek* is an energetic round dance in triple meter. It is popular among the Polish-Americans, although not as much as the polka.

*Goals:*

Recognize changes in tonalities (key changes; modulation).

Recognize the sounds of major chords and major tonality.

Identify the phrase structure (form).

*Guide:* Count in triple meter, a moderate one beat to the bar. An "x" denotes chords other than I and V. The following structure for the musical example is repeated.

| | 1 | 2 | 3 | 4 | 5 | 6 | 7 | 8 | 9 | |
|---|---|---|---|---|---|---|---|---|---|---|
| a | x | x | V | I | x | x | V | I | | |
| a | x | x | V | I | x | x | V | I | | |
| b | V | I | V | I | V | I | V | I | | Higher key |
| b | V | I | V | I | V | I | V | I | | |
| a | x | x | V | I | x | x | V | I | I | Extra bar leads into next phrase |
| c | I | V | I | I | I | V | I | I | | Original Key |
| c | I | V | I | I | I | V | I | | | Repeat (except one bar short to balance extra bar in earlier phrase) |
| a | x | x | V | I | x | x | V | I | | |
| a | x | x | V | I | x | x | V | I | | |

***Reflections:*** The form is aabbaccaa. Note that the first contrasting phrase (*b*) is in a higher key with a different chord progression. The second contrasting phrase (*c*) returns to the original key but with a different melody.

# Example 3

**"Galanica"** (Pretty One)—Jewish music

A folksong of the Sephardic Jews (Spain)

Sung by Gloria Levy, voice and guitar

Gloria Levy learned this folksong from her mother.

## *Goals:*

Recognize the sound of Oriental-based modal music, and differentiate this sound from Western major tonal sounds.

Identify the motive on which this piece is based.

Recognize strophic form.

***Guide:*** Count in a moderately fast duple meter, two beats to the bar.

| | | |
|---|---|---|
| Intro. | 8 bars | Instrumental; main theme |
| a | 8 bars | Vocal; open cadence |
| b | 8 bars | Vocal; closed cadence |
| Interlude | 8 bars | Instrumental; main theme |
| a | 8 bars | Vocal; open cadence |
| b | 8 bars | Vocal; closed cadence |
| Interlude | 8 bars | Instrumental; main theme |
| a | 8 bars | Vocal; open cadence |
| b | 8 bars | Vocal; closed cadence |

***Reflections:*** The *a* and *b* phrases represent antecedent/consequent phrase groups.

The melody is simple and step-wise; the form is strophic. The structure is three stanzas with introduction and instrumental interludes. The piece is built on a four-bar motive.

# Example 4

**"Sheyebonei"** (excerpt)—Jewish music

Music of the synagogue—a cantorial chant

Jan Peerce, tenor, with symphony orchestra

The chant is sung by a cantor who is considered a creative musician and a spiritual leader in the Jewish community. The roots of the chant lie in Oriental modes and melismas and in Western harmonies. They are considered the moving, spiritual embodiment of prayers and poetry, an outpouring of emotion, a feeling of sublime communication.

The cantor possesses outstanding singing ability with great vocal beauty and dexterity. Traditionally, the possessor of a magnificent voice is considered to have received a "heavenly gift."

*Goals:*

Differentiate between free and metric rhythm.

Recognize melismas (melismatic passages) and differentiate from syllabic settings.

Identify fermatas, accelerandos, and ritards.

Be aware of the Oriental, modal scale structure. Contrast this structure with the Western scale structure and harmonies heard simultaneously in the orchestra.

*Guide:* The piece is sectional; the first section is *A,* the second section *B.* Capital letters are used to refer to larger sections of music that may have structural subdivisions, in which case, lower case letters would be used.

```
Intro.                  5 bars          Fermatas in third and fifth
                                        bars; tempo fluctuates in last
                                        two bars

A       Chant--in free rhythm,
        with elaborate
        melismas and a high
        degree of emotional
        expression
B       Song
        a     1---2---3---4---
        a     1---2---3---4---
        b     1---2---3---4---         Fermatas
        b     1---2---3---4---         Fermatas
        a     1---2---3---4---
A       Chant--a return--
        again, in free rhythm,
        with elaborate
        melismas and a high
        degree of emotional
        expression
```

*Reflections:* This example displays a mixture of free and metric rhythm, fermatas (held notes), and accelerandos (speeding up) and ritards (slowing down). It is a modal and oriental-sounding chant supported by Western-sounding harmonies played by a Western-type orchestra. The chant, at times, has a florid line with much ornamentation. It is highly melismatic, with many notes to one syllable of text. Differentiate between a melismatic and a syllabic setting (one note of music given to one syllable of text).

# Example 5

**"Y'Vorach"**—Jewish music

Dance music of the Chassidic Jews

(Listen to SS1/4 and refer to chart on pages 24 and 25.)

# Example 6

**"Bhimpalasi"** (two excerpts)—music of India

An afternoon rāga

Ravi Shankar, sitār; Chatur Lal, tablā; and N. C. Mullick, tamburā

The tāla or rhythmic cycle used in the gat, the last section, is Ada Chautal, a cycle of fourteen beats. The sitār is the lead instrument, and the tablā is the percussion instrument. The drone is played on the tambura.

*Goals:*

Recognize the timbre of the sitār and the tablā. Identify the drone sound.

Recognize when the music is in free rhythm and when it generates a sense of meter.

*Guide:* After a descending glissando, the sitār presents the rāga in free rhythm, setting forth its pitches and its intended character. Many slides, pitch bending alterations, and ornaments enhance the melody. The drone continues throughout.

The entering of the tablā creates a distinct pulse and a more active rhythm. As the rāga develops, the complexities of the rhythm and the melodic improvisation intensify.

*Reflections:* Notice the improvisation and the melodic embellishments, such as glissandos and pitch bending. Be aware of the sound of music that is based on a non-Western scale structure.


# Example 7

**"Rokudan No Shirabe"** (two excerpts)—Japanese classical music—music for koto

(Listen to SS2/4 and see page 34.)


# Example 8

**"Variations on a Lullaby"** (excerpts)—Japanese music

A Japanese lullaby by Inzan Tanaka composed for koto and shakuhachi (bamboo flute)

Three contrasting excerpts are included: the slow beginning section, a faster section, and, again, a slow section. This piece is based on a gapped, six-tone scale.

*Goals:*

Be aware of the sounds created by the gapped scale.

Identify the sound of the koto and of the shakuhachi.

Describe elements of rhythm and harmony heard in the music, particularly those that seem to make the music sound non-Western.

*Guide:* The introduction, played on the koto, is comprised of two phrases, each one ending on a held tone, the last one preceded by an ascending glissando.

The slow section contains four phrases of equal length. The shakuhachi takes essentially the same melody stated in the introduction at half the speed and expands on it.

The fast section is built on a recurring five-note motive and includes melodic interplay between the two instruments. The rhythm is regular, and the phrase structure is irregular.

The example ends with a return to a slow tempo with a shakuhachi solo in free rhythm, ending with a banjo-like strumming on the koto.

*Reflections:* Compare the sound of the shakuhachi with the sound of a flute, oboe, or clarinet. Compare the sound of the koto with that of a guitar, banjo, or harp. In what ways is this piece appropriate as a lullaby?

# Example 9

**"Sado Okesa"** (excerpt)—Japanese music

A folk song with shamisen accompaniment sung and played by a Geisha from Okayama City

The Geisha have popularized many Japanese folk songs, singing them in a more sophisticated style for entertainment.

## Goals:

Recognize the sound of a shamisen.

Recognize ostinato.

Describe the metric feeling.

*Guide:* Count at a moderately slow pulse.

Intro.   11 beats (6 + 5)
Vocal    Number of beats to each phrase and phrase group
        16
        15
         8 + 11 + 4
        14
         8 + 6 + 18 + 5
        14 + (fade)

*Reflections:* This love song has a lilting character in regular rhythm. The vocal line, based on a gapped scale, is highly ornamented. The voice has a tight, nasal, stylized quality. The accompaniment is played on the shamisen.

As can be seen from the phrase organization presented previously, describing the number of strong beats in a phrase and phrase group, balanced phrases or regular patterns of contrast and repetition do not occur.

Notice the scale pattern that features an interval wider than a whole step. Thus, the melody is based on a gapped scale.

# Example 10

**"Magonde"** (Song for the Chief)—music of Africa

Mbira music

This example is from the nation at one time known as Rhodesia, now Zimbabwe. It is an old traditional tune played on an mbira-type instrument known as *Njari dza MaNjanja;* it has twenty-seven reeds and two manuals on a board with external resonators. All lines in the texture are performed by Chabarwa Musunda Moyo Sinyoro, from Rusapi, Zimbabwe.

## Goals:

Identify the sound of the mbira.

Recognize ostinato patterns, syncopation, and multiple layers of sound.

Recognize the vocables.

*Guide:* The piece begins with an introduction of seven chords that increase in speed and lead into an mbira ostinato pattern that has a strong metric feeling and is maintained throughout the excerpt. The first melody, played on the mbira, is syncopated and has many rhythmic patterns that contrast with the mbira ostinato pattern. Both the melody and the ostinato pattern are played by one person on one mbira.

The next addition to the texture is the singer who uses words and some vocables. His rhythms, too, are in contrast to the mbira ostinato. The mbira is played to some extent in dialogue with the singing.

*Reflections:* Notice the interplay among the differing rhythms sounding at the same time and the energy created by the syncopation. What Western instruments are most like the mbira?

# Example 11

**"Singing and Drumming for Farmers"**—music of Africa

Music of the Hausa people from Nigeria

This music is an example of a praise song of the *masu-gangan noma,* a group of drummers who sing special words of praise for specific young farmers in a cooperative work group. They extol a farmer's strength, his greatness, and his success in love.

The song leader beats the big farm drum or *gangan noma.* His adult son beats a much smaller drum or *kazagi* and sings the refrain with the help of a praise shouter.

## Goals:

Recognize the call-and-response technique.

Recognize ostinato patterns.

Be aware of subtle changes in the singing and drumming patterns.

*Guide:* The piece begins with drumming in irregular rhythms and shouting in the background.

The drums move into a machine-gun-type repetitive pattern, then into a highly syncopated, intricate style. The drummers develop an ostinato accompaniment with subtle variations and accents that provide rhythmic interest in the music.

The singing moves more and more into a regular, ostinato pattern in call-and-response style.

*Reflections:* Be aware of the shifts from irregular to regular rhythmic feeling. Be aware of the difference in sound between the solo "caller" and the "responders."

The joyful shrilling of a female bystander can be heard near the end of this piece.

This music is repetitive, making generous use of ostinato patterns and call-and-response techniques. However, even in the repetition, with careful listening, changes in the singing and in the drum patterns can be noted.

# Example 12

**"Nkende yamuyayu"** (The waist of the wild cat)

Africa—music of the Soga people of Uganda

(Listen to SS1/5 and see page 11.)

# Example 13

**"Akasozi Mwiri"**—music of Africa

Music of the Soga people of Uganda

This piece, sung by a group of boys from Busoga College, is based on a traditional Soga folk song. It is in verse/chorus form, with each verse utilizing the call-and-response technique. The music is full of energy and excitement, particularly the choruses.

*Goals:*

Recognize the verse/chorus form and the specific formal organization of this piece.

Recognize regular pulse but no meter in the Western sense. Be aware of the patterns of rhythmic organization.

*Guide:* The pulse is fairly fast and regular, but without meter. Each cycle (phrase) must be counted in the number of beats rather than number of bars. In this piece, all cycles have twelve beats.

| | |
|---|---|
| Chorus | 2 cycles |
| Verse | 6 cycles |
| Chorus | 2 cycles |
| Verse | 7 cycles |
| Chorus | 2 cycles |
| Verse | 8 cycles |
| Chorus | 2 cycles |

*Reflections:* The music is repetitive, utilizes very few pitches, and is highly syncopated.

*Discography*

**Ex. 1** Krestyanskyj Orkestr. "Malenky Barabanshtchik." *Old Country Music in a New Land: Folk Music of Immigrants from Europe and the Near East.* New World Records. NW 264. :50.

**Ex. 2** J. Baczkowskiego Orkiestra. "Oberek Pulawiak." *'Spiew Juchasa/Song of the Sheperd: Songs of the Slavic Americans.* New World Records. NW 283. 1:35.

**Ex. 3** Levy, Gloria. "Galanica." *Sephardic Folk Songs.* Folkways FW 8737. 1:26.

**Ex. 4** Peerce, Jan. "Sheyebonei." *Cantorial Masterpieces.* Vanguard VSD-2134. 4:55.

**Ex. 5** "Y'Vorach." *Chassidic Dances.* Tikva Records T-62. 2:15.

**Ex. 6** Shankar, Ravi. "Bhimpalasi." *The Sounds of India.* Columbia WL 119. 4:05.

**Ex. 7** "Rokudan No Shirabe." *Japanese Music for Koto and Shakuhachi.* Toshiba Records Th 7002. 3:35.

**Ex. 8** "Variations on a Lullaby." *Japanese Music for Koto and Shakuhachi.* Toshiba Records Th 7002. 3:35.

**Ex. 9** "Sado Okesa." *Folk Music of Japan.* Folkways FE 4429. 2:20.

***Ex. 10***    "Magonde." *Music of Africa Series, Musical Instruments II/Reeds.*
Kaleidophone Records KMA 2. 1:37.

***Ex. 11***    "Singing and Drumming for Farmers." *An Anthology of African Music.*
Barenreiter Musicaphon BM 30, L 2306. 1:55.

***Ex. 12***    "Nkende yamuyayu." *Music of Africa Series, Uganda I.* Kaleidophone
KMA 10. 1:08.

***Ex. 13***    "Akasozi Mwiri." *Music of Africa Series, Uganda I.* Kaleidophone
KMA 10. 1:55.

*Summary*

Having now assimilated a portion of world music, you have learned that musical styles and musical languages differ from country to country, region to region, and culture to culture. Yet, we find ourselves using the same descriptive language for all styles. As examples, the musical concepts of melody, harmony, rhythm, texture, and form are useful in describing music of any and all cultures. Musical instruments used by the many cultures may differ, but all are plucked, shook, hit, blown, or bowed, giving us a common descriptive frame of reference.

Musical functions (why music exists in a culture), performance practices (the setting, the dress, the degree of formality), and performer-audience relationships may differ among cultures. However, these issues are common to all cultures and provide a common vocabulary for studying world music.

Finally, all cultures value, use, create, perform, and listen to music in a variety of ways. We become aware of music's importance to people whose values about music and life may be quite different from our own. Yet, somehow, it can be a humbling but enriching experience to realize that Western music represents only a fraction of the world's musical styles and preferences and that people from different backgrounds and cultures have values, likes and dislikes, and preferred musical practices that suggest to us that they are important people as well, and worthy of our respecting the music that they value.

*Terms and Concepts*

**Non-Western music**          ***Tamburā***
**World music**                ***Gagaku***
**Gamelan**                    ***Kabuki***
**Hammered dulcimer**          ***Koto***
**Accordian**                  ***Shakuhachi***
**Fiddle**                     ***Shamisen***
**Melisma**                    ***Nagauta***
***Rāga***                     ***Mbira***
***Talā***                     ***Polyrhythms***
***Sitār***                    ***Call-and-response***
***Tablā***

# Part IV
# Listening to Classical Music

The classical music that is part of American culture has its roots in the history and traditions of Western European civilization. Its development proceeds through distinct yet overlapping historical periods, each period reflecting characteristics different from that which preceded it. These changes emerge from cultural and technological developments in society, from shifting progressive and conservative attitudes, and from tendencies to bring secular styles into the church followed by the church's purging itself of these accumulated secular influences. Cyclical patterns of emphasis on personal feeling, imagery, and romantic notions about music contrasted with a more objective, intellectual, classical attitude that placed emphasis on form and structure, balance, and craftsmanship in the creation of music also were sources of change.

Throughout history, these
accumulated changes are
sufficiently identifiable to be
treated as specific periods of
musical development that
scholars have labeled the
Medieval (200–1450 A.D.),
Renaissance (1450–1600),
Baroque (1600–1750), Classical
(1750–1820), Romantic (1820–
1900), and Modern (1900 to the
present) historical periods. These
dates must be considered
approximate, allowing for the
overlap of musical styles,
composers, and influences.

Chapters 8 through 13 trace
this development from the
beginnings of the Christian era to
the present with chapter 12 and
13 focusing on twentieth-century
European and American classical
music. Chapter 14 concludes the
text with an examination of
music in American society.

# Chapter 8
# Music to 1600

The towers of the cathedral at Chartres offer two radically different phases of medieval architecture. The tower on the right illustrates old Romanesque and Norman styles and the tower on the left is late Gothic style.

Western European/American classical music—and much of American vernacular music—are part of a musical tradition traced to the theoretical writings and teachings of famous scholars from the ancient Greek civilization. This period spanned from the time of Pythagoras in about 500 B.C. to Ptolemy around 200 A.D., including Aristotle and Plato.

It was the theory, not the practice, of the Greeks that influenced Western music. It was the influence of the doctrines and descriptions rather than the music itself. The Greek scholars wrote about the nature of music, its place in the universe and in society, and its materials and principles of composition. They examined the effects of music on people, particularly in defining the relationships between music and mathematics, morality, poetry, education, and character or personality. The Greek writers began our vocabulary for discussing and describing music. In terms of the music itself, however, the history of Western practice is traced from the beginnings of the Christian era.

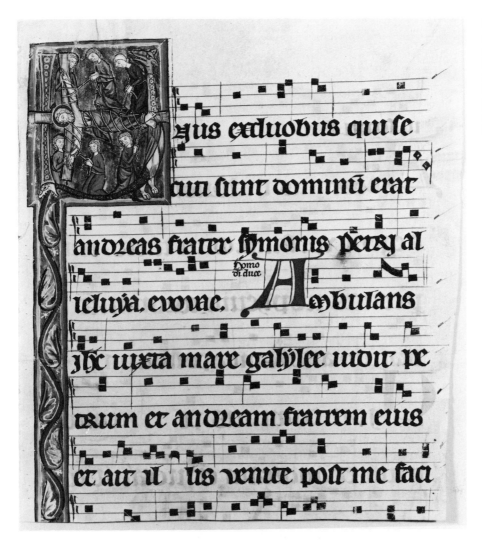

Crucifixion of St. Andrew from an Antiphonary. French-Rhenish, ca. 1230–1240, illumination on parchment, 31.8 × 27.5 cm. Courtesy of The St. Louis Art Museum.

The church of Rome dominated the history of Western music for its first 1400 years. This period is frequently divided into the Medieval period or the Middle Ages (up to the early fifteenth century) and the Renaissance (from about 1450 to 1600).

## The Beginnings of Western Music (to about 1450 A.D.)

Whereas the theory of Western music was derived from the Greek philosophers, the religious ritual (liturgy) of the Catholic church and its music were borrowed and adapted from the Jewish synagogue services: hymn singing, psalm singing, prayers, the position of cantor (chief solo singer), and responsorial or antiphonal singing (similar call-and-response techniques have been observed in other styles and traditions). Additionally, as the Roman Catholic church spread into Africa, parts of Asia, and Europe, its music absorbed elements from these diverse areas.

The liturgy of the early Western churches was varied, as local churches at first were relatively independent. The predominant musical style of religious music was the **chant** with the various regions developing their own distinct liturgies and chant repertoires (refer to discussion on pages 194–195). These regional versions, by the eighth century, either disappeared or were absorbed into the single uniform practice established by the leaders who from the fourth century were established in Rome.

## The Renaissance (1450–1600)

The Renaissance in Europe saw a magnificent flourishing of knowledge and productivity in the arts and letters. It was the age of Michelangelo and Leonardo da Vinci, Raphael and El Greco, Luther and Shakespeare, and many other of the world's great artists and writers. It was also the Golden Age of polyphonic choral music created by the first significant group of master composers that included Josquin des Prez, Giovanni Pierluigi da Palestrina, and Giovanni Gabrieli.

The Renaissance was an age of humanism, optimism, and reform. Artists and scholars expanded their interests into secular society, and arts patronage began shifting from the church to the courts. Developments that were important in shaping Western culture occurred during the Renaissance. The inventions of gunpowder and the compass changed the course of history. The art of printing books, perfected by Gutenberg in the fifteenth century, led to the dissemination of printed music and books about music in the fifteenth century.

Listen to SS8/2 and 3.

## The Reformation

In 1517, Martin Luther began a reform that was to separate the Christian church into two major divisions: Catholic and Protestant. This reform had a dramatic impact on the history of music. In the Baroque period, there was a shift from Gregorian chant and polyphonic pieces based on chant and sung in Latin to the following types of music:

1. Lutheran **chorale** melodies sung by the congregation in the vernacular and in unison (analagous to modern hymn tunes)
2. Polyphonic settings of chorale melodies performed by a choir with the text in the vernacular
3. By the end of the seventeenth century, chorale harmonizations in a simple, chordal, homophonic, strophic, hymnlike style for congregational singing. Listen to SS9/2.

A version of this reform (the Calvinist churches) led to congregational singing of texts that adhered rigidly to the Bible, particularly to the psalms. Psalm singing involved rhymed, metrical translations of the psalms that were published in psalters (hymn books—see chapter 3). Among the best known and most widely used psalters were the *French Psalter* (1562), the *Scottish Psalter* (1564), and the *Ainsworth Psalter* (1612). Versions of these books became important sources of hymn singing in American churches, beginning with the *Ainsworth Psalter* which was brought to New England by the Pilgrims in 1620.

In 1534, the Church of England separated from the Catholic Church, paving the way for even more church music to be sung in the vernacular. The anthem, sung in English, became the Anglican counterpart of the Latin **motet** (a choral genre intended to be sung by choirs of trained singers, rather than by congregations).

Of course, the Roman Catholic church countered with its own reforms (Counter-Reformation). Palestrina was given the responsibility of improving church music. He was to establish a model to make liturgical music more worshipful, dignified, and easier to understand. These goals, however, were more successfully attained by later composers.

## Musical Characteristics

The earliest examples of Western classical music were Gregorian chants, relatively short pieces used in the liturgy of the Catholic church (see pages 194–195 for a fuller discussion of Gregorian chant). Notation (a system of visual symbols) was developed to reinforce the singer's memory of a chant melody learned from oral tradition. Notation was developed also to specify pitches so that melodies for chants would be uniform throughout the far-flung Roman Catholic church. In figure 8.1 an example of medieval, square notation can be compared with its counterpart in modern notation.

Orlando di Lasso and the private music chapel of the Duke of Bavaria. Miniature from the Milan codex. Sixteenth century. Illuminator Hans Meilich. Bavarian State Library, Munich.

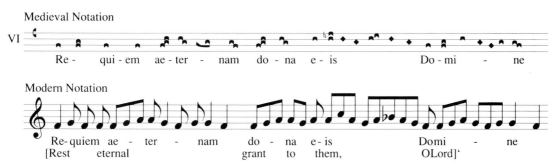

**Figure 8.1**
Medieval square notation and modern notation.

**Figure 8.2**
Excerpt from a Josquin
motet demonstrating
rhythmic independence.

The ninth through thirteenth centuries provided fundamental changes in Western music. Composition was becoming structured, adhering to certain principles and techniques. Chant was not only an entity in itself but was becoming a basis of other compositions. By the eleventh century, musicians had added a second melodic line to a chant creating vertical sounds (harmony) and polyphonic texture. These melodies either moved with the same rhythm or, more commonly, had contrasting rhythms and sense of movement (one melody moving faster than the other). Polyphony became a common technique in creating music. Another system of notating music was devised in order to convey several melodic lines of polyphonic music for others to perform, specifying not only pitch but rhythmic patterns in order to maintain an orderly performance of increasingly complex music. Singers, thus, were taught to read this notation.

It is obvious that notation was a great aid in teaching polyphonic music to others. By the thirteenth century, music in three parts was common and the person who created a piece of music (the composer) was no longer anonymous but acknowledged in the notated manuscripts. An important region for the development of notation was northern France, and the first known composers of notated polyphony were Leonin and Perotin.

The various melodic lines of Renaissance polyphonic music were considered equal in importance. No line was dominant as in a melody with accompaniment. Each line was a singable melody with rhythmic independence from the other lines. In figure 8.2, notice that each voice enters separately in a rising contour and the words, *absalon fili mi,* are not sung at the same time.

It was common for composers to write in imitative **counterpoint,** wherein each voice entered separately but imitated the one that started the previous phrase. This technique was usually devised so that each voice would begin with the same melodic and

**Figure 8.3**
Imitative counterpoint.
Excerpt from a Josquin
mass. From Kamien,
*The Norton Scores,* Vol.
1, 4th edition. Copyright
© W. W. Norton
Company, New York,
NY.

rhythmic pattern, perhaps on a different pitch and then soon deviate from the pattern.
Because melodic lines were moving independently, the strong beats would fall at different times. The music was metered, but the rhythmic independence among the lines
minimized the metric feeling, with a resulting gentle, flowing rhythm. The Josquin
example in figure 8.2 also is written imitatively. Notice the identical contour of each
entrance of *absalon fili mi.* A second example of imitative counterpoint is shown in
figure 8.3. It is a page from the Agnus Dei from Josquin's *Missa L'Homme armé.* The
words, *dona nobis pacem,* in the second voice (second staff from the top), are an exact

repetition of the first voice. The imitation then extends with repetitions of *pacem* treated in a four-voice texture. The notes in the bottom two voices are part of a very slow-moving melody that is not part of the imitation.

Imitation gives unity to a piece but also makes it sound complex and more challenging for the listener. Renaissance choral polyphony may be challenging, but it is also beautiful and noble music, ranking among the most inspired choral music in Western literature. The multiple independent lines and overlapping imitative parts, however, tend to obscure the clarity of the text, a problem particularly devastating to the liturgy.

Composers of both sacred and secular choral music, by the end of the sixteenth century, were paying more attention to the vertical sounds—the harmonies or chords. In fact, much choral music, especially secular music, placed sufficient emphasis on its harmonic aspects to be considered having homophonic rather than polyphonic texture. This is in contrast to the thirteenth- or fourteenth-century composer who created pieces with independent lines whose vertical sonorities were quite incidental and of little concern.

Historical information about secular music, the prevalent folk and entertainment music of an era, dates to around the twelfth century. Secular music was not notated until the late Middle Ages. It involved dances, was more metric, and had a stronger rhythmic feeling. It also included instruments for accompanying songs and dances. This music was often performed in the context of other forms of entertainment, such as acting, storytelling, poetry, juggling, acrobatics, and dancing. Secular music and drama were occasionally added to the church liturgy. By the thirteenth century, these insertions developed into what are now known as liturgical dramas, dramas that eventually became entities in themselves that were performed outside of church. The two most common liturgical dramas, dating from the twelfth century and found on modern recordings, are *The Play of Daniel* and *The Play of Herod*. These dramatic expressions used such instruments as flutes, trumpets, and percussion instruments.

## Choral/Vocal Music

Choral music is music for more than one voice to each part, such as for a choir of sopranos, altos, tenors, and basses (SATB). Vocal music refers to solo pieces or ensemble works intended for one singer to each part.

Music of the Middle Ages was predominantly choral/vocal. Instrumental and keyboard genres were virtually unknown until around the fourteenth century. This music was predominantly choral/vocal because most music, at least that which has been preserved, was centered in the life of the church.

## Gregorian Chant

From the fifth to the seventh centuries, the music of the church took significant strides forward. The church developed boy choirs, established schools for training boys and men as church musicians, and revised its liturgy and music. The most significant reform of the music came under the papacy of Pope Gregory I at the end of the sixth century. Pope Gregory established an order to the liturgy, assigning particular items to the various services throughout the church year, and developed a uniform repertoire of chant for use by churches in all countries. His improvement became standard practice for centuries and was so highly regarded that this body of chant repertoire became known as **Gregorian chant.**

A chant is a type of song with text found in many cultures and traditions. Chants range from the intoning of a two-note melody to an elaborate, melismatic melody with ornamentation and improvisation.

**Plate 11**

Illustration from *Der Weisskunig*. Hans Burgkmair, circa
1514–1516, woodcut. The Metropolitan Museum of Art,
gift of William Loreng Andrews, 1888.

**Plate 12**

Mathis Grunewald. *Isenheim Altarpiece,* 1515, detailed
*The Angelic Concert.* Incidents in the life of the painter
Mathis Gothart Nithart, known as Grunewald, are
dramatized in Paul Hindemith's opera Mathis der Maler.
The movement of the symphony derived from the opera
depict the scenes from the Isenheim altarpiece illustrated.
Scala/Art Resource, Inc. New York.

**Plate 13**

Jean Antoine Watteau. *Music Party,* circa 1719.
25½″ × 36¼″. (68.6 × 90.5 cm). Wallace Collection,
London (Reproduced by Permission of the Trustees).

**Plate 14**

G. B. Panini. *The Concert: Performance of La Contea dei Nami* by Leonardo da Vinci, given in Rome on November 27, 1729 in the Polignac Palace. Paris, Louvre. On the stage is an orchestra and chorus whose composition is similar to that of the classical orchestra. Scala/Art Resource, New York.

**Plate 15**

Nineteenth-century grand opera tradition remains alive at
the Metropolitan Opera.

**Plate 16**

The production of *Giselle* was first performed in 1841 at
the Paris Opera. The most modern version follows the
choreographer of Marius Petipa, with some changes by
Frederic Franklin.

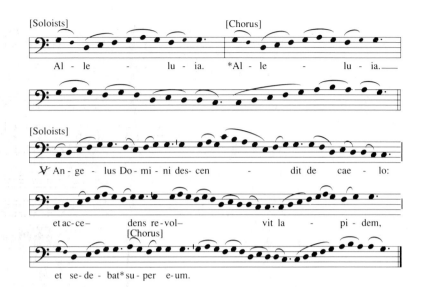

**Figure 8.4**
Notated example of
Gregorian chant. From
Davison & Apel,
*Historical Anthology of
Music.* Copyright
© 1966 Harvard
University Press,
Cambridge, MA.

A Gregorian chant traditionally was an integral part of the liturgy of the Roman Catholic church. It was sung in Latin by a priest or a cantor, the men and boys of the choir, or the congregation. Originally, these chants were performed without instruments, although organ accompaniment was common by the thirteenth century. In recent years, much of the Catholic liturgy including music is presented in the vernacular language (the spoken language of the people).

A Gregorian chant (SS8/1) is monophonic in texture, of relatively short duration, and sung in an unhurried manner. Its rhythm is fluid, reflecting the natural inflection of the text. Its accents are compatible with the accents of the prose text, that is, without regular accent and without a strong metric feeling. These chants were not originally notated. The manuscripts containing notated chants date to the ninth century, and many were done in beautiful handwritten calligraphy. The composers of Gregorian chants were unknown priests and monks.

The text can be treated in a **syllabic** manner with one note to each syllable of text; in a florid, melismatic manner with several and sometimes many notes to a single syllable; or frequently in a combination of these two treatments. The shape of a chant melody is fairly flat, is mostly stepwise, and encompasses a small range. Figure 8.4 shows the typically flat contour (conjunct melody). It illustrates the relationship of notes to text. Recognize both the melismatic and the more syllabic portions of the chant.

The scale patterns of Gregorian chants are derived from a system that preceded the major/minor tonal system, a system of church modes (scales) that gives the chants their oriental, mystical quality. This modal quality is found in much American traditional folk music and recent jazz and popular music. The modal system formed the basis of Western music for over a thousand years.

Chant was functional music. It was an aid to worship, rather than music that people would passively listen to. The several thousand chants make up a significant body of literature in Western music. Many have been used as bases for other types of musical compositions, such as the polyphonic settings of the mass and church motets prevalent during the sixteenth century.

The Mass of St. Gregory. Engraving. Serman School Prints Anonymous. The Mass was symbolic in relating worship to sacred music. The Metropolitan Museum of Art, Harris Bresbame Dick Fund, 1924.

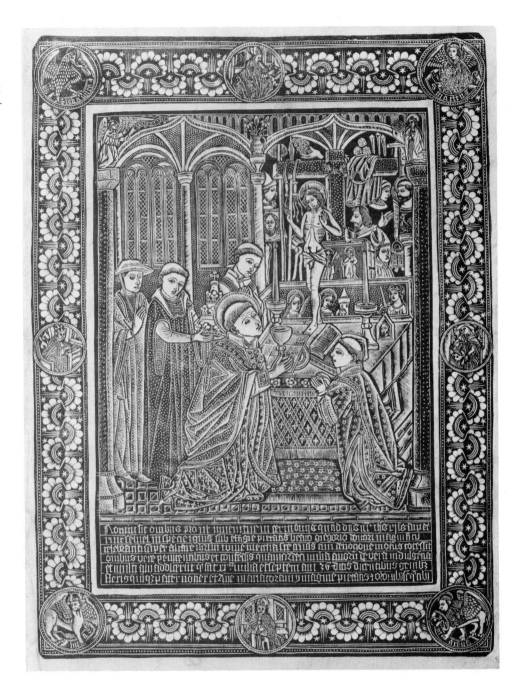

## The Mass

The part of the liturgy that has produced the most important sacred music literature is the **mass,** particularly the music from the Ordinary of the High Mass.

In the Low Mass, the priest intones or recites the prayers in a low voice with the congregation remaining silent. In the High Mass, the service is recited in a high voice and sung either in Gregorian chant or in a combination of chant and polyphonic choral settings sung by the choir.

The High Mass is comprised of the Proper, which varies according to the season of the church year or the particular commemoration, and the Ordinary, which does not vary.

The music of the Ordinary is usually sung by the choir. Its five parts are the *Kyrie, Gloria, Credo, Sanctus and Benedictus,* and the *Agnus Dei.* It is polyphonic settings of these sections of the mass that have produced much of the greatest choral literature in Western music, some of it not intended for liturgical use but for concert performance. This music has been sung in both church and concert performances by Catholic, Protestant, and secular choirs, sometimes preserving the Latin language, other times with a text translated into the vernacular.

The first important polyphonic setting of the mass was the *Notre Dame Mass,* composed by the Frenchman, Guillaume de Machaut, in the mid-fourteenth century. The significance of this work was in its unity. Previously, little concern was given to the relationship between style, mode, or thematic idea from one part of the Ordinary to another. Machaut regarded his mass as a complete composition.

Two other important composers of masses are the Franco-Belgian who worked many years in Italy, Josquin des Prez (c. 1450–1521), whose best known mass is *Missa L'homme armé* and the Italian, Giovanni Pierluigi da Palestrina (c. 1525–1594), whose most influential work is the *Mass of Pope Marcellus.* Josquin and Palestrina rank among the foremost of the early "master" composers.

The composition of polyphonic settings of the mass has occurred consistently since the late Middle Ages but was prevalent in the history of Western music through the sixteenth century, particularly in Italy.

The motet (listen to SS8/2) is a sacred polyphonic composition sung in Latin without accompaniment (a cappella). During the Renaissance, a motet usually had from four to six independent melodies, in contrast to the more common three-part melodies of the thirteenth century motets.

**The Motet**

The thirteenth-century polyphonic motets were composed anonymously in France and England, frequently in three voices with a different text in each voice—either in Latin or in the vernacular. One voice, usually the tenor, was based in whole or in part on a chant. Its movement would be slow with the other composed melodies being more rhythmically active. This chant that was used as the basis for the polyphonic composition—either a motet or a section of the Mass—was known as the **cantus firmus** or fixed melody. Because the cantus firmus had no liturgical function, it was frequently sung in the vernacular or played on an instrument. The Kyrie by Dufay in figure 8.5 is based on one of the most popular songs used in polyphonic composition. The original melody is presented first. Its shape in the polyphonic texture can be observed by following the arrows.

The popularity of the motet spread throughout Western Europe. The cantus firmus continued to be borrowed not only from the chant repertoire but also from popular songs of the day. Composers freely borrowed melodies, texts, or fragments of either from preexisting sources. Motets usually were not intended to be sung as part of the liturgy but became common repertoire for trained choirs in church services and concert settings and are still performed in those settings today.

Renaissance choral music culminated in the great **polychoral motets** (motets for multiple choirs) of Giovanni Gabrieli. Although polychoral music was established before Gabrieli, he was able to exploit it most effectively. St. Mark's Cathedral in Venice was constructed in such a way that Gabrieli, who was the choirmaster and a noted composer, was able to have two or more independent choirs placed to allow music to be sung antiphonally (two or more choirs singing in alternation or one in response to the other). With the cathedral's two great organs and his interest in writing sacred choral music that included not only organ but a variety of wind and string instruments, Gabrieli composed motets and other choral pieces for several choirs with numerous, independent melodic lines. These works also featured homorhythmic sections where the text was sung by all voices at once, making the words more understandable.

**Figure 8.5**
An example of the cantus firmus used in polyphonic
composition. Excerpt from a Kyrie by Dufay. From
Davison & Apel, *Historical Anthology of Music.* Vol. 1
Copyright © Harvard University Press, Cambridge, MA.

Gabrieli's use of instrumentalists performing lines that were independent of the voices and his use of multiple choirs contrasting with each other and with the instruments became basic principles of the baroque style emerging at the turn of the seventeenth century. Gabrieli's music and the natural acoustics of the cathedral must have provided a thrilling and exalting musical experience for the parishioners.

The Basilica of St. Mark's interior, Venice. Alinari/Art Resource, New York.

## Madrigal

The Renaissance **madrigal** (SS8/3) is in four or five parts with one singer to a part; thus, it is considered vocal chamber music. It is a secular composition, reflecting the growing independence of the arts from the church. In the vernacular language, the poetic text is about love, a pastoral theme, or other secular topic. The music, usually more metrical and lively than a motet, combined elements of the ancient modal scales with the harmonies of modern major tonalities and combined both polyphonic and homophonic textures.

Madrigals, flourishing in Italy and England, were sung at court festivities, social gatherings, and meetings of learned societies. Because the madrigal did not have to adhere to the strictures of the church, composers were more free to experiment with harmonic boldness, pictorial and expressive writing, or even the baroque notion of a solo part contrasting with a harmonic bass line or with a chordal background.

Jean Antoine Watteau. *Mezztin.* An Italian comedienne who traveled from one estate to another playing for families and guests.

## Instrumental Music

Instrumental music—music for drums and other percussion instruments, lyres, and various kinds of flutes—must have existed throughout prehistory, before recorded history. In many cases, instrumental music was more metric, more lively, and less polyphonic than sacred, liturgical music. During the Middle Ages, instrumental music probably was not conceived for its own sake but for its important accompanying role in singing and dancing. By the twelfth century, it probably played an important part in liturgical dramas.

The harp, lyre, psaltery, and vielle were instruments in common use in the Middle Ages. The vielle, a bowed instrument, was a forerunner of the viol, which itself was a forerunner of the violin. Instruments common in the Renaissance were recorders, viols, shawms, krumhorns, and cornetts, and a popular social instrument was the lute. The most common keyboard instruments were the harpsichord and the clavichord. The organ as we know it today became popular during the sixteenth century.

For the most part, Renaissance instrumental music modeled itself after the vocal style, and it was common for a vocal line to have an instrument either double or substitute for a vocal part. Music was sometimes written for a **consort** of like instruments, such as soprano, alto, tenor, and bass recorders or a group of viols of various ranges.

In the sixteenth century, instrumental music had advanced to the point that composers wrote pieces specifically for instruments, and the first instrumental music genres evolved: the ricercar and the canzona. The ricercar was written for keyboards or an instrumental ensemble and was modeled after the polyphonic motet. The less sober canzona was similar to the madrigal or the French chanson. It was entertaining, fast-moving, metric, and contrapuntal but in a light and easy manner.

## Composers

### Josquin des Prez (c. 1440–1521)

Josquin was born in the border region between France and what is now Belgium. He became a successful court musician and composer, particularly in Italy. Much of his music, published in printed collections, includes eighteen masses, one hundred motets, and seventy secular songs with French texts (chansons).

The mass, by its restricted nature, offered few opportunities for experimentation; thus, Josquin utilized the motet genre to create his most innovative and influential works. In his motets, he was able to use a wider range of texts and to develop a more progressive and innovative compositional style with flowing melodies, rich harmonies, and less restricted rhythms. He was able to convey through this music a much more humanistic, Renaissance attitude that provided an expressive power and a more vivid and clear text.

His mark of genius was in his ability to combine the intricacies of polyphonic composition with emotional expression. In so doing, he was able to further the development of music by exceeding the limits of the musical language of his time. Josquin's role in history places him as one of the great masters of the Renaissance.

### Giovanni Pierluigi da Palestrina (c. 1525–1594)

Born near Rome, his entire professional life was spent as a choirmaster and composer in Rome, including the last twenty-four years of his life at St. Peters. His music is primarily sacred and includes 102 masses, 450 motets and other liturgical compositions, and 56 spiritual madrigals with Italian texts.

His music is characterized by its purity (detached from secular influences) and its appropriateness for the formal ritual of the Roman Catholic liturgy. It serves as the model of the best in sixteenth-century imitative counterpoint, capturing the essence of the conservative elements of the Counter-Reformation. Palestrina set out to show through his music that polyphony is not necessarily incompatible with a reverent spirit nor with an understanding of the text.

Palestrina's contrapuntal texture is not overly elaborate; his melodies are diatonic, mostly stepwise, and easily singable. A large number of his sacred polyphonic pieces are for four voices, each given equal importance. Cadences (ends of phrases) overlap because of the polyphonic textures. Palestrina incorporates much chordal, homorhythmic writing with clearly perceivable chord progressions. These sections end with strong, full cadences that generate tonic/dominant relationships and clear tonal centers. This signals a shift away from modal writing and foreshadows the emerging major/minor tonal system that becomes fully established in the seventeenth century.

### Giovanni Gabrieli (c. 1557–1612)

The organist and choirmaster at St. Mark's Cathedral in Venice from 1585 until his death, Gabrieli was exemplary in composing sacred works for multiple choirs and for combinations of voices and wind and stringed instruments.

Performances by multiple choirs spaced in different areas of a cathedral, although not begun by Gabrieli nor in Venice, flourished there because of the design of this cathedral and the receptiveness of the people of Venice to the grandiose music of multiple choirs with contrasting instrumental sonorities. His music for multiple choirs utilized the antiphonal, dialogue technique (echo) and chordal, homorhythmic writing contrasted with rich, contrapuntal textures.

Gabrieli's role in history, as Josquin before him, places him at the crossroads of two historical eras. He was a master of the older, polyphonic, Renaissance style, yet his uses of contrasting sonorities foreshadowed much of the essential qualities of the Baroque era to follow.

# A Study in Sound
*Music to 1600*

# Example 1

### Gregorian chants

Choir of the Vienna Hofburgkapelle (comprised of former Vienna choirboys)

Gregorian chants are songs that function as an integral part of the liturgy of the Roman Catholic church. They serve as aids to worship, many having specific purposes in the ritual of the mass.

## Goals:

Identify the musical characteristics of the chant, particularly its melodic shape, texture, and rhythm.

Recognize monophonic texture.

Recognize the relationship of music to words, noticing especially the phrasing and accents and whether the treatment of the words is melismatic or syllabic.

*Guide:* The slashes (/) denote phrase endings.
Communion for Easter Sunday

> ### Latin
> *Pascha nostrum/immolatus est/Christus,/alleluia;/itaque epulemur/in azymis sinceritatis et veritatis,/alleluia, alleluia, alleluia.*
>
> ### Translation
> *Christ our Paschal lamb is slain, Alleluia; let us eat our Easter meal with the unleavened bread of truth and sincerity, Alleluia, Alleluia, Alleluia.*

Antiphon for Easter Sunday in Praise of Mary

> ### Latin
> *Regina caeli laetare, alleluia./Quia quem meruisti portare, alleluia./ Resurrexit, sicut dixit alleluia;/ora pro nobis Deum, alleluia.*

*Translation*
*Rejoice, Queen of the Heavens, Alleluia; He whom you were worthy of*
*bearing, Alleluia; has risen as He promised, Alleluia; pray to God for*
*us, Alleluia.*

**Reflections:** Notice the flexible pulse. It is nonmetric, because the music flows with the natural inflection of the text.

Although the chant is sung by a group of men rather than a soloist, the texture is monophonic in that the one melodic line exists by itself without accompaniment or supportive harmony.

Notice the frequency with which syllables of text are treated melismatically. Typically, how long are the melismas?

# Example 2

**"Tristis est anima mea"**—a five-voice motet

Composed by Orlando di Lasso (1532–1594)

This Latin motet, a masterpiece of Renaissance polyphony, exemplifies the finest in liturgical music of the mid-sixteenth century. Its expressiveness, unity, and polyphonic control demonstrate the highest achievement of the art at that time. The work is a Response for Maundy Thursday.

## Goals:

Recognize polyphonic texture, imitation, cadences, and points at which all voices move with the same rhythm, creating vertical sonorities (chords).

Listen for voice parts other than the soprano.

**Guide:** Count in a moderately slow four. Follow the music and the text. Listen for entrances of melodic patterns or phrases, identifiable motives, and points of imitation.

*Latin*
*Tristis est anima mea usque ad mortem:*
*sustenete hic, et vigilate mecum:*
*nunc videbitis turbam, quae circumdabit me:*
*vos fugam capietis,*
*et ego vadam immolari pro nobis.*

*Translation*
*My soul is very sorrowful, even unto death;*
*remain here, and watch with me:*
*Now ye will see the multitude that will surround me:*
*Ye will take flight,*
*and I shall go to be sacrificed for you.*

**Reflections:** Since this is polyphonic music in which melodies move independently one from the other, phrases cadence at different times, creating an overlap of phrases and a sense of ongoing movement until two very clear closed cadences occur, one at the end of the first line of text and one at the end of the piece.

Notice that this piece combines a restrained dignity yet a highly expressive quality, polyphonic control yet a tender, human feeling, and bold harmonic progressions yet a humble simplicity.

# Example 3

**"April is in My Mistress' Face"**—a madrigal

Composed in 1594 by Thomas Morley (1557–1602)

Morley was an English composer known primarily for his madrigals and balletts (both secular choral compositions of the Renaissance) and for an important teaching book on music, the first of its kind in the English language.

"April is in My Mistress' Face" is a madrigal for four voices. Although the voices move polyphonically, even imitatively, they come together more frequently in homophonic texture than they typically would in the sacred polyphonic music of the same time period.

### *Goals:*

Be aware of the shifting of polyphonic and homophonic textures.

Identify the metric organization.

Recognize the equal emphasis given to each vocal part (SATB).

Recognize imitation and modified imitation.

### *Guide:* The text follows:

> *April is in my mistress' face,*
> *And July in her eyes hath place,*
> *Within her bosom is September,*
> *But in her heart a cold December.*

The numbers represent pulses counted at a moderately slow tempo. Each line coincides with a phrase pattern, a number of which begin with pickups.
First phrase—eighteen beats; soprano and alto start, then tenor and bass join; beats are grouped as follows:

```
1 2 3 4 5
1 2 3 4 5 6
1 2 3 4 5 6 7
```

Second phrase—twelve beats; modified imitation; entrances in order: soprano and alto, bass, tenor.
Third phrase—sixteen beats, grouped as follows:

```
1 2 3 4
1 2 3 4
1 2 3 4 5 6 7 8
```

Fourth phrase—fourteen beats; imitation; entrances in order: soprano, tenor, bass, soprano and alto, bass.
Fourth phrase (repeated)—fifteen beats; imitation; entrances in order: alto, tenor, soprano, bass, soprano and alto, bass;
Ends with big ritard; hold on last beat.

### *Reflections:* Differentiate within this piece between a texture in which several melodic lines are equal in emphasis (polyphony) and a single, dominant line that is supported by a secondary chordal texture or accompaniment (homophony).

Compare the mood and style (musical characteristics) of this piece with the mood and style of the Di Lasso piece presented earlier. In particular, describe the degree of rhythmic vitality and the dominance of one texture over another. What makes music sound sacred? What makes it sound secular?

*Ex. 1*     "Communion for Easter Sunday." and "Antiphon for Easter Sunday in Praise of Mary." Gregorian chants. Performed by the Choir of the Vienna Hofburgkapelle. Vox SDLBX 5206.

*Ex. 2*     di Lasso, Orlando. "Tristis Est Anima Mea." Dover 97269-0. 3:17.

*Ex. 3*     Morley, Thomas. "April is in My Mistress' Face." Vanguard BG 577. 1:26.

*Discography*

Although the beginning of Western music is traced from ancient civilizations, for our purposes we have traced it from the beginnings of Christianity and the liturgy of the Roman Catholic church. Gregorian chant, in common use in the church since about 500 A.D., represents the first body of music literature in Western civilization, a literature on which much later music was to be based.

Adding a second line, then a third or more lines, to Gregorian chant created polyphonic texture, stabilizing by the sixteenth century at four or five parts when most polyphonic compositions were created independently of a chant. The development of notation facilitated this kind of composition. Notation allowed composers to communicate a more complex music in a way that others could perform it. By 1600, the invention of printing greatly facilitated the dissemination and preservation of music. Printing also greatly expanded the communication of information and ideas about music.

During the Renaissance, the first professional composers and performers of classical music began to devote their lives to creating and making music for their livelihood. The initial employers were the churches; later, the aristocracy became important employers of musicians. Creators of music became known for their talents and their contributions, the most outstanding becoming our first master composers.

The main genres after Gregorian chant were choral settings of the mass, the Renaissance motet, and the Italian and English madrigals. Instrumental music was used mainly to accompany dancing and the singing of folk and popular songs. When it did exist as a separate entity, it was patterned after choral music. No distinct instrumental genres had yet emerged.

This period of Western music, dominated by influences of the Roman Catholic church, culminated in the Golden Age of Choral Music—the music of Josquin, Palestrina, and Gabrieli.

Finally, the Protestant Reformation opened up new directions in sacred music: church music in Protestant churches was now sung in the vernacular in hymn style by the congregation rather than sung in Latin in chant form by the priest or the choir as practiced in the Catholic church. It also began a rich heritage of Protestant polyphonic choral music, much of it based on hymn or chorale melodies, in much the same way that earlier polyphonic music was based on Gregorian chants.

*Summary*

| | | *Terms and* |
|---|---|---|
| *Greek civilization* | *Syllabic* | *Concepts* |
| *The Christian era* | *Melismatic* | |
| *Liturgy* | *Modal system* | |
| *Anthem* | *Mass* | |
| *Counter-Reformation* | *Motet* | |
| *Notation* | *Madrigal* | |
| *Polyphonic texture* | *Polychoral motets* | |
| *Cantus firmus* | *Antiphonal* | |
| *Imitative counterpoint* | *Homorhythmic* | |
| *Secular music* | *Consort* | |

Chapter 9

# Music of the Baroque (1600–1750)

Monastery church,
Melk. An example of
baroque architecture.

The Baroque, a period of absolute monarchy that flourished in Italy, France, Germany, and England, was marked by pomp and splendor, a dynamic and dramatic spirit, and an emotional expression full of color and movement. It was romantic and grandiose, an age of innovation and adventure. This era saw major advancements in science, philosophy, and the arts from the contributions of such men as Galileo, Newton, Descartes, Spinoza, Milton, Rubens, and Rembrandt.

The courts, in addition to the churches, were the patrons of the arts. The rulers of the courts were wealthy monarchs, building magnificent palaces and maintaining court composers and musicians for orchestras, chapel choirs, and opera companies. Although folk and entertainment music and music for the churches continued, secular classical music was performed for the courts and the elite upper class.

In addition, city governments now joined churches and courts as centers of music and culture and as employers of musicians. Musicians were needed to fulfill the demand for church music, for the entertainment of the courts, and for festivals, ceremonies, and other public occasions in the cities. The people's interests and enthusiasms were for the music of the local composers, the contemporary composers, not for the old-fashioned (polyphonic) music "where you could not understand the words."

As the Catholics were rebounding from the effects of the Reformation, the Protestant church became firmly established and added significantly to the repertoire of Western music. They contributed particularly in the development of the Lutheran chorale and various compositional forms based on chorale melodies.

New techniques of composition, new musical forms, the development of opera and the orchestra, and the establishment of the major-minor tonal system are hallmarks of the Baroque period. It now was common for composers to write music with specific instruments in mind, for the specific tone colors that they would produce. Judging from the music composed particularly during the first half of the eighteenth century during the late Baroque period, instrumental performers became more proficient, placing greater emphasis on technical skill and virtuoso performance than ever before. Additionally, solo keyboard performers and organists in some contexts added their creative instincts to a performance by improvising ornamentations and otherwise embellishing a melodic line.

**Musical Characteristics**

Many genres and forms, particularly for instruments and keyboards, emerged that remain in common use today. Many instruments and musical sounds that we know and feel comfortable with today came into common use during the Baroque period.

One of the first major developments in the Baroque period was the shift in emphasis from a horizontal to a vertical texture. This was a change from composition that stressed the combination of two or more melodic lines (polyphonic texture) to harmonic or chordal writing with one predominant melody and harmonic background (homophonic texture).

**Homophonic Texture**

Composers still wrote polyphonic music but now created much music with homophonic texture, an essential ingredient in the development of opera (discussed more fully on pages 218–220). In the late Baroque period, it became common to create polyphonic textures in instrumental and keyboard music as well as sacred choral works. For purposes of comparing textures, figures 9.1–9.3 illustrate polyphony (a fugue for organ; see page 218 and SS10/3), homophony (a Bach chorale—see SS10/2), and a polyphonic setting of a chorale melody (based on the above chorale). Follow the chorale tune as it appears within the brackets.

Another development of great importance was the establishment of the major/minor tonal system. This shifted the basis of composition from the system of church modes (modality), discussed briefly in chapter 8, to the major-minor tonal system, the system of scales and keys that produce sounds of which most of us have a high degree of familiarity (tonality). It is the system of the tonic, the chord of rest, and the dominant, the chord of movement.

**Major-Minor Tonal System**

We perceive "tonicness," the home tone or tonal center of a key, and we perceive modulation, a change of tonality from a key of stability (tonic) to a key of contrast or instability (frequently but not always dominant). It is the system that provides diatonic writing (notes in the key) and additional color and means for modulation through chromatic or altered tones (notes outside of the key). Much baroque music is diatonic.

**Figure 9.1**
Polyphony. J. S. Bach.
Organ Fugue in G minor
(Little). From Kamien,
*The Norton Scores,* Vol.
1, 4th edition. Copyright
© W. W. Norton
Company, New York,
NY.

**Figure 9.2**

Homophony. J. S. Bach, *Wachet auf* Cantata No. 140. Copyright © European American Music, Valley Forge, PA.

**Figure 9.2**
*Continued*

**Figure 9.3**

Polyphonic setting of a chorale melody. J. S. Bach, *Wachet auf* Cantata No. 140. From Hoffer, *The Understanding of Music,* Fifth Ed. Copyright © 1985 Wadsworth Publishing Co., Belmont, CA.

**Figure 9.3**
*Continued*

Final adjustment being made to a newly completed two-manual harpsichord. Its construction reflects the authentic baroque music.

**Continuo**

The importance of solo keyboard and organ improvisation was mentioned earlier. The **continuo** included another type of improvisation that played a significant role in baroque performance practice. It was common for keyboard players to fill in harmonies based on chord symbols and a bass line. The technique was useful in providing a harmonic basis to the new homophonic, tonal (rather than modal) music. The continuo involved two players: a cellist or player of another bass instrument to play a simple, continuous bass line that emphasized the principle notes of the harmonies or chords (similar to the walking bass in jazz), and a keyboard player, usually a harpsichordist, to fill in or improvise on the chords dictated by the symbols and the bass line. This technique of improvisation is sometimes known as "realizing" (bringing into reality) the harmonies (as a jazz pianist or guitarist does). The continuo supported harmonically one or more instrumental or vocal melodic lines (SS9/1).

A musical shorthand (chord symbols) was devised to assist the keyboard player. The notes of the chords were not written out; rather, numbers were placed below each chord in the bass line identifying the chord so the keyboardist could improvise the realization. The shorthand was called **figured bass.** Such improvisation expanded in scope, becoming a high art and a coveted skill among keyboard performers in the late Baroque period. Figure 9.4 is an example of a continuo with figured bass.

**Other Musical Characteristics**

Baroque music is music of contrasts: voices and instruments, loud and soft, tonic key and a contrasting key, an *A* section and a *B* section, and a small group of instruments (concertato) contrasted with a large group (ripieno) or the small and large groups together (tutti). Rhythm is regular, metric, and often energetic. A steady pulsation is often maintained in the bass. "Classical" pieces often were derived from popular and court dances, further enhancing the tendency toward a dynamic baroque rhythm. Yet this strong metric feeling is in contrast to the free rhythm of the recitative and the free rhythm common in improvised passages, especially in keyboard works.

**Figure 9.4**
Figured bass. J. S. Bach,
*Wachet auf* Cantata No.
140. Copyright
© European American
Music, Valley Forge,
PA.

Melody is often perceived as a continuous expansion of an idea, without short, regular phrases. Dynamics (loudness levels) are contrasting and abrupt, achieved through adding or taking away instruments or voices rather than gradually changing the loudness of the music. This technique is known as terraced dynamics.

**Tone Painting**

**Tone painting** began during the Renaissance as composers realized the ability of music to convey the moods and meanings of the text, to express musically a wide range of ideas and feelings. Triumph or Resurrection, for example, might be described musically in a very different manner from Death or Crucifixion.

The interest in tone painting became even more pronounced and sophisticated during the Baroque period. Composers went to great lengths to depict not only specific images but the emotions of the text, to mirror the text in the music as literally as possible.

**Instruments**

Instrumental music for the first time in Western music became equal in importance to vocal music to composers and listeners. Although orchestras were made up of instruments similar to those of today, there was no standard set of instruments or instrumentation. The baroque orchestra was not as large or as varied as the modern symphony orchestra. The instruments generally were smaller and quieter than their modern counterparts, and the primary instruments were those of the violin family plus trumpets, oboes, and flutes.

The lute was a popular plucked instrument, and the primary keyboard instruments were the harpsichord and organ. The forerunner of the modern piano, the pianoforte, was invented but not widely used during the Baroque period.

**Musical Forms and Genres**

New musical forms or genres that developed in the Baroque period ranged from keyboard works and chamber music to multimovement orchestral pieces, large choral works, and operas. Old forms, of course, continued. Renaissance polyphony and imitative counterpoint were adapted to baroque instrumental music in such forms as the ricercar and fantasia. These one-movement pieces (without sections) eventually led to the fugue (see page 218). The sectional canzona form led to the baroque sonata.

**Orchestral Works**

The two orchestral forms that reached their peak in the late Baroque period are the **concerto** and the concerto grosso. The concerto involved one solo instrument with orchestra, and the concerto grosso included a small group of soloists, usually two or three. The element of contrast between the soloist(s) and the orchestra was germane to these as well as other baroque forms. Both concerto forms were in three movements, fast, slow, fast, with the slow movement in a contrasting key.

Another popular genre was the French **overture.** Its original aim was to create a festive atmosphere as an opening to an opera. It later became an independent instrumental genre. The French overture was in two parts, the first in a slow, majestic, homophonic style and the second in a faster, yet serious, polyphonic style. It often ended with a reference to at least the rhythm of the opening section.

Finally, the **dance suite** was sometimes written for orchestra, sometimes for keyboards. It is a set of contrasting dances combined to form a single, multimovement work. The main dances are the allemande, courante, sarabande, and gigue, but most dance suites are created in a flexible format that include additional or substitute dances or perhaps movements other than dance forms.

**Chamber Music**

The typical forms for a small number of instruments are the church **sonata** and the chamber sonata, both written for various instrumental combinations. Both sonatas typically included either one solo instrument with continuo (solo sonata—three performers) or two solo instruments with continuo (**trio sonata**—four performers).

These compositions usually were comprised of contrasting sections or movements, frequently in dance forms. The church sonata is usually a four-movement work in a slow-fast-slow-fast pattern. The chamber sonata is the ensemble form of the dance suite, although composers frequently incorporated additional dances or movements other than such dances as a prelude or an aria.

## Keyboard Works

The toccata, prelude, fantasia, and fugue were important single-movement, keyboard compositions of the Baroque. The toccata and prelude were improvisatory in character, sometimes having a contrapuntal middle section or sometimes paired with a fugal composition in performance. The fantasia was a larger, more complex work that may have employed a series of contrapuntal variations on a single theme. A composer may have written one of these pieces with a particular instrument in mind, either the harpsichord or the organ, but in actual practice, the instruments were interchangeable, later including the piano.

**Fugue** is a compositional technique that may be used within any composition, but it often described the structure of an entire piece. A fugue is an imitative, contrapuntal form built on a single theme—a procedure for "working out" the musical possibilities of a simple melodic idea. It represents the epitome of baroque polyphonic music.

Other keyboard works should be mentioned: the chorale prelude, an organ work based on a chorale tune that acts as a theme for a set of variations; the passacaglia and chaconne, both of which use a repeated bass line—an ostinato—as the basis of the composition; and the dance suite, discussed previously as an orchestral genre.

## Choral Music

The two major choral forms of the Baroque period were the **cantata** and the **oratorio.** Both were dramatic forms with the oratorio being of much larger proportions than the cantata, usually longer and more complex. The oratorio was intended for concert performance rather than for the worship service as was the cantata. Both were sacred works, the cantata becoming an integral part of the German Lutheran church service. Secular oratorios and cantatas did exist. One of the best known secular cantatas was J. S. Bach's "Coffee Cantata."

Both cantatas and oratorios included vocal solos (arias and recitatives), solo ensembles and choruses, and instrumental accompaniment. The **aria** typically was more song-like, melodic, and metric than the recitative. The **recitative** played a more important part in oratorio than in cantatas. This technique was important in opera wherein the action could be described in a way that all could understand. It was sung speech, in free rhythm and declaimed the natural inflection of the words, with a minimal accompaniment of simple chords. Soloists other than the narrator typically introduce their arias by means of the recitative. A dramatic character known as the narrator was often included in the oratorio.

The solo ensemble was a small group of solo voices. The choruses (sung by a choir) were often contrapuntal, even fugal. The accompaniment for the cantata was often organ, occasionally with a small group of instruments. An organ and often an orchestra accompanied the oratorio.

## Opera

The development of **opera** around 1600 resulted from the following interests:

1. A renewed interest among scholars in the famous Greek tragedies and a desire among a small group of scholars in Italy to set dramatic works to music with costumes and staging
2. A heightened interest generally in drama and theatrical elements in music
3. The tendency in the early Baroque period for composers to use music to depict the meanings of words and the emotions of the text

A commemoration of
Handel in Westminister
Abbey. The assembly of
British nobility. Drawn
by. E. F. Burney and
engraved by J. Spilsbury.

The Santa Fe Opera
featuring Carmen
Balthrop and Judith
Forst in 1986 production
of Monteverdi's
*L'incoronazione
di Poppea.* Photo by
Hans Fahrmeyer.

4. The shift from a polyphonic to a homophonic texture that presented words in
   an understandable manner
5. The use of accompanied monody, which was a new, expressive, solo singing
   style designed to recapture what was thought to be the texture and style
   of ancient Greek music
6. The creation of the aria and recitative as viable means for carrying forth
   dramatic action and developing a plot

In baroque opera, the singer dominated. Improvisatory, dazzling vocal effects and
stereotyped practices too often had little to do with the plot; the purpose was to display
the virtuosic abilities of the star singers. Little attention was given to characterization
and dramatic action. The recitatives, arias, and choruses became a series of numbers

that did little to enhance dramatic flow. The da capo aria served as a basic pattern of solo song. It had a first section, a contrasting second section, and concluded with a return to the first section, establishing the ternary (ABA) form.

The first operas were produced around 1600 in Italy. The most important and durable early operas were *Orfeo* by Claudio Monteverdi, produced in 1608, and *Dido and Aeneas* by Henry Purcell, produced in 1689. The late Baroque included the operas of Handel (operas in the Italian style produced in England by the great German master) and the beginnings of ballad opera, the English genre that satirized Italian opera. Ballad operas included popular tunes or ballads and had tremendous popularity both in Europe and the Americas.

## Composers

The most important early baroque composer was Claudio Monteverdi, known for his early madrigals in the old-fashioned or Renaissance polyphonic style and for his later madrigals that foreshadowed many important baroque features that were to become commonplace. He was especially known for his operas composed in the new, baroque style. His operas, *Orfeo, The Return of Ulysses,* and *The Coronation of Poppea,* are found today on recordings and staged by university and professional opera companies.

Between Monteverdi and the giants of the late Baroque era, Johann Sebastian Bach and George Frideric Handel, are the following composers:

1. Jean Baptiste Lully, important in the development of French opera
2. Archangelo Corelli, a violin virtuoso known for his development of modern violin technique, his trio sonatas, and his contribution to the concerto grosso form
3. Henry Purcell, England's foremost native composer of the seventeenth century whose success was founded on his composition of numerous anthems and other religious works, trio sonatas, and his most famous opera, *Dido and Aeneas*
4. Antonio Vivaldi, probably the most celebrated of all Italian composers who wrote operas, oratorios, and church music but whose fame rests in his concerto grossos and solo concertos of which he composed more than four hundred

The most famous of baroque composers who rank among the greatest of the masters of Western music are Bach and Handel.

## Johann Sebastian Bach (1685–1750)

Bach, a member of an illustrious German musical family, lived and worked entirely in Germany. The first part of his professional career was in Weimar where he was court organist and chamber musician to the Duke of Weimar and composed his most significant organ music. Bach then went to Cöthen where he was chapelmaster and director of chamber music to the Prince of Anhalt and composed important chamber and orchestral music. He ended his career in Leipzig where he was cantor of St. Thomas church and school and composed his monumental choral works.

Bach was a master of baroque forms and genres, taking them to their fullest potential. His organ music continues among the best of organ literature. His tonal counterpoint in choral music, chord progressions in chorale harmonizations, and fugues for keyboard instruments have been and continue to be studied perhaps more than music of any other composer. Among Bach's most important attributes was his phenomenal grasp of the technique of composition, particularly in his ability to master the grand art of polyphony and the newer art of harmonic writing.

*The Master of Leipzig.* This artist's impression shows the Bach family at morning prayers, with Bach himself playing the clavichord, accompanied by one of his sons on the violin. Music Division, The New York Public Library at Lincoln Center: Astor, Tilden, and Lenox Foundations.

Among his most important works are *Mass in B Minor, The Saint Matthew Passion,* and his church cantatas, of which he composed more than three hundred; numerous chorale preludes, toccatas, fugues, and other works for organ or harpsichord; *The Art of Fugue, The Goldberg Variations,* and *The Well Tempered Clavier* for keyboard instruments; *Six Solo Suites for Unaccompanied Violoncello;* and the six *Brandenburg Concertos.*

Bach's music was not performed much after he died until it was rediscovered in the early nineteenth century. His music continues to be played today in churches and concert halls throughout the world.

## George Frideric Handel (1685–1759)

Handel was a native of Germany who learned well the Italian musical style, particularly of opera, and achieved his most notable successes during the nearly fifty years he spent in England. Unlike Bach, Handel was internationally famous during his lifetime. His initial fame was in his composition and production of Italian operas in England, but his most lasting fame was in his composition of oratorios. His best known work is, of course, *Messiah.*

Handel also is well known for his instrumental music in virtually all the common baroque forms, notably concerto grossos, harpsichord suites, organ concertos, and two widely recorded orchestral pieces, *Water Music* and *Music for the Royal Fireworks.* Handel composed for a wide audience and became a master in the grand style of the late Baroque.

King George II rises to his feet at the performance of Handel's "Hallelujah" chorus.

## A Study in Sound

*Music of Bach and Handel*

## Example 1

**"Behold, I Tell You a Mystery"** (recitative) and **"The Trumpet Shall Sound,"** (bass aria) from Part III of *Messiah*

Composed by George Frideric Handel

Composed in 1741

Text from the Scriptures

*Messiah* is undoubtedly the most famous of all oratorios; it has been heard repeatedly, year after year, for more than two centuries. The style is typical of many of Handel's works and is consistent with the common compositional practices of the day. It is a work of epic proportions and dramatic entertainment and was intended to please public and private supporters.

Part I is the section on prophecy and Christ's birth; Part II on His suffering and death; and Part III on the Resurrection and Redemption. *Messiah* has been performed by professional and amateur musicians, for large and small choruses and orchestras, and in both churches and concert halls. Many institutions maintain long-standing traditions of performing at least Part I of *Messiah* during every Christmas season.

## Goals:

Recognize the styles of recitative, aria, and continuo. Learn the structure of the da capo aria.

Be aware of the relationship of the music to the meaning of the words.

Recognize the sound of the baroque trumpet, contrasting instrumental sounds, and traditional chord progressions.

*Guide:* Recitative—prepares the listener for the mood and character of the aria to follow. The recitative is declamatory, in free rhythm, and states the text with minimal accompaniment in a manner that the words can accurately be expressed and clearly understood. As is typical in a baroque recitative, the last notes of singing are without accompaniment and are followed by the final cadence played by the orchestra. The text follows:

Behold I tell you a mystery; We shall not all sleep, but we shall all be changed, In a moment, in the twinkling of an eye at the last trumpet.

Aria—for bass voice is in a large ABA form, a da capo aria (first section; a second, contrasting section; and a repeat of the first section).

Section A—exalting and majestic, particularly when the orchestra is full and features the baroque trumpet, a small trumpet useful for playing in the high register. The text follows:

. . . the trumpet shall sound, and the dead shall be raised incorruptible, and we shall be changed.

Section B—more lyrical and legato than the *A* section; the continuo, played principally on a bass instrument and harpsichord, is prevalent throughout this section. The text follows:

For this corruptible must put on incorruption, and this mortal must put on immortality.

Section A—the return coincides with the return of the text, "The Trumpet Shall Sound. . . ."

*Reflections:* Notice the different musical treatments of such words as mystery and sleep, then the change of mood as the text states that we shall be "changed in a moment . . . at the last trumpet." This is a good example of word painting common in baroque vocal music.

Cadences are clear, and the meter is regular and strong. The music is diatonic, essentially homophonic, and rooted in traditional harmonic chord progressions. The text is frequently presented with lengthy melismas, that is, with many running notes sung to a single syllable of text.

The solo and orchestra are often in dialogue (a question and answer context) with sudden contrasts of dynamics, instrumentation, and texture.

The continuo is heard throughout the *B* section and in some solo passages in the *A* section that are accompanied by a smaller instrumentation than full orchestra.

# Example 2

**Cantata No. 140—"Wachet auf"** (Sleepers, Awake!)—I; VII

Composed in 1731 by Johann Sebastian Bach

The chorale tune, "Wachet auf," was composed by Philipp Nicolai (1556–1608).

The seven parts follow:

    I  Instrumental introduction and polyphonic chorus

   II  Recitative—tenor

 III  Duet—soprano and baritone

 IV  Chorus—based on the chorale tune

   V  Recitative—baritone

 VI  Duet—soprano and baritone

VII  Final chorus—the stately chorale setting

For this example, only movements I and VII are included. They are presented in reverse order in order to hear the chorale setting first.

## *Goals:*

Recognize the hymnlike setting of a Lutheran chorale.

Recognize a polyphonic chorus based on a chorale tune. Be able to identify the chorale melody and to describe its relationship to the other voice parts in the polyphonic texture.

## *Guide:*

VII  Final chorus—chorale setting; written in a hymnlike style with all voice parts moving virtually in the same rhythm. Count in a moderately slow four (a slash denotes a pause in the phrase):

```
1---2---3--/-4---5---6--/-7---8---/
1---2---3--/-4---5---6--/-7---8--/
-1---2--/-3---4--/-5--/-6---7--/-8---9--/
```

 I  Instrumental introduction and polyphonic chorus.
Introduction—seventeen bars; in triple meter; count in a moderate three; and notice the question-answer dialogue in strings and oboe in the fifth, sixth, seventh, and eighth bars, and the ascending scales in bars nine through twelve.

Polyphonic chorus—The chorale tune begins on the final chord of the introduction and has the same meter and tempo. The chorale tune, in the soprano voice, is in very simple and very slow rhythm and is always surrounded by intricate, independent lines. Each phrase of the tune is usually separated by instrumental material.

*Reflections:* Compare the chorale style with "Sherburne" and "Amazing Grace," two hymns presented in chapter 3.

The polyphonic chorus is based on the chorale tune. It is the most elaborate and complex of all the movements of this cantata. Notice that the tune is in slower rhythm than the other parts, and its phrases are separated.

Be aware of outer voices (sopranos and basses) and inner voices (altos and tenors). Notice the moving parts wherein other voices move for a beat or two in faster rhythm than the notes of the soprano melody.

Identify recurring motives, imitation, and contrasting sounds. Be aware of the various layers of sounds—the various lines, whether vocal or instrumental.

# Example 3

**Fugue in C Minor—No. 2** from *Well-Tempered Clavier,* Book I

Composed by Johann Sebastian Bach

Performed on the harpsichord by Wanda Landowska

This music is an example of a three-voice fugue. The fugue, a polyphonic compositional technique used in many types of pieces, is sometimes an independent, identifiable composition such as this example. It begins with a subject (theme) by itself (a single line). The same theme enters shortly at a different pitch level while the first voice continues independent of, yet consonant with, the second voice. A third voice or even a fourth voice may enter subsequently while the other voices continue independently. The result is a complex, polyphonic interplay of melodic lines.

## Goals:

Recognize polyphonic texture and entering voices in a fugue.

Be aware of the sounds of a minor tonality.

*Guide:* Count in a moderately slow four. The music starts with a two-note pickup on the second half of the first beat. Thus, the first strong beat is the second beat. The letters, A, B, and C identify the initial entrances of each voice. After the entrances are made, the fugue is developed.

```
( 1 )---2---3---4---5---6---7---8---
      A        B              C
```

*Reflections:* The fugal subject (theme) is based on a five-note motive that opens the fugue. The first statement of the subject (A) is in the middle voice (compared with the pitch areas to follow), the second entrance is in the high voice (B), and the third is in the low (C).

After the entrance, the fugue subject is developed in a variety of ways, including varying the subsequent entrances of the motive and making the setting more chromatic and unstable.

Listen for the motive throughout the piece as Bach develops the fugue. Notice the two ritards approaching the final cadence. Be aware of the sound of the minor tonality and the shift of the last chord from the expected minor sound to major, offering a surprise chord quality in the context of the previous minor tonality.

**Additional
Listening**

# Example 1

***Brandenburg Concerto* No. 5 in D Major**

1. Allegro

2. Affetuoso

3. Allegro

Composed in 1721 by Johann Sebastian Bach

For flute, violin, and harpsichord soloists

The six *Brandenburg Concertos* were composed for Bach's own use while employed at the Cöthen Court and were dedicated to Markgraf Christian Ludwig of Brandenburg. They were composed for various solo instruments:

No. 1—violin, oboe, and horn

No. 2—trumpet, recorder, oboe, and violin

No. 3—no soloists

No. 4—violin and two recorders

No. 5—flute, violin, and harpsichord

No. 6—two violas and a violoncello

The orchestra is typically small, but the first three concertos add trumpets, oboes, and bassoons to the strings, whereas the last three add only recorder and flute. They are not numbered in the order that they were composed. No. 5, for example, was thought to be the last of the six to be completed. Listening to any of the six concertos would provide insight into baroque orchestral style.

*Guide:* Recognize contrasting textures, points of tension and resolution, and essentially diatonic melody that is supported by the underlying chord structure. Recognize also the timbre and both the supportive and featured roles of the harpsichord. Be aware that the harpsichord in a continuo performs a harmonic, supportive function, but in this concerto, the harpsichord is given a soloistic role equal to the violin and the flute.

**First movement**—the fast rhythm can be felt in duple meter at a moderate tempo. Notice the constant, almost perpetual motion and the relative lack of a clear and balanced phrase structure;

Main theme—seventeen bars; stated by the full orchestra; based on a motive of an ascending tonic arpeggio;

The main body of the movement features dialogue between solo flute and solo violin and the constant harmonic motion of the harpsichord supported by the bass line in the cello. The main theme is heard by the orchestra several times throughout this section.

The harpsichord precedes the concluding statement of the theme with an elaborate passage that is improvisatory in nature.

The movement ends with a complete statement by the full ensemble of the original seventeen-bar theme.

**Second movement**—slow; soloists and harpsichord;

The main theme on which the entire movement is based is stated polyphonically at the beginning, first by the violin then answered immediately by the flute, then the harpsichord. Be aware of the varied ways that Bach used this motive throughout the movement.

**Third movement**—fast; duple meter, with a triple subdivision of the pulse;

The motive on which the entire movement is based is stated by the violin at the beginning, answered immediately by the flute, then the harpsichord.

*Ex. 1*    Handel, George Frideric. *Messiah,* Nos. 47–48. Columbia 2-CBS-MG-603. 9:05.

*Ex. 2*    Bach, Johann Sebastian. "Wachet auf."

*Ex. 3*    Bach, Johann Sebastian. Fugue in C Minor, No. 2. Angel CDCB-49126. 1:45.

*Discography*

Sacred, polyphonic choral music dominated the styles of Western music through the late Middle Ages and the Renaissance. The Baroque period, itself, was divided in emphases fairly equally between choral and instrumental and between sacred and secular music.

The major-minor tonal system, homophonic texture, and orchestral writing became standard practice during the Baroque period. Instruments as we know them today became common during this period, laying the foundation for the symphony orchestra and classical chamber ensembles, such as the string quartet, that became standard during the Classic era.

The Baroque period also gave us the beginnings of opera, incorporating the aria and the recitative and their ability to carry forth dramatic action. It brought a proliferation of keyboard works for harpsichord and organ, the fugue as the primary polyphonic compositional technique, the oratorio and cantata as important choral genres, and the concerto as an important instrumental genre.

It produced many composers who are well known today: Corelli, Vivaldi, Monteverdi, Couperin, Scarlatti, Lully, and Purcell, but giants among them were Johann Sebastian Bach and George Frideric Handel, whose deaths in the 1750s marked the end of the old music and the beginning of the modern age.

*Summary*

| | |
|---|---|
| *Virtuoso performance* | *Fugue* |
| *Baroque improvisation* | *Chorale* |
| *Implied harmony (chords)* | *Oratorio* |
| *Figured bass* | *Cantata* |
| *Concerto* | *Opera* |
| *Overture* | *Accompanied monody* |
| *Suite* | *Aria* |
| *Sonata* | *Recitative* |
| *Keyboard genres* | *Da capo aria* |

*Terms and Concepts*

# Chapter 10
# Music of the Classic Period (1750–1820)

The minuet. An eighteenth-century royal ballroom scene.

The sounds of the classical music of the late eighteenth century as well as those of the nineteenth century are familiar to twentieth-century American ears. Many of the pieces and many of the composers are household words. This music is widely performed today by school, community, and professional musical organizations, and recordings of this music frequently are purchased by the American consumer. Who has not heard or at least heard of the music of Mozart, Haydn, and Beethoven or some of their music: Beethoven's "Fifth Symphony" or his "Moonlight Sonata," Haydn's "Surprise Symphony," or Mozart's *The Magic Flute* or *The Marriage of Figaro*?

We can refer to the Classic period of the late eighteenth century as the beginning of the Modern era. Developments of this time period that form the groundwork for the musical practices of the next 150–200 years are the sonata, symphony, and string quartet; the instrumentation of the modern symphony orchestra; and the establishment of public concerts available to everyone.

The Classic period was centered in the courts and communities of Austria and Germany. It was a sophisticated and aristocratic society. The courts valued artistic and social status and demanded the very best in entertainment, but this period also saw an increase in community concert halls and opera houses as music became more available to common people through public performances. It was a day that saw the church's influence decline in shaping the direction of Western music. Although the creation of liturgical music for the Catholic church continued to flourish, more than for the Protestant church, the Classic period saw a rise in the dominance of instrumental music.

## Musical Characteristics

Whereas the Baroque period was a time of opulent splendor, ornamentation, decoration, and emotional expression, the Classic period reflected the Age of Reason: emotional restraint, balance, clarity, symmetry, clear and precise formal structure, and simplicity.

The classical emphasis was on the predominance of melody with all other factors subordinate to the melody. Thus, homophonic texture was much more important than contrapuntal or polyphonic writing to the classical composer. The baroque continuo and figured bass were no longer needed in the Classic period, as all parts were written out. The keyboard was not used as an accompaniment instrument in an ensemble as it was when part of the continuo, and the continuo concept did not lend itself well to the classic ideal of shorter, more regular phrases.

Melodies were typically lyrical with smooth, step-wise contours; phrases ended with obvious tonic-dominant cadences; diatonic melodies prevailed, and to a large extent they reflected the underlying harmonies. Rhythm was uncomplicated, simple, and predictable.

Music was tonal, in a major or minor key, for the harmonic practices were based on a logical extension and refinement of the tonal system established during the Baroque period. Harmonies were simple, and tonalities were clear. Chord progressions revolved around what had come to be common practice in the use of the primary tonic, subdominant, and dominant chords, with the continued use of dissonances such as the dominant seventh chord that demanded resolution.

Modulations to new keys were common, and the element of key relationships took on new significance—relationships of keys from one phrase group to the next, one section to the next, and even one movement of an extended work to the next. New keys represented instability that was resolved only when the tonal center returned to the original tonic. This interest resulted in a strong preference for the *ABA* formal structure, with *A* in the tonic key, *B* in a contrasting key, and a return to the tonic key in the return to the *A* section. The concept of unity and variety, of contrast and return, was valued in classical music and was applied most commonly in the forms developed during the Classic period.

## Instruments

As stated earlier, the Classic period was an age of instrumental music. The families of instruments of modern orchestras and bands became standard: strings, woodwinds, brass, and percussion (see Appendix B), and the piano replaced the harpsichord in popularity. The instrumentation of the modern orchestra, the string quartet, and other chamber ensembles also became standard during this period:

1. The orchestra included the string section of first and second violins, violas, cellos, and double basses; winds in pairs (flutes, clarinets, oboes, bassoons, trumpets, horns, and sometimes trombones); and timpani, the only widely used percussion instrument.
2. Chamber music ensembles included a wide variety of string, wind, and piano combinations, ranging commonly from three to eight musicians (trios to octets). Among these ensembles were the following:

   String quartet—two violins, one viola, one cello

   Piano trio—violin, cello, and piano

   Piano quintet—a string quartet plus piano

## Genres

The genres of the Classic period grew out of those of the Baroque period. At the same time, these genres changed and stabilized sufficiently in terminology and concept that they became models of formal structure on which much music was based during the next 150 years. Again, keep in mind that descriptions apply to common practice but that many exceptions to each generalization exist.

A modern chamber orchestra with violin and viola soloists.

## Instrumental Genres

The primary instrumental genres of the Classic era are comprised of multimovement works, usually three or four movements: the **sonata** for one or two instruments, the **symphony** and **concerto** for orchestra, and **chamber music** (the string quartet and other small chamber music groups).

Chamber music is distinguished from orchestral music in that in chamber music each part is played on only one instrument. In orchestral music, more than one instrument may play the same part. For example, eight double basses might be playing the bass part, or twelve violins might be playing the violin part.

Typical multimovement works will have the following arrangement and structure of movements:

I     Fast—sonata-allegro form
II    Slow—a broad ABA form is common, sometimes the
          theme and variations form
III   Dance—usually a minuet and trio or, later, a scherzo
          and trio—omitted in most three-movement sonatas,
          particularly the concerto
IV    Fast—usually a rondo, sometimes a sonata-allegro form

The sonata is a work for one or two instruments. Solo piano sonatas are the most common. Sonatas for two instruments are usually written for an orchestral instrument and piano. Violin sonatas are the most common. It is not accurate to describe them as works for solo instrument with piano accompaniment, because the piano parts are often as important as the solo instrument.

The concerto features a solo instrument, frequently the piano or the violin, with the full symphony orchestra. It typically is in three movements. The dance movement is the one omitted, for the texture of solo with orchestra does not lend itself to the spirit of the dance. A classical concerto typically features a cadenza, which is that portion of the solo where the orchestra stops and the soloist engages in an extended virtuoso passage that highlights the soloist's technical abilities. The cadenza frequently conveys an improvisatory character and includes long passages in free rhythm.

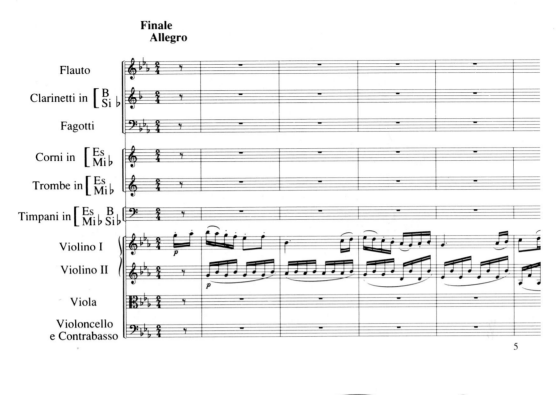

The symphony is a work for the full symphony orchestra, usually in four movements and featuring the varied tonal colors of all the orchestral instruments. Figures 10.1 and 10.2 are pages from the conductor's score of two classical symphonies. Notice the difference in instrumentation between Mozart's Symphony No. 39 composed in 1788 (see SS10/1) and Beethoven's monumental Ninth Symphony composed in 1824.

**Figure 10.1**

Part of a conductor's score from Mozart's Symphony No. 39. Edwin F. Kalmus & Co., Inc.

**Figure 10.2**
Part of a conductor's
score from Beethoven's
Ninth Symphony.

Figure 10.2
Continued

An artist's impression of
Haydn leading a
rehearsal of a string
quartet.

The most common chamber music ensemble of the Classic era is the string quartet (two violins, viola, and cello). As stated before, chamber music as a genre encompasses works for a variety of small ensembles from trios to octets, including those that combine strings and piano or that involve wind instruments.

**Vocal, Choral, Opera**

The primary vocal/choral genre of the Classic period was opera. Composers continued to write oratorios, masses, and other sacred choral music. However, these genres no longer reigned supreme in the musical developments of the late eighteenth and nineteenth centuries as they did through the time of Bach and Handel.

The opera of the Classic era strengthened the relationship between music and drama and between singers and orchestra. The trend was toward ongoing music and continuous drama arranged in scenes, rather than a series of recitatives, arias, and choruses that interrupted the flow of natural dramatic action as was common in baroque opera. The recitative and aria were still common, but their accompaniments were now more complex and were intended to enhance the atmosphere of the text, rather than be totally subservient to the singer. The recitative provided narrative; the aria provided commentary on the plot; and the solo ensembles and choruses along with staging, costumes, and orchestral accompaniment enhanced the plot and added musical and dramatic interest. The opera orchestra in the Classic period was used, more than in the Baroque era, to create the proper mood in support of the drama. It incorporated more lyrical melodies rather than mere accompaniment patterns and became a more integral part of the drama.

The most famous operas of the Classic period are those by Mozart, including *The Marriage of Figaro, The Magic Flute,* and *Don Giovanni.* Classical choral works include Haydn's oratorio, *The Creation,* Mozart's *Requiem,* and Beethoven's *Missa Solemnis.*

The following formal structures, all related to instrumental music, were common to classical music but seldom were adhered to in a strict sense. They became flexible models used as the basis of much nineteenth- and twentieth-century music. The challenge to listeners is to learn to recognize the factors that create form, such as the elements of contrast and repetition and the changes in mood, tonality, or instrumentation.

**Forms**

The **sonata-allegro** form was common in all classical orchestral and chamber music. It was most often used as the basis of the first movements of sonatas, symphonies, concertos, and string quartets. A typical first movement form would include an introduction, exposition, development, recapitulation, and coda.

**Sonata-Allegro**

After the introductory material, the exposition presented the primary theme in the tonic key, followed by a secondary theme in a contrasting key and usually in a contrasting mood. Frequently, a short transition section moved the music from one key to the next. The second section ended in the new key, meaning it did not return to the tonic key but ended with a feeling of instability, with an expectation to continue. The exposition sometimes was repeated.

The development section was that portion of the movement in which the composer's imagination could flourish. It was music based on prior material, such as a melodic fragment of the first theme, perhaps of the second or even both themes. The fragments became the basis of experimentation, of the composer's ability to use an idea and let it grow. Tonalities would be changed or avoided. The pitch contour of melodic fragments might be altered. Dynamics, rhythms, harmonies, and tempos might be modified, or a fragment might be passed from instrument to instrument, from a high to a low pitch area, from the brass to the woodwinds. Contrapuntal imitation might be inserted in an essentially homophonic texture, or the density (thickness) of the texture might be varied by adding or taking away the number of instruments playing at any time. Any or all of these devices created an unstable, restless music, a dramatic sense of conflict and tension that at some point demanded a return to stability.

The recapitulation provided the return to stability, the return to the tonic key, the primary theme of the exposition. Sometimes it was a literal repeat of the exposition, except the second theme area usually was kept in the tonic key rather than modulated to a new key as in the exposition. Other times the recapitulation was modified in a variety of ways, particularly at the point of bringing the movement to a close.

The coda was the concluding section, in effect, serving as an extension of the tonic ending but creating an anticipation of, a building up to, the final cadence.

The formal structure of the sonata-allegro form can be depicted as follows:

Introduction

Exposition (often repeated)

  a  (home key—stability)

  b  (contrasting key—instability)

Development (an expansion of the exposition, that is, music derived from previous material—instability)

Recapitulation (return to the tonic key—stability)

  a  (home key—stability)

  b  (home key—stability)

Coda

**Theme and Variations**

Any large instrumental work or movement of a work could be built on the statement of a **theme** followed by a series of variations on that theme. Variations were achieved in a variety of ways, such as changing tempo, dynamics, articulation (separated or connected notes, known as staccato or legato), tempo, tonality, mode (shift from major to minor), instrumentation, and texture. The variations were continuous, without clear stops, or sectional, with clear breaks between each variation.

**Minuet and Trio**

The **minuet and trio** is a stately dance movement in triple meter. It usually is the third movement of a symphony or string quartet. The minuet is a carry-over from the stylized dance forms popular during the Baroque period. In fact, this dance was the only one that maintained popularity during the Classic period. In the nineteenth century, this form was often replaced by a scherzo and trio, also in triple meter but played at a fast tempo with great rhythmic drive.

The minuet is in two parts with repeats; the trio is in a contrasting mood, also in two parts with each part repeated. The minuet returns but is traditionally played without repeats. Again, contrasting key relationships and returns to tonic are important in this form. A common minuet and trio form can be depicted as follows:

| Minuet | A | a (repeated) |
| (Part I) | | ba (repeated) |
| Trio | B | c (repeated) |
| (Part II) | | dc (repeated) |
| Minuet | A | ab |
| (Part I repeated) | | |

**Rondo**

The principle of contrast and return is integral to the **rondo.** It is based on two or more contrasting theme areas, areas in which changes are made in melody, mood, and tonality, each followed by a return to the original section. The concluding movement of a sonata, symphony, or string quartet frequently is in rondo form, which might be depicted as follows:

abaca or abacaba or abacada

**Composers**

After Johann Sebastian Bach and George Frideric Handel, the most famous composers of Western European art music are Franz Joseph Haydn, Wolfgang Amadeus Mozart, and Ludwig van Beethoven—all Austrians. (Beethoven was born in Germany but from the age of twenty-two spent the rest of his life in Austria.)

To illustrate the magnificent popularity of Mozart, Haydn, and Beethoven, music by these composers continues to be performed today, after two hundred years, by virtually every amateur and professional symphony orchestra, chamber group, choral organization, and opera company throughout the world. Their music is currently available on audio recordings numbering in the thousands. In fact, as of this writing, over 2,000 currently available compact disc recordings or sets of recordings feature the works of Haydn, Mozart, and Beethoven. Almost 1,000 of these recordings are by Mozart alone.

**Franz Joseph Haydn (1732– 1809)**

Haydn is the best example of a composer working successfully within the aristocratic, patronage system. For thirty years, he was chapelmaster and court composer to the Prince of Esterhazy in Austria. He wrote music for every occasion the court demanded and had a court orchestra and opera company at his disposal, an ideal circumstance for a composer.

Haydn was not a revolutionary, but he devised many new ways of putting music together to the delight of the people who bought his music and attended his concerts. His works were known throughout the German-speaking world, in France, Spain, Italy,

Leopold Mozart with his children Maria Anna and Wolfgang Amadeus. After a painting by L. C. de Carmontel.

and especially in England where he acquired his greatest fame and fortune. The best illustrations of his genius—his imagination, inventiveness, craftsmanship, and amazing productivity—are his sonatas, symphonies, and string quartets.

Haydn built on the past, absorbed romantic impulses just beginning to emerge, and brought the classical style of the late eighteenth century to its pinnacle of sophistication and perfection. He was innovative, a champion of new forms, yet his music was logical and coherent. He drew on the folk songs of his native Austria and on the dance music of the Baroque era. He drew on the dramatic power of modulation and changes of tonality and took to new heights the notions of thematic development and the use of motives as building blocks in the compositional process.

Haydn has enriched the literature of Western classical music immensely. His compositions include 104 symphonies, approximately 35 concertos for various solo instruments, 82 string quartets, and 60 solo piano sonatas. His most famous symphonies are No. 94, the "Surprise"; No. 100, the "Military"; No. 101, the "Clock"; No. 103, the "Drum Roll"; and No. 104, the "London." Of his string quartets, perhaps Op. 76, No. 3, the "Emperor," is his most famous. Best known among his many concertos are those for cello, harpsichord, organ, trumpet, and violin. Finally, he composed several widely performed masses and two oratorios, the most famous being *The Creation*.

## Wolfgang Amadeus Mozart (1756–1791)

Mozart was a prodigiously gifted child and a product of the Austrian aristocratic system. Since art music in the last quarter of the eighteenth century was not the sole province of the church or the aristocracy, Mozart was willing to sacrifice the security of the patronage system for personal freedom and the risks of earning a living from commissions, concerts, and the sale of his published music. He had a superior education, both from his father, Leopold, a court musician, and from his extensive travels to Italy,

**Figure 10.3**
Benjamin Franklin
playing his glass
harmonica.

France, England, Germany, and the Austrian imperial court in Vienna. His childhood was serene, but his adult life was one of struggle. He never sustained an important, permanent court post, had to struggle for recognition and income, and died in poverty.

Mozart was a genius with few peers in Western music. He was prolific and inventive, and he composed in virtually every popular form of the day. He brought to his music an unmatched lyricism and a profound expression that allows the devoted listener to gain deeper insights into his music from repeated hearings of the same works. His music conveys the elegance of court music at its best. It is sophisticated and urbane, reflecting the cosmopolitan culture of Salzburg and Vienna.

In his short life, Mozart created over 600 compositions. The final six symphonies are noteworthy. The last three—No. 39, No. 40, and No. 41 (the great "Jupiter" Symphony)—were not commissioned nor were they performed in his lifetime. Yet, they now rank among the most substantial of his instrumental works. He wrote concertos for bassoon, clarinet, horn, flute, flute and harp, and oboe, plus twenty-five piano and seven violin concertos. His "entertainment" music—the divertimentos and serenades—continue to be popular, especially the Serenade in G, commonly known as "Eine kleine Nachtmusik." His most unique works may well be his pieces written for glass harmonica (see fig. 10.3), an instrument invented by Benjamin Franklin, but the music is now more commonly performed on musical glasses. Mozart's chamber music continues to be widely performed and listened to, including his twenty-three string quartets, quintets for clarinet and strings and for piano and winds, and piano quartets and

Beethoven holding his
*Missa Solemnis.*

quintets. Professional solo pianists will have one or more of his seventeen piano sonatas in their repertoire. His *Requiem* stands out among his many excellent choral works.

As stated previously, *The Magic Flute, The Marriage of Figaro,* and *Don Giovanni* are Mozart's most famous operas. He had an affinity for opera and was able to combine the best of Italian and Germanic traits that dominated the operatic styles of this era. His gift for creating beautiful, lyrical melodies was combined with a strong sense of drama. With his collaborators, he infused opera also with a sense of humanity, a depth of feeling, and character development. Rather than stereotypical caricatures, human beings that were real and recognizable were central to Mozart's operas. More than lively tunes with light accompaniment, his music provided emotional and dramatic support for the characters and the plot.

**Ludwig van Beethoven (1770– 1827)**

Beethoven's earlier music fits the classical style, but his later and, for many scholars, his superior works display many of the characteristics of music associated with the Romantic period to follow. For this reason, he is frequently considered both a classic and a romantic composer, or perhaps more accurately, a composer who exemplifies a transition from the classic to the romantic style.

Beethoven began his career in the employment of the Bonn Court in his native Germany and, at the age of twenty-two, moved to Vienna where he spent the rest of his life and earned a comfortable living from the sale of his compositions. He was the first composer to live independent of the exclusive patronage of the aristocracy.

As with many of the great composers, their creative lives sometimes can be divided into discrete periods. With Beethoven, scholars identify three periods: (1) his first thirty-two years—his education and formative years—during which he became established as a great composer; (2) his middle life which produced many of his most famous works, and (3) his final period which produced fewer but intensely serious and personal works.

Beethoven freed music from the restraints of classicism by creating works that were models of subjective feeling and personal expression. His works influenced not only his contemporaries but numerous composers in later generations. He made significant contributions to virtually every musical form and every medium of musical expression from solo sonata to symphony to grand opera.

Beethoven's music can be beautiful and tender, but much of it is described as heroic, tempestuous, and powerful. It can be energetic, unpredictable, and highly emotional. In addition, his techniques for creating his powerful, personal statements include fragmentation of themes, harmonic clashes, and sustained tension. His works, compared with those of Mozart and Haydn and his own early works, can be lengthy as can be sections of movements, such as development sections or codas. In fact, the first movement of his ninth symphony lasts longer than his entire first symphony. Beethoven was an innovator in his use of the voice in traditionally instrumental works (his ninth symphony) and his dramatic, coloristic use of the piano.

His masterpieces are numerous and include his nine symphonies of which Nos. 3, 5, and 9 are considered monuments of symphonic literature; five piano concertos of which No. 5, the "Emperor" concerto, is the best known; a widely performed and recorded violin concerto; thirty-two piano sonatas of which the "Pathétique," the "Appasionata," and the "Moonlight" are the best known; chamber music, including sixteen string quartets, nine piano trios, and a quintet for piano and winds; numerous concert overtures including *Egmont* and *Prometheus;* an opera, *Fidelio;* and the great choral masterpiece, *Missa Solemnis.*

# A Study in Sound
*Music of Mozart, Haydn, and Beethoven*

# Example 1

**Symphony No. 39 in E♭—IV**

Composed in 1788 by Wolfgang Amadeus Mozart

Sonata-allegro form

The two most important principles in a sonata-allegro form are (1) contrast and repetition and (2) development; this movement exemplifies both quite clearly.

    The sonata-allegro form is comprised of the exposition (two theme areas), development, and recapitulation.

## Goals:

Be aware of the principles of stability/instability, tension/release, and contrast/repetition

Recognize the strong, identifiable nine-note motive at the beginning and be aware of the development of that motive.

Be aware of the basic characteristics of the sonata-allegro form.

Be aware of modulation (change of key) and return to the home key (tonic).

*Guide:* Count in a moderate two. The movement starts with the opening theme.

### Exposition

a     8 bars—main theme area; diatonic melody; soft; strings; open cadence;

       7 bars—loud; full orchestra; closed cadence;

    26 bars

    Extended material and bridge to second theme area;

       First segment (8 bars); starts simultaneously with end of previous phrase; full orchestra; Second segment (8 bars); continuation;

       Third segment (10 bars); full orchestra; chromatic, unstable; transition (bridge) to next section

b     12 bars—second theme area in new key; soft; motive related to first theme; thin texture; violins answered by woodwinds;

      8 bars—dialogue between flute and bassoon;

    43 bars

    Concluding section;

       First segment (17 bars); loud; thick texture (full orchestra);

       Second segment (20 bars); thin texture;

       Third segment (6 bars); full texture to final cadence of exposition.

**Development**—motivic development; main motive passed around from instrument to instrument, altered in many ways; chromatic; unstable; varying textures.

**Recapitulation**—return to material, style, and form of exposition.

*Reflections:* Recognize various changes, contrasts, and returns, particularly the return to the stable, tonic key after the unstable development section. Equate instability with tension and stability with release of tension.

Identify and retain in memory the initial motive in order to recognize it in its many manifestations as the piece unfolds.

# Example 2

**String Quartet in C, Op. 76, No. 3—II (excerpt)**

Composed by Franz Joseph Haydn (1732–1809)

Theme and variations form

The "Emperor" is one of the last of Haydn's eighty-two string quartets. It was composed in 1797 when Haydn was sixty-five years old. The second movement includes the hymn that Haydn was asked to write for the birthday of Emperor Francis. It was to become the Austrian national anthem. Melodies in other movements are equally lyrical or are delightfully folklike as in the fourth movement of this quartet.

## *Goals:*

Recognize the sounds and musical lines of each instrument.

In each variation, recognize and describe ways that Haydn varied the setting of the theme.

Recognize staccato/legato, tension/release, and simple/elaborate (florid) melodies.

*Guide:* For the listening guide, see Additional Listening, Ex. 1, page 245.

*Reflections:* Be aware of the varying roles or styles given to the instruments, considering such issues as foreground/background roles, simple/elaborate lines, or melody/countermelody. Recognize polyphonic/homophonic settings.

Discuss the values of the theme and variations form.

# Example 3

**Piano Sonata in C, No. 58—II**

Composed in 1789 by Franz Joseph Haydn

Rondo form

The sonata as it evolved in the Classic era was a multimovement work, usually in four movements, for solo piano or for solo violin and piano. Its movements were fast (sonata-allegro form), slow (ABA or other form), dance form (minuet and trio), and fast and spirited (frequently in rondo form). Even in the Classic period, many exceptions to these generalizations existed.

The rondo form typically has two or more contrasting sections, each followed by a return to the main theme area. Forms depicted as abaca or abacaba may be described as rondos.

This piano sonata is an exception; it has only two movements. Since this example is the second and last movement, it is not surprising that its tempo is fast and that it is in rondo form.

## *Goals:*

Recognize contrasting theme areas and returns to main themes and original keys.

Describe elements of balance and form in the classical style.

Recognize characteristics of tension and its resolution.

*Guide:* Count in a moderately fast two; the main theme, starting with a pickup, begins the movement.

a    12 bars—descending/ascending melodic contour;
   8 bars—four-note question/answer motive;
  12 bars—return to main motive.
b    Extended section; main motive in new key; increased chromaticism, tension, and instability; in two distinct segments, each ending quietly in a rising motion with tension (forward energy) that is resolved, after a pause, with the beginning of the next phrase.
a    12+4+14 bars—return to key of stability (the tonic key).
c    Extended section; in minor key; chromatic passages in middle obscure tonality that stabilizes again as it prepares for the return; as before, this section ends with a quiet, rising motion to an unstable chord that is resolved with the beginning of the return.
a    Extended section; in tonic key; is repeated after short transition and moves into diatonic concluding section and final cadence in original tonality.

# Example 1

**Additional
Listening**

**String Quartet in C, Op. 76, No. 3 "Emperor"**

1. Allegro

2. Poco adagio cantabile

3. Minuet and trio

4. Finale: Presto

Composed by Franz Joseph Haydn

For background information, see SS10/2, page 243.

## Guide:

**First movement**—sonata-allegro form; fast; duple meter

| Exposition | a | Main theme in the main key<br>Transition |
|---|---|---|
| | b | Second theme in a contrasting key (exposition repeated) |
| Development | | Based on both previous themes; ends with dancelike version of the first theme in major, then minor |
| Recapitulation | a | Main theme in the main key<br>Transition |
| | b | Second theme in the main key; (development and recapitulation repeated with modification) |
| Coda | | Coda begins after the quiet passage and energy stop, at the loud return to tonic; extends to final V–I cadence |

**Second movement**—theme and variations (comments provided for theme and first four of seven variations); a hymnlike melody; in a slow four, starting with two-beat pick-up on third beat

Main theme

| a | 4 bars | Primary phrase |
|---|---|---|
| a | 4 bars | Repeat |
| b | 4 bars | Contrasting phrase |
| c | 4 bars | New melodic idea starts on high note, then descends to V–I cadence |
| c | 4 bars | Repeat |

Variation 1 For two violins; melody in second violin; fast-moving; florid first violin part; shifting staccato and legato passages

Variation 2 Melody in cello; legato harmonization in second violin; harmonic "fill" in viola; more elaborate, syncopated countermelody in high first violin part

Variation 3 Melody in viola; polyphonic setting involving other three parts in equal, independent melodic lines

Variation 4 Melody in first violin; first phrase in chorale setting; second, third, and fourth phrases each shift to higher, more intricate interplay of parts; ends with four-bar extension, descending to a quiet cadence wherein all parts hold one dissonant chord until tension is resolved on the final tonic

**Third movement**—minuet and trio; triple meter; moderate tempo

| Minuet | A | a | Main theme; in two parts; starts in tonic key; ends in contrasting key |
|---|---|---|---|
| | | a | |
| | | b | More chromatic, unstable |
| | | a | Returns to and ends in tonic key |
| | | b | |
| | | a | |

| Trio | B | c | Lyrical; minor tonality |
|---|---|---|---|
|  |  | c |  |
|  |  | d | Similar theme; unstable tonality; then stable tonality in a different, major key |
|  |  | c | Returns to and ends in minor |
| Minuet | A | a |  |
|  |  | b |  |

**Fourth movement**—sonata-allegro form; in a fast duple meter

The entire movement is built on two motives, both stated at the opening. The second motive is derived rhythmically from the opening theme of the first movement. Listen to the polyphonic interplay and the imaginative use of imitation throughout; notice the fast triplet accompaniments and shifts between the minor and major modes.

| Exposition |  | a | In a minor key; |
|---|---|---|---|
|  |  |  | Motive 1—three loud, short chords |
|  |  |  | Motive 2—a quiet two-bar answer |
|  |  |  | Transition; quiet passage |
|  |  | b | Major tonality |
| Development |  |  |  |
| Recapitulation |  | a | Minor mode; modified repetition |
|  |  |  | Transition; high energy passage ends on dominant chord followed by a pause |
|  |  |  | Quiet, fragmented entrance to major key |
| Coda |  |  | Concluding section and final cadence. |

# Example 2

### Piano Sonata No. 8 in C, Op. 13 "Pathétique"

1. Grave; Allegro di molto e con brio

2. Adagio cantabile

3. Rondo: Allegro

Composed in 1799 by Ludwig van Beethoven

The "Pathétique" Sonata is one of Beethoven's most respected and best known works. It maintains many of the traditional classic ideals of clarity and balance. However, with its dramatic contrasts, powerful chords, and extreme ranges of emotional content, this sonata foreshadowed much of the nineteenth-century romantic spirit and of the intensely personal expressions to emerge in his later, more mature works.

## *Guide:*

**First movement**—sonata-allegro form; in C minor

| Introduction |  | Slow, solemn, dramatic |
|---|---|---|
| Exposition | a | Fast, energetic main theme; ascending followed by descending contour; in a minor key |
|  | b | Ascending then descending contour; in a different minor key |
|  | a |  |
|  | b | Return to slow introductory material |
| Development |  |  |
| Recapitulation |  | Ends with return of introductory motive |
| Coda |  | Based on first theme |

**Second movement**—rondo form (abaca) with two contrasting
sections; a slow four; in a major key

| a | 8 bars | Slow, hymnlike melody with simple, broken-chord accompaniment |
| a | 8 bars | Second phrase an octave higher |
| b | 12 bars | An ornamented melody with repeated blocked-chord accompaniment |
| a | 8 bars | Melody in low octave with broken-chord accompaniment |
| c | 14 bars | In minor mode; triplet figures prominent in accompaniment and in low-register answering figures |
| a | 8 bars | Triplet accompaniment continues |
| a | 8 bars | Melody an octave higher; seven-bar extension or coda concludes with series of V–I progressions |

**Third movement**—rondo form (abacaba); lively, dancelike; in the tonic key of C
minor

| a | Extended phrase |
| b | Three subparts; major key; aggressive triplet patterns |
| a | Tonic minor |
| c | Legato; soft syncopation; builds in energy and intensity; major key; ends like the second theme, with long high note and descending scale to sustained, unstable chord |
| a | Tonic minor |
| b | Derived from subparts of *b* section |
| a | Tonic minor; long extension and coda |

*Discography*

***Ex. 1***   Mozart, Wolfgang Amadeus. Symphony No. 39 in E♭ (IV). Columbia MDK-44648. 4:05.

***Ex. 2***   Haydn, Franz Joseph. String Quartet in C, Op. 76, No. 3. Haydn Society HS9058. 5:10.

***Ex. 3***   Haydn, Franz Joseph. Piano Sonata in C, No. 58 (II). Columbia IMT 37792. 3:20.

*Summary*

The Classic period was an outgrowth of the aristocratic life of Austria, but it also saw the decline of the aristocracy throughout Europe, the rise of the middle class, the beginnings of the industrial revolution, and the urbanization of western societies.

Musically, Bach and Handel exemplified a culmination of all that went before; their deaths marked the end of an era. With the music of many Germans, Austrians, and Italians, but particularly, the music of Mozart, Haydn, and Beethoven, a new style emerged, resulting in a tremendous wealth of literature—the so-called masterworks. These masterworks are still in common use today: music for piano; for orchestral instruments and the symphony orchestra, the development of the sonata, symphony, concerto, and chamber music genres; and the standardization of the sonata-allegro and other forms that have maintained continuity to this day.

In many respects, the mid-eighteenth century—the Classic period—signals the beginning of the modern age in music.

*Terms and Concepts*

| | |
| --- | --- |
| ***Symphony orchestra*** | ***Cadenza*** |
| ***Chamber music*** | ***Sonata-allegro form*** |
| ***Symphony*** | ***Coda*** |
| ***Concerto*** | ***Opera*** |
| ***Sonata*** | |

# Chapter 11

# Music of the Romantic Period (Nineteenth Century)

Frederic Chopin playing in the salon of Prince Radziwill. Painting by Siemisadszki.

Beethoven was an individualist, defying the aristocracy and rejecting the rigidity of the classical forms. Caught up in the spirit of the French Revolution and with the rise of the capitalistic middle class, he sought to express his own personal convictions in his music with emotion and with imagination. Beethoven desired to be different.

These attributes of Beethoven summarize the attributes of the Romantic period—highly individual, highly personal. One composer's beliefs and practices often were frequently in opposition to another's. The Romantic period saw little unity of musical expression. The rise of individualism and the decrease in aristocratic patronage, in effect, put composers "on their own."

The business of music became an important factor in the Romantic period as the patronage system shifted from the aristocracy to the public—from court-employed composers and performers to musicians who had to cultivate their own support through audience development and publishing. They had to "sell" their music to the public. This need to sell created new jobs in the music profession: concert managers (or impresarios as they were then known), music publishers, and music critics. It became apparent that an artist with a dynamic and colorful personality would have a significant asset.

It was found that the public craved virtuosity and dazzling displays of technical skill. The greatest virtuosos became great stars, whether performers or composers. The orchestra conductor also became a virtuoso due to the increased size and complexity of the orchestra. Many conductors also developed "star" personalities and became popular celebrities.

Music of the nineteenth century, because much of it was technically demanding, was no longer intended for amateur performance. The demand for professionals created a demand for teachers. Thus, in the nineteenth century, the teaching of music became an established profession. The nineteenth century was a period of polarities that ranged between the extremes of tradition and experimentation, music for huge orchestras and intimate pieces for solo instrument or voice, classical forms and new forms, nationalism and internationalism, and absolute music and program music. A composer may very well have been active at both ends of these polarities or at any point in between.

Two twentieth-century virtuosos (a) Leonard Bernstein, (b) Luciano Pavarotti with Zubin Mehta.

*a.*

*b.*

## Musical Characteristics

Music created for its own sake without any extramusical connotation is known as **absolute music.** It typically is characteristic of such genres as the sonata, symphony, or concerto. In the nineteenth century, **program music** became a prevailing interest. This music was created to depict moods, images, stories, and characters. Program music reflects the composers' and the audiences' interests in poetry, the unity of music and words, and the use of music to create imagery suggested by a text. Romantic composers also went to greater lengths than before to create music without text that could stimulate subjective feelings, moods, and images of places or things and to associate specific musical ideas with characters in a story.

Music in the nineteenth century was primarily homophonic, with a predominance of singable, lyrical, "romantic" melodies. Folk melodies or melodies in a folk style became common as composers sought not only new modes of expression but successful ways of reaching wider audiences. Melodies usually related directly to the underlying harmonies and harmonic progressions, particularly in the first half of the century. The second half of the century saw an increase in chromaticism and dissonance in an attempt to create musical tension and intensified emotion in the music. Much music was highly emotional with strong contrasts, unexpected chords, and long buildups to exciting climaxes. The increase in chromaticism and dissonance brought with it a decrease in tonal clarity—a weaker sense of tonal center. By the beginning of the twentieth century, tonality in much music was obscure even to the point of being nonexistent.

Rhythm was less regular and more complex in nineteenth-century music, increasingly so in the second half of the century. Composers increasingly avoided the regular stress on each downbeat, used more polyrhythms and more syncopation, and made frequent use of tempo changes. These tempo changes included accelerandos (getting faster), ritardandos (getting slower), and rubato (a slight speeding up and slowing down that creates a flexible pulse and a highly expressive manner). The increase in complex rhythm brought with it a decrease in the sense of meter.

The nineteenth-century orchestra was bigger, more lush, and thicker in texture than the classical orchestra. The use of the tone color of instruments became an art in itself—the art of orchestration. Composers used the instruments of the orchestra not only to play melodies and harmonies but to create special sonorities unique to individual instruments or special combinations of instruments. As the industrial revolution dawned in the early nineteenth century, instrument manufacturers sought ways to enhance the resonance and range of all orchestral instruments. New instruments were added to accommodate the creative needs for new expressions and new tonal colors. Some new instruments carried the names of their makers or musicians responsible for their use. Two such examples are the saxophone, named for Adolphe Sax, and the sousaphone, named for John Phillip Sousa.

## Forms and Genres

The multimovement sonata genre, whether a solo piece, symphony, concerto, or chamber work, continued as a basic structure in the Romantic period, as was the sonata-allegro form and other classical forms discussed in the previous chapter. These, however, were flexible models that few composers adhered to rigidly. Forms were not as precise or as clear and not as symmetrical or balanced as in the music of the classic composers. Phrases tended to be longer and less regular than in classical music with internal cadences frequently less clear, suggesting an ongoing momentum rather than an obvious ending to a phrase or a section.

Many composers excelled in writing symphonies, concertos, or chamber works, especially Beethoven, Schubert, Brahms, Mendelssohn, Tchaikovsky, and Mahler. Important new instrumental genres that became popular during the nineteenth century were the **symphonic poem,** forms derived from stage productions (the overture, prelude,

Calvin Simmons conducting a large symphony orchestra.

suite, and incidental music), and the woodwind quintet (flute, oboe, clarinet, horn, and bassoon), a genre established for virtuosic wind playing to complement the firmly established string quartet.

The symphonic poem is a one-movement work with contrasting moods and is derived from the romantic interest in music that describes something (program music) in contrast to most symphonies and concertos that do not carry any nonmusical associations (absolute music).

The overture or prelude begins an opera or ballet. The suite is an orchestral arrangement of songs or dances from within an opera or ballet. The incidental music was performed between acts of a production. Many times these instrumental works, performed as symphonic concert pieces, were more widely performed, became more well-known, and were more lasting than the original stage productions.

Opera with its sense of drama and its combining of music, poetry, drama, and visual effects had tremendous emotional impact in the nineteenth century and was a major medium of romantic expression. The great nineteenth-century composers of opera were Verdi, Wagner, Rossini, Puccini, and Richard Strauss. Opera flourished during the eighteenth and nineteenth centuries in France, Germany, and Italy and continues to appeal to a public that enjoys music with action, plots, and spectacle—attributes that typically do not characterize symphonic music or chamber music. Operas continue to include arias, recitatives, solo ensembles, choruses, and orchestral accompaniment. The orchestra plays the overture, preludes to acts, any incidental music, and the accompaniments to singers and dancers.

Grand operas, with their large number of singers, elaborate scenery and effects, and serious plots, often include visual diversions through pageantry and ballet. Comic operas and operettas, in contrast to grand opera, generally are lighter in mood, less complex, often satirical, and frequently include spoken dialogue. The **libretto** is the text of the opera and is created to allow the plot to be interrupted, perhaps enhanced, by the various songs, choral numbers, and dances. Whereas singers in choruses are identified as

A scene from a
nineteenth-century
ballet, Tchaikovsky's
*Swan Lake*.

sopranos, altos, tenors, and basses, opera singers are known as coloratura, lyric, or dramatic sopranos, mezzo-sopranos, contraltos, lyric or dramatic tenors, baritones, and basses.

Opera is very popular in the United States with professional companies existing in virtually every large metropolitan area. Additionally, performances may be seen and heard by many regional semiprofessional or amateur companies and by productions in large departments or schools of music in colleges and universities.

Another form of stage production that became popular in the nineteenth century was the **ballet,** which at first was part of opera and was then created as an independent genre. It featured both solo and ensemble dancing and represented the highest form in the art of dance. Tchaikovsky composed the most memorable music for ballet in the nineteenth century, including *Sleeping Beauty, Swan Lake,* and *The Nutcracker.*

Along with the large orchestras and orchestral forms and the elaborate stage productions, there emerged new, miniature forms at the other extreme: short "character pieces" for solo piano and the solo song with piano accompaniment. The one-movement, **character pieces,** exemplified by the solo piano works of Chopin, are expressive, at times lyrical, at times dramatic, and often technically demanding virtuoso pieces. These ballades, capriccios, impromptus, intermezzos, nocturnes, mazurkas, polonaises, rhapsodies, preludes, waltzes, and études each have their own distinctive mood and character. They rank among the best of solo piano literature from the nineteenth century, continue to appear in the repertoire of any concert pianist, and are studied by virtually all advanced piano students.

The songs, known as **art songs** or lieder (singular: lied), are best exemplified in the works of Schubert who wrote over six hundred of them. Most are short and are set to the works of German poets, notably Goethe. The interest among German poets in creating lyric poetry stimulated interest by composers in creating art songs. The emergence of the piano in the nineteenth century as the primary keyboard instrument in concert halls and homes also contributed to the development of the art song. Its expressive power was well suited as a means of enhancing the varying moods and images of the art song.

The German lieder are known for their beautiful, expressive melodies. Many are strophic (same music for each verse of the poetry), but in some songs the music changes to reflect the changes of character or mood of the text. Today art songs from the nineteenth century are programmed regularly on recitals by both professional and amateur singers.

## Composers

At least thirty composers from the nineteenth century are well-known to large numbers of Americans, and their music is performed regularly in concert and on stage in the United States each year. All are men. It is unfortunate but not surprising that the two most prominent women artists and composers of the nineteenth century are usually presented in history books not as musicians in their own right but in relationship to other composers who happen to have been important men in their lives. These women were Clara Schumann, a concert pianist and composer who was married to Robert Schumann, and Fanny Mendelssohn, the sister of Felix Mendelssohn and an important composer in her own right.

All who claim even a minimal knowledge of Western European, classical music should have some acquaintance with the contributions and the music of at least the most prominent among the great romantic composers.

## Franz Schubert (1797–1828)

Schubert was endowed with a prodigious natural gift for music. He composed 143 songs before he turned nineteen and 179 more works the following year, including major choral and symphonic pieces. His entire adult life, however, was a constant struggle against illness and poverty. Without position or patronage, he eked out a precarious existence from the generosity of friends and a few commissions, the sale of a few pieces to publishers, and some private teaching.

Schubert is best known for his more than 600 lieder. These art songs embody a wide range of feelings, from elegant simplicity to bold, dramatic expression—from simple folklike songs to elaborate ballads of great musical sophistication. The outstanding qualities of his compositions are lyrical melodies, colorful harmonies, and sensitivity to the poetic expression of the texts. "The Erlking," "Who is Sylvia," and "Serenade" are among his best known solo songs, although some of his most important songs are found in his two song cycles (sets of songs with a common unifying factor), "Die schöne Müllerin" and "Winterreise."

His nine symphonies reflect the classical ideals of form and structure yet are infused with the songlike qualities of Viennese romanticism. Of these works, No. 8, the "Unfinished" (a symphony in two movements) and No. 9, "The Great," are the most important. His short piano pieces, including the impromptus, the twenty-two solo piano sonatas, and the "Moments Musicaux," are widely performed today. His best chamber works include the "Death and the Maiden" quartet, the "Trout" piano quintet, the Quintet in C for strings, and two piano trios. The *Mass in G* is included among his best choral works.

## Felix Mendelssohn (1809–1847)

Mendelssohn came from a wealthy, educated German family of high social and cultural status. His home was a gathering place for musicians and intellectuals. He was surrounded by the finest opportunities for an aspiring musician, including the resources of a private orchestra. He was widely traveled and became famous throughout Europe and England.

His music had wide appeal. It was traditional and closely aligned to the classical ideals of form and structure. His classical spirit was reflected in his orderly, elegant, graceful expression, whereas his romantic spirit showed through primarily in the emotional expressiveness and sentimentality of his melodies. He is best known for his "Scotch" and "Italian" symphonies, the oratorio *Elijah,* the Violin Concerto in E Minor, "The Hebrides Overture," and incidental music to *Midsummer Night's Dream.*

**Frédéric Chopin
(1810–1849)**

Born and educated in Poland, Chopin spent his entire professional life in Paris. He was a virtuoso pianist but did not seek to develop an extensive concert career. He preferred private performances in the aristocratic salons and intimate gatherings of wealthy Parisians. In Paris, Chopin was profoundly influenced by his lover, George Sand (her pen name). She was a cigar-smoking novelist and feminist with whom he lived for nine years. Many of his greatest and best known works were created during this period.

Chopin is known almost exclusively for his short, one-movement piano compositions: études, preludes, mazurkas, waltzes, scherzos, impromptus, polonaises, nocturnes, and ballades. He also wrote three solo piano sonatas and two piano concertos. His piano "miniatures" included stylized dances (not intended for dancing), pieces that reflected the spirit of the Polish people, and virtuoso pieces that retained beautiful melodic invention. He expanded the pianistic concept to a greater extent than his contemporaries or predecessors by expanding the use of chromaticism and creating more elaborate, decorative melodies, particularly in subsequent repetitions of a theme. He incorporated more bold, colorful harmonies with daring dissonances, unresolved tensions, and unusual modulations. He freed adherence to the pulse by increased application of rubato and developed new uses of the pedal that allowed a smooth, sustained quality and that enhanced the harmonic texture through innovations in the left-hand technique.

**Johannes Brahms
(1833–1897)**

Born in Germany, Brahms moved to Vienna at the age of thirty and lived there for the rest of his life. He worked mostly as a freelance composer and pianist. He became world famous and part of a mid-nineteenth century controversy between the traditionalists of which he was the acknowledged master and the musical revolutionaries led by Richard Wagner. Such controversies were fed by the propensity of composers like Schumann and Wagner to function also as music critics and essayists.

While touring, Brahms met and became friends with Robert and Clara Schumann, friendships that shaped the course of his artistic and personal life. He fell in love with Clara, creating an intense personal conflict between loyalty to a friend and his love for Clara. He also was torn between love and freedom, for when Robert died, Brahms never married Clara (nor anyone else). He preferred a separate but intimate friendship with Clara that continued until her death in 1896.

Brahms' music is full of passion. It is often introspective, mellow, and full of rich, dark sonorities. His melodies are lyrical, even with complex rhythms or intricate polyphonic textures. His phrases can be irregular, at times conflicting with the prevailing meter. He was a romanticist in his emotional expressiveness but a classicist in his formal organization. Devoted to the principles of the sonata form, his orchestral music was full and massive. He was interested in absolute music, writing little program music except for his songs and choral works.

Brahms is best known for his four symphonies; a violin concerto; two piano concertos; Hungarian Dances; the Liebeslieder waltzes, important trios, quartets, quintets, and sextets; two serenades; the *German Requiem;* sonatas for piano, cello, violin, and clarinet; and numerous short piano pieces, songs, and choral works.

**Richard Wagner
(1813–1883)**

Wagner was a German composer of opera who was caught up in the revolutionary movements of his time. He was raised in a theatrical family and was virtually self-taught as a musician and composer. He studied the scores of previous masters, notably Beethoven. Active in the revolution of 1848, he was forced to flee his country and took up exile in Switzerland. While there, he set forth his theories about art, describing an ideal art form in which music, drama, poetry, and stagecraft would all have equal emphasis. He called this form music drama rather than opera. In the German town of Bayreuth, a theater designed by Wagner was built to produce his operas, and to this

Johannes Brahms.

day it serves as a center for lovers of Wagnerian opera. As a composer and author, Wagner's artistic philosophies influenced both contemporary and future musicians as well as other artists and writers.

Wagner's music dramas were symphonic in nature with strong emphasis on orchestral color, notably the sounds of the powerful brass instruments. The music was continuous, and dramatic flow was without interruption from arias, recitatives, and ensembles in the traditional sense. Wagner used chromaticism, dissonance, vague or nonexisting cadences, and unresolved tension. Much of his music had virtually no sense of tonality and no sense of symmetry or balanced phrase structure. He made extensive use of the *leitmotif,* which is a recurring musical motive associated with a character or a mood. It contributed unity to his music in the absence of more traditional forms and structures.

His theories were exemplified in his cycle of four operas known as *The Ring of the Nibelung,* which took twenty years to complete, and in *Tristan and Isolde,* a work of great beauty, sustained tension, and dramatic expression. Wagner was his own librettist, further contributing to his ability to fuse the arts into a unified whole. He was aided greatly by a wealthy patron, King Ludwig of Bavaria, who helped Wagner complete *The Ring* and create a lavish production of the cycle in Munich in 1876.

**Guiseppe Verdi (1813–1901)**

Verdi was the greatest figure of Italian opera—a national hero. He had a wealthy patron, a secure job, and became a world-renowned figure. He became famous in America and was invited to help open Carnegie Hall in 1891.

Verdi composed for a population whose main source of musical enjoyment was opera. He maintained the traditions of the aria and recitative and included choruses and ensembles as in earlier operas. He enriched his operas with superb melodies and a strong theatrical sense. Conventional harmonies and predictable rhythms and meters characterize most of his music.

Verdi's early operas had little continuity of dramatic action and in some cases were nationalistic and political. His next operas, *Rigoletto, La Traviata,* and *Il Trovatore,* are among his best known and durable works. They are in the repertoire of virtually any modern opera company. These operas portray violent emotions and such dramatic behaviors as dishonor, seduction, and murder. His last operas, including *Aida,* provide a greater sense of drama and spectacle, richer harmonies, and a more important orchestra than in his earlier operas. In these, he lessened the differences between the aria and the recitative.

The librettos were invariably unhappy with tragic endings. They portrayed real-life passions and emotions conveyed through both heroes and villains. The dramatic action was typically swift-moving, energetic, and full of conflict and tension.

Among his few nondramatic works are two successful, large choral compositions: the *Te Deum* and *Requiem.*

**Peter Ilyich Tchaikovsky (1840–1893)**

The most famous Russian composer, Tchaikovsky, was appointed professor of composition at the Moscow Conservatory at the age of twenty-five. He benefited from a wealthy patroness, Mme. Von Meck, which enabled him to quit his teaching position to devote his life to composition.

Tchaikovsky's music is both nationalistic and international, capturing the spirit of Russian folk song but also influenced by Italian opera, French ballet, and German symphonies and songs. His music is tuneful, accessible, sometimes exciting, sometimes sentimental, and tremendously popular to this day. It has a directness and a range of emotional expression that has wide appeal. It is music full of beautiful melodies, striking contrasts, powerful climaxes, and passionate emotions.

His best known works include the violin and piano concertos; his symphonies, particularly Nos. 4, 5, and 6 (the "Pathétique"); the "1812 Overture"; and "Romeo and Juliet," a symphonic overture-fantasia. The ballets, *Swan Lake, Sleeping Beauty, The Nutcracker,* and orchestral excerpts taken from these ballets, are also well-known works.

**Plate 17**

Performance of Tchaikovsky ballet, *The Nutcracker.*

**Plate 18**

P. A. Renoir. *Young Girls at the Piano.* Joslyn Art
Museum, Omaha, Nebraska.

Marc Chagall. *Green Violinist,* 1923–1924. Oil on canvas
78″ × 42″ × ¾″. Solomon R. Guggenheim, 1937.
Photo: David Heald. #37.446.

Georges Braque. *Man with Guitar,* 1914. Paris, Museum
National Art Moderne. Giraudon/Art Resource, New
York.

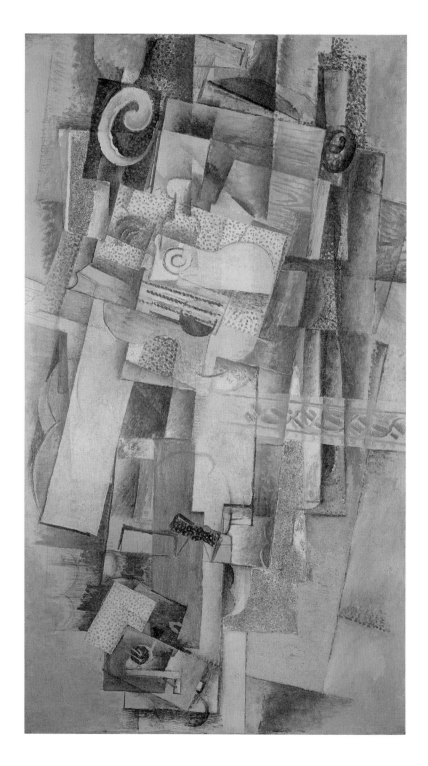

**Plate 20**

Henri Matisse. *Piano Lesson,* 1916. Oil on canvas,
8′½″ × 6′11¾″. Collection, The Museum of Modern
Art, New York. Mrs. Simon Guggenheim Fund.

**Plate 21**

Andy Warhol. *Green Coca Cola Bottles,* 1962. Oil on canvas, 82¼″ × 57″. Collection of Whitney Museum of American Art, New York. Gift of the Friends of the Whitney Museum of American Art.

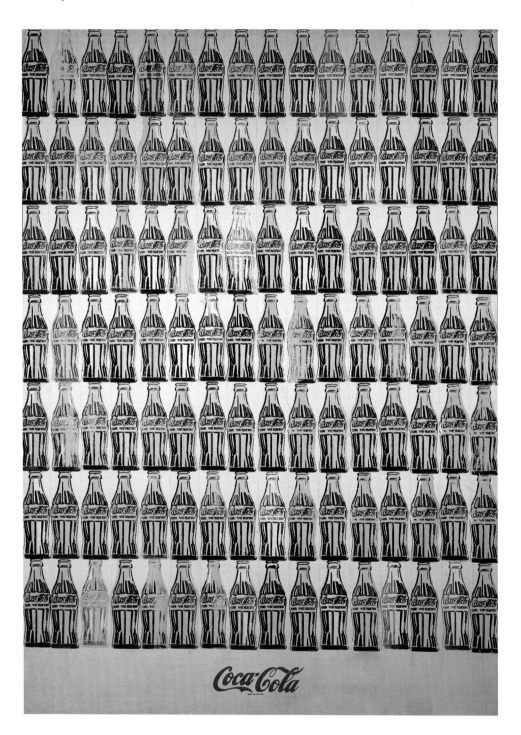

# Example 1

**"Der Wanderer"** (The Wanderer)—1816

**"An Silvia"** (Who is Sylvia?)—1826

Two art songs composed by Franz Schubert (1797–1828)

Schubert had a remarkable gift for creating melodies that were expressive, emotional, dramatic, sad, or mysterious. In them, he epitomized the essence of romanticism. His songs, for solo voice and piano accompaniment, ranged from short, simple pieces to extended, more dramatic, and emotionally complex works.

## *Goals:*

Recognize diatonic melody and when the melody deviates from the key, perhaps becoming more chromatic.

Recognize diatonic, consonant harmony and places where the chords deviate from the key, adding color to the music and at times creating modulation.

Be aware of expressive qualities in music.

## *Guide:* "The Wanderer"

The restless, unhappy wanderer, roaming the world in search of the land of his dreams, expresses his longing, his questioning, and concludes that his happiness is in the land where he is not.

The music is not strophic. It changes to reflect the changing content and moods of the text. It provides different music for each verse of poetry.

"Who is Sylvia?"

A simple accompaniment of a bass ostinato and repeated chords supports one of Schubert's most beloved songs. It is strophic (the same music used for each verse of poetry), yet one hears dramatic changes of mood as each verse of the poetry is repeated.

The text is from Shakespeare and was translated into German by one of Schubert's friends. It honors Sylvia, extolling her beauty, her grace, and her kindness, but it does not answer who Sylvia is! The text follows:

*Who is Sylvia? What is she*
*That all our swains commend her?*
*Holy, fair, and wise is she,*
*The heaven such grace did lend her*
*That she might admired be.*

*Is she kind as she is fair?*
*For beauty lives with kindness:*
*Love doth to her eyes repair*
*To help him of his blindness:*
*And, being help'd, inhabits there.*

*Then to Sylvia, let us sing,*
*That Sylvia is excelling;*
*She excels each mortal thing*
*Upon the dull earth dwelling;*
*To her let us garlands bring.*

**Reflections:** Compare the musical characteristics of these two examples. Is one more chromatic than the other? more tense and dramatic? more symmetrical in its structure? more complex? more expressive?

Discuss the differences in the two accompaniments.

Differentiate between a song that is strophic and one that is not. Discuss the advantages and disadvantages of each.

# Example 2

**Preludes, Op. 28**—Nos. 1, 6, 16

By Frédéric Chopin (1810–1849)

Composed in 1839

Chopin's twenty-four preludes, each in a different major or minor key, have no structural or stylistic similarity, whereas his other sets of pieces (polanaises, noctunes, and ballades, for example) share common musical characteristics.

The preludes are varied in style and mood. They may be short, miniature pieces or extended works having contrasting moods, and they may range in emotion from quiet serenity to chromatic restlessness. They are examples of absolute rather than program music.

## Goals:

Differentiate between absolute and program music. Compare the preludes with Schubert's art songs.

Recognize chromatic tension and resolution. Identify chromaticism in melody.

Recognize rubato, arpeggios, inner and outer "voices" on the piano, and left-hand/right-hand pitch areas on the piano.

## *Guide:*

### No. 1 in C Major

From the complex interplay of sound, listen to the following:

1. The harmonic progressions
2. The bass line, played on each downbeat
3. The melody with many off-beats
4. Arpeggios that constitute the inner voices

### No. 6 in B Minor

Differentiate between the left-hand melody (rubato and many repeated chords) and the right-hand accompaniment (a rise-and-fall contour within each phrase).

Listen for the phrase structure and points of repetition, contrast, and return.

### No. 16 in B♭ Minor

An introduction of six accented chords followed by a pause prepares the listener for the fast and furious melody of constantly running notes, a perpetual motion in the right hand with a simple, crisp, ostinato accompaniment in the left hand.

The contrast is in the harmonic structure and its developing chromatic intensity. Listen for the point this intensity ceases, when the harmonic movement stops, and when the melody continues with a slight ritard.

This point prepares the listener for the return of the main theme (this is similar to the turn-around or break in jazz).

*Reflections:* What makes the preludes absolute music? Give a programmatic title to each one. Could they, then, be classified as program music. Is the determining factor only the title?

What musical characteristics in the preludes enable them to be classified as romantic music?

In what ways are they different from a piano sonata?

Discuss the relationship between right-hand and left-hand functions in each example.

## Additional Listening

## Example 1

**"Romeo and Juliet"**—an overture-fantasia

Composed in 1869 by Peter Ilyich Tchaikovsky (1840–1893)

Revised and published in 1881

The concert overture is a musical genre new to the nineteenth century and the history of Western music. It is a one-movement concert piece that is not associated with a stage production but is based on a nonmusical idea such as a literary work. In this sense it is considered program music. One can appreciate the music on its own merits, however, whether or not one knows the relationship of this music to Shakespeare's play.

***Guide:*** Composed for large symphony orchestra; in sonata-allegro form.

### Introduction

> Opens with slow, somber melody in chordal texture in simple, direct rhythm; the first statement is in clarinets and bassoons;
>
> Second part—an extension beginning in the strings and upper woodwinds. It rises to thick texture with full orchestra;
>
> Restatement of first part in new guise; stated in the woodwinds to the accompaniment of running notes in the strings;
>
> Chordal theme in upper strings with running accompaniment in oboes, bassoons, and violas;
>
> Extended to its greatest point of intensity; loud chords derived from opening theme; suddenly quiet, then accelerando to exposition.

### Exposition

a    The conflict theme; sharp, crisp, syncopated motive; loud, fast; full orchestra; extends with full orchestra, then drops out suddenly at transition to the second theme.

b    The love theme—first part; lyrical, romantic—one of the best known melodies in classical music; opens with English horn and viola; light texture, small orchestra; simple, chordal accompaniment in horns;

> The love theme—second part; provides a gentle, rocking motion; violins; straight rhythm in groups of four, but each group starts on the fourth beat of each bar;
>
> Theme repeated an octave higher; flutes and oboes; this time, accompanied by a rocking, two-note motive in the horn;
>
> Transition to the development section; energy diminishes through a static, sustained passage with harp ostinato.

### Development

> Starts with opening theme of the exposition; this as well as material from the introduction and the love theme are developed;
>
> Fast, furious scale passages in the strings lead to recapitulation.

### Recapitulation

> Begins with first theme of exposition;
>
> The love theme recurs in a context of great swells—ascending scales leading to huge climaxes;
>
> Recapitulation ends when energy diminishes to the low sustained note in the cellos and basses.

### Coda

> Begins quietly with motive derived from both parts of the second theme of the exposition;
>
> Fullness of texture increases, ending with a powerful timpani roll and concluding chords.

# Example 2

**Symphony No. 3 in F Major**

I. Allegro con brio

II. Andante

III. Poco allegretto

IV. Allegro

Composed in 1883 by Johannes Brahms (1833–1897)

This work is scored for full symphony orchestra: woodwinds in pairs plus contrabassoon; two trumpets, four horns, three trombones; strings; and tympani. It is in the classical form of four movements and represents a balance of romantic and classical ideals.

First movement—sonata-allegro form; in F major; fast, energetic.

### Introduction

Three chords in the woodwinds and brasses, the third chord overlapping the beginning of the first theme.

### Exposition

a   First theme area; descending arpeggio in the violins; loud, forceful; in F major;

Transition to second theme area—extended; new thematic idea—ascending, legato, stepwise motion; stated first in violins and cellos.

b   Second theme area—lyrical melody with a contour of rather quick rises and falls; stated first in clarinet, then answered by oboe and violas; in A major;

Transition to development—extended; builds to big climax through ascending chromatic scales followed by huge descending, syncopated arpeggios.

### Development

Begins with huge syncopated chords followed immediately by the *b* theme stated in the bassoon, violas, and cellos;

Transition—begins with soft, low chords—a slowing of rhythmic movement, then a slow statement of the opening theme followed by descending scale passages.

### Recapitulation

Forceful return of the descending arpeggios (*a* theme) in F major, followed by other material from the exposition including the *b* theme now in D major;

Transition to the coda—similar to transition to development section; starts quietly then builds through ascending chromatic passages, then strongly syncopated descending chords to the return of the *a* theme, which begins the coda.

### Coda

Starts forcefully with the *a* theme in F major, then after several ascending arpeggios and one final descending statement of the theme, the movement ends quietly.

**Second movement**—sonata-allegro form; in C major; slow, quiet.

### Exposition

a   Opening theme stated in woodwinds and brasses, melody in clarinet; in dialogue with strings; simple, diatonic; five-note motive characterized by rocking motion ending with descending interval; in C major;

Transition—quiet, descending, slowing activity.

b   Soft, quiet melody; small range; starts in clarinet and bassoon, then oboe and horn; in A minor;

Second part—in the strings, answered by woodwinds—features legato, descending, scalelike melody.

### Development

A short section derived from principle theme, starting with bassoons and cellos accompanied by a countermelody in the violins; then main theme in violins.

### Recapitulation

In high woodwinds; beginning statement in slower rhythm than original motive.

### Coda

Begins with slow, lush romantic texture—melody in violins; procedes through a surging, ascending passage; then a final statement of the theme by the clarinet; finally subsides to a quiet ending.

**Third movement**—ABA; in C minor; triple meter but only slightly dancelike.

A     First section

a   Long, flowing main theme—starts on third beat; twelve bar phrase; melody in cellos.

a   Melody in violins.

b   Subordinate, bridgelike passage—sixteen bars; begins with a sense of major tonality, then back to minor for return of first theme; ends with ascending arpeggios in cellos, then clarinet.

a   Melody in horn and high woodwinds.

B     Second section

c   In A♭ major; eight-bar phrase; more spritely than first theme; rhythmic three-note motive begins repeatedly on third beat.

c   Increased activity in accompaniment with arpeggios in strings.

d   Strings; legato; chromatic; unstable tonality; rise and fall of pitch and dynamics; pattern of ascending intervals, each successively higher.

c   Woodwinds; arpeggiated accompaniment.

d   Strings; as energy diminishes and texture sustains, woodwind patterns above strings signal return of first theme.

A     Return.

a   In C minor; horn.

a   Oboe.

b   Contrasting material in clarinets and bassoons, ending with ascending arpeggios in cellos, then flute.

a   Violins in octaves.

**Coda**

> Begins with unstable chords in woodwinds, each starting on second beat of the bar; woodwinds first, then woodwinds and strings combined; descends to quiet cadence in C minor.

## Fourth movement—ABABA; in F minor/F major; fast.

A a   In F minor; strings and bassoons in octaves; low register; repeated with modification, noticeably the rhythm; upper woodwinds.

  b   Shifting tonality; chordal; dark instrumentation (strings and woodwinds in low register); triplet figure prominent; answered by loud, contrasting chords and crisp rhythms, interrupted by a brief return of the first theme in the low strings and bassoons.

B c   In C major; small orchestra; light character; triplet figures in rising arpeggios; announced in cellos and horns; answered by violins and upper woodwinds.

  d   Loud, energetic, syncopated; full orchestra; subsides, signaling return of main theme by use of fragments of that theme.

A a   In F minor; upper woodwinds answered by woodwinds an octave lower; descending scales prepare for new material; descending, scalelike chords in simple, regular rhythm; short fragments derived from opening motive.

  b   Shifts to forceful, triplet rhythms and chords in woodwinds—derived from triplet pattern in second part of *A* section—and fast, highly chromatic accompaniment in the strings; full orchestra.

B c   Suddenly soft and legato; announced in cellos and horns.

  d   Full orchestra; a brief statement in F minor presented in a different guise precedes the coda.

**Coda**

> An extended section with different parts; some different material, but more like a development of the main theme; begins quietly with a tripletized version of the main melody; first, unstable harmony, then settles back in the main key of F major. As music approaches the symphony's conclusion, there appears subtly in the violins the F major arpeggio—the opening motive of the symphony—descending to a quiet ending.

# Example 3

**"The Moldau,"** from *My Fatherland*

Composed in 1874 by Bedrich Smetana (1824–1884)

A symphonic poem; program music

The Moldau is the second from a set of six symphonic poems depicting the folk songs, dances, legends, and the countryside of Smetana's native Bohemia, now Czechoslovakia. This poem depicts the scenes and episodes as the mighty Moldau river makes its way, sometimes rippling, sometimes turbulent, from two springs in the Bohemian woodlands to its majestic expanse as it approaches the city of Prague.

  This work is one of the best-known musical examples of late romantic tone painting and nationalistic music. It was scored for full orchestra: strings, woodwinds in pairs plus piccolo, two trumpets, four horns, three trombones, tuba, bass drum, cymbals, triangle, and harp.

Introduction—the rippling figure of two flutes as the two springs unite in a rushing brook that becomes the mighty Moldau.

a    The river's theme, stated in the violins, appearing sometimes serene, sometimes majestic, as the river wends its way.

b    Through dense woods, the horns convey the joyous sounds of the hunt.

c    Through meadows and fields, a wedding is celebrated in song and dance.

d    On moonlit nights, the water nymphs dance on the shimmering waves. Then, as the river passes fortresses and castles, it recalls glories of bygone days.

a    The main theme returns as the river appears in its fullest majesty. It then passes through the Rapids of St. John, where it takes on its most turbulent character.

e    A mighty chorale conveys the glory of The Moldau and all it represents—as it approaches Prague, then disappears into the distance.

**Discography**

**Ex. 1**    Schubert, Franz. "Der Wanderer" and "An Sylvia." Angel 35699. 8:30.

**Ex. 2**    Chopin, Frédéric. Preludes, Op. 28, Nos. 1, 6, 16. Columbia M-33507. 4:03.

**Summary**

The nineteenth century produced an amazing quantity and quality of composers and great works that are known, loved, and listened to extensively by people worldwide as we approach the twenty-first century. The purpose of this chapter has been to draw attention to the characteristics of nineteenth-century romanticism and to the composers and their compositions that best exemplify these characteristics.

For many, nineteenth-century music is a person's entree into the world of classical music. It is this music, plus that of Mozart and Haydn from the Classic period, that one first listens to, because these sounds are familiar and the music is to a great extent accessible at first hearing. At the same time, these masterpieces wear well. They can unfold subtleties and reveal new insights upon repeated hearings, and their ability to communicate feelings and to stimulate responses among large numbers of people spans generations, even centuries. These are the factors that separate a masterpiece—a great work of art in any medium or style—from the trite, the obvious, and the predictability of works of lesser quality and substance.

**Terms and Concepts**

| | |
|---|---|
| *Individualism* | *Prelude* |
| *Virtuoso* | *Suite* |
| *Absolute music* | *Incidental music* |
| *Program music* | *Grand opera* |
| *Accelerando* | *Libretto* |
| *Ritardando* | *Ballet* |
| *Rubato* | *Character piece* |
| *Orchestration* | *Lieder* |
| *Symphonic poem* | *German poetry* |
| *Overture* | |

# Chapter 12
# Music of the Twentieth Century
*Part I*

By the end of the Romantic period, the typical symphony orchestra had become more than twice the size of the orchestra of Mozart's time. Composers wrote for larger numbers of string instruments but also added a variety of additional brass, woodwind, and percussion. Instrumental compositions had become much longer and more involved, but new short forms for both piano and voice had emerged.

Chromaticism had increased and harmony had become complex, at times reducing the clarity of tonality to the point of an absence of tonal center. Melodies were longer, phrases were less clear, and form was more difficult to discern.

The nineteenth century was a time of great diversity of musical style. Composers created from a more personal viewpoint and, to a great extent, were interested in creating program music, depicting images, moods, and other nonmusical associations in their music. We see all these characteristics in the music of the twentieth century—and more.

Composers largely have returned to the classical ideals of order and objectivity, and we see a renewed interest in polyphonic texture. Modern music, as might be expected, has been subject to advancements in technology. It has been, like everything else, affected by the rate of speed of technological accomplishments in this century. As in the music of every past era, it reflects the good and the bad of the society in which it was created.

Many contemporary composers cannot easily be classified. In their search for originality, they will at different times experiment and discover new possibilities but will at other times return to selected practices of the past. When a composer returns to an old style, the music usually combines certain elements of the old with the new musical languages of the day. Other composers—the avant-garde—branch out into new directions, perhaps minimizing influences from the past and developing new musical language, compositional techniques, or aesthetic ideas.

As radical and extreme as much contemporary music may seem, it most likely does not represent any greater extreme than some of Monteverdi's music when compared with Palestrina's, or Beethoven's music when compared with Haydn's, or Wagner's music when compared with Brahms'. Stravinsky's ballet music of 1910–1913 was considered radical and barbaric at the time but is now ranked among the classics of the twentieth century.

Classical music from all historical periods is readily available through the broadcast media, recordings, and concerts. Listeners of classical music know the music of the past and for the first time in history prefer the music of the eighteenth and nineteenth centuries, rather than the music of contemporary, living composers. Many twentieth-century composers, however, create music not for the general public but for highly trained, professional musicians and scholars. This is the dilemma of contemporary music: its ability to speak in a twentieth-century language to a public that prefers a nineteenth-century language.

## Musical Characteristics

About the only generalization one can make about modern, classical music is to say, again, it is diverse and complex. Composers have written for every conceivable medium from a single, solo instrument to a huge symphony orchestra. They have written for conventional orchestra instruments, expected performers to play conventional instruments in nonconventional ways, and written for nonconventional instruments, adding them to the orchestra or creating new ensembles.

Composers have written for a tremendous diversity of instrumental combinations, many of them small in number and many incorporating the solo voice. When a composer wrote for large orchestra, the texture frequently was more thin and transparent than was common in orchestral writing toward the end of the nineteenth century.

To a great extent, modern composers have placed considerable emphasis on timbre and rhythm rather than on melody and harmony, creating the need for a different way of listening to music than when a melody predominates. Silence has become a conscious compositional device in modern music and not just a time for a performer to rest. Silences frequently have powerful aesthetic impact because of their extended length and place in the music.

The organization and form of music also is diverse and complex, ranging from totally controlled to free and improvisatory music. In controlled music, the composer gives minute instructions about how the music should be played. Conversely, in the more free music, performers, in some cases, are given instructions to improvise passages, usually within certain guidelines and restrictions. Much of this music is organized in time segments, measured in seconds, rather than bars and phrases.

The horizontal pitch organization is typically angular and disjunct, moving with wide intervals or skips, rather than in a smooth and conjunct manner as in traditional sounding melodies that move with a more stepwise contour. Melodic lines span wide, even extreme, ranges. They cannot be described as singable.

Balanced phrases, symmetrical patterns, forward energy culminating in clear cadences, and regular meter are not common in modern music. Traditional tonic/ dominant chord progressions are rare. Dissonance is the rule, and unresolved dissonances and sustained tension are common.

Modern music may be tonal, but any sense of a major or minor key most likely will be obscure. Some music lacks any sense of key feeling, and some may sound in two or more keys at the same time. Frequently, pitches are based on scales other than major or minor. They may incorporate scales found in other cultures or scales invented by the composer. The five-note pentatonic scale and a whole-tone scale, which excludes half steps, are common in some modern pieces. Many modern composers, however, are experimenting with a return to tonal music.

Essentially, the twentieth-century musical language is extremely different from the language common in the nineteenth century, and for much of contemporary music, a new notation had to be devised (see figure 12.1) to accommodate the sounds and the new concepts. It is a language with which many people feel uncomfortable, perhaps because it is a language they haven't completely come to understand.

## Major Composers and Stylistic Developments

Most developments in the history of Western art music evolved logically from past practices as composers sought to create music in new and inventive ways while building on existing forms. The continuum ranged from such conservative traditionalists as Mendelssohn and Brahms to such radical innovators as Berlioz and Wagner.

New developments occurred because composers reacted against what they considered excesses of the past or a particular style then in common practice. New developments also occurred because of external circumstances: economic factors, shifts in patronage expectations, or political upheavals.

As we approach the twenty-first century and look back on the present century, we can identify the master composers and see a number of important styles and techniques used by these composers that influenced other composers and that rightfully are considered major new developments in the history of Western music.

## Claude Debussy (1862–1918)

Debussy was an adventurous, French composer, who rejected many of the established musical styles, forms, and techniques. He is considered an "impressionist" composer, but he did not set out to compose impressionistic music; others gave his music that label.

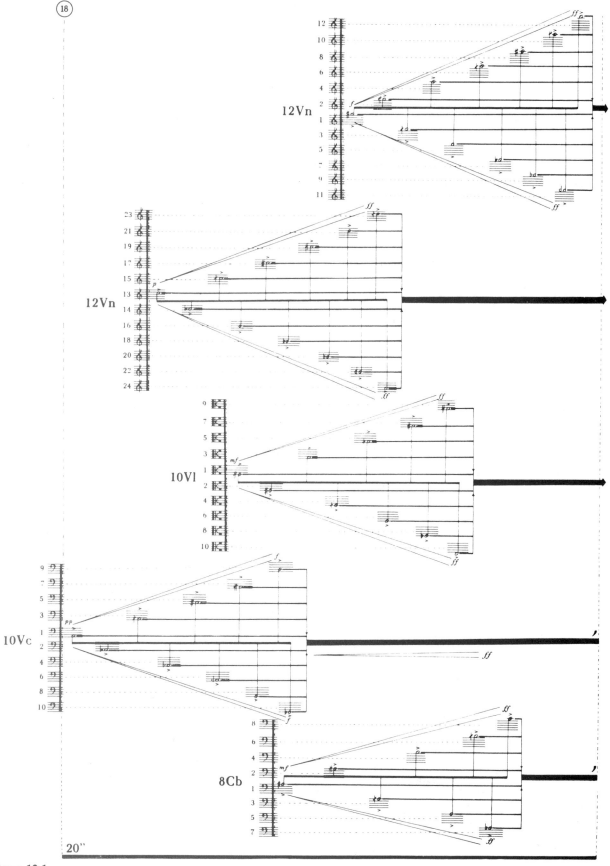

**Figure 12.1**
A page from a contemporary classical piece using a new musical language—a new notation. It is from Penderecki's *Threnody for the Victims of Hiroshima*. © 1961 DESHON MUSIC, INC. and PWM EDITIONS. All Rights Reserved. Used by Permission.

**Impressionism** is derived from the philosophy and practice of a group of French painters, notably Monet and Renoir, in the last few decades of the nineteenth century. Debussy sought to evoke moods and to convey impressions of images and feelings rather than to produce literal descriptions. In fact, he also was influenced by the symbolist poets, notably Mallarmé, and oriental music, especially the gamelan music of Indonesia.

Impressionism in music was a reaction to the massive, intellectual Germanic music as practiced by Brahms, Wagner, and Mahler. It is best typified in the music of Debussy and is marked by the delicate sonorities of flute, harp, and strings rather than massive sounds of brass, and by subtle shadings rather than dramatic contrasts of tone color. Impressionistic music is sensuous and beautiful, seldom harsh.

Debussy, more than any other composer, represents the transition from nineteenth-century romanticism to the diverse and more complex practices of the twentieth century. He wrote in virtually every medium, but his piano and orchestral music stand out. Among his best known works are *Prelude to the Afternoon of a Faun*, 1892–1894, for orchestra; *Nocturnes,* 1893–1899, a set of three descriptive pieces for orchestra; *La Mer* (The Sea), 1903–1905, a large, programmatic, three-movement orchestral work; *Syrinx,* 1912, for unaccompanied flute; *Images for Piano*, Books 1 and 2, 1905, 1907; and *Preludes for Piano*, Books 1 and 2, 1910–1913. He also composed one string quartet, one opera, and his most popular piece, "Clair de Lune."

**Igor Stravinsky (1882–1971)**

Stravinsky was a Russian composer who lived and worked in Russia, Switzerland, France, and, for the last thirty-two years of his life, in the United States. He became an American citizen in 1945. He is by all accounts a legendary composer who, for many generations to come, undoubtedly will be regarded as one of the great composers of the twentieth century.

His claim to fame began around 1910 in Paris where he composed three large-scale ballets for Diagilev and the Russian Ballet: *The Firebird, Petrushka,* and *The Rite of Spring.* The collaboration produced revolutionary ballet and ballet music. As frequently happens, the lasting qualities of this ballet music came through orchestral versions. Each has become a masterpiece of twentieth-century symphonic repertoire.

Because of an economy affected by World War I, Stravinsky turned to smaller works, such as *The Soldier's Tale* (1918), a theatre-piece with an "orchestra" of seven solo instruments that incorporated elements of jazz, ragtime, marches, a waltz, a tango, and a fiddling dance.

Many contemporary composers, Stravinsky included, have valued the importance of form and structure in their music, in many cases returning to the common practices and aesthetic values of the past. These composers are known as neoclassicists, or they are known to have composed one or more pieces in a **neoclassical** style.

As mentioned previously, contemporary composition may be derived from past practices, but its language is not. A neoclassical piece by Stravinsky does not sound like Mozart, but it may have commonalities with the classic ideals of control, order, emotional restraint, adherence to formal structure, minimal instrumentation, and transparent texture.

Stravinsky's neoclassical music began in the early 1920s and included his "Back-to-Bach" music: *Symphony for Wind Instruments* (1920) and *Concerto for Piano and Wind Orchestra* (1924). Other neoclassical works include the opera-oratorio, *Oedipus Rex* (1927); *Symphony of Psalms* (1930), a three-movement sacred work for chorus and orchestra that omits violins, violas, and clarinets; and the *Symphony in Three Movements* (1945), one of Stravinsky's most unique works. An opera, *The Rake's Progress* (1951), culminated his neoclassic period when he was nearly seventy years old.

(a) A scene from
Stravinsky's *The Rite of
Spring* (*Le Sacre du
Printemps*), a twentieth-
century ballet, (b) a pen
and ink sketch of
Stravinsky: *Le Sacre du
Printemps*.

*a.*

*b.*

He then began his modern period, during which he produced his more experimental works. He continued his compositional activity into the 1960s, but most critics agree that his greatest and most memorable works came from his earlier, neoclassical period. Stravinsky's contributions lie in his use of the following techniques:

1. Rhythmic imagination and complexity wherein he explores irregular meters and shifting accents to create imbalance, minimizing the effect of the pulse and regular metric feeling
2. Innovative approaches to orchestration in using extreme ranges and unusual instrumental combinations
3. His ability to produce tonal music in new ways
4. His success in creating new music from old material, particularly baroque and classic forms and techniques, and from other existing styles, such as jazz and ragtime rhythms and Russian folk melodies.

**Arnold Schoenberg (1874–1951)**

Schoenberg, an Austrian, became a leader of contemporary musical thought in the 1920s. He assumed an important post as professor of composition in Berlin in 1925. With the rise of Hitler, he moved to the United States in 1933. His longest post was as professor of composition at the University of California at Los Angeles where he remained until his retirement at age seventy. He became an American citizen in 1940.

Schoenberg's first compositions were in the highly chromatic but tonal postromantic style reminiscent of Brahms, Mahler, and especially Wagner. His most important early work is *Verklärte Nacht* (1899). In his next stage as a composer, Schoenberg rejected the major/minor tonal system entirely and created atonal pieces in which any establishment of tonal centers was deliberately avoided (atonality). In traditional tonal music, compositions are based on sets of whole-step/half-step patterns (major or minor scales) that establish key centers. A composer can modulate from one key center to another, and dissonance typically resolves to a consonance.

In **atonality,** the twelve tones of the chromatic scale are used in patterns that avoid rather than create a tonal center, and because there are no key centers, modulation is not possible. Also, dissonance has been emancipated from consonance. It no longer needed to resolve and could stand alone, unresolved.

In Schoenberg's music, the melodies tended to be predominantly disjunct rather than stepwise. The texture was polyphonic, and he preferred small orchestras and chamber ensembles of both standard and unconventional instrumental combinations to the huge resources of postromantic music. Phrases were of irregular length, and melodic repetition and chord progressions were deliberately avoided. The music sounded complex and fragmentary. Unity was achieved in different ways in different pieces, often through some transformation of short motives.

Schoenberg's outstanding pieces from this period are *Five Pieces for Orchestra,* Op. 16 (1909), and perhaps his most popular work, *Pierrot Lunaire* (1912), for female reciter and an ensemble of five players playing eight different instruments. The reciter "sings" in an unusual style that combines speech and singing.

From 1914–1920, Schoenberg produced few works. Instead, he contemplated ways of organizing the twelve tones of the chromatic scale in some cohesive system. These efforts concluded with a system we know as **serial composition** or **twelve-tone technique.** It revolutionized music. It gave us a system that provided an alternative to the major/minor tonal system.

The essence of the system is a set of pitches, a tone row, that is the basis of the composition, much as the traditional major or minor scale was. The tone row is subsequently used in various forms in its entirety, never repeating a tone until the entire row is completed. In addition to its original order of pitches, the row may be used backwards, upside down, or upside down and backwards. The art is in the imaginative manipulation of the row: rhythmically, melodically, harmonically, in varying textures and timbres, and in contrasting dynamics. Serialism is a means of organizing music; it is not something we can identify as we listen.

In Vienna, Schoenberg gathered students around him, the most talented being Anton Webern and Alban Berg, both of whom became significant composers. In fact, composers since Schoenberg have experimented and produced significant compositions in which other musical factors have been serialized, basing their compositions not only on tone rows but on specific sequences (rows) of nonrepeated, contrasting dynamic levels, note values, or timbres. When several factors have been serialized, the music is said to be **totally controlled,** thus leaving little creativity to the composer once the serial decisions were made. The growth of the composition is determined in great detail by previous decisions in establishing the various rows.

Schoenberg's most famous serial compositions date from the early 1920s. His first composition based solely on a single row is *Suite* for piano, Op. 25. *Variations for Orchestra* (1928) is considered one of his best serial compositions. An entire opera, *Moses and Aaron* (1930–1932), is based on a single tone row. He continued to write serial music throughout his American career, at times experimenting with combinations of tone row technique and tonality in the same piece.

Atonality and serialism have been controversial, some people thinking the music too cerebral, complex, and without emotion. Others feel serial composition is the logical path on which to base future musical developments. However, few composers in the late twentieth century base entire compositions on a single row of twelve tones, instead building in a more flexible manner on the cohesive principles of organization suggested by Schoenberg's revolutionary system.

## Béla Bartók (1881–1945)

Bartók, the greatest of Hungarian composers, taught piano at the Budapest Academy of Music for twenty-seven years (1907–1934) and gave recitals throughout Europe. In the early years of his career, he did not gain much acceptance as a composer in his native land. As an intense anti-Nazi, he felt compelled to leave Hungary and emigrated to the United States in 1940. He settled in New York City where he died in 1945.

In the early part of his career, Bartók became interested in the nationalist movement that had spread throughout Europe. He sought to preserve the folk music of Hungary and let the world know that Hungary possessed a traditional folk repertoire that included more than gypsy music. He, with Zoltan Kodály, went into the small villages and rural communities in the first decades of this century and recorded their songs on cylinder recording machines. They were able to succeed in their efforts because they lived with the peasants, gaining their confidence and trust. As a result, they developed a treasury of folk songs numbering in the thousands, including songs collected and recorded as they moved into other parts of eastern Europe and northern Africa. This folk music was to have a profound effect upon his compositional style.

Bartók's highly individual style combines the spirit of eastern European folk music, forms of the classic era, and the musical language of contemporary Europe, a language he expanded in many exciting and innovative ways. His music transcends many styles, techniques, and systems. His music is tonal, often modal, sometimes polytonal. It frequently slides into highly chromatic atonality, because he did not adhere rigidly to the major/minor tonal system. His harmony is dissonant, often harsh, and his rhythms have vitality and are often pounding, nonsymmetrical, and syncopated. He often treats the piano as a percussion instrument, using pounding chords and tone clusters as elements of rhythm. His scoring for instruments brought a variety of imaginative tone colors, particularly from the many percussion instruments that he frequently used.

Béla Bartók, a great Hungarian composer (at left).

Bartók's greatest compositions are in the piano and orchestra mediums. *Mikrokosmos* (1926–1937) is a set of 153 piano pieces in six books of varying levels of difficulty. They not only have pedagogical value but summarize his compositional styles and the styles of European composition flourishing at the time. His six string quartets (1908–1939) rank among the finest works in the chamber music repertoire, and *Music for Strings, Percussion, and Celesta* (1936) is one of his greatest works.

His best known compositions are from the years he spent in the United States, which were not happy years. He was poor, felt isolated and unaccepted, could not get his music performed, received few commissions, and developed leukemia. While hospitalized, he did receive a commission from Serge Koussevitsky for which he composed *Concerto for Orchestra* (1943). This was to become his most popular work. It led to a series of other commissions. Unfortunately, he was to live only one more year. His last completed work was his *Third Piano Concerto* (1945). Ironically, after Bartók's death, he became famous and his music became in demand in the United States.

The composers just presented are identified with individual developments—impressionism, neoclassicism, serialism, folk music—because of their significant roles in shaping those developments. Other composers, as well, were associated with these styles at the same time or, in many cases, as followers. The developments presented in this section are not associated in an outstanding way with a single composer, are not as widely accepted by the public, or are too new to have withstood the test of time as styles and techniques presented previously.

In every generation, a small group of composers tries new styles, techniques, forms, timbres, or concepts in order to develop a new approach to composition, new aesthetic notions, or a new language for expressing music. These composers are said to be in the **avant-garde.** Their pieces, being experimental, will have varying degrees of impact.

## New Sounds in Music: The Experimentalists

For some experimentalists, the musical outcomes of an experiment are far less significant than the actual process of the experiment itself. Such compositions may have been more important as musical ideas than as music itself.

It is through the work of the experimentalists that the history of music progresses. Musical styles which advance through history are usually not represented by specific experimental pieces but pieces that follow. These later pieces show the influence of the experimentalists but more likely blend new concepts and the more tried and acceptable practices. It is not unusual for pieces by an experimentalist to gain wide acceptance as concepts and techniques are refined in his or her own subsequent compositions.

The creative process, itself, suggests a certain amount of experimentation, but composers have ranged from creating in bold and innovative ways to creating in a language that is known and proven acceptable. Typically, however, they settle into one end of the continuum or the other, depending where they feel most comfortable and potentially successful.

Music history evolves, sometimes very gradually, sometimes quite suddenly. Compositional style always moves ahead while being influenced by experimental music but always building on acceptable practices of the past. No new musical developments totally reject the past.

## Electronic Music

Although primitive electronic instruments existed in the first half of this century, electronic music as a medium did not appear until the 1950s. The impetus came from the development of magnetic tape recording. Technicians in Paris experimented with *musique concrète,* a name given to the technique of manipulating tape recorded sounds from existing natural sources. Recorded sounds generated from musical instruments or voices could be altered by changing the speed of the tape, playing the tape backwards, and cutting and splicing the tape. The altered sounds, perhaps combined with natural sounds, could then serve as sound sources for a composition.

The next development in electronic music was the construction of sound generating equipment and synthesizers in which the electronic sound generation was combined with sound modification. Composers could now control every detail of their creation—rhythm, dynamics, pitch organization, timbre, reverberation (echo), and even how a tone is begun and released (attack and decay). What the composer created was immediately on tape ready for any listener; no performer was necessary. Synthesizers are common today. They are greatly reduced in size and operational complexity, and used in the performance of classical, jazz, rock, and commercial music.

Most electronic music today is created to be used with live performance. The performance may include standard instrument(s) with prerecorded tape or a standard instrument using tape for sound modification, such as digital tape delay. Early experiments not only involved live performers with electronically generated sounds but also with real or modified tape recorded sounds from nature, such as the sounds of fire, water, birds, or whales.

The most recent development that will most likely dominate the field in generations to come is computer-generated music. Here the composer plots desired sounds in numerical sequence, feeds them into a digital-to-analog converter, and records these sounds on tape. Software programs now make this process easy for professionals and amateurs through MIDI (Musical Instrument Digital Interface) that connects a computer with a synthesizer to store sounds (samples) and produces sounds for tape recording or for immediate playback in live performance. Important composers of electronic music include Edgar Varèse, Milton Babbitt, and Morton Subotnik.

**Chance music** represents a compositional style on the opposite end of the spectrum from totally controlled serial music (see previous section devoted to Schoenberg and the twelve-tone technique). Rather than the composer controlling all the details of a composition, chance music allows the performer to participate in the creative process.

This process can include the random selection of sounds, selection by chance, or improvised passages within the structure of a composition. However, it is not uncontrolled music. The overall structure may be indicated in a score, but details are left to the performer. A work utilizing techniques of chance music will never be performed the same way twice. The most noted exponent of chance music is John Cage.

## Chance Music

A recent development is a style of composition that attempts to achieve the greatest effect from the least amount of material. **Minimalism** is a reaction against the complexities of serialism and the uncertainty of chance music.

The technique of minimalism is to take a musical pattern or idea and repeat it incessantly, creating slow subtle changes in rhythm, chord movement, or other musical elements. The rhythmic activity may be fast, but the speed of change in the activity will be slow. The technique represents a way of controlling the music other than through serialization, and it also represents a return to tonal music in that the repetition generates clear centers of tonal feeling.

Minimalist music allows the listener to concentrate on few details, thus enhancing the possibility of increased perception. Its adherants have kinship with jazz and rock music and the music and ideas of India and Africa. Time will tell if minimalism will have a significant impact on the development of Western classical music. The most prominent composer of minimalist music is Phillip Glass.

## Minimalism

Not all twentieth-century music is abstract, complex, and challenging to listen to. In the early part of the century, such neoclassicists as Stravinsky returned to practices of the past, yet their music was put in a context and a fresh musical language that made it sound like it belonged in the twentieth century.

Other composers preferred a return to nineteenth-century romantic aesthetics, forms, and techniques. They wrote program music, symphonies, or concertos, and they created personalized, expressive music with singable melodies. Their music was tonal with relatively simple rhythms, conventional playing or singing ranges, and traditional instrumental combinations. Their harmonies were colorful, even bold, but generally within the accepted techniques of the major/minor tonal system.

Composers may have adopted a traditional style because of their own comfort with accepted practices or perhaps from their desire to counter the complexities of other modern music by simplifying the musical language. They were most likely motivated by a desire to serve an audience that would not be alienated by their music, would find it accessible and enjoyable, and, of course, would pay to hear it in concerts or on recordings.

Folk songs and regional ethnic music have been the source of inspiration for many composers. Bartók, as mentioned previously, became intimately involved in folk music. Whereas some composers, such as Bartók, incorporated the spirit of folk music rather than specific songs in their music, other composers included specific folk material—melodies, rhythms, dances—as the basis of a composition. Because of the literal reference to folk material, such music frequently was tuneful, rhythmically comfortable or even exciting, and created in a traditional rather than experimental context.

Many of the great composers found the balance between innovation and a style that would find wide acceptance. Interestingly, such acceptance may have come decades later, even after a composer's death. Those whose music is never forward-looking seldom

## Familiar Sounds in Music: The Traditionalists

contribute much to the development of music. Conversely, it is the great innovators—Monteverdi, Beethoven, Wagner, Stravinsky—that give vitality to music and move it forward. Representative composers of a traditionalist nature include Heitor Villa-Lobos (Brazil), Samuel Barber (United States), Serge Prokofiev (Russia), and Ralph Vaughan Williams (England).

# A Study in Sound
*Twentieth-Century Music*

## Example 1

*La Mer*—II

  I  De l'aube à midi sur la mer
     (From Dawn to Noon at Sea)

  II  Jeux de vagues
     (Play of the Waves)

  III  Dialogue du vent et de la mer
     (Dialogue between the Wind and the Sea)

Composed in 1903–1905 by Claude Debussy (1862–1918)

A programmatic multimovement work for large symphony orchestra

The orchestra, in addition to the normal string section and winds in pairs includes piccolo, English horn, a third bassoon and contrabassoon, two additional horns, a third trombone, and a tuba. The percussion section includes three timbales, gong, cymbals, triangle, two harps, and a glockenspiel.

This "symphony" paints a tonal landscape, evoking Debussy's impression of the wind and sea. The music conveys the surges and swells of the undulating waves, with moods ranging from serene when the sea is calm to furious during the storms.

This musical example is the second movement, "Play of the Waves." It is light and playful. Listen to musical details as specified in the guide but also to the overall sounds, letting the soundscape create images in your mind.

### Goals:

Be aware of texture, timbre, and mood more than clearly stated melody and harmony.

Recognize music whose tonality is obscure and whose sounds are derived from scales other than major or minor.

Recognize chromatic and dissonant harmony.

Recognize assymetrical meter and phrasing.

*Guide:* In a fast triple meter

Introduction—quiet; sustained winds and harp arpeggios followed by descending flute;

    Repeated staccato notes in the trumpets that signal the start of the first theme.

Theme A—stated in English horn (motive is ascending, four-note, whole-tone scale which is then repeated and extended);

    Answered by oboe in high range in different key area; with ascending harp arpeggio;

    Music builds in intensity then recedes, descending to low trills in cellos, signaling beginning of second theme.

Theme B—stated in upper strings (shimmering, flat contour);

    Answered by flutes, then harp arpeggios and horns in dialogue;

    Repeated, staccato notes in high woodwinds signal the start of the third theme.

Theme C—long, legato theme stated in English horn; joined shortly by solo horn;

    Short, loud brass figures accompanied by flurry of descending, ostinato figures passed between high woodwinds and high strings;

    Solo clarinet, then solo violin, then legato, solo horn followed by increasingly animated passage.

    Suddenly quiet as oboe line is accompanied by countermelody in flute and horn;

    Legato strings and horns with flute arpeggios;

    Staccato horns and trumpets signal return of theme C.

    Theme C restated in cellos; staccato figures continue; builds and subsides;

Theme A—stated in oboe and clarinet;

    Builds to peak—solo trumpet—then subsides;

    Dialogue in the upper woodwinds, beginning with oboes and English horn, then clarinet and flute;

    Descending string scales answered by ascending scales in the woodwinds with horn melody; builds to climax;

    Subsides to quiet, sustained trills in upper strings.

Theme B—stated in flute then oboe;

    Legato passage in violas and cellos; horns and clarinets soon added;

    Theme restated in oboes and bassoons;

    Many lush, ascending and descending passages in strings over ascending pizzicato scales in cellos, contrasting with fragments in upper woodwinds, horns, and trumpet solos; builds to huge climax.

Coda—sound subsides and texture thins;

    Ascending and descending harp arpeggios;

    Answered by sustained horns with fragments of the first theme;

    Ends with slow harp figures and one final statement of theme A; short ascending lines by the harp, then flute in the low range, a glockenspiel arpeggio, and finally a single tone on the harp.

***Reflections:*** The music is chromatic, with little sense of tonality and traditional chord progression. Melodies constantly seem to emerge and recede, flowing in and out of the sound fabric, ranging from a light and airy texture to the sonority of the full orchestra that is never brassy or percussive.

# Example 2

*Symphony of Psalms*—a multimovement work for chorus and orchestra—Part I

Composed in 1930 by Igor Stravinsky (1882–1971)

*Symphony of Psalms* was composed "to the glory of God" and dedicated to the Boston Symphony Orchestra on the occasion of its fiftieth birthday anniversary. The instrumentation is for symphony orchestra but excludes violins, violas, and clarinets. The text is from the Psalms and taken from the ancient, Latin version of the Bible—the vulgate.

The musical style is neoclassical in that it is restrained and controlled, is in clear form, and uses consistent, cohesive patterns and traditional unifying techniques, such as repetition, ostinato, and fugue. Additionally, the piece somehow evokes a sense of the past, perhaps through melodic suggestions of ancient chant traditions. Yet the work unmistakably is derived from the musical language of Stravinsky's time. It is one of the masterworks of the twentieth century.

### Goals:

Recognize dissonant harmonies, unusual melodies, and assymetrical rhythm and phrasing.

Recognize ostinato patterns.

Be aware of varying degrees of tension.

***Guide:*** (See page 285 for a guide to the complete work)

First movement (excerpt)—moderate tempo in mixed meter with slow rhythmic activity in the choir

Introduction—broken chords punctuated by occasional single, blocked chords; strings introduce first theme, a two-note melody

Chorus enters with main theme in alto voice over constant patterns of two different ostinatos, followed by soprano, tenor, and bass voices

***Reflections:*** In listening to *Symphony of Psalms,* one will not hear many dominant-tonic progressions. Functional harmony has not been a big part of twentieth-century musical language. This is unconventional tonal music, but any sense of key center is achieved by ways other than through traditional chord movement and cadences. One at times may notice a sense of suspension in time, a lack of forward energy, a sense of stasis. At other times, the music moves forward, building to powerful climaxes.

# Example 3

*Pierrot Lunaire*

"Mondestrucken" and "Columbine"

Composed in 1912 by Arnold Schoenberg (1874–1951)

For voice and ensemble of five performers: piano, flute and piccolo, clarinet and bass clarinet, violin and viola, and cello

Poetry by Albert Giraud

This song cycle is comprised of twenty-one numbers grouped by sevens into three parts. The musical example includes the first two songs of Part I.

The music is atonal and includes the use of *sprechstimme,* when written, a new way of fusing music and words. It is a technique of pitch declamation that is half spoken, half sung, and sung on approximate pitches.

## *Goals:*

Be aware of unusual treatment of words and music.

Recognize thin texture, angular melody, and polyphonic interplay of voice and instruments.

Identify various instrumental timbres.

*Guide:* Follow the phrases of the text. Be aware of various musical characteristics and the changes of mood. The German and English texts follow:

### *Part I*

1. *"Mondestrunken"*
   *(for voice, flute, violin, cello, and piano)*

   *Den Wein, den man mit Augen trinkt,*
   *Giesst Nachts der Mond in Wogen nieder,*
   *Und eine Springflut überschwemmt*
   *Den stillen Horizont.*

   *Gelüste schauerlich und süss,*
   *Durchschwimmen ohne Zahl die Fluten!*
   *Den Wein, den man mit Augen trinkt,*
   *Giesst Nachts der Mond in Wogen nieder.*

   *Der Dichter, den die Andacht treibt,*
   *Berauscht sich an dem heilgen Tranke,*
   *Gen Himmel wendet et verzückt*
   *Das Haupt und taumelnd saugt und schlürit er*
   *Den Wein, den man mit Augen trinkt.*

  2. *"Columbine"*
    *(for voice, flute, clarinet in A, violin, and piano)*

    *Des Mondlichts bleiche Blüten,*
    *Die weissen Wunderrosen,*
    *Blühn in den Julinächten—*
    *O bräch ich eine nur!*

    *Mein banges Leid zu lindern,*
    *Such ich am dunklen Strome*
    *Des Mondlichts bleiche Blüten,*
    *Die weissen Wunderrosen.*

    *Gestillt war all mein Sehnen,*
    *Dürft ich so märchenheimlich,*
    *So selig leis—entblättern*
    *Auf deine braunen Haare*
    *Des Mondlichts bleiche Blüten.*

### Part I

  1. *"Moondrunk"*
    *The wine that only eyes can drink*
    *Pours nighttimes from the moon in waves,*
    *And its springtime tide floods over*
    *The horizon's quiet bowl.*

    *Aching lusts, shocking and sweet,*
    *Float beyond measure in the gushing philter!*
    *The wine that only eyes can drink,*
    *Pours nighttimes from the moon in waves.*

    *The poet, under piety's cover,*
    *Gets fuddled on the holy brew;*
    *Towards Heaven, rapt, tilts back his head*
    *And giddily reeling laps and swills*
    *The wine that only eyes can drink.*

  2. *"Columbine"*
    *The moonlight's pallid blossoms,*
    *The white and wondrous roses,*
    *Bloom in midsummer midnights*
    *O! could I pluck but one!*

    *To still my luckless grieving*
    *I seek in Lethe's murky stream*
    *The moonlight's pallid blossoms,*
    *The white and wondrous roses.*

    *All my yearning would be sated*
    *Could I, in fairytale secret,*
    *In gentle bliss . . . rip petal from petal*
    *And scatter in your auburn hair*
    *The moonlight's pallid blossoms.*

*Reflections:* Discuss ways that Schoenberg's melodies differ from the nineteenth-century concept of melody. Notice that angular melodies are comprised of many wide intervals. Stepwise motion is minimized.

Discuss cadences and phrase structure. Notice the role of the instruments before and after the poetry.

# Example 4

**"Threnody for the Victims of Hiroshima"** (excerpt)

Composed in 1960 by Krzysztof Penderecki (1933–        )

For string orchestra

In the late 1950s, Poland revolted against the oppression of Russian Stalinism, creating a new Polish government. This government encouraged cultural independence and artistic freedom. The result for music was that Poland became the leader of the European avant-garde practices in composition, with Penderecki one of its most notable figures.

Penderecki was greatly affected by the Polish Jews who were killed by the Nazis. This stimulated his compassion for the plight of other human beings, which, then, influenced his composition. He wrote "Threnody" in 1960, but it is uncertain whether his feelings about the devastation wreaked by the explosion of the first atomic bomb inspired the work. The title may have been provided after the piece was completed. Penderecki also wrote "Dies Irae" in 1967, a piece memorializing the victims of Auschwitz, the German concentration camp at which hundreds of thousands of Jews were killed.

"Threnody" was written for fifty-two string instruments. Spectacular and novel sounds from conventional instruments produce an extremely intense musical fabric that is not comfortable to listen to. The music is noisy, sounding almost as though it were electronically produced. "Threnody" is agonizing music, as is the event it commemorates.

## Goals:

Recognize unusual timbres of string instruments and discuss methods of their tone production.

Be aware of programmatic elements in this music.

Describe elements of melody, harmony, and rhythm.

Be aware of shifting textures.

*Guide:* The rhythm is nonmetric. Musical events are organized in time segments, rather than according to regularly recurring bars and phrases.

Compositional techniques include the use of clusters of sounds, instruments played in extreme ranges, microtones (tones smaller than a half step), glissandos, percussive effects from the string instruments, and vocal sounds produced by the performers.

*Reflections:* Discuss the aesthetic implications of this music. Is "ugly" an acceptable and appropriate way to describe this music in an objective, nonjudgmental sense? Select other descriptive words that do not reflect a personal opinion, biased or otherwise.

Describe ways the sounds are produced. Which ways could be considered nontraditional methods of tone production?

Discuss the musical characteristics in relationship to musical language, comparing this language to nineteenth-century language.

# Example 5

**"Bachianas Brasileiras No. 5"** (excerpt)

  I  Air (Cantilena)—1938

 II  Dansa (Martelo)—1945

Composed by Heitor Villa-Lobos (1887–1959)

For soprano voice and eight cellos

The Air is very slow with a broad, lyrical melody sung on the neutral syllable, "ah." Melodically, it is reminiscent of Bach's famous "Air for the G String" from his orchestral piece, Suite No. 3 in D. The Portuguese poetry by Ruth Valadares Correa is sung in the *B* section of this ABA structure and is not included in the listening example.

    The lively Dansa is evocative of the Brazilian folk dance, the martelo. It is in duple meter and has an ABA formal pattern. The text is by the Brazilian poet Manoel Bandeira.

## *Goals:*

Describe nontraditional and traditional musical language.

Describe roles of solo and accompaniment.

Recognize sequential patterns (sequences).

Compare this musical language with that used for the music represented by examples 1–4.

Describe the nationalistic elements in this music.

*Guide:* For phrasing and structure, follow the numerical groupings. Each number represents one pulse felt at a slow tempo. The slash (/) represents a slight break or pause in the phrasing.

"**Air**"—notice that the cello doubles the vocal line throughout, then repeats the melody without voice.

```
Introduction--instrumental
1 2 3 4 5
1 2 3 4 5                          Ritard on bars 4 and bars 5
Theme--vocal
1 2 3 4 5 6 7 8 9 10 11 12 13
1 2 3 4 5 6 7 8 9
1 2 3 4 5 6 7 8 9 10 11
1 2 3 4 5 6 7 8
1 2 3 4 5 6 7 8                    Ritard on bars 7 and bars 8
1 2 3/4 5 6 7 8 9
1 2 3 4/5 6 7 8/9 10 11 12         Descending sequence
1 2 3 4 5/6                        Ritard on bars 5 and 6
Interlude--instrumental
1 2 3 4 5 6 7 8 9 10 11            Ritard on bars 10 and bars 11
```

```
Theme--cello
1  2  3  4  5  6  7  8  9  10  11  12  13
1  2  3  4  5  6  7  8  9
1  2  3  4  5  6  7
1  2  3  4/5  6  7  8/9  10  11  12
1  2  3  4  5  6  7  8
1  2  3  4  5
```

Ritard on bars 7 and 8
Ritard on bars 4 and 5;
hold on bar 5

**"Dansa"**—fast tempo; energetic; more active rhythmically

**First section**

```
1  2  3  4  5  6  7  8  9  10
```

Instrumental; voice enters
with pick-up to bar 10

```
1  2  3  4  5  6  7  8
```

Vocal

```
1  2  3  4  5  6  7  8/9  10  11  12
1  2  3  4  5  6/7  8  9  10
```

Hold on bar 10

**Second section**

More complex; assymetrical rhythm and phrasing; changing styles and moods; several new motives and themes; notice the highly rhythmic vamp that introduces a contrasting, middle part; a new melodic motive introduced by the cello serves as a countermelody to the vocal line.

**Return**

First section followed by an abbreviated second section; leads to a brilliant ending.

*Reflections:* Describe the differences in the "Air" and the "Dansa" melodies.

Recognize the vamp and sequential patterns in the middle part of the second section.

In what ways does this music reflect twentieth-century musical language and culture? To the extent that it does not, is it therefore to be considered old-fashioned, traditional, and perhaps unworthy music? Is new and experimental music worthy music, and is traditional, noninnovative music unworthy music? Is it the other way around? Is the element of enjoyment a factor in judging worth?

# Additional Listening

# Example 1

### Symphony of Psalms

Composed by Igor Stravinsky (1882–1971)

(For background information, see Study in Sound, example SS 12/2, page 280)

This is a three-movement work for chorus and orchestra. The instrumentation is for symphony orchestra but excludes violins, violas, and clarinets.

## Guide:

Part I—moderate tempo in mixed meter with slow rhythmic activity in the choir.

Introduction—broken chords punctuated by occasional single, blocked chords; strings introduce first theme, a two-note melody.

First verse—chorus enters with main theme in alto voice over constant patterns of two different ostinatos, followed by soprano, tenor, and bass voices.

Interlude—featuring a fast, descending oboe line.

Second verse—the choral parts incorporate increasingly wide melodic intervals;

Music builds to a great climax, then continues mainly in block chords over the double ostinato;

Approaches the final cadence through slow, powerful, dissonant chords whose tension is resolved at the final, major chord, a chord that gives the expectation of continuing.

Part II—double fugue (one in the orchestra followed by a different one in the chorus); slow; duple meter; chromatic; wide melodic intervals (angular melody).

Instrumental fugue—first statement in oboe, second in flute, third in second flute (low register), and fourth in second oboe; ends with interplay of three flutes.

Choral fugue—first statement in soprano characterized by descending interval; theme of instrumental fugue heard in orchestra; entrances follow in altos, tenors, then basses, with voices accenting their descending intervals;

Continues in polyphonic interplay;

Ends with an a cappella passage reminiscent of Renaissance sacred polyphony.

Instrumental interlude—derived from instrumental fugue; in order of entrances: trombone, French horn, English horn, oboe, and flute and trombone; a pause sets up the final section.

Last section begins with chorus in powerful, blocked chords, all parts moving with the same rhythm; ends with suddenly quiet passage with voices in unison and octaves.

Part III—contrasting moods

Introduction—short; instrumental.

First verse—"Alleluia. Laudate, Dominum"; quiet, hymnlike, chordal.

Interlude—instrumental; powerful and energetic; fast, repeated staccato chords in horns;

Ostinatos in low range and in trumpets;

Fast, triplet figures.

Second verse—a mixture of polyphonic and homophonic settings; three motives: first, "Laudate," a stepwise, flat contour; second, very rhythmic and syncopated on a single tone; and, third, "Laudate," a rising interval in the men's voices

Interlude—slow instrumental chords; return of "Alleluia."

Third verse—"Laudate"; forceful, homorhythmic (voices move with same rhythm), in octaves and unisons, then melodic fragments;

Moves directly to instrumental interlude without a cadence

Interlude—brilliant horn solo and powerful, intense orchestra;

Suddenly quiet passage preceding entrance of fourth verse;

Fourth verse—begins with surprising new theme in a major key; slow; imitative, polyphonic setting;

Builds to climax;

Quiet, chordal, homophonic section with a simple, undulating melody; flat contour;

Concludes quietly with return to the opening "Alleluia. Laudate, Dominum."

*Discography*

**Ex. 1**    Debussy, Claude. *La Mer*. Columbia ML 6154. 7:07.

**Ex. 2**    Stravinsky, Igor. *Symphony of Psalms*. Columbia MS 6538. 3:22.

**Ex. 3**    Schoenberg, Arnold. *Pierrot Lunaire*. Nonesuch H-71251. 3:16.

**Ex. 4**    Penderecki, Krzysztof. "Threnody for the Victims of Hiroshima." RCA. 5:40.

**Ex. 5**    Villa-Lobos, Heitor. "Bachianas Brasileiras No. 5." Angel CDC 47357. 7:31.

*Summary*

The twentieth century is the first time in music history in which the public is more interested in dead composers than in those still living and writing music—the contemporary composers.

One major reason for this circumstance is that this century has seen advances in scholarly research of old music and has seen advances in accessibilty and availability of all kinds of music in their published form as well as on recordings.

Another reason for the popularity of music of the past is that the twentieth century is an age of experimentation in the sciences and the arts. The modern aesthetic in music calls for composers to "do their own thing," express as they feel, try new techniques even new notations, and have artistic integrity above the need to appeal to the masses or sell more music. For the most part, the audience is less important to the twentieth-century composer. Likewise, the modern composer's music is less important to the contemporary audience.

A third reason has to do with the kind of society that the twentieth century has generated. Two world wars, the atomic age, a continual threat of more devastation, and rapidly advancing technology affecting every facet of our lives. Communications and media provide immediate information about tragedy and turmoil wherever in the world they occur, and a highly mobile society reduces our feelings of security. In music as well as the other arts, the production of works reflect this unsettled world. Society is not all pleasant, a state reflected in its arts.

*Terms and Concepts*

*Twentieth-century language*
*Diversity of instrumental combinations*
*Emphasis on timbre and rhythm*
*Silence*
*Controlled music*
*Free music (improvisatory, chance music)*
*Impressionistic music*
*Neoclassical style*
*Atonality*

*Serial composition*
*Folk elements*
*Electronic music*
**Musique concréte**
*Synthesizer*
*Computer music*
*MIDI*
*Minimalism*

# Music of the Twentieth Century
*Part II*

Consistent with a goal of this text to experience a broad spectrum of music that is important to our time and to our nation, this chapter will continue a presentation of twentieth-century music with emphasis now on American classical music.

American classical music normally means music of the United States of America, rather than of North America or of all the Americas. It also means music created by Americans, not Mexicans or Canadians or Brazilians.

Chapter 13 will explore issues related to the development of American classical music, particularly in the twentieth century. It will present a sampling of important works by American composers who sought to create interesting, important music—some experimental, some traditional, and some unquestionably American.

## Perspectives on American Classical Music

This section will draw attention to a number of issues related to the history and development of classical music in the United States:

1. Varying relationships between cultivated, high art music (classical) and vernacular, folk art, or commercial music (popular)
2. Varying relationships of American music to foreign influences, particularly to the creation of music that is based on European styles as opposed to that which reflects uniquely American qualities
3. Education, women and minorities, and American nationalistic music
4. The dichotomy between the production of sophisticated, complex music for professional virtuoso performers and simpler, more accessible music that can be better understood and appreciated by the ticket-buying public

## The Classical/ Popular Dichotomy

The previous discussion on popular music (chapter 5) revealed that, in the eighteenth and early nineteenth centuries, very little distinction was made between classical and popular music in America. The most loved and best known songs were from the classics or similar in style to classical art songs or songs from operas, especially the English ballad operas. These operas included songs, waltzes, marches, and an overture. They were very popular in the United States, and the music was tuneful and appealing.

It was in the second half of the nineteenth century that the separation took place as popular songs took on a more rhythmic, syncopated feel—most evident in the minstrel songs. New songs emerged from the influences of cross-cultural interaction among Anglos, blacks, Creoles, and all sorts of immigrants. This new music widened the gap between classical and popular music in terms of musical style and people's acceptance of these styles. The dichotomy became established. Classical music became an elite art, and popular music was geared toward mass audiences.

This dichotomy was enhanced by the United States being a middle class, rather than aristocratic, society from the beginning. Musical performances were directed to involvements by amateurs and professional performers whose financial support was dependent upon paying audiences. This circumstance affected the repertoire that was performed. It had to be appealing to encourage the largest possible audiences. The more advanced, complex, modern pieces became even more for the elite, further separating composers from their audience. In turn, this created more demand for the more accessible eighteenth- and nineteenth-century music. Many modern composers, however, resisted innovation and complexity in music so their music would be more widely accepted.

Additionally, the separation was enhanced by the rise of the music industry, particularly the selling of sheet music and the touring of virtuoso artists and performing groups. Marketing and promotion affected and continue to affect peoples' taste, what they will buy, and what kind of concerts they will attend.

This dichotomy became even more pronounced by the mid-twentieth century as some classical composers consciously created innovative and complex music. By then, universities became their patrons, employing them to teach and compose as they saw fit, without dependency on the patronage of the public.

Judging by some evidence of a growing eclectic taste among the general population, the most recent trend is lessening the extremes of this dichotomy. A number of factors have contributed to many crossover and fusion styles among pop, rock, country music, jazz, and classical styles. These factors include:

1. The recording industry, broadcast media, film, and live concerts have contributed significantly to making music in many styles widely known and available.
2. Electronic music began in the classical context then branched to rock, jazz, and popular music.
3. Increased influences from world music have affected classical music throughout this century and, in recent years, both jazz and rock.
4. Music courses and curricula have to varying extents expanded well beyond a devotion to their more traditional goal of stimulating the love of classical masterworks.
5. The natural cycle of changing tastes was combined with the not always gentle help of media manipulation through marketing and advertising.
6. The Federal Government through the National Endowment for the Arts has, since 1965, sought successfully to expand audiences for music in many styles, particularly classical music, and to preserve and stimulate involvement in many of our nonclassical folk, jazz, and ethnic repertoires.

For these and perhaps other reasons, an increasing number of both musicians and listeners are involved to a greater or lesser extent in the music of more than one style within the jazz, classical, and popular repertoires. The result is a broadening of peoples' tastes and a lessening of a view of classical music as an elite art. It may be worth contemplating and discussing the extent to which this broadening of interest and taste is true and the extent to which it indeed does affect how Americans view classical music.

## The European Preoccupation

With the initial immigration to the United States coming primarily from the British Isles, the first main musical influence was English music. Immigrants brought their folk songs, their psalmody, and their love for amateur musical participation as performers and as patrons. These immigrants settled in cities on the east coast (Boston, Charleston, Philadelphia, New York) and developed centers of musical activity for both professionals and "genteel amateurs." Among the better known of these early American gentleman musicians were Thomas Jefferson, Benjamin Franklin, and Francis Hopkinson.

Public concerts and opera were prevalent by the mid-eighteenth century. The most popular types of art music included songs, waltzes, and marches—not what we call "highbrow" music. The first important classical genre popular in the United States was the English ballad opera. Other popular types included overtures, variations on familiar tunes, and program music. In the nineteenth century, the piano became the most important household instrument. It was valued not only for musical performance but also as a cultural symbol.

As more immigrants came from mainland Europe during the early part of the nineteenth century, the music of the German and Austrian composers—Haydn, Mozart, and Beethoven—became known and appreciated. Much of their music was produced and made available by American music publishers. These immigrants contributed significantly to the shaping of America's taste in art music.

Jenny Lind. The Jenny
Lind picture appeared in
Volume 19, Number
482, of *Punch*, 1850.

**JENNY LIND AND THE AMERICANS.**
*From our own Reporters.*

CORONATION OF JENNY THE FIRST—QUEEN OF THE AMERICANS

## Romanticism and the Virtuoso

Germany by the mid-nineteenth century was at the peak of romanticism. Americans valued the romantic characteristics of individualism, personal freedom, and the virtuoso performer. European artists began to present concerts in America. Many became very popular as star performers and entertainers. Musically naive American audiences became enamored with the artists' personalities and their technical proficiencies more than with the quality of their music.

Among the most famous performers who achieved great success in America in the mid-nineteenth century were the Norwegian violinist, Ole Bull, and the "Swedish Nightingale," Jenny Lind. Americans were in awe of European virtuosity, and those who aspired to become professional musicians went to Europe, especially Germany, for their musical education. They returned knowing European music; thus, those who were composers created music in the European style.

Inferences that can be drawn from this preoccupation with European music were that music created in America was inferior to European music, that America's educational opportunities had not yet developed sufficiently to adequately prepare our own professional musicians, and that German music, especially, represented the ultimate in art music.

This love of German romanticism and European music created a dilemma for American music. The values of personal freedom and individualism came into conflict with the taste of the ticket-buying public. The taste, then as now, tended more toward the tried and true, the familiar, the simple, and the less innovative and individualistic.

Symphony orchestras began to tour the United States, their conductors taking on the starlike aura of the virtuoso performers. In imitation of the Europeans, the big, Eastern cities soon established their own symphony orchestras: New York in 1842, Boston in 1881, and Chicago in 1891. Most American orchestras hired European conductors. Again, this perhaps reflected an American inferiority complex or a belief that our educational system had not yet developed sufficiently to prepare the professional conductors needed by these organizations and desired by the public. It must be pointed out, however, that this infatuation with European artistry continued well into the mid-twentieth century.

Artistic relations between the United States and France had improved by the early part of the twentieth century. By the 1920s, American composers were flocking to France—not Germany—for the following reasons:

*The French Connection*

1. The environment in France encouraged artistic interaction as poets, composers, dancers, and intellectuals flocked to Paris.
2. France also provided a sense of the exotic, for many American and French composers were influenced by the cosmopolitan musical environment found in Paris: Russian folk music, oriental and north African music, Latin American sounds and rhythms, and jazz.
3. Many American composer/teachers were now receptive to the new French impressionistic music as an alternative to the excesses of German romanticism and the conservatism of many Germanic composers such as Brahms and Schumann.

Composers studied at the Paris Conservatory, the Schola Cantorum, or later at the American Conservatory in Fountainebleau. The American Conservatory originally was a music school for American soldiers serving during World War I. It was established in 1918 as a means of providing musically talented soldiers a world-class musical education. The school closed in 1919 at the end of the war. However, through the efforts of Walter Damrosch, then conductor of the New York Philharmonic Orchestra, it reopened in 1921 as the American Conservatory.

The Conservatory's most notable teacher was Nadia Boulanger, probably the twentieth century's preeminent compositon teacher of American composers. An unusually large number of American composers went to France to study with her. Many, such as Aaron Copland, Elliott Carter, Roy Harris, Roger Sessions, and Walter Piston, now are considered among America's most illustrious composers.

By the 1920s, European composers had been exposed to jazz and American popular music from their trips to the United States and also from jazz already being performed in Europe. Well-known pieces by composers such as Debussy, Ravel, Stravinsky, and Milhaud included these American vernacular sounds, giving respectability to the incorporation of American idioms in classical music (Americanist music).

American classical music matured considerably from the 1920s through the next several decades. Americans had gone to Europe; Europeans were now coming to the United States. American composers since the 1940s have sought to become part of an international musical style, rather than to continue seeking a uniquely American music. This effort was given impetus by the arrival of a number of important European immigrant composers.

Millions of immigrants have come to the United States since the late nineteenth century, many of whom were fleeing persecution and hardship and were adventurous enough to seek a new life in the "land of opportunity." In some cases, these immigrants were peasants, laborers, farmers and not of the educated, upper classes. One circumstance that led to the immigration of artists, craftsmen, scientists, and other educated people was the political climate affecting Jews from Russia, Germany, and eastern Europe in the 1930s. America benefited as many artists and scientists came to the United States for the freedom to practice their chosen skills and to further develop their knowledge and careers.

*Immigrants*

Through the years, composers who faced political or religious persecution or who were deprived of artistic freedom have journeyed to the United States to benefit from what had become, by the mid-twentieth century, a center of musical excellence with abundant opportunities. Among these immigrants were several of the world's most renowned composers: Igor Stravinsky, Arnold Schoenberg, Paul Hindemith, and Béla Bartók. Their influences were felt through their music, and in several cases, through their writing and teaching in American universities.

## Musical Education

Americans in the nineteenth century realized the importance of music education, both formal and informal. As mentioned in the previous discussion of religious music (chapter 3), singing schools were established to raise the standard of hymn singing in America. Secular counterparts of the singing school were the choral and instrumental organizations established in the eastern cities to promote and perform the new European music. The first and most famous of these organizations was the Handel and Haydn Society of Boston, founded in 1815.

Private instruction was a common form of music instruction. In 1838, Lowell Mason established in Boston the first formal music program in the public schools. At the collegiate level, music conservatories were founded to develop professional virtuoso performers of European classical music. The most famous of these conservatories exist to this day: Peabody Institute of Baltimore founded in 1860 and conservatories in Oberlin, Boston, Cincinnati, and Chicago founded in 1865. The first music curriculum in an American university began at Harvard in 1875. It was taught by John Knowles Paine, America's first professor of music.

## Women and Minorities

The purpose of this section is to draw attention to twentieth century women and black musicians, particularly composers. The purpose is not to explore issues except to say that some women and black composers have achieved distinction in spite of their environments. Women and blacks have not had the same opportunities and societal incentives as white males to develop their skills, to get their music published, and to get it performed and recorded. Society is changing. In the past few decades, an increasing number of opportunities have become available to composers from these groups. An increasing number of these musicians are developing distinguished careers.

This section focuses briefly on the music of several representative women and black composers who reached high levels of achievement. The music of additional modern women and black composers is presented in A Study in Sound.

## Amy Cheney (Mrs. H. H. A.) Beach (1867–1944)

Given the period of time in which Beach lived, she pursued a successful career as a performer and composer. Her "Gaelic" Symphony was the first symphony to be composed by an American woman. She was also the first woman to have music premiered by the Handel and Haydn Society of Boston and the New York Philharmonic Orchestra. Much of her music is recorded and still available.

Beach's compositions for solo piano, in particular, may sound conservative to our contemporary ears. They incorporate impressionistic sounds and are programmatic, carrying such titles as "By the Still Waters" and "From Grandmother's Garden." Her instrumental music, including a piano concerto, string quartet, and piano quintet, is more innovative and complex.

## Ruth Crawford (1901–1953)

She was an active and important composer when, in the early 1930s, she married Charles Seeger, distinguished ethnomusicologist and folk song collector. She then stopped composing because of family responsibilities and to pursue, along with her husband, her interest in American folk music.

Sarah Caldwell, an
illustrious American
conductor.

Crawford was in the vanguard of musical developments and serialization of elements other than pitch. In 1930, she was awarded a Guggenheim Fellowship, the first woman to win one. It enabled her to study in Berlin and Paris. She composed songs, suites for various instruments, nine Preludes for Piano, a well-known string quartet, and a woodwind quintet composed in 1952.

*William Grant Still (1895–1978)*

Still's career took him from his home state of Mississippi to New York and Boston. He worked or studied with W. C. Handy in Memphis, Eubie Blake and Noble Sissle on Broadway, George Chadwick at the New England Conservatory, and Edgar Varèse in New York. While Still was staff arranger and composer for radio stations in New York City, he came into contact with such famous entertainers as Artie Shaw, Sophie Tucker, and Paul Whiteman.

Still's 1934 Guggenheim Fellowship enabled him to devote more of his time to classical composition. Settling in Los Angeles, he pursued an active career in composition. He produced operas, large numbers of orchestral works, and vocal, keyboard, and chamber pieces. His style, conservative and nondissonant, combined elements of French impressionism and Afro-American music. His most representative and perhaps best-known work is the *Afro-American Symphony,* composed in 1930.

*Ulysses Kay (1917–      )*

Kay is one of the most honored of American composers. He received a Fulbright, a Guggenheim, and the Prix de Rome. He pursued a successful career as a moderately conservative tonal composer. Much of his music is in small instrumental and choral forms, but he also composed operas and music for television and films. Much of his music would be considered neoclassical because of its formal and orchestral balance. It is known that he was encouraged to become a composer by William Grant Still.

**American Experimentalists**

Charles Ives was perhaps the first great experimentalist in twentieth-century music. He was followed by Edgar Varèse and Henry Cowell who continued the line of experimentalists and helped shape the mid-twentieth century avant-garde movement, particularly in America. In the 1950s, impetus was given to experimental musical activity through the music and writings of Cowell's student, John Cage, and Varèse's activities in the newly developing electronic medium.

One must be aware of different musical characteristics when listening to twentieth-century experimental music. The emphasis is more on texture, color, and rhythm than on melody, harmony, and thematic development. By definition, the music of the experimentalists is not in the mainstream of repertoire known and appreciated by the general public. However, some of it gradually becomes part of the mainstream. Experimental music, however, is performed and recorded. It is thus available for others to study, particularly composers who help shape the course of musical development.

*Charles Ives (1874–1954)*

Ives, symbolic of America's rugged individualist, felt he could be more free and independent as a composer if he did not have to depend on it for his livelihood. He became very successful in the insurance business. Ives was well educated in music and received a degree in music from Yale. Working in Connecticut and New York, far from the major European music centers, his style stood outside the generally accepted European tradition. His music represents virtually every major compositional innovation in the twentieth century, but Ives "discovered" the new techniques decades ahead of everyone else.

Ives experimented musically but was guided by larger issues. Music was more than the sounds. It was the spirit that emanated from the creator of those sounds. It was a musical manifestation of life itself. His music was infused with quotations of melodies or fragments of melodies from familiar, American vernacular music, mostly hymns, patriotic songs, and marches—recreating sounds from life. He did not consider this use of quotations as producing nationalistic music as much as using available materials to create something larger. It was the recognition that all of life is vital and substantial and that art and life do not need to be separate. In this way, his music synthesized American classical and vernacular traditions.

Ives has been well known only since the 1940s, although he stopped composing in 1921. Recognition of his work came later, most of it after his death in 1954.

Although much of Ives's music is extremely complex to perform and listen to, his music now is widely recorded and performed, particularly choral pieces and songs from the nearly 200 that he wrote. His instrumental music is widely recognized, particularly the four symphonies, the third of which was awarded the Pulitzer Prize in 1947; *Three Places in New England,* a set of tone poems (Additional Listening example 1, page 305); and *The Unanswered Question,* for trumpet, four flutes, and a string orchestra to be played off stage. Of his two piano sonatas, Sonata No. 2—the "Concord"—is best known.

*Edgar Varèse (1883–1965)*

Varèse was born and educated in Paris but came to the United States in 1915 where he pursued his entire career. He, like Cowell, Copland, and others, was active in the promotion of new music.

Varèse accepted any sound, whether perceived as pitches or noise, as potential material for musical composition. In the 1920s, he used a wide variety of percussion instruments and even sirens. In the 1950s, he incorporated electronically taped sound sources. His music is frequently described as static, sound masses, or collages of sound having little to do with chord progressions or melodic movement.

His most influential music was composed in the 1920s and 1950s. The earlier music, reflecting his lifelong interest in science and technology, included *Hyperprism, Octandre, Intégrales, Arcana, Ionization,* and *Density 21.5.* His later music, incorporating manipulated taped sounds, is best represented by *Déserts* and *Poème électronique.*

Cowell's influence was as a composer but also as a teacher, author, and promoter of new music. A number of his values and practices from the 1920s became commonplace by the 1950s.

*Henry Cowell (1897–1965)*

Cowell was committed to exploring ways of merging Western music with the folk and traditional music of other cultures. He searched for new sound sources and new ways of organizing sound and created new notational devices to communicate his new techniques.

One of his most famous compositional devices, dating as far back as 1912, is the tone cluster, a grouping of adjacent pitches played simultaneously. On the piano, the cluster is often achieved by depressing the keys with the fist or the entire forearm. He found new sources of sound in a myriad of percussion instruments and in the percussive use of the piano by means of tone clusters but also by plucking, strumming, scraping, and hitting the strings inside the piano.

The best-known of Cowell's over 5,000 compositions includes a number of symphonies, a series of Hymn and Fuging Tunes, and music for solo piano.

Cage's influence is through his music but, perhaps more, through his writings. He, like his predecessors, explored new sounds and new ways of organizing sound. He is best known for areas of influence broadly symbolized by the following terms: prepared piano, chance music, and silence.

*John Cage (1912–    )*

His early activity stressed percussive sounds, including the piano. His best-known technique was to alter the sound of the piano by placing screws and other things inside, touching the strings in ways that affected the sound. His most famous work in this manner is *Concerto for Prepared Piano and Chamber Orchestra (1951).*

Whereas some composers extended concepts of serialism to gain total control of every nuance of sound, Cage reduced control, allowing outcomes of a performance to be unpredictable. He provided for the performer to make conscious choices in the creative process (chance music). Rather than put things together, Cage was willing to "let things happen." He is well known for his piece for multiple radios set at different places on the dial, including static. He accepted the sounds, whatever they were, as the piece of music.

Cage became aware that there was no such thing as silence, that we always will be able to hear sounds—of our own body, air circulating, and people moving, breathing, or coughing. These sounds, then, become sources of sound for music. Silence, more than at any time in music history, has become a conscious part of musical composition. Cage has helped us understand it better.

Prior to the 1920s, American composers may have quoted folk tunes, spirituals, and other types of vernacular music, but European-style music dominated. Since the 1920s, certain composers, notably Aaron Copland, sought a national music style that would be immediately recognizable as uniquely American. Such composers are known as Americanist composers. Their style would become a matter of national pride and would also contribute to reaching a broad audience.

**American Nationalism**

One begins with the premise that something American is in some way reflective of events, places, or characteristics, musical or otherwise, that are important and known to a large segment of Americans. It is something that does not apply to other nations or regions and is a characteristic that is national rather than universal in nature.

This American nationalistic music might convey a sense of the spaciousness of the wide open spaces; might reflect its vernacular music, such as the syncopated rhythms of its jazz and popular music; or might include suggestions of its well-known religious, folk, or patriotic songs. Perhaps this ideal to cultivate a distinctively American musical style was derived from the notion that America was a melting pot where various cultures blended into one "American society." However, America already was too diverse. Perhaps it was true that certain immigrant groups had largely assimilated into mainstream society, but other groups retained significant elements of their distinctive, native character, including taste in food, songs and dances, dialect, and values.

The music of both mainstream America and all its ethnic groups provided a mosaic of musical styles that was as diverse as it was enriching. Adding to this mosaic was the large number of American composers who developed their own styles but without a consciously American flavor. These composers focused more on abstract, experimental music, others on atonality and serialism, and still others on a return to earlier models of styles and structures (neoclassical or neoromantic styles). Many of these composers produced works representative of more than one focus. Yet, it was all American music, having been created in America by Americans. It is this diversity that is the core of the American musical language.

**Americanist Composers**

The first well-known composer of American classical music was Louis Gottschalk (1829–1869). He was a virtuoso pianist, a well-known composer of piano music, and a star entertainer in Europe and throughout the United States, Canada, and South America. He grew up in New Orleans but lived and studied in Paris for almost eleven years. Thus, much of his music is based on Negro and Creole songs but set in a Europeanlike, virtuoso context that demonstrated to the utmost his pianistic skills. However, his Americanist music did not wear well and had little lasting influence on future composers. His best-known works are the solo piano pieces, "The Banjo" and "Bamboula."

After Gottschalk, it is Charles Ives, Aaron Copland, and George Gershwin who rank at the top among those composers who incorporated American vernacular elements in their music or otherwise attempted to capture, musically, the American spirit.

*Charles Ives (1874–1954)*

Ives is considered an experimentalist composer, but he also incorporates many Americanist characteristics in his music. He was presented earlier under American experimentalists.

*Aaron Copland (1900–     )*

Copland, without a doubt, is the best known and most successful of all American composers of classical music. He was the first of the idealistic Americans in Paris in the 1920s who wanted to elevate the stature of American music and help shape the American musical personality. He is one of the number of American-born Jews—including George Gershwin, Jerome Kern, Irving Berlin, and Leonard Bernstein—who have contributed so much to the development and vitality of American music.

Copland, like Ives, was interested in merging elements of classical and vernacular traditions. He wanted to do more than quote hymns, spirituals, or American Indian chants, as others before him had done. His value was in using vernacular elements, however regional, to help shape more universal thoughts that were representative of the whole country.

Copland was interested in innovation but not at the expense of past developments. He felt that music had to move ahead but should be built on past practices. He was influenced, as were other Americans in Paris in the 1920s, by Stravinsky, whose first musical achievements took place in Paris fifteen years earlier. The Stravinsky influence was neoclassicism—combining a new musical language with old forms, structures, and musical values.

Three outstanding "American" artists: Seiji Ozawa, conductor; Aaron Copland, composer; and Leonard Bernstein, conductor, composer, pianist, author, and television personality.

In the 1920s and 1930s, along with Henry Cowell, Roger Sessions, and others, Copland was active in organizing concerts that featured new works by American composers, however experimental or modern. Copland was active also in writing about this music in order to disseminate information and to help people understand it. There was an audience for these concerts for a time, but in the mid-1930s, it began to dwindle. The gap between composer and audience began to widen as composers began to be ultramodern, abstract, and separated from the tastes of the public. As audiences for new music declined, Copland became concerned about composing in a vacuum without listeners. In the late 1930s, he began exploring ways of reaching a wider public, of composing with artistic integrity but in an understandable, more accessible language.

The results were tone poems, ballet music, music for films and radio, and patriotic works that reflected the American spirit and drew upon much vernacular music. This music included cowboy songs, popular Mexican songs, church music, jazz, and blues. It was music of rural America with urban rhythms and harmonies. It created a lasting, distinctive manner for Copland's music.

Copland's best known ballets are *Billy the Kid, Rodeo,* and *Appalachian Spring* (Additional Listening example 2, page 308). His patriotic music includes *Fanfare for the Common Man* and *Lincoln Portrait.* His best-known movie music was for *Red Pony* and *Our Town.* Copland has experimented with serial technique, particularly in the 1950s, and his piano music ranks among his best abstract, modern works.

Gershwin is known as a successful Tin Pan Alley composer of songs, musicals, and film music (see chapter 5). He is also known as a successful composer of jazz-oriented classical music. When considering both of these accomplishments, he must be considered one of the most popular, effective, and successful of all American composers. His classical music is widely known, universally loved, and extensively performed. The following are some of his most popular compositions: *Rhapsody in Blue,* for piano and orchestra (1924); *Concerto in F,* for piano and orchestra (1925); *An American in Paris,* for orchestra (1928); three *Preludes for Piano* (1926); and *Porgy and Bess,* a folk opera (1935). All rank as classics of American music literature.

*George Gershwin (1898–1937)*

# A Study in Sound
*Twentieth-Century Music*

## Example 1

**"Echoes of Time and the River"**—I (excerpt)

Four Processionals for Orchestra

| | |
|---|---|
| I | Frozen Time |
| II | Remembrance of Time |
| III | Collapse of Time |
| IV | Last Echoes of Time |

Composed in 1967 by George Crumb (1929–    )

"Echoes of Time and the River" was premiered by the Chicago Symphony Orchestra and won for Crumb the Pulitzer Prize in 1968. Crumb is a Pennsylvanian and has received grants from the Rockefeller and Koussevitsky Foundations and was a Guggenheim recipient. He has been on the faculty at the University of Pennsylvania.

In live performance, "Echoes" provides the double impact of both aural and visual experiences. These experiences are achieved from watching the performers, at times, move about on stage, marching in varying steps to the music they are performing. The percussionists play numerous instruments, and other instrumentalists also play certain percussion instruments, such as a violinist playing the antique cymbal.

The orchestration calls for three flutes and three clarinets but no oboes; all the brass instruments except tubas; a full string section; two pianos, a harp, and a mandolin; and a vast amount of regular and exotic percussion instruments, including a variety of sizes and types of cymbals; two sizes of gongs; glockenspiel, vibraphone, and xylophone; bamboo wind chimes and Chinese temple gongs and bells; conga drums, bongo drums, and timbales; and cowbells, sleigh bells, and tubular bells.

The composer has indicated every detail in the score, not only of what and how all notes are to be played but where performers are to be placed on the stage—a different placement for each of the four movements.

## *Goals:*

Be aware of the organization of music by time segments as opposed to bars and phrase structure.

Describe the musical language in terms of melody, harmony, and rhythm.

Identify glissandos.

Identify altered tones produced inside the piano.

*Guide:* The following outline specifies prominent musical events as they occur in seconds lapsed from the beginning:

| | |
|---|---|
| :00 | Loud bell sound is the antique cymbal. |
| :15 | Low register glissandos by three trombones. |
| :24 | Timbales—two notes a fifth apart. |
| :38 | Voices—staccato, only approximate pitches. |
| 1:05 | Timpani up-and-down glissandos. |
| 1:52 | Loud chord—all previous instruments sounding at once, starting with antique cymbal. |
| | Followed by eight pitches altered by touching strings inside the two pianos. |
| 2:16 | A loud chord begins a long series of rising and falling glissandos in the strings that move from the high pitch area of the violins down to the low pitch area of the basses. |
| 3:08 | Low, rumbling sound made inside the pianos, followed by eight piano tones, some altered. Followed immediately by upper voice mandolin, then shimmering glass chimes, and altered piano sounds (strings hit with mallets); pattern continues with decreasing activity to the end. |
| | Movement ends with three high notes played on the mandolin. |

# Example 2

**"Piano Piece"** for piano and electronic sounds (excerpt)

Composed by Olly Wilson (1937–   )
Natalie Hinderas, piano

Wilson is a currently active composer and teacher. He is one of the few black composers to create works in the electronic music medium.

The piano itself is capable of a wide range of expressions, from delicate touches to banging clusters. This diversity of expressive possibilities becomes a vast array of sonorities when the inside of the piano is used as a sound source. Sounds are produced inside the piano by plucking or hitting unaltered strings or "prepared" strings whose sounds are altered by the insertion of items, such as thumb tacks placed against certain strings in a manner that affects their timbre.

The composer directs that the piano for "Piano Piece" be altered by adding a light weight ruler with metal edge, three metal rings (notebook type), and three metal protractors approximately 3¾ inches in length.

## *Goals:*

Recognize the expanded sonorities of the piano.

Recognize electronically produced sounds.

Describe the musical language in terms of melody, harmony, and rhythm.

*Guide:* Excerpt can be perceived in three distinct parts.

First part—loud, nervous, energetic; repeated tones on the piano with irregular punctuations (single, loud sonorities) produced electronically; flat melodic contour; Another layer of sound is added—a rustling, shaking sound; the punctuated electronic sounds lengthen.

Second part—acoustic piano; soft, slow pace; detached notes; angular melodic contour. Electronic music follows in same style and mood; piano and tape interact and build in intensity.

Third part—similar style and mood as first part, except for more angular melodic lines.

*Reflections:* Describe and compare the synthetic sounds of the electronic music rendered on tape and the diverse sounds of the acoustic piano.

Discuss the functions of this music.

Discuss implications of modern technology for the production of great art music.


# Example 3

**Three Places in New England—II**

    I. The "St. Gaudens" in Boston Common
      (Col. Robert Gould Shaw and his Colored Regiment)

  II. Putnam's Camp, Redding, Connecticut

 III. The Housatonic at Stockbridge

Composed by Charles Ives (1874–1954)

Three Places in New England is a set of three pieces for large orchestra. The listening example is the second movement, "Putnam's Camp."

## *Goals:*

Identify unresolved dissonances, mixed meter, and assymetric phrasing.

Recognize Ive's selection and use of melodic motives.

Identify the many sounds of individual instruments.

Be aware of the range of expression in this piece.

*Guide:* (For more complete background information and the Guide to the second movement, see Additional Listening example 1, page 305.)

*Reflections:* Discuss aesthetic benefits of cacophony in music (noise).

Discuss communication in music, Ives musical language, and his selection of musical materials in relation to his aesthetic intentions.

Discuss the extent, nature, and purpose of dissonance in Ives' music.

Discuss the range of expression in this piece—the dramatically contrasting moods.


# Example 4

**"Afro-American Symphony" in four movements—III**

Composed in 1930 (revised, 1969) by William Grant Still (1895–1978)

This symphony, the first composed by a black American, is rooted in the blues and in the syncopated popular music of the time.

## *Goals:*

Identify the principle motive and recognize the modifications and variations of this motive as the piece progresses.

Recognize blue notes and the call-and-response technique in symphonic music.

Recognize diatonic and tonal American music.

## *Guide:*

The syncopated motive on which the entire movement is based is stated in the introduction and at the beginning of the first theme. The movement is basically a series of variations of that motive. It is passed throughout the orchestra, often in a question/answer, call-and-response format.

A second theme—songlike, bluesy, and legato—follows and returns only once near the end of the movement.

## *Reflections:*

This movement, diatonic and tonal, has songlike themes. It is light-hearted and bouncy. The regular, dancelike rhythm is enhanced by the strumming of the banjo. Notice the abundance of blue notes.

# Example 5

**Preludes for Piano, No. 1**

Composed in 1926 by George Gershwin (1896–1937)

Composed for his own recital at the Hotel Roosevelt in New York City, the Preludes are usually performed as one three-movement composition in a fast-slow-fast order. Each movement is in a contrasting key.

## *Goals:*

Recognize jazz and Latin elements in a classical context.

Recognize the vamp.

## *Guide:*

The first movement opens with a blue note motive. The left-hand vamp precedes the entrance of the opening theme, and the accompaniment takes on a distinctively Spanish flavor.

## *Reflections:*

The movement is in classical form and context but incorporates the syncopated, bluesy sounds of 1920s popular music and jazz.

Compare this prelude with the Chopin and Crawford preludes. (SS11/2, page 260; SS13/6, page 303)

# Example 6

**Preludes for Piano, No. 8** "Leggiero"

Composed by Ruth Crawford (Seeger) (1901–1953)

From a set of nine preludes completed in 1928

Ruth Crawford was an important part of the American avant-garde scene in the 1920s. Among her most important works are a string quartet (1931) and these piano preludes, some of which utilize compositional techniques rare at the time but that were later to become commonplace.

*Goals:*

Describe the rhythmic characteristics and the approach to melody and harmony.
   Recognize motives and patterns of repetition that give the piece cohesion (unity).

*Guide:* The piece, in ABA form, is bold and innovative. It has imaginative rhythms and harmonies, first, lively and dancelike with irregular, crisp rhythms, then, a contrasting, quiet, middle section followed by the return.

*Reflections:* Compare this work with other piano pieces, such as the Gershwin prelude (SS 13/5), the Chopin prelude (SS 11/2, page 260), the Haydn sonata (SS 10/3, page 244), and the Wilson piece (SS 13/2). Discuss the appropriateness of each of these works for the age in which they were created.

# Example 7

**Toccata for Piano**

Composed in 1979 by Emma Lou Diemer (1927–   )

A prolific, American composer who has received many awards and grants, Diemer has composed in the electronic medium and for virtually all standard and many nonstandard vocal and instrumental ensembles.

*Goals:*

Be aware of the expanded coloristic uses of the piano.
   Recognize a variety of contemporary compositional techniques.

*Reflections:* Unusual pianistic techniques applicable to this piece include (1) damping strings by hand inside the piano, (2) strumming strings by hand inside the piano, and (3) hitting undamped strings.

   Contemporary compositional techniques that are used in this piece include:
1. The percussive use of the piano
2. The wide range of pitches—using the entire keyboard
3. The lack of melody and harmony in the traditional sense
4. The use of fast, staccato repeated notes
5. Melodic contour ranging from a flat shape with a narrow range of pitches to a wide-ranging, angular use of pitches
6. Energy ranging from a flurry of activity to a considerable use of silence

# Example 8

**Symphony No. 1—III—in three movements**

Composed by Ellen Taaffe Zwilich (1939–   )

Zwilich won the 1983 Pulitzer Prize for this work. She was the first woman to win this coveted prize. She has composed solo works, chamber music for a variety of ensembles (her *String Quartet 1974* received much acclaim), and music for orchestra. Her style combines modern musical language with links to the past. She likes to develop large-scale works based on a germinal idea and values the richness and variety found in modern orchestras.

## Goals:

Recognize main motives and elements of contrast and repetition.

Identify entrances of main theme areas.

Be aware of the sounds of modern, tonal music.

*Guide:* First theme area—fast, vibrant, forceful; begins with timpani, followed by the main, ascending motive and by many staccato, repeated-note patterns.

Second theme area—begins with a bell sound; slow and quiet.

Return—timpani, then the original ascending motive.

Third theme area—again, begins with the bell sounds; legato, soft, and slow.

Return—fast and spritely, making use of the earlier, repeated-tone patterns; the intensity builds; the ranges of the violins are at times extreme, and the piece ends conventionally, providing a clear sense of tonic.

*Reflections:* This movement has characteristics of a rondo but not with traditional sounds or formal clarity.

Compare the musical characteristics of this music, particularly the orchestral sonorities, with those of Stravinsky, Brahms, and Bach.

# Additional Listening

# Example 1

**Three Places in New England**

   I. The "St. Gaudens" in Boston Common (Col. Robert Gould Shaw and his Colored Regiment)

  II. Putnam's Camp, Redding, Connecticut

 III. The Housatonic at Stockbridge

Composed by Charles Ives (1874–1954)

*Three Places in New England* is a set of three pieces for large orchestra. It was begun in 1903, completed in 1914, and revised in 1929 for chamber orchestra.

The work was first performed publically in 1931 in Boston's Town Hall by the Boston Chamber Orchestra under the direction of Nicholas Slonimsky. In that year, other performances took place in New York, Havana, and Paris. The original performance was urged by Henry Cowell, and partial financial support was provided by Ives.

This piece was Ive's first commercially published work. Although it was published in 1935, it was not performed again until 1948 when it was revived by the Boston Symphony Orchestra, Serge Koussevitsky, conductor, at the urging of Slonimsky. In 1974, it was revised by James B. Sinclair for large orchestra, combining the best of the 1914 and 1929 versions.

In 1931, Ives wrote a letter of encouragement to Slonimsky's musicians in Paris, who were discouraged by rehearsal problems:

The concert will go alright. Just kick into the music as you did in Town Hall—never mind the exact notes, they're always a nuisance. Just let the spirit underneath the stuff sail up to the Eiffel Tower and on to Heaven.

The instrumentation for the 1974 version of *Three Places in New England* is the common, large orchestra of winds in pairs plus piccolo, English horn, contrabassoon, an additional two horns, an additional trombone, and one tuba; and piano, celeste, organ, harp, and a gong.

*Guide:* I. The "St. Gaudens" in Boston Common

This movement is a tribute to the dedicated, valorous men of the first black regiment (the 54th) of the Massachusetts Volunteer Army and to its leader, Colonel Robert Gould Shaw. St. Gaudens refers to a sculpture by Augustus St. Gaudens, admired by Ives, which was part of a monument to the 54th Regiment located in the Boston Common across from City Hall.

It is a slow movement—rhythmically complex, syncopated, and dissonant. It has mostly full texture in the strings and mostly thin texture in the winds, with occasional bursts of full orchestral, even, brassy sonority. Notice the many widely spaced, short motives, particularly in the upper woodwinds and horns.

**First section**—quiet, full strings, little forward energy. The sonority builds primarily through rising pitches in the violins to a prominent motive of an ascending, five-note scale in the string basses and bassoons;

Additional prominent motives follow by oboe, then clarinet in low register, then flute playing a fragment of a familiar patriotic song;

A mildly, thumping bass ostinato punctuated by off-beat piano chords highlights the transition into the second section.

**Second section**—a little faster; harder syncopation; strings set the tone, then upper woodwinds provide the first long melody of the movement;

Intense increase in dynamics followed by a fanfare in the upper brasses, then a quiet horn solo;

Full orchestra builds to a huge, brassy climax; subsides immediately to the strings with punctuated piano chords, leading to the third section.

**Third section**—a return to the quiet mood and slower tempo of the first section;

A long, lyrical melody by the flute, derived from the previously suggested patriotic song;

Violins become prominent, interspersed by a short passage for two solo violins, then solo cello;

An oboe motive, then a flute motive—with strings and harp—bring the movement to a quiet close.

II. Putnam's Camp, Redding, Connecticut

In the winter of 1778–1779, General Israel Putnam's soldiers were camped near Redding, Connecticut. At this location now is a small park preserved as a Revolutionary War memorial.

Ives inspiration for this movement was derived from the following story:

> A child went to this park on a picnic. Wandering away, he hopes to catch a glimpse of some of the old soldiers. As he rests on the hillside of laurel and hickories, the tunes of the band and the songs of the children grow fainter and fainter. Over the trees on the crest of the hill, he sees a tall woman standing who reminds him of a picture of the Goddess of Liberty. With a sorrowful face, she pleads with the soldiers not to forget their cause and the great sacrifices they have made for it. But they march out of camp with fife and drum. Putnam is coming over the

hills in the center—the soldiers turn back and cheer. The little boy awakens, hears the childrens' songs, and runs down past the monument to listen to the band and join in the games and dances.

A number of fragments of popular childrens and patriotic songs are heard in this movement. They provide continuity and cohesion and some familiar sounds in this dissonant, complex, though highly programmatic music.

The music is traced to Ives' two pieces for theatre orchestra, "Country Band" march and the overture and march, "1776," composed around 1903.

The movement is mostly loud and marchlike, in mixed meter, and at times with several different melodies (and different tonalities) all happening at once. It is a cacophony of sound, just like the real-life sounds of a picnic and a band concert in a town park, yielding a variety of unrelated sounds all happening at once.

**Introduction**—marchlike in quick-step time.

**First section**—first theme stated in the violins, the first phrase ending with a few syncopated piano chords. The next phrase is an interplay of two melodies in the woodwinds and strings;

Then, Ives introduces his first cacophony of sound. Different songs are played by the trumpet; the trombone and tuba; the oboe, first clarinet, and violas; the flute and second clarinet; and the violins. Suddenly, a lovely, quiet children's song appears in the first violin, followed by an interplay among the various instruments.

This section ends with a low, static, passage in the clarinets and violins that decreases in pitch, dynamics, and texture. A dissonant chord in the strings and piano prepares the next section.

**Second section**—soft and sustained;

The quiet strings interact with melodic fragments in the upper woodwinds. Both soon are supported by short, syncopated piano chords. The fragments soon become an extended melody.

This section gradually moves into the loud, faster, marchlike spirit of the first section, with its several returns of the cacophony of sound.

Builds with intense fervor to huge climaxes, once suddenly returning to the quiet childrens song heard in the first section;

The movement returns to the town band/picnic environment before building to its most intense, most furious climax.

The movement ends on a highly dissonant, unstable, crashing chord.

III. The Housatonic at Stockbridge
    In 1908, shortly after Ives was married, he walked with his wife in the meadows along the Housatonic River, and heard distant singing from the church across the river. The mist had not entirely left the river bed, and the colors, the running water, the banks and elm trees were, for Ives, a memorable experience. He then made a brief musical sketch, capturing the atmosphere of that experience.

**Beginning**—very slow with the shimmering sounds of the strings;

**Hymn tune**—long, majestic melody; solo horn with violas, then with English horn;

Later, the cellos and bassoons sing the sonorous melody. The shimmering background takes over and evolves into a powerful, complex sonority from the full orchestra, ever increasing in intensity and speed;

Music drives to the final, crashing chord, answered by a delicate, quiet fragment of the hymn tune to end the piece.

# Example 2

**Appalachian Spring**—a ballet and a concert piece based on the music of the ballet

Composed in 1944 by Aaron Copland (1900–   )

In eight sections played as one continuous movement

For thirteen instruments, enlarged by Copland for his orchestral version to include wood-winds in pairs plus piano, harp, and percussion; percussion section adds xylophone, glockenspiel, and wood block to the standard instruments

Awarded the Pulitzer Prize in 1945

The setting is early nineteenth-century America. It is a "pioneer celebration in spring around a newly-built farm house in the Pennsylvania hills. . . ."

The characters include a bride-to-be, the farmer/groom-to-be, and a revivalist and his followers. The ballet, portraying the simplicity of the Quaker life, celebrates an awakening of life, both for the couple and the crops.

The music is considered very American, portraying barn dances, fiddle tunes, and revival hymns. The music is characterized by much syncopation and many changes of meter. It is tuneful and tonal yet has the stamp of the unique musical personality of Aaron Copland.

## *Guide:*

**Section 1:** A slow introduction that depicts the setting of a peaceful countryside.

Theme A—based on three ascending chords, outlined melodically (arpeggios);

First motive—stated in the clarinet (a motive much used in later sections);

Second motive—two successive chords (arpeggios), one on top of the other, stated in the violins.

**Section 2:** Lively.

Theme B—a dancelike tune characterized by the opening octave jump and many ascending and descending arpeggios passed around from instrument to instrument;

A choralelike hymn emerges in the brasses, interacting with theme B;

Theme B and ascending arpeggios (from the second motive of theme A) are developed with vitality until the hymn returns; Ends quietly with the motives from theme A appearing in various solo woodwind instruments.

**Section 3:** Quiet.

Bassoon introduction in irregular meter. Theme C—legato melody, a motive of an ascending arpeggio; in clarinet, then oboe, then combination of woodwinds;

Strings in more intense, dissonant section;

The main theme of this section returns in the oboe, then clarinet, then flute; intense string passage returns briefly; quiet ending.

**Section 4:** Lively.

Introduction—short melodies bounce around the orchestra, first in the upper woodwinds;

Theme D, first part—a dancelike tune stated first in the strings; the second part, also dancelike, stated in solo trumpet;

Theme D develops with fragments of each part of theme D;

A majestic passage, based on a descending motive, brings the section to a close as the oboe quietly recalls theme C from section 3.

**Section 5:** Very lively.

Continues with the spirit of Section 4, combining new material with elements of previous themes, particularly theme B from section 2.

**Section 6:** A short, quiet section beginning with legato solo violin; it is thematically derived from the ascending motive of theme C.

**Section 7:** A quiet introduction with material derived from theme A.

Theme E—a Shaker hymn tune, "Simple Gifts," and a set of variations based on this tune; stated first in the clarinet after quiet introductory material that recalls the ascending motive of theme C.

**Section 8:** Soft, serene.

Theme F—a quiet, legato, choralelike passage in the strings;

Theme C returns again;

The last statement is the opening motive of theme A, which brings the composition to a quiet close.

*Discography*

*Ex. 1*  Crumb, George. "Echoes of Time and the River (I)." Louisville 5-711. 3:21.

*Ex. 2*  Wilson, Olly. "Piano Piece." Desto DC7102-3.

*Ex. 3*  Ives, Charles. Three Places in New England. Columbia MS 7015. 5:34.

*Ex. 4*  Still, William Grant. "Afro-American Symphony (III)." Columbia P19426. 3:23.

*Ex. 5*  Gershwin, George. Preludes for Piano, No. 1. Columbia IM-39699. 1:17.

*Ex. 6*  Crawford, Ruth. Preludes for Piano, No. 8. Northwestern NR 204.

*Ex. 7*  Diemer, Emma Lou. Toccata for Piano. Coronet 3105. 5:47.

*Ex. 8*  Zwilich, Ellen Taaffe. Symphony No. 1 (III). New World Records. NW 336. 4:04.

*Summary*

Chapter 13 focuses on classical art music in the United States of America. The classical tradition has been dominated by Western European culture but in the twentieth century has become a worldwide phenomenom, with the United States taking a place at the forefront of modern developments in classical music.

An "American Musical Language," to some, means nationalist music that reflects various aspects of American life (Americanist music). This chapter conveys more than that. It suggests that modern American music has been created by those who value explicitly American idioms but also by those Americans who continue in cultivating the European styles, who experiment while searching for a new musical language, or who write in a personal style of expression that fits no particular label and that is perhaps neither American nor European. It is the sum of all these musics that comprise the American musical language.

Finally, twentieth-century America has raised the social conscience of its citizens in matters of race relations and minority and women's concerns, a fact that has permeated every aspect of our society, including music. This chapter has drawn attention to the status of America's music by women and minority composers by focusing on a few representative composers and their works.

*Terms and*
*Concepts*

*Cultivated music*
*Vernacular music*
*European influences*
*How Americans view classical music*
*The ultimate art music*
*The ticket-buying public*
*Cosmopolitan musical environment*
*Nadia Boulanger*
*Experimental (avant-garde) music*
*A distinctively American musical style*

# Chapter 14
# Cultural Factors and Functions

This chapter seeks to promote an understanding of those cultural factors common in the United States that can enrich the study of music. It will focus on the following points:

1. Ways music functions in the United States of America, that is, how music is used by Americans
2. The roles Americans play as music creators, performers, and listeners, as well as the roles that people, as nonmusicians, play in support of musicians and of the musical life of their communities, regions, or nation.

The information is organized in three broad areas:

1. *The music industry.* Comprised broadly of merchandising (making and selling things for profit) and performance (producing and selling live or recorded music for profit or as a service)
2. *Music and the media.* Includes broadcasting, film, and advertising
3. *Music in our communities.* Encompasses (a) Professional, semiprofessional, and amateur musical activities (b) The promotion and development of music and the other arts

## The Music Industry

Music is big business, one of the largest and most complex in the United States. The music industry, as has been stated, is comprised of selling products and live and recorded music. It can be broken down into five overlapping categories that can assist in understanding more clearly what the industry is and how it functions. The categories are manufacturing, publishing, merchandising, performance, and management.

## Manufacturing

The making of goods includes research, design, and development. To present a variety of manufactured goods essential to the music industry will suffice to illustrate its scope, variety, and impact on our lives:

1. Musical instruments
   a. Band and orchestra instruments that serve thousands of school, community, and professional bands and orchestras
   b. Electronic instruments, mostly keyboards, guitars, drums, and synthesizers with their links to computers through MIDI technology that serve the vast professional, semiprofessional, and amateur entertainment industry
   c. Pianos and pipe organs that serve homes, schools, churches, and concert halls
   d. Traditional folk instruments such as dulcimers, autoharps, and acoustic banjos and guitars that serve mostly amateur music making that varies from region to region
   e. Educational instruments such as recorders, various drums and tone bars or other mallet instruments, guitars, and keyboard instruments that are used especially in elementary school music classes
2. Audio equipment
   a. Stereo systems that include record and/or playback capability for cassette tapes, long play records, compact discs, videotapes, and videodiscs
   b. Receiver capability for stereo FM, AM, and TV broadcast
   c. Audio reinforcement and enhancement from amplifiers, graphic equalizers, and speaker systems
3. Uniforms and robes—for the thousands of school, college, and community choirs, orchestras, and bands

A recording in progress in a modern commercial studio

Sting adjusting sound at a mixing board

4. Accessories—the many supportive goods that all musicians need, such as replacement strings for guitars and violins, music stands, lubricants, patch cords, disc or tape cleaners, and other goods that for the most part represent high profit items for music stores.

## Publishing

The heart of the music publishing industry is the popular song in its recorded not printed form. It is all connected with making a hit and realizing the fullest commercial potential of a song.

From the days of the minstrel shows in the second half of the nineteenth century, America became enamored with a vernacular music that we call popular music. By 1900, with the establishment of large publishing houses and the development of sophisticated merchandising methods, the music industry was big business. It was a business based on the "making a hit" concept, a concept still central to the industry today. By the 1920s, hits were made with the aid of Tin Pan Alley song pluggers and songs from musical theatre and vaudeville shows. The primary means of dissemination of a song was the sale of sheet music. In the swing era of the 1930s, songs were plugged by the lead singers of the big bands. In the 1940s, and 1950s, many former big band singers became solo performers independent of big bands and promoted their songs. Since the 1950s, the disc jockey and the quantity of airplay became the hitmakers. In the 1980s, it is clear that the impact of video airplay is playing a significant role in making a song commercially successful.

The first measure of commercial success was the sale of popular songs in the form of sheet music. With the establishment of the copyright law in 1909, composers, lyricists, and publishers became the copyright owners of popular songs and were able to make a profit from the royalties collected from the use of these songs in live and recorded performance. Copyright holders were granted exclusive rights to authorize use of their music for a limited time and to collect fees for such uses. Anyone *performing* copyrighted material had to obtain performance rights by paying for a license or by paying royalties. Anyone *recording* copyrighted material had to obtain mechanical rights and pay the established fees. Anyone using copyrighted material in *film* had to obtain synchronization rights and pay the appropriate fees.

Licensing agencies (ASCAP, BMI, SESAC) have been established to collect these fees and distribute them to the copyright holders. With the revised copyright law that went into effect in 1978, colleges and universities now pay these agencies the cost of "blanket" performance licenses to cover royalties for a year's collective use of copyrighted material (rather than of individual works) controlled by the agencies and performed by school marching and concert bands, stage bands, choirs, and other performing ensembles.

Publishers build catalogs of music with the greatest commercial potential. They use the following process:

1. Seek out composers and songwriters
2. Negotiate and obtain rights for their music
3. Manage and promote their music to realize maximum profit
4. Negotiate contracts for producing, manufacturing, distributing, and selling recordings
5. Cause a song, usually after it has become a hit, to be released in sheet music or songbooks (folios).

Some publishers specialize in printed music for churches, schools, and colleges—the Christian, educational, and concert music markets. Another market for printed music is the large group of amateur music makers who buy pianos, organs, electronic keyboards, and guitars for home use and who need to buy sheet music, folios, and

A home entertainment center.

instructional "how to" books. One area of music publishing that is very large but typically is not included as part of the music industry is the music book industry, including textbooks and magazines about music. Usually, these materials are published by houses that specialize in writing, producing, and distributing books or other materials in more than one discipline.

## Merchandising

Music merchandising is the pricing, distribution, promotion, retailing, and servicing of music and music-related products. For the most part, it is ultimately the exchange between the music store retailer and the consumer. The consumer may be a music teacher buying band or choral music, an instrument, or instruction books; a professional musician always on the lookout for a better instrument or new music; parents supporting the musical interests of their children; teenagers checking out the latest in electric guitars; adult amateurs who keep active musically as an avocation; or anyone seeking to add to their record or tape library.

The merchandising exchange may not be in a music store but at a concert where consumers can buy merchandising "tie-ins" (posters, tote bags, T-shirts, recordings) that identify the artist or music organization. Such merchandising is common for performers of all types of music—popular, rock, folk, religious, country, and classical. Sales of tie-in merchandise add to the profits of the musician or organization. At the same time, as long as the products are used and seen, they advertise the musician or organization. Virtually all organizations producing classical music, including opera companies, consider the merchandising of tie-ins to be an essential component of their business operation.

Recorded music is sold mostly in stores specializing in the sale of records and tapes, but it is also sold in department stores, in discount houses, through record clubs, and from direct TV offers. Inventories of large record stores are usually maintained by the retailer who purchases directly from record distributors who are associated exclusively with a major label (record company) or who handle (represent) many labels. The inventory of nonspecialized stores (department stores, discount houses, and perhaps book stores) or any store that maintains racks of records and tapes is supplied and controlled by the "rack jobber." The rack jobber pays to the retailer a space rental fee or commission on sales or both. In large record and tape departments, the rack jobber may actually function as a retailer, controlling the sales and cash flow through his or her own checkout counter and financial management. Almost all record stores or departments, in responding to the changing technology and the changing markets, now stock videos and perhaps video equipment for sale or rent.

Specialized audio stores serve mostly the semiprofessional and the sophisticated amateur consumer—the audiophile. These stores provide expertise and service, and you pay for it. Department stores and discount houses that sell audio equipment usually stock the middle to low end of the quality spectrum and provide little expertise and service. You pay less and you get less. Almost all these stores, in responding to changing technology and changing markets, now stock video equipment. Professional consumers of audio equipment deal directly with manufacturers or through sound design consultants in maintaining sophisticated recording studios or other sound reinforcement businesses.

Printed music, band and orchestra instruments, guitars, pianos, organs, and electronic instruments of various types are sold in music stores that range from a highly specialized shop to the full-line, comprehensive store that maintains a wide variety of inventory. Most stores specialize to some degree. Some serve their local or regional school music programs through the sale of band and choral music and the sale or rental and servicing (repair) of band and orchestral instruments. Some serve the local or regional amateur or semiprofessional entertainment market with an inventory of drums, guitars, and electronic instruments and equipment. Others limit themselves to the sale of pianos and organs.

The size and scope of music stores range from small, "mom and pop," family owned and operated shops to large mail-order houses with a national market. The largest market for music stores is the amateur market, mainly because it includes the more than 100,000 school music ensembles whose memberships total in the millions and the vast amount of music making that takes place in our communities, churches, and homes.

## Performance

The performance of music, of course, permeates every aspect of the music industry and, indeed, of society itself. Thus, it overlaps, relates to, and is served by every topic under consideration in this chapter. Music is performed live in concert halls, gymnasiums, parks, fair grounds, and hotel lounges. It is performed, recorded on discs or tapes, distributed, and sold to consumers, broadcast over radio or television, placed on the sound tracks of films and commercials, and used in elevators, offices, and department stores.

As they say, it "all begins with a song." This is literally true in the entertainment industry and, metaphorically, is true for all aspects of the industry. The business of music begins with a creative work, whether composed in notated form, created spontaneously through improvisation, or composed orally as a means of expression with no thought of writing it down. In the context of the music business, music, whether created recently, decades ago, or even centuries ago, is presented to a paying audience, the consumer, who buys recordings or pays to listen to live music.

The previous section on publishing discussed the process in the entertainment industry of commercially exploiting a song under the "make a hit" concept, from the writing of a song through getting it recorded, distributed, played on the air, and sold. This process usually precedes a song becoming a hit and the performer becoming well known. A song becomes a hit when enough people listen to it on the radio or "hear" it on TV and then buy recordings of it, either as a single or in an album. It also precedes a performer having a sufficient name to attract a paying audience to live concerts. Live concerts can provide income for a performer but can also increase income from the

Examining a program announcing a professional concert series.

sale of recordings. Live performances might be single concerts that are part of a regional or national tour or multiple engagements at a single location such as a hotel lounge. To achieve fame, sell recordings, and have successful tours are also major goals for many professional classical, folk, and jazz artists.

One of the biggest "buyers" of those musicians who tour are colleges and universities. Most institutions of higher education offer "artist series" sold preferably as packages of concerts (commonly known as subscription series or season tickets) with considerable savings over costs of individual concerts. Communities also frequently sponsor artist series comprised of touring performers. Organizations such as Affiliate Artists and Community Concerts exist to assist communities in providing high quality music at the lowest possible costs. Affiliate Artists assist communities in sponsoring residencies in which musicians live in a community for extended periods of time, usually from one to six weeks. The artists present recitals but also involve themselves in the musical life of the community in as many different ways as possible. Community Concerts assist in developing artist series for communities, including many in small rural areas.

One way many communities and colleges reduce costs is through the concept of block bookings, wherein artists who can play several concerts in a region with minimal travel between locations will perform for reduced fees. This concept saves them time and energy because of the more efficient travel schedule and earns them more money, even with reduced fees, because of a schedule that can allow more concerts in less time.

Most communities offer their own local music performances in every conceivable style, depending upon the size and population mix of the area. Large cities with a diverse ethnic makeup can offer a tremendous diversity of live musical performances to appeal to every taste. Many communities sponsor festive occasions such as folk festivals, bluegrass festivals, fiddlin' contests, or Renaissance fairs. Most of the larger cities maintain symphony orchestras, community bands, and even opera companies, some of which are fully professional, some strictly volunteer.

A symphonic band
concert

The majority of the community orchestras hire semiprofessional musicians who play for pay but at a level that requires them to earn their major source of income elsewhere, usually from teaching. Many of the performers have chosen professional careers outside of music and play music for their own enrichment, enjoyment, and perhaps supplemental income. Many semiprofessional or amateur musicians play jazz, rock, or country music in local nightclubs, lounges, private social clubs, and for school or community dances, or they may be hired to perform church music regularly or on special occasions.

The maintenance of a vital and active musical life, for many communities, is a source of civic pride; a symbol of a progressive attitude that stresses human, cultural, and artistic values; and a strategy for economic development, including the promotion of tourism and the recruitment of new business and industry.

## Management

Virtually no professional musician achieves successful career advancement without the assistance of people other than a paying audience. The performer needs help in finding jobs, negotiating contracts, hiring attorneys, handling the intricacies of the copyright law, creating an image, designing and writing publicity materials, organizing publicity campaigns, stimulating media coverage, obtaining recording or publishing contracts, organizing concerts and tours, and managing finances.

An aspiring professional with limited funds begins with an agent whose responsibility is to find jobs for the performer and to exploit the performer's talents to their greatest potential. The agent may be a friend of the performer or a representative of a talent agency who handles many clients. The second step would be to hire a personal manager with responsibilities for handling the artitst's money as well as every aspect of the artist's career. As the performer achieves financial success, the specialized functions described above may be assigned to more specialized people or to one or more people who are put on the performer's payroll. The performer may establish a corporation, perhaps a publishing company, to handle the business and keep expensive fees and commissions "in-house."

In the classical field, careers typically are handled by representatives of artist management firms who serve the dual roles of personal manager and booking agent for concert artists.

## Music and the Media

The purpose of this section is to explore briefly fundamental relationships between music and various forms of communication (media), with emphasis on how music benefits the media and how the media benefits music. The media (or mediums) most closely aligned with the musical life of our society are those that reach the largest number of people, namely, radio, television, and newsprint—the mass media. Of these, perhaps radio has had the greatest impact on music, particularly in its role in "making a hit" in the entertainment or popular music industry. Yet, it may be that, in the 1980s, music videos are changing the relationship of radio to music in our society, a relationship to be discussed further. Another relationship between music and the media worthy of exploring is that created by music in advertising. The newsprint medium (newspapers and magazines) provides a significant relationship to be explored, involving the music critic.

## Radio

Fundamental factors in the relationship between music and radio programming follow:

1. Music remains at the core of programming.
2. Music is part of virtually all advertising.
3. Airplay promotes the sale of recorded music.
4. Airplay provides income from royalties for jingle writers, song writers, publishers, and other holders of copryrighted music used by stations either in advertising or programming.
5. Musicians are hired for the production of some commercials and recorded program material.

Soon after its beginnings, radio was found to be a medium for reaching large numbers of people, and the best format found to reach that goal was to broadcast popular music. Live programming in radio was common through the 1940s. It included comedy, drama, variety, swing music, and opera.

Responding to the impact of television programming, radio in the 1950s settled on a music/news/weather format. The music was recorded, and the programs were hosted by DJs (disc jockeys). Typically, programming was laid out in one-hour blocks, with news at the top of the hour followed by music and an abundance of commercials and chitchat by the DJ. Promotions, contests, gimmicks, interviews, or remotes (live broadcasts from outside the studio, perhaps at a store or shopping center) were common. Most radio shows were locally oriented, and the personality of the DJ was a valued commodity, particularly if a rapport with his or her audience could be established.

Because of the importance of the music to programming and the importance of airplay to the success of songs and their performers, music publishers were highly competitive and assertive in encouraging DJs to air the songs of their clients through their latest releases. The competition was fierce, for there was only so much broadcast time available for new releases. Frequent replays of songs were common, and dozens if not hundreds of new releases appeared on the market each week. Airplay was essential to a song becoming a hit and a performer becoming famous and financially successful. In recent years, however, airplay has become less essential for established performers and for those concentrating on promotion by means of music videos.

A radio disc jockey.

In the 1980s, two related factors have modified if not completely changed the format of radio broadcasting, particularly programming: automation and increased syndication. New computer technology has allowed radio stations to be partially or totally automated. Stations can program equipment to air taped music, commercials, and station identifications or logos on reels or carts (broadcast cartridges) automatically, without the need for a disc jockey or an engineer.

Production companies (syndicators) develop prepackaged program or "canned" material compatible with the station's programming policy and format. Many of the Top Forty-type shows are now syndicated, as well as many news and sports programs. This minimizes the spontaneity and local color brought by the traditional DJ who has become less of a factor in local radio and the promotion and sales of recordings.

Paid advertising is the primary source of income for commercial radio, but most regions of the United States are served by public or noncommercial radio. Such stations, funded by grants and contributions, are free to program less popular material such as jazz, classical, and folk music, extended news programs, and special features that appeal to a more sophisticated audience in the region. Many public radio stations are affiliated with colleges and universities.

**Music in Advertising**

Virtually all commercials on radio and television use music to help sell a product or service. That music has to be created and performed, providing jobs for both musicians and jingle writers (composers). Many commercials use electronic instruments only, and the creator frequently is also the performer.

It has been found, intuitively and through documented research, that music has the psychological power to affect both the conscious and subconscious emotions of listeners. Music in advertising can be in the foreground, accompany dancing, or serve as background for spoken material. It can create an image or a mood, establish an association, and enhance the positive and minimize the negative attributes of a product or service. It can attract attention, create unity, and provide memorability. It can be catchy, simple, and repetitive, and it can serve as a catalyst for an entire ad campaign. Music for an ad may be derived from a popular song, or it may be converted into a popular song. Either way, the intent is to capitalize on the exposure and popularity of the other.

Examine the qualities of familiar commercials or virtually any current ones on radio or TV. What are their attractive qualities? What makes them potentially effective? How do you respond to them?

It is worth pointing out that the broadcast media air commercials for which they are not paid a fee. Public Service Announcements (PSAs) are available to nonprofit groups such as educational institutions, arts organizations, and charitable agencies. The production of PSAs may cost, but most are produced locally and inexpensively. Many times they involve no music, only a spoken message.

**Music Videos**

A music video is a commercial for recordings, a tool for promoting a song and its performer, and another method of getting a performer before the public. It is a means of communication whose impact, as of this writing, is not yet fully known or understood. However we do know that music videos' impact is significant.

Part of the attraction of music videos, in addition to the music itself, is the innovative production techniques and imaginative visual creativity. Many videos incorporate dance, movement, dramatic action, montages, graphics, and other special effects. Such effects might be produced by means of editing techniques but also might be computer generated.

Music videos at first were distributed free to nightclubs, discos, and other places that would expose them to potential buyers of recordings. With their success and with rising production and performance costs, they are now sold not only to commercial establishments but to the public. They originally promoted rock music and became prominent on cable television, notably MTV, and now are produced to promote music in many styles, including jazz, country, and classical music. They are aired over a variety of cable channels as well as network television and are usually aired at a time to coincide with the release of its soundtrack as a commercial recording.

**Newsprint**

The basics of the relationship between music and the newsprint medium (newspapers and magazines) involve two overlapping styles of writing:

1. *Music journalism.* Presents information about upcoming musical events and produces feature articles about artists and artistic developments—local, regional, or national
2. *Music criticism.* Presents reviews of newly released recordings or commentary, interpretation, and critiquing of musical events that have just occurred

Music journalism typically refers to the reporting of information without personal commentary or interpretation. On the other hand, music criticism, presented in a by-lined column or article (author's name identified), informs but also entertains and editorializes with the interest of the public (perhaps more than the artist) in mind.

Reviews of jazz, popular music, rock, as well as classical music are found regularly in various music magazines and in newspapers, particularly in the larger metropolitan areas. These reviews can provide a way for consumers to be more knowledgeable in purchasing recordings and in selecting which live performances to attend. Positive reviews are, of course, hoped for by any artist, and negative reviews can be damaging, particularly in the context of repeated presentations such as a musical show. Bad reviews have been known to cause the premature closing of Broadway shows.

## Music in the Community

Music making, music listening, and music learning are favorite pastimes for large numbers of Americans. Most of these musical involvements take place outside of the formal music education programs in our schools and colleges. They take place in the community.

### A Diverse Musical Life

Outside of formal educational surroundings, musical activities take place in such diverse locations as streets, malls, playgrounds, civic auditoriums, community music schools, senior citizen centers, prisons, mental health clinics, and in the privacy of homes with family and friends. The extent and nature of the musical activities taking place in these contexts reflect the vast amount of amateur music making in our society. These examples also suggest that Americans value and enjoy a wide diversity of styles of music, from children's songs to chamber music, from square dance music to ballet, from mariachi music to blues. Additionally, considering the extent to which Americans attend live concerts and buy radios, stereos, cassettes, albums, and compact discs, music listening as well as music making are valued activities in our society. Again, it is easy to document the variety of musical styles people listen to by examining radio programming among the various stations in a community; record sales; the various topics used for the sales "charts," such as Hot Soul Singles, Hot Country LPs, Top 50 Adult Contemporary, Jazz LPs, Spiritual LPs, and Classical; and the types of concerts publicized in newspapers and arts and entertainment magazines. This is not to say that people as individuals are eclectic in their listening preferences. They probably are not and choose to listen only to a limited number of styles. However, collectively, a wide variety of music is performed and listened to in our society.

The performance of music in the community by professional and semiprofessional musicians was discussed previously in the context of the music industry. That discussion concluded with reference to the value of a vital musical life to a community. That reference is equally important in the context of amateur music making and music listening. It is the sum of the community's musical life, both professional and amateur, that can help build civic pride, promote tourism and economic development, and convey a community's human, cultural, and artistic values. A community's musical life does not happen automatically. If it is to be successful and vital, it needs to be developed, promoted, and nourished.

### Promotion and Development

Just as in the entertainment industry where many people fulfill nonmusical functions in order to make the industry work (agents, managers, bookers, promoters, etc.), many paid professionals and many more unpaid volunteers fulfill nonmusical functions in support of a community's artistic life.

#### Government Support

Government agencies exist at all political levels in support of music and the other arts. At the national level, the National Endowment for the Arts provides grants to performing and visual arts organizations that must be matched by the requesting agency, thus, stimulating fund-raising in the private sector. It also provides funds to regional agencies and state arts councils who in turn support programs throughout their constituencies. These programs include facilitating block booking of touring groups, selecting and supporting residencies, offering grants to worthy programs which in turn generate even more local fund-raising as these grants have to be matched by the requestor. Many of these grants support programs of local community arts councils.

This form of government subsidy has a marvelous rippling effect as it filters down to the local level. When individuals support a program with money, typically they become involved personally and attend any public events. Thus, the Endowment, since its establishment in 1965, has generated directly or indirectly dramatic increases in private and corporate support of the arts in both financial backing and audience attendance. Additionally, the support of the Endowment lends an air of credibility to a program and causes private and corporate contributors to feel a gift will be a good investment. Many arts organizations, however, are well known in a community, have a good track record of quality production, and attract repeated contributions each year.

*Corporate Support*

Many large corporations, such as Ford, Kresge, and Atlantic-Richfield, have established foundations to handle their corporate giving. Others will contribute funds directly from their operating accounts.

Typically, business and industry support arts programs in areas in which they operate as a means of helping their employees have a better place to live. Such support sends a message that acknowledges and communicates to others that the arts do contribute to an improved quality of life in their communities and are important in the workplace.

*Civic Support*

Local community support from the private sector comes from the volunteer work of boards of directors of professional arts organizations, committees of chambers of commerce and local government, local arts councils, and volunteer support groups (Friends of Music, the Symphony Auxilliary, the Opera Guild).

Board members are appointed for their professional expertise, such as lawyers or accountants, for their capacity to contribute money, or for their ability to raise money and encourage contributions from their peers. Arts councils usually involve both professionals and lay people who work together to develop important community projects. Volunteer groups are usually associated with a professional organization or educational institution. The volunteers may help the parent organization in a host of ways. They may sell tickets, work with local and state government and arts councils in supporting and enacting legislation affecting the arts, promote a concert or festival, plan fund-raising activities and related social activities, usher at concerts, or schedule concerts or special programs in schools or for community organizations.

Large and active volunteer organizations also cause a ripple effect in increased contributions and larger and perhaps better informed audiences at live concerts. Many, perhaps most, arts organizations would not exist without the dedication and hard work of the community volunteers.

*Summary*

Music is an aural art, either high art (classical music), vernacular art (folk and popular music), or hybrids of both as in religious music and jazz that can be studied for its own value as art and works of art. Whichever classification, the way people use music, the value it has for their lives, and the function it has in society all create a cultural context that enables music to be observed and studied outside of the realm of music as an art. One example is the study of music as an industry.

This chapter has examined music as a multibillion dollar industry that employs hundreds of thousands of people as musicians and nonmusicians. It has looked at music's involvement with the mass media, particularly through the entertainment and advertising industries. It has discussed the various and diverse roles that music plays in our communities—how music functions, who is involved, and how it does or does not thrive depending upon community values about music and the extent to which lay people (the consumers, patrons, and advocates) become involved in their community's musical life.

*Terms and Concepts*

*Song pluggers*
*Sheet music*
*Disc jockey*
*Airplay*
*Copyright law*
*Exclusive rights*
*Licensing agencies*
*Folios*
*Retailer*
*Consumer*
*Tie-in merchandise*
*Rack jobber*
*Music stores*
*Artist series*
*Block booking*

*Agent*
*Personal manager*
*Music videos*
*Music in advertising*
*Jingles*
*Automation*
*Syndication*
*Music journalism*
*Music criticism*
*National Endowment for the Arts*
*Arts councils*
*Matching grants*
*Government subsidy*
*Volunteer organizations*

# Appendix A
## *Acoustics of Music*

Acoustics is the science of sound and the physical basis of music. Sound consists of wave motion from a sound producing object. The wave motion involves tiny disturbances or changes in air pressure.

**Sound-Producing Agents**

Sound-producing agents are objects that, when struck, shaken, rubbed, blown, bowed, or plucked, produce movement in such a way that they generate exactly the same movement in the air (sympathetic vibrations). Such objects include voices, musical instruments, a siren, waterfall, train, animals, and electronic synthesizers. More specifically, it includes such vibrating objects as violins, guitars, piano strings, drum heads, the reeds of a clarinet or saxophone, organ pipes, rattles, cymbals, and maracas. The vibrations (sound waves) are received by the ear and perceived (heard) as either musical sound or noise.

| **Physical Properties of Sound** | **Musical Elements** |
|---|---|
| Frequency | Pitch (register) |
| Intensity (amplitude) | Loudness |
| Duration | Duration |
| Complexity (shape) | Tone quality (timbre) |

**Frequency**

The rate of speed of a sound wave is measured in hertz (Hz)—the number of sound waves per second (the number of cycles or vibrations per second).

| A = 440 | The pitch, A above middle C on the keyboard, is 440 cycles per second or 440 Hz. |
|---|---|
| A = 220 | One octave lower than A 440 |
| A = 880 | One octave higher than A 440 |
| C = 256 | Middle C on the keyboard |

Keyboard frequencies (all numbers can vary slightly)

Middle C

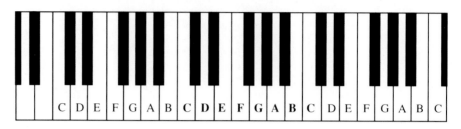

|  | 220 Hz   256 Hz | 440 Hz | 880 Hz |
|---|---|---|---|
| Bottom of hearing range 16 Hz | ‹----- Lower Pitches | Higher Pitches -----› | Top of hearing range 20,000 Hz |

**Pitch**

When we can perceive a single tone, we call it a pitch. Most melodies are made up of individually recognizable pitches. Sometimes an exact pitch cannot be determined but can be grouped in a high range (a cluster of high frequencies), middle range, or low range. The entire range of frequencies sounding at once is called white sound or white noise (radio static, the roar of a waterfall). The absence of frequencies is silence. The faster a frequency, the higher the pitch; the slower a frequency, the lower the pitch.

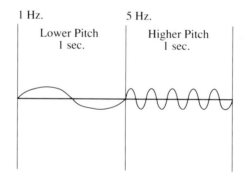

**Loudness (Dynamics, Volume)**

The loudness or softness of sound is generated by the amplitude of a wave (the height of the wave), that is, the intensity or energy of tone production.

ff = fortissimo; very loud
f = forte; loud
mf = mezzo forte; medium loud
get louder = crescendo
get softer = decrescendo (diminuendo)
accent = extra stress (intensity) on one tone

mp = mezzo piano; medium soft
p = piano; soft
pp = pianissimo; very soft

The length of time a tone is produced.                    **Duration**

Patterns of long and short durations.                    **Rhythm**

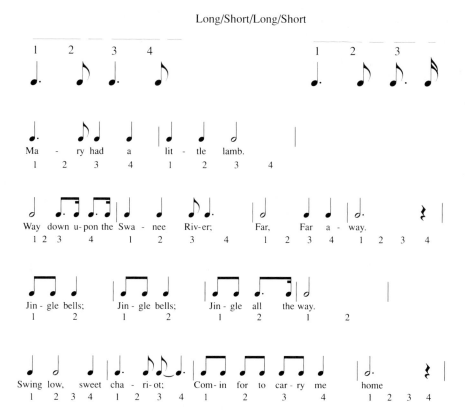

**Articulation**

The shape of a sound wave determines the tone quality (timbre). The shape is deter-    **Shape**
mined by the intensity (loudness) of the fundamental frequency (pitch) and its various    **(Complexity)**
overtones. Most pitches are complex, that is, comprised of a fundamental tone and a
variety of overtones of varying degrees of loudness. Pitches with a relatively pure tone
quality, such as those produced by a flute, are comprised of the fundamental and very
few heard overtones. More complex tones, such as those produced by oboes or saxophones, have several overtones perceivably present. You will hear these overtones but

will not be able to distinguish one from the other. You will typically not recognize individual overtones. However, they do contribute to the shape of the sound waves and thus to the quality of the sound.

| | | | | |
|---|---|---|---|---|
| Seventh overtone (third octave) | = C | = D | = F | = G |
| Sixth overtone (seventh) | = B♭ | = C | = E♭ | = F |
| Fifth overtone (fifth) | = G | = A | = C | = D |
| Fourth overtone (third) | = E | = F♯ | = A | = B |
| Third overtone (second octave) | = C | = D | = F | = G |
| Second overtone (fifth) | = G | = A | = C | = D |
| First overtone (first octave) | = C | = D | = F | = G |
| Fundamental pitch | = C | = D | = F | = G |

A relatively simple tone — essentially one peak per cycle.

(the fundamental)

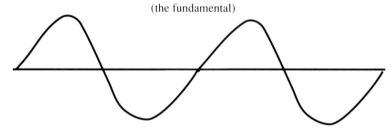

A more complex tone with multiple peaks per cycle.

(fundamental pitch with louder overtones)

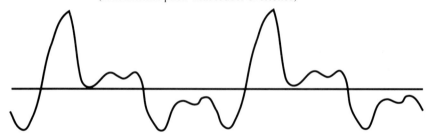

## Architectural and Audio Acoustics

Attaining proper acoustics in an auditorium, recording studio, or home requires knowledge, skill, and planning. Acoustical characteristics must be designed into such a facility. The size, shape, wall and ceiling material, structure, and type of seating must be consistent with the purpose of the room. Different physical characteristics are required depending on the needs, whether it is to be used for speech, chamber music, large performing groups, home listening, or professional recording. Some of the characteristics that acoustical engineers (professional or amateur) can consider are: blend, brilliance, clarity, ensemble, fullness, intimacy, liveness, reverberation, and warmth.

## Blend

The sounds of the music blend properly if they are well balanced and are heard at appropriate loudness levels throughout the ensemble (in a studio or concert performance) and throughout the room or hall. The blend of sound refers to the mixing of the sound from all the instruments or voices in the ensemble over all points in the room. In a concert hall having poor blend, an audience member may hear one section or player louder than another in ways that were not intended by the composer or performers, or people in different parts of the hall will hear the sounds differently. The simplest technique for achieving proper blend is to use appropriate reflecting surfaces surrounding the performance area. The purpose is, in effect, to mix the sound on stage before distributing it to the audience.

The high frequencies are predominant. It is the opposite of warmth and exists if the reverberation time for high frequencies is larger relative to that of the low frequencies.

**Brilliance**

Sounds do not run together; all lines (parts) are heard distinctly. It is the opposite of fullness. This is obtained when the intensity (loudness level) of the reflected sound is low relative to the intensity of the direct sound. Great clarity is required for optimum listening to speech and is particularly important when performing orchestral music. In general, greater clarity is achieved from shorter reverberation times.

**Clarity**

Good ensemble playing is determined by the extent to which a performing group plays together with precision. To do so, the musicians must hear each other. To achieve good ensemble playing, reflections must not prolong the sound beyond the duration of the fast notes in the music being performed.

**Ensemble**

A room will have fullness if the intensity of the reflected sound is high relative to the intensity of the direct sound. In general, greater fullness implies longer reverberation time.

**Fullness**

Sound has intimacy if the live or recorded sound seems close to the listener. This is a situation easily found in small halls where reflected sound reaches the listeners very quickly. For large halls, intimacy can be enhanced by placing a reflecting canopy above the performers, directing the reflected sound toward their audience. A canopy is sometimes used in large cathedrals above the pulpit to achieve intimacy of the speaker's voice in relation to the congregation. A canopy also forms the basic part of the structure of a bandshell, helping to increase the sound level by reflecting the upward sound out toward the audience.

**Intimacy**

The longer the reverberation time, the more live a room is.

**Liveness**

The length of time a sound will bounce around a room (reverberate) determines the reverberation time. A live room will have lengthy reverberation time, whereas the sound waves in a dead room will be absorbed immediately without time to reverberate. Reverberation time is one of the more important acoustical considerations in room design.

**Reverberation (Echo)**

A room is considered to have warmth (as opposed to brilliance) when the reverberation time for low frequency sounds is somewhat greater than the reverberation time for high frequencies.

**Warmth**

In the construction of auditoriums or in designing rooms for home listening, there are several factors that influence the sound:

**Other Acoustical Factors**

1. Type of material used in walls, whether hard surfaces
(reflective) or soft (absorptive)
2. Size and shape of room, whether rectangular with all corners at 90° or
having corners at angles other than 90°
3. Types of rugs, drapes, and furnishings
4. Quality of audio equipment, especially speakers
5. Placement of speakers as recommended by the manufacturer

In most cases, there is not much one can do to alter room size and shape or the building materials without great expense. If deadening the room is needed it may be possible to install absorbent tiles or to hang rugs on the walls. If the desire is to retain as much liveness as possible, furnishings can be obtained that offer little absorption of sound. Placement of speakers can be of considerable importance, particularly in listening to stereophonic programs. The distance between speakers is critical. The larger the room, the farther apart. An average home listening room probably would require speakers placed about eight feet apart. The listening area should begin some distance back from the speakers. Space is required for sound to spread out evenly. Equalizers can be used to "tune" the sound to fit the room. If certain frequencies are lost due to the construction of the room they can be boosted through the equalizer.

**Audio Equipment**

Purchasing a turntable, compact disc (CD) player, tape deck, speaker system, or microphones can be confusing because of the quantity and types of equipment from which to choose and the language used to describe the equipment. A good strategy for understanding such language as wow and flutter, signal-to-noise ratio, impedance, harmonic distortion, frequency response, is to look at specifications (specs) in a high quality audio store and ask questions of a salesperson. Recommendations, test reports, and specs on the latest equipment can be found in current magazines such as *Stereo Review, Audio Review,* and *High Fidelity.*

**Acoustics of Instruments**

The basic sound-producing mechanism of string instruments is the vibration of the string by plucking or bowing. These vibrations are transmitted by a bridge to the belly and back of the instrument causing the wood to oscillate sympathetically with the frequencies present in the vibrating string.

**Stringed Instruments (Chordophones)**

The strands of the bow are usually hair from the tail of a horse that grips the string during bow strokes. Sound is produced when the bow grabs or a finger pulls (plucks) a string. The string, when it reaches its maximum point of elasticity, moves in the opposite direction as far as it can, then returns as far as it can, thus setting up vibrations that continue only if given additional stimulus from bowing or plucking the string.

**Piano**

The piano consists of individually tuned strings encased in a wooden body. The keyboard has eighty-eight keys, thirty-six black and fifty-two white, which when depressed causes hammers to strike the strings. The upper notes of the keyboard consist of three strings per hammer, while the lower ones have single or two strings. When pressed, the left pedal (soft pedal) moves the entire keyboard slightly to the side so a hammer that would normally strike three strings only hits two strings. The middle pedal (sustain pedal) on many grand pianos (absent from most uprights and some grand pianos) sustains only those keys that are being held at the time the pedal is pushed. It simply acts as a damper pedal for the notes in the low range.

**Wind Instruments (Aerophones)**

The trumpet and trombone of the brass family use basically cylindrical tubes. As in the woodwinds, conical tubes are also used in brasses, although the acoustical difference between conical and cylindrical tubes is not as dramatic for brass instruments as it is for reed instruments. For woodwind instruments, there are three primary elements that determine the characteristic tone quality:

1. The source of the sound, for example, the vibration of the reed in clarinets and saxophones
2. The size and shape of the bore (wood or metal tube—the body of the instrument)
3. The size and position of finger holes or keys

Of all the instrument families, the percussion family has the greatest variety of sound, both in dynamics and sound quality. Basic to percussion is sound that is produced by striking the instrument, whether it is a marimba, timpani, cymbal, or drum. Important in considering percussion instruments are the unique timbres of the many instruments and the unique attack and decay of the sound.

**Percussion (Idiophones and Membranophones)**

With the technological explosion during the last few decades, many new instruments and ways to make music have been developed. In the 1950s, the tape recorder became influential in the creation of classical music. Electronic music originally resulted from the taping of sounds from nature and the environment and sounds of both traditional and nontraditional musical instruments. Music was created by manipulating these taped sounds (for example, changing the direction and speed of the tape and by tape splicing), selecting the new sounds, and organizing them into a piece of music recorded on another tape.

**Electronics (Electrophones)**

Subsequently, electronically generated sounds as from a synthesizer became commonly used, first in classical music, then in rock music and jazz. Synthesizer keyboards as well as guitar and drum synthesizers can now be purchased through music stores just as traditional instruments.

Electronic technology includes computer applications, MIDI technology, and sampling. MIDI (Musical Instrument Digital Interface) is the technology that allows an electronic musical instrument to "speak" to a computer and visa versa. The sampling feature can be found on many small, inexpensive, electronic keyboards as well as highly sophisticated, expensive models. One can digitally record and store in memory one or more sounds, and these "samples" are stored in memory to be retrieved as a sound source for later playback on a synthesizer or other electronic instrument. The quantity of sound samples is limited only by the capacity of the computer memory.

Most electronic music today, whether in live or recorded performance, combines electronically produced sounds with those from traditional instruments.

# Appendix B
## Classification of Instruments According to Methods of Tone Production

I. Aerophones
  A. Flute
      1. Piccolo
      2. Panpipes
      3. Flute (alto flute)
      4. Shakuhachi
      5. Recorder (soprano, alto, tenor, bass)
  B. Reeds
      1. Single reed
        a. Clarinet (soprano, alto, bass, contrabass)
        b. Saxophone (soprano, alto, tenor, baritone)
      2. Double reed
        a. Oboe
        b. English horn
        c. Bassoon
      3. Free reed
        a. Harmonica (mouth harp)
        b. Accordian
  C. Pipe organ
  D. Brass
      1. Trumpet
        a. Cornet
        b. Flugelhorn

      2. Horn (French horn)

      3. Trombone (bass trombone)

      4. Euphonium (baritone)

      5. Tuba (sousaphone)

II. Chordophones

  A. Violin family

      1. Violin (fiddle)

      2. Viola

      3. Violoncello(cello)

      4. Double bass (string bass, bass fiddle)

  B. Viols

  C. Harp

  D. Zither

      1. Dulcimer (plucked, hammered)

      2. Autoharp

      3. Koto

  E. Lute

      1. Sitār

      2. Shamisen

      3. Mandolin

  F. Guitar

      1. Banjo

      2. Guitarron

      3. Charango

      4. Tamburā

      5. Ukelele

III. Idiophones

  A. Clappers

      1. Claves

      2. Castanets

      3. Cymbals (also a hitter)

  B. Shakers

      1. Maracas

      2. Rattles

  C. Hitters

      1. Xylophone

      2. Marimba

      3. Vibraphone (vibes)

      4. Steel drums

  D. Pluckers

      1. Mbira (sansa, kalimba)

IV. Membranophones

  A. Double head

      1. Snare drum

    B. Single head
      1. Bongos
      2. Timpani (kettle drums)
      3. Tablā
V. Electrophones
    A. Keyboards
      1. Synthesizer
      2. Electronic organ
    B. Guitars
    C. Drum machine (drum synthesizer)

## Descriptions of Representative Instruments

Accordian: A portable, free-reed aerophone with keyboard for melody and buttons for chords. Its wind is supplied by bellows worked by the player's arm that compresses and expands the air supplied to the reeds.

Autoharp: A zither that has a series of chord bars that lie across all the strings. Grooves in the bars are placed to allow strings that produce pitches in the chosen chords to vibrate while other strings of nonchord tones are damped to prevent vibration. The autoharp is commonly used in elementary school music programs and in the performance of folk music of the southern mountains.

Banjo: A plucked chordophone of black African origin, a long guitarlike neck, and a circular, tightly stretched parchment of skin or plastic against which the bridge is pressed by the strings.

Baritone: *See* euphonium.

Bass fiddle: *See* double bass.

Bassoon: A double reed tenor/bass instrument made of a wooden tube doubled back on itself. It dates from the seventeenth century. Also, there is a contrabassoon that plays one octave lower than the bassoon.

Bongos: An Afro-Cuban, single-head, membranophone usually played in pairs. The two are of the same height but of different diameters and are joined. Bongos are often played in jazz and rock groups featuring Latin American rhythms.

Cello: *See* violoncello.

Charango: A small guitar from South America. It is made of dried armadillo shell or carved wood and used mainly by the Indians and mestizos in the Andean mountains. Most models have ten strings tuned in pairs.

Clarinet: A single reed woodwind instrument dating from the late seventeenth century. The clarinet family consists of the soprano in E♭, soprano in B♭ and A, alto in E♭, basset horn in F, bass in B♭, and contrabass in B♭. The soprano clarinet is common in many parts of the world and is an important melody instrument in Western European (and American) bands, symphony orchestras, and chamber music ensembles and jazz groups.

Claves: Idiophones consisting of two cylindrical hardwood sticks that are clapped together. They are usually used in the performance of various Latin rhythms.

Cornet: A trumpetlike instrument that has a bore and bell slightly different than the common trumpet and achieves a more mellow, less brilliant tone quality. In earlier decades of the twentieth century, it was common as the main melodic high brass instrument in European and American concert bands and American dixieland jazz groups.

Cymbal: An idiophone of indefinite pitch. It is a round, metal plate of varying sizes that is hit with a stick or played in pairs (clapped together; crash cymbals). The high hat and ride cymbals are common in jazz.

Double bass: The bass instrument of the violin family. It is the standard bass instrument of the symphony orchestra (the bass section). At least one is found in many symphonic bands, and it is standard in any traditional jazz combo or big band. In modern jazz and rock, it has largely been replaced by the electric bass. The double bass is often known as the bass, bowed bass, stand-up bass, acoustical bass, bass fiddle, or string bass.

Drum machine: A drum synthesizer used in modern jazz and rock groups. Some groups will carry the traditional drum set and the drum "synth."

Dulcimer: A name applied to certain zither-type instruments. Certain dulcimers are plucked with the fingers. Others are hammered (strings struck with curved mallets).

Electronic organ: *See* organ.

English horn: An alto oboe that looks similar to an oboe but is larger and has a bulb-shaped bell. It has a slightly more mellow sound than the oboe.

Euphonium (baritone): A valved brass instrument that has the same playing range as the trombone.

Fiddle: A generic name for a bowed instrument having a neck. It is the common name for the violin, particularly when used to play folk or country music.

Flugelhorn: Similar to the trumpet but with a bore and bell that gives it a more mellow, sweeter tone. It is a favorite melody instrument among some jazz artists.

Flute: A woodwind instrument generally made of either wood or metal. There are two types of flutes: vertical flute (recorder; panpipes) and transverse flute (the flute in general use today in American bands and orchestras).

Gong: An idiophone in the form of a circular, shallow, metal plate of various sizes that is hit usually with a soft-headed beater. It is hung vertically, and its tone characteristically swells after the gong is struck.

Guitar: A flat-backed, plucked chordophone of Spanish descent. It is traced from the thirteenth century and is now used worldwide in folk, jazz, popular, and classical styles of music.

Guitarron: A bass guitar used in Spain and throughout Mexico and Latin America. It is common in modern mariachi groups.

Harmonica: A free-reed aerophone. The reeds are placed in a small rectangular box. Grooves lead from the reeds to openings on one of the long sides of the box into which the player exhales or inhales air. The player changes pitches by moving his or her mouth back and forth along the side of the box.

Harp: A chordophone with ancient heritage. Its strings are placed perpendicular to the sound board (sound resonator). Generally, they are triangular in shape and are placed on the floor and played vertically. Concert harps have pedals to play chromatically altered tones and all the major and minor keys. Folk harps typically are smaller and do not have these pedals and the tonal flexibility.

Harpsichord: A keyboard instrument characterized by strings that are plucked with little leather quills rather than struck with hammers as with the piano. It will have one or two manuals and little capability for expressive contrasts. It dates to the Renaissance and was a popular baroque keyboard instrument.

Horn: A generic name for a variety of lip-vibrated wind instruments of the trumpet variety, with or without valves. It is also a name for a specific brass instrument whose bore spirals and culminates in a large, flaring bell. This instrument is sometimes known as the French horn.

Kalimba: *See* mbira.

Kettledrums: *See* timpani.

Koto: A long zither with thirteen strings, each with a moveable bridge, traditionally placed horizontally on the floor. It is sometimes considered the national instrument of Japan.

Lute: An ancient, plucked or bowed chordophone with a round back and a neck (the guitar family of instruments has flat backs). The tuning pegs in many versions were placed perpendicular to the neck. The lute family includes the Arabic *ud,* the Japanese shamisen, the mandolin, and instruments of the viol and violin families.

Mandolin: A plucked chordophone of the lute family. It dates from the early eighteenth century and is in common use today, mainly in Italy and in the United States. Although it is chiefly used in folk and country music, it occasionally is used in classical compositions.

Maracas: A pair of gourd rattles, most commonly oval gourds usually containing dried seeds or beads. They are originally of South American Indian cultures but are now commonly used in playing Latin American dance rhythms.

Marimba: An idiophone (xylophone) comprised of tone bars under which are gourd or tubular resonators. The bars are hit with sticks (mallets). Its antecedents are in sub-Sarahan Africa.

Mbira (thumb piano, kalimba, sansa): An African, plucked idiophone comprised of tuned metal tongues (as are common in music boxes) and sometimes gourd resonator boxes. The ends of the tongues are free to vibrate as they are depressed and released (plucked) by the thumbs of the performer.

Oboe: A double-reed, woodwind instrument whose tone can be described as nasal and piercing. The oboe is often used as a solo instrument in the classical symphony orchestra, modern symphonic bands, and woodwind chamber ensembles.

Organ (pipe organ, electronic organ): The pipe organ is a wind instrument consisting of one or more ranks of individual wooden or metal pipes. Each pipe produces a specific tone color at a specific pitch. Each rank is comprised of a set of pipes for each tone quality. There are usually from two to four manuals (keyboards). The larger organs will have thousands of separate pipes. The tones are generated from air supplied by a blower supported by action that is dictated by the organist at the keyboard and that directs the air to the appropriate pipes. The various tone colors of the electronic organ are generated by electrical circuitry rather than air pressure. These sounds are similar (but inferior?) to those of the pipe organ. In fact, some electronic organs attempt to imitate the pipe organ sounds.

Panpipes: Sets of end-blown flutes of different pitches combined into one instrument. There are no finger holes as the player changes pitches by blowing air across the end-holes of the different pipes. Panpipes are used in all regions of the world. They often are associated with the Inca civilization of the Andes mountains in Peru and Bolivia.

Piano: A keyboard instrument whose eighty-eight strings are struck by rebounding hammers. Its origin dates back to the early eighteenth century. In the nineteenth century, the piano replaced the harpsichord as the popular keyboard instrument in Western music.

Piccolo: A small, transverse flute. It sounds an octave higher than written and often doubles the flute part an octave higher.

Pipe organ: *See* organ.

Rattles: Any shaken idiophone.

Recorder: An end-blown, vertical flute used from the Middle Ages until the eighteenth century but has seen a resurgence in popularity in modern times. Often, recorders come in sets that consist of descant (soprano), treble (alto), tenor, and bass recorder.

Saxophone: A single-reed, woodwind instrument made of metal. The family of saxophones includes the soprano in B♭, alto in E♭, tenor in B♭, baritone in E♭, and the less common bass in B♭. The alto and tenor saxophones are the most common and are integral to band instrumentations and to jazz ensembles. They are occasionally used in symphony orchestras.

Shakuhachi: An end-blown Japanese flute usually made of bamboo with five finger holes. With roots in China dating back to the tenth century, it is used today as a solo instrument and as part of various instrumental ensembles, sometimes with koto and shamisen.

Shamisen: A three-stringed, long-necked Japanese lute. It is used as part of ensembles, sometimes with koto and perhaps the shakuhachi, and is used also to accompany traditional Japanese songs.

Sitār: A large, fretted long-necked lute. It has from four to seven metal strings, movable frets, and several drone strings. The sitār is the main melody instrument in the classical music tradition of northern India.

Snare drum: A side drum with a set of snares (wires) stretched across the lower head. The tension of these wires can be adjusted to change the quality of sound.

Steel drum: A tuned idiophone usually made from an oil drum. Steel drum bands were first popular in the Caribbean, particularly Trinidad, and are now popular in the United States.

String Bass: *See* double bass.

Sousaphone: A type of tuba used in marching bands. It is distinguished by its shape that wraps around the body for ease in carrying and its overhead, widely flaring bell.

Synthesizer: An electronic instrument capable of generating and processing a wide variety of sounds (drums, keyboard, and guitar).

Tablā: A pair of small, tuned, hand played drums of north and central India, Pakistan, and Bangladesh. They are used to accompany both vocal and instrumental art, popular, and folk music. They are particularly well known in performances of the classical music of northern India as a frequently intricate accompaniment in rāga performances.

Tamburā: A long-neck, plucked lute of India. It has four wire strings used only for drone accompaniments in both classical and folk styles.

Timpani (kettledrums): A single-headed drum consisting of a large bowl-shaped resonating chamber or shell (usually of copper). The large head can be tightened or loosened to produce different pitches. It is struck with a pair of mallets. A band or orchestra usually uses a pair of timpani in two sizes. Some music calls for four timpani with the additional ones extending the pitch range higher and lower.

Trombone: A brass aerophone characterized by a telescopic slide with which the player varies the length of the tube, thereby manipulating the pitch. It is a common harmony and melody instrument in the tenor range used in bands, orchestras, brass chamber music, and jazz ensembles of all kinds.

Trumpet: A treble brass instrument played with a cup-shaped mouthpiece. Its brilliant tone makes it an ideal melody instrument in bands, orchestras, chamber music ensembles, and jazz groups. It is found frequently in Mexican and Latin American popular music groups. Various versions of the trumpet, many made from animals' horns, date from ancient times and are found in many world cultures. The invention of the valves in 1813 as a means of changing pitch has made it the versatile and popular instrument it is today.

Tuba: The bass instrument of the brass family.

Ukulele: A small guitar originally from Portugal but popularized in America through Hawaiian music.

Vibraphone (vibraharp, "vibes"): A xylophone with metal bars and metal resonator tubes suspended below each bar that help to sustain the tones. An electric motor drives propellers affixed at the top of each resonator tube that produces its characteristic pulsating pitches (vibrato).

Viol: A bowed string instrument with frets usually played vertically on the lap or between the legs. Viols were built in three sizes: treble, tenor, and bass (viol da gamba). They flourished in Europe in the sixteenth and seventeenth centuries and subsequently became one of most popular Renaissance and baroque instruments. By the middle of the eighteenth century, they were replaced by the more resonant violin family of instruments.

Viola: The alto or tenor member of the violin family. The viola is slightly larger than the violin and creates a slightly more mellow sound.

Violin: The soprano and most prominent member of the violin family. Its versatile, expressive quality is unequaled. The history of the violin dates to the early seventeenth century in Cremona, Italy. It was here that the great masters worked—Niccolo Amati, Antonio Stradivari, and Guiseppe Guarneri. The violin is the main melody instrument of the Western symphony orchestra and chamber music ensembles such as the string quartet. It is also used in folk music (fiddle), jazz (both acoustic and electric versions), and in music of many other cultures.

Violoncello (cello): The tenor or bass instrument of the violin family. Its beautiful, lyrical quality makes it ideally suited to play melody as well as harmonic and bass lines.

Xylophone: A percussion instrument consisting of two or more wooden tone bars of varying lengths to produce varying pitches. The bars are struck with knobbed sticks. Modern versions have the bars laid out similarly to a piano keyboard with each bar having a metal resonator suspended below it. With roots in Asia, the xylophone was introduced in the Americas by Africans.

Zither: A folk instrument, but also a class of chordophones whose strings are stretched between two ends of a flat body, such as a board or a stick. The hammered dulcimer, piano, and harpsichord are board zithers.

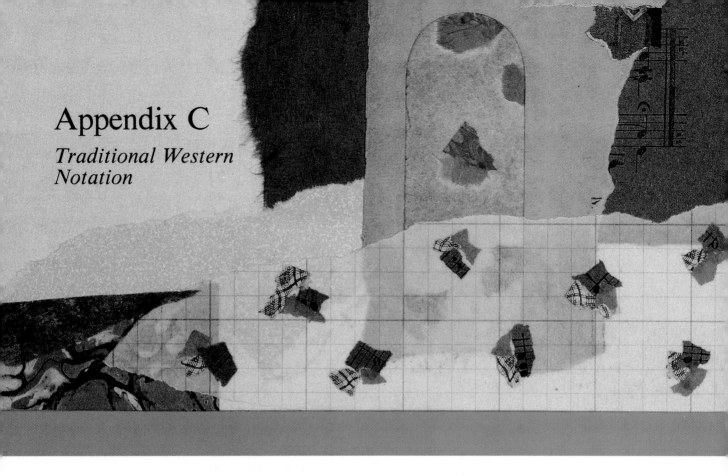

# Appendix C
## Traditional Western Notation

Musical notation is the use of written or printed symbols to represent musical sounds. It was first used as a memory aid. For example, the notation of Gregorian chant did not depict rhythm but merely served as reminders of pitch direction. The first visual representation of music making can be found around 3000 B.C. in the hieroglyphic writings of the ancient Egyptians. They show what appears to be a system of arm, hand, and finger signs by which the leader signaled melody and rhythm to performers. The first musical notation to employ the use of the alphabet occurred sometime before 500 B.C.. It was a mixture of Greek letters and archaic signs to represent a continuous diatonic series of notes over three octaves.

The development of polyphonic music during the Middle Ages brought about the need for the performers of the various melodic lines to stay together. This, in turn, brought about the need for regular meters and for a system of notation that would precisely indicate rhythm and pitch. Early notational systems subsequently evolved by the sixteenth century into our modern staff notation with notes that indicate exact pitch and exact rhythm.

The notation of music in manuscript or in printed form enhanced the possibility for music to be preserved in its original form rather than in the more flexible manner found in oral traditions. Notation also shifted the musical culture from anonymous creators of music to known composers— first, church musicians and, by the eighteenth century, professional composers.

## Durations

In the current system of Western notation, note values are based on arithmetical proportions. Certain terms and symbols contain particular meanings.

A stem is added to a whole note to divide its value in half. The half note is then made into a solid note known as the quarter note. To further divide the note value, a flag is added to the stem creating eighth notes, and so on as follows:

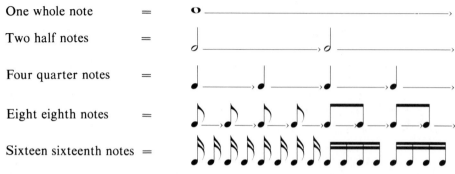

The same principle is true of rests (symbols of silence).

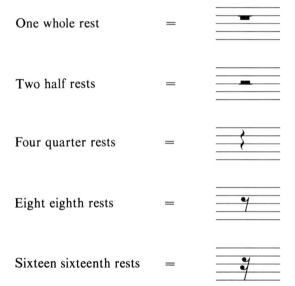

Horizontal beams are used to group two or more notes containing flags in order to make them easier to read. Beams mean the same as flags (they divide a note's value by half). One beam equals one flag, two beams equal two flags, etc.

A dot after a note increases the value of that note by half. For example, a dotted quarter note equals a quarter note plus an eighth note, and a dotted half note equals a half note plus a quarter note.

The note placement on the staff determines whether the stem is placed up or down. If the notehead is above the middle line of the staff, the stem is placed downward. If the notehead is below the middle line of the staff, the stem is pointed upward. If the note is on the middle line of the staff, the stem is placed either direction depending on the notes surrounding it.

A time signature is placed at the beginning of a piece and reveals the metric pulse of that piece. The lower number in the time signature explains which note value contains one beat. For example, in 2/4 time, the lower number is 4; this means that the quarter note gets one beat. If the lower number is 2, then the half note gets one beat. If the lower number is 8, the eighth note gets one beat, etc. The upper number in a time signature explains how many beats are in each bar (measure). For example, in 4/4 time, there are four quarter notes to each measure. In 2/4 time, there are two quarter notes to each measure. In 2/2 time, there are two half notes to each measure, etc. If the upper number in the time signature is 2 or a multiple of 2, then the piece is said to be in duple meter (2/4, 4/4, etc.). If the upper number is 3 or a multiple of 3, then the piece is said to be in triple meter (3/4, 3/2, etc.). Each beat typically is subdivided into two (1 + 2 + 3 + 4 +). There is also compound meter, the most common type being 6/8. This is six beats to the measure with an eighth note getting a beat, but it is often felt as a duple meter with a triple subdivision of the beat, particularly at a fast tempo:

**Metric Organization**

```
1  2  3  4  5  6 / 1  2  3  4   5  6
1  + +2  + +/ 1   + +2  + +
```

Additionally, two symbols to exemplify two common time signatures is the "C." One is used to depict the "common" 4/4 time. The other is the symbol for 2/2 time, also known as cut time.

Notation reveals the rhythm of the notes, but it also reveals the pitch. The first aspect in understanding how the pitch is described is to understand the "chart" that is used to do this. The notes are written on a chart known as a staff. In addition to the time signature being placed at the beginning of each staff, a clef sign is also used. The two most common clef signs are the treble clef (G clef) and the bass clef (F clef). Other types of clefs are the tenor clef and the alto clef, each indicating the placement on the staff of middle C.

**Pitch**

Also found at the beginning of each staff is a key signature. This determines which notes are raised or lowered a half step. The easiest way to understand this concept is to examine a keyboard.

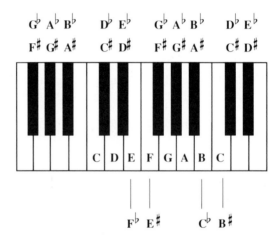

The white keys are labeled A to G. If you lower a note by one half step (to a black key, for example), then this lower note is called a flat. The symbol for a flat is (♭). If a note is raised a half step, it is known as a sharp (♯). When no black key exists between two white keys for the half step, the next adjacent white key then becomes the sharp or flat.

A key signature contains one or more sharps or flats near the beginning of the staff to indicate that all the notes they represent are adjusted throughout unless indicated by a cancellation sign—the natural (♮). Occasionally sharps or flats are added that are not in the key signature. They are called accidentals.

**Examples**

5. Conductor's score for a full symphony orchestra— traditional notation.

Staffs
Clef signs
Meter signatures
Bar lines
Note values
Rest values
Expression marks
Tempo markings
Ties
Slurs
Staccato
Ties/beams
Instrumentation

6. Nontraditional use of traditional notation.

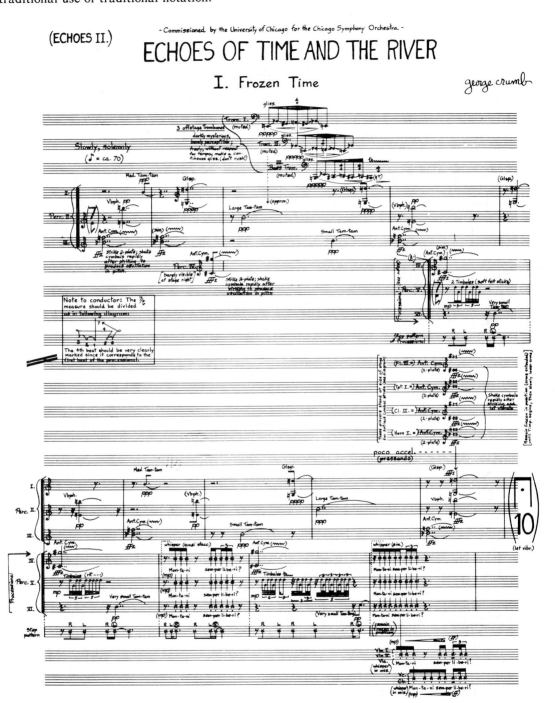

## 7. Nontraditional notation—a new musical language.

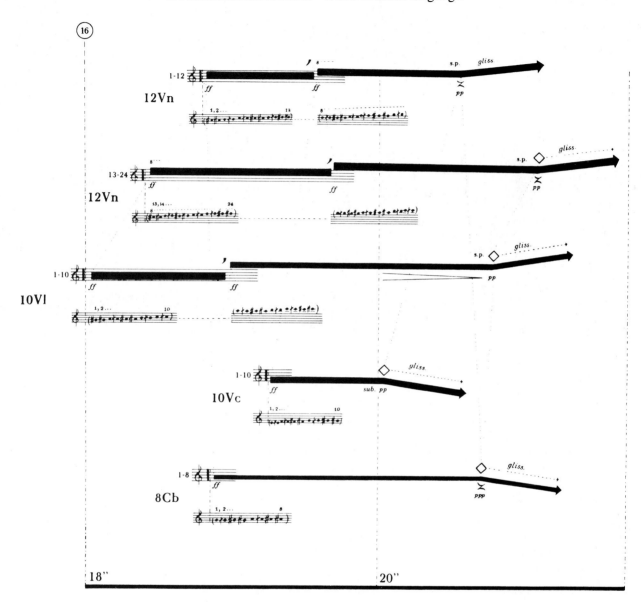

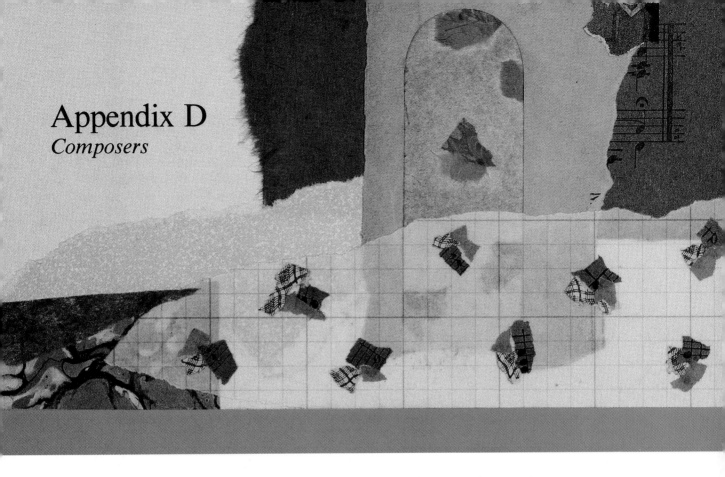

# Appendix D
## *Composers*

The purpose of this appendix is to provide information about twenty-five composers representative of each historical period. This is not an exhaustive list. Many great composers, particularly from the nineteenth and twentieth centuries, have been omitted for the sake of brevity. Three criteria for selection have been applied: (1) influence on future composers and the future course of music history, (2) the extent to which a composer's music is known and performed today, and (3) the author's preferences.

**Renaissance (1450–1600)**
Josquin des Prez
Orlando di Lasso
Giovanni da Palestrina

**Baroque (1600–1750)**
Claudio Monteverdi
Antonio Vivaldi
Johann Sebastian Bach
George Frideric Handel

**Classic (1750–1820)**
Wolfgang Amadeus Mozart
Franz Joseph Haydn
Ludwig van Beethoven

**Romantic (1820–1900)**
Franz Schubert
Frédéric Chopin
Johannes Brahms
Felix Mendelssohn
Giuseppe Verdi
Richard Wagner
Peter Ilyich Tchaikovsky
Richard Strauss

**Modern (1900–   )**
Claude Debussy
Igor Stravinsky
Arnold Schoenberg
Béla Bartók
Sergei Prokofiev
Charles Ives
Aaron Copland

Names of
Composers by
Historical
Period

**List of Composers with Brief Biographical Information**

1. ***Bach, Johann Sebastian** (1685–1750).* Living and working entirely in Germany, Bach became a master of that which existed in common practice, having taken many baroque forms and genres to their fullest potential. He mastered the grand art of polyphony and the newer art of harmonic writing. Bach's chorale preludes; cantatas and other extended vocal and choral works; preludes, fugues and other works for keyboard instruments (organ or harpsichord); and instrumental music ranging from suites for solo cello to the popular *Brandenburg Concertos* continue to be played today in churches and concert halls throughout the world.

2. ***Bartók, Béla** (1881–1945).* The greatest of Hungarian composers, Bartók was a nationalist, a serious collector of Eastern European folk songs, and an individualistic composer whose music transcends many styles, techniques, and systems. In many innovative and exciting ways, he combined in his music the spirit of this folk music, forms of the Classic era, and the musical language of contemporary Europe. His music is tonal, often modal, sometimes polytonal, yet frequently slides into highly chromatic atonality, He did not adhere rigidly to the major/minor tonal system. His harmony is dissonant, often harsh. His rhythms have vitality and are often pounding, asymmetrical, and syncopated, and he uses a variety of imaginative tone colors. His greatest successes came after his death in New York City.

3. ***Beethoven, Ludwig van** (1770–1827).* Born in Germany, Beethoven spent his adult life in Vienna composing and selling his compositions. He was the first important composer to live independently of the exclusive patronage of the aristocracy. Beethoven created works that freed music from the restraints of classicism and that were models of subjective feeling and personal expression. His works foreshadowed the romantic spirit that was to dominate nineteenth-century music. The symphonies, piano concertos, and overtures are among his works that are commonly found in the repertoire of every symphony orchestra today. Also frequently performed are his piano sonatas, the violin concerto, and string quartets and other chamber music compositions.

4. ***Brahms, Johannes** (1833–1897).* Brahms was a German who, from the age of thirty, lived and worked in Vienna. He was a romanticist in his emotional expressiveness and rich, dark sonorities, yet he also was a traditionalist in his devotion to classic forms and structures and in his interest in absolute music. His four symphonies, a violin concerto, two piano concertos, chamber music, the great *German Requiem,* sonatas for various instruments, and numerous short piano and choral works are widely performed today.

5. ***Chopin, Frédéric** (1810–1849).* Born and educated in Poland, Chopin spent his entire professional life in Paris. He was a virtuoso pianist who composed almost exclusively for the piano. He preferred the short, one-movement "miniatures," including the preludes, études, polonaises, mazurkas, impromptus, ballades, and nocturnes. Chopin expanded the concept of piano playing by developing new uses of the sustain pedal and by creating more elaborate pianistic textures and techniques. He created more decorative melodies, utilized the expressive rubato, and incorporated colorful harmonies with dissonances, unresolved tensions, and unusual modulations. Chopin in some cases acknowledged his heritage by capturing in music the spirit of the Polish people.

6. ***Copland, Aaron (1900–   ).*** Undoubtedly the best known and most successful of all American composers, Copland was interested in merging elements of classical and vernacular traditions. In his music, he quoted hymns, spirituals, patriotic songs, and Indian chants but with a purpose of shaping universal, musical thoughts that were representative of the whole country. He tried to bridge the ever-widening gap between composer and audience by creating music with artistic integrity but in an understandable and more accessible language. Orchestral settings of his ballets— *Billy the Kid, Appalachian Spring,* and *Rodeo*—rank among his best known works.

7. ***Debussy, Claude (1862–1918).*** A French Impressionist composer, Debussy rejected many of the established forms and massive sonorities of German romanticism. His music, instead, is typified by subtle shadings, delicate, sensuous sonorities, and a preference for flute, harp, and shimmering strings rather than powerful brass sounds. Debussy represents the transition from nineteenth-century romanticism to the diverse and more complex practices of the twentieth century. Among his best known works are the *Prelude to the Afternoon of a Faun, La Mer, Preludes for Piano,* a string quartet, and the opera, *Pélleas and Mélisande.*

8. ***Handel, George Frideric (1685–1759).*** Handel, a native German who became a master of the Italian musical style, notably opera, achieved his greatest successes in England. His lasting fame rests in his oratorios (*Messiah*), orchestra pieces (*The Water Music*), and a variety of harpsichord suites, concerto grossos, and organ concertos.

9. ***Haydn, Franz Joseph (1732–1809).*** Haydn, an Austrian, is the best example of a composer working successfully within the aristocratic, patronage system. He wrote music for every occasion that the court demanded. He brought unity to the classical style. Through his orchestral music, he helped to establish the symphony as an important instrumental genre and to standardize the instrumentation of the symphony orchestra. He also established the string quartet as an important chamber music genre.

10. ***Ives, Charles (1874–1954).*** The first great composer of uniquely American music, Ives was a musical pioneer and an innovator. He used modern compositional techniques before they were fashionable. He used such techniques as harsh dissonances, tone clusters, polytonality, asymmetrical rhythms, and mixed meters. Recognition came to Ives late in life. He was awarded the Pulitzer Prize for his third Symphony when he was seventy-three years old.

11. ***Josquin des Prez (c. 1440–1521).*** Josquin, perhaps the most important composer of the middle Renaissance, was born in the border region between France and what is now Belgium. He became a highly successful court musician and composer, particularly in Italy. Much of his music, published in printed collections, includes eighteen masses, one hundred motets, and seventy *chansons.*

12. ***Lasso, Orlando di (1532–1594).*** Di Lasso, one of the most important composers of the late Renaissance, was a prolific and versatile composer and widely admired in Europe in his own time. A court composer, Lasso's output consists of over 2,000 works, primarily vocal settings of the Mass and Passion. A large number of motets, madrigals, chansons, and songs also are included.

13. ***Mendelssohn, Felix (1809–1847).*** Mendelssohn grew up in an educated German family of high social and cultural standing. He was surrounded by the finest opportunities for an aspiring musician. He was widely traveled and became famous throughout Europe and England. His music is appealing and is closely aligned to the classical ideals of form and structure, and his romantic spirit is revealed in the emotional expressiveness and sentimentality of his melodies. His symphonies, the oratorio *Elijah,* the violin concerto, and the incidental music to *A Midsummer Night's Dream* are included among his most important compositions.

14. ***Monteverdi, Claudio (1567–1643).*** Monteverdi, an Italian and an influential figure in the history of music, represents the transition from the sixteenth to the seventeenth centuries (from the Renaissance to the Baroque). He composed in the "old-fashioned" polyphonic style, particularly in his early madrigals, and helped create the new baroque style, particularly through his late madrigals and operas. He was the first important opera composer.

15. ***Mozart, Wolfgang Amadeus (1756–1791).*** A product of the Austrian aristocratic system, Mozart was a genius with few peers in Western music. He was prolific and inventive, and he composed in virtually every popular form of the day. In his short life, Mozart created over 600 compositions, including symphonies, concertos, "entertainment" music (the divertimentos and serenades), chamber music, piano sonatas, choral works, and operas. His music continues to be widely performed and listened to today.

16. ***Palestrina, Giovanni Pierluigi da (c. 1525–1594).*** Born near Rome, his entire professional life was spent as a choirmaster and composer in Italy including the last twenty-four years of his life at St. Peter's. He composed a large amount of sacred music including 102 masses, 450 motets and other liturgical compositions, and 56 spiritual madrigals with Italian texts. His music is characterized for its purity, for its appropriateness in the formal liturgy, and as a model of the best in sixteenth-century imitative counterpoint.

17. ***Prokofiev, Sergei (1891–1953).*** Prokofiev, a Russian, is respected by musicians and popular with the public. Many of his works today are widely known and frequently performed in the United States. He is a classicist and a tonal composer, one who has combined pungent dissonances with lyrical qualities and humor. Among his best known works are the "Classical Symphony," Symphony No. 5, the third Piano Concerto, the second Violin Concerto, orchestral music from the opera *The Love of Three Oranges,* the symphonic suite *Lieutenant Kije, Peter and the Wolf,* and excerpts from his ballet *Romeo and Juliet,* in addition to a variety of successful piano works and chamber music.

18. ***Schoenberg, Arnold (1874–1951).*** Schoenberg, an Austrian, became a leader of musical thought in the 1920s. Previously, he wrote in the highly chromatic but tonal, German, postromantic style. He later rejected the major/minor tonal system entirely, preferring to deliberately avoid tonal centers (atonality). He set out to find a way of organizing the twelve tones of the chromatic scale as an alternative to the major/minor tonal system. His conclusion was the development of serial composition or twelve-tone technique, a system that was to revolutionize music.

Compared with traditional music, Schoenberg's music would seem to sound cerebral, fragmentary, and complex. His melodies are disjunct, his textures are polyphonic, his phrases are of irregular length, chord progressions are deliberately avoided, and he preferred small instrumental ensembles of both standard and unconventional combinations. Yet, his highly significant contribution to the history of music lies in his influence on his immediate followers and on generations of future composers.

19. ***Schubert, Franz*** *(1797–1828)*. Schubert was an Austrian who had a prodigious natural gift for melody. He composed more than six hundred songs (*lieder*). These art songs as well as his piano "miniatures" embody a wide range of feelings from elegant simplicity to bold, dramatic expression. His orchestral and chamber music reflect the classical ideals of form and structure yet are infused with the songlike qualities of Viennese romanticism.

20. ***Strauss, Richard*** *(1864–1949)*. Best known for his symphonic poems (tone poems) and his operas, Strauss ranks as one of the best late romantic composers who distinguished himself in writing for the orchestra. His best known works are the programmatic symphonic poems, *Don Juan, Till Eulenspiegel, Ein Heldenleben, Death and Transfiguration,* and *Also Sprach Zarathustra.*

21. ***Stravinsky, Igor*** *(1882–1971)*. Stravinsky was a Russian who for the last thirty-two years of his life lived and worked in the United States, becoming an American citizen in 1945. He will undoubtedly be recognized as one of the great composers of the twentieth century. The orchestral settings of his early ballets, *The Firebird, Petrushka,* and *The Rite of Spring,* composed in Paris, have become masterpieces of twentieth-century symphonic repertoire. Stravinsky is known as a neoclassicist for having valued the classical ideals of form and structure in music and having adopted many common practices and aesthetic values from the past. However much his music is derived from past practices, it is very much couched in the idioms of twentieth-century musical language. His music minimizes regular metric feeling, preferring shifting accents, mixed meter, and rhythmic complexity. His orchestrations are innovative, using extreme ranges in some instruments and unusual instrumental combinations. His music is tonal but with tonality produced in new ways. He created new music from old or preexisting material such as jazz, ragtime, and Russian folk melodies.

22. ***Tchaikovsky, Peter Ilyich*** *(1840–1893)*. Tchaikovsky, a Russian, composed music in an international style. Although at times he would capture the spirit of Russian folk song, much of his music incorporated influences from Italian opera, French ballet, and German symphonies and songs. His music has a wide range of expression. It is full of beautiful melodies, striking contrasts, and powerful climaxes. His music is sometimes sentimental, sometimes exciting, and extremely popular to this day, particularly his symphonies, the piano and violin concertos, the orchestral piece *Romeo and Juliet,* the ballets (especially *The Nutcracker*), and the *1812 Overture.*

23. ***Verdi, Giuseppe*** *(1813–1901)*. Verdi was the greatest figure of Italian opera in a country whose main source of musical enjoyment was opera. He maintained the traditional use of arias, recitatives, and ensemble choruses but enriched his operas with superb melodies and a strong

theatrical sense. Conventional harmonies and predictable rhythms and meters permeate his music. Virtually any opera company today has in its repertory at least one Verdi opera.

24. ***Vivaldi, Antonio*** *(1678–1741).* Vivaldi is counted among the most original and influential Italian composers of his generation. His contributions to musical style, violin technique, and orchestration were substantial. In Vivaldi's more than 500 concertos (more than 230 for violin) are found a variety of forms, instrumentations, and imaginative compositional techniques, although his approximately ninety sonatas for different instruments and instrumental combinations are more conservative in form and style. His sacred choral music, subject to the operatic influences of the time, includes the widely performed *Gloria.*

25. ***Wagner, Richard*** *(1813–1883).* Wagner was a revolutionary, German opera composer. His ideal was a work whose music, drama, poetry, and stagecraft all would receive equal emphasis. He called it music drama rather than opera. His music was symphonic in nature with an orchestral color that featured the powerful brass instruments. Wagner's operas had a continuous, dramatic flow uninterrupted by the traditional arias, recitatives, and ensemble choruses. His music is highly chromatic and dissonant, some of which would provide no clear sense of tonality. His phrase structure is mostly asymmetrical with vague or nonexisting cadences. He at times would achieve unity in part by the use of a *leitmotif,* a recurring musical motive associated with a character or a mood.

# Glossary

## A

**Absolute music** Music created for its own sake without extramusical connotation. It is characteristic of such genres as the sonata, symphony, concerto, and string quartet as well as preludes, fugues, études and other works whose titles depict only form or function. Program music depicts images, moods, stories, characters, and other nonmusical associations. It includes all music with text and many instrumental forms common during the Romantic period, including the symphonic poem and some symphonies that were created with programmatic associations.

**Accent** A stress or emphasis on a particular tone.

**Acculturation** The blending of cultures. The process by which a culture assimilates or adapts to the characteristics and practices of another culture.

**Acoustics** The science of sounds and the physical basis of music.

**Aerophone** A wind instrument. The sound producing agent is air set in vibration either within the body of the instrument or outside of the instrument. *See* Appendix B, aerophones.

**Aesthetics** The study of the emotional and expressive aspects of music.

**Airplay** The number of times a popular song is broadcast on radio. Airplay can generate record sales and can contribute to making a song a hit.

**Aria** A lyrical song found in operas, cantatas, and oratorios. It may comment on the text presented in a recitative that preceded the aria.

**Arrangement** A setting (rescoring) of a piece of music for a genre or ensemble for which it was not originally intended, such as a pop song arranged for big band or an orchestral piece arranged for wind ensemble.

**Art music** Music that is formal, sophisticated, urban, and appreciated by an educated elite. It is music derived from a cultivated tradition based largely on notated music. Therefore, it requires a certain amount of musical training to be able to create and perform art music.

**Art song** *See* miniature.

**Assimilation** The process whereby immigrant groups gradually adopt the characteristics of the host society. It is also the process by which a primitive culture is modified by contact with an advanced culture.

**Atonality** The avoidance of tonal centers and tonal relationships in music. This is highly chromatic, dissonant music without traditional, functional chord progressions, modulations, and tuneful melodies. Dissonances stand alone, without the need to resolve to consonances as in traditional music.

**Avant-garde** Experimental composers who are in the forefront of musical developments and who are the leaders in the development of new and unconventional musical styles. They experiment with untried techniques, forms, timbres, or concepts in developing new approaches to composition, new aesthetic notions, or a new language for expressing music.

# B

***Ballads*** Songs with a story having a beginning, middle, and end. The music is strophic and may have many stanzas. A ballad singer is a storyteller.

***Ballet*** A stage production featuring formal, stylized dance performances with story or unified theme. It has, at times, been part of opera, but also developed popularity as an independent genre in the nineteenth century.

***Bar*** *See* meter.

***Bebop*** A combo jazz style that emerged in the 1940s. It is characterized by high energy, virtuoso solo improvisation, complex rhythmic patterns, and more novel and chromatic harmonies than were used in previous styles.

***Big band jazz*** Music for large jazz ensemble, usually from twelve to twenty musicians. It is notated music (charts) that may be original compositions but more frequently are arrangements of preexisting songs. Arrangements are scored for the brass section (trumpets and trombones), the sax section, and the rhythm section.

***Binary*** *See* form.

***Black gospel*** *See* gospel music.

***Bluegrass*** A style of country music that combined a return to the rural, folk traditions of hillbilly music and the urban, commercial music that was part of our national, popular culture. The typical bluegrass instrumentation includes the acoustic guitar, fiddle, mandolin, bass fiddle, and banjo— no electric instruments.

***Blues*** A style of music that has exerted considerable influence on jazz, rhythm and blues, soul, rock, and other forms of recent American popular music. Blues refers to a three-line poetic stanza, a twelve-bar musical structure with a specific chord progression, a scale having the flatted blues notes, or a melancholy, soulful feeling.

***Boogie woogie*** A piano jazz style popular in the late 1920s and 1930s. It is characterized by a left-hand ostinato figure underlying a rhythmically free and highly syncopated right-hand melodic texture. Most boogie woogie pieces are based on the standard, twelve-bar blues chord progression.

***Break*** A stop of the music in a jazz piece during which a soloist will improvise, usually for two bars. A break will occur at the end of a phrase, providing transition to the next phrase.

# C

***Cadence*** The ending of a musical phrase.

***Cadenza*** *See* concerto.

***Cantata*** An extended solo or choral work that flourished during the Baroque era. It was intended for the German Lutheran worship service, although some cantatas have secular texts. Choral cantatas, particularly those by J. S. Bach, include harmonized chorales, polyphonic choruses, arias, recitatives, solo ensembles, and instrumental accompaniment.

***Cantus firmus*** A term meaning "fixed melody" that denotes a preexisting melody, often a Gregorian chant, which a composer from the Renaissance used as the basis of a polyphonic composition.

***Chamber music*** Works for solo instruments performing together in small ensembles, such as a string quartet, a woodwind quintet, or a piano trio. Each part is played on one instrument (no doubling). In the Classic era, the string quartet (first and second violins, viola, and cello) became the standard chamber music genre. The quartet, typically, was a four-movement work with a fast-slow-dance-fast pattern, although many exceptions to this pattern exist.

***Chance music*** A compositional technique whereby a composer does not control all the details of a composition, allowing the performer to make creative choices through improvisation or other means of selecting sounds within the structure of the composition. John Cage was a major influence in developing chance music.

***Chant*** A simple song found in many cultures and traditions. It is a monophonic song without accompaniment, of relatively short duration, of limited melodic range, and with a fluid pulse reflecting the rhythm of the text. Gregorian chants, sung in Latin, are those used in the liturgy of the Roman Catholic church. They date from the end of the sixth century A.D. when Pope Gregory was thought to have ordered a collection and classification of chants used throughout the far-flung Roman church.

***Character piece*** *See* miniature.

***Chart*** A weekly record of sales of songs in a variety of categories, such as rock, jazz, rhythm and blues, and country. It is used to measure a song's popularity. The most widely used charts are produced by *Billboard Magazine.* Also, the written or printed arrangement of a popular song or a jazz tune for an ensemble, such as a rock group, studio orchestra, or a jazz band.

***Chorale*** Originally a hymn tune of the German Lutheran church sung by the congregation in unison and in the German (rather than Latin) language. It was an outgrowth of the Reformation and the rise of the Protestant church. Chorale tunes, especially during the Baroque era, were used as the basis for other compositions: they were harmonized in four-part settings for singing by choirs and congregations; they were used as the basis of sacred polyphonic compositions for trained choirs, and they formed the basis of organ pieces known as chorale preludes.

***Chord*** A meaningful (as opposed to random) combination of three or more tones. The primary chords in Western European harmonic practice are the tonic (I chord), the subdominant (IV chord), and dominant (V chord).

***Chordophone*** A stringed instrument. The sound producing agent is a stretched string that is plucked or bowed. *See* Appendix B, chordophones.

*Chromatic* Proceeding by halfsteps, using sharps or flats. Notes outside of a standard major or minor scale. A melody is chromatic if many of its pitches are not derived from the standard major or minor scale.

*Combo jazz* A small jazz group, usually from three to six musicians.

*Comping* The syncopated chords and melodic figures played by a jazz pianist while accompanying a solo improvisation, adding rhythmic punctuation and vitality.

*Concerto* A three-movement work for solo instrument and orchestra that emerged during the Baroque period and has been a common instrumental genre ever since. The concerto grosso was an important genre of this period that featured a small group of soloists with orchestra. The arrangement of the movements is fast-slow-fast. Many concertos since the Baroque era include a cadenza, an unaccompanied passage in free rhythm in which the soloist displays his or her greatest virtuosity.

*Conjunct* *See* melody.

*Consonance* A relatively stable, comfortable sound that seems to be at rest as compared with a dissonant, restless sound.

*Consort* A group of like instruments, such as soprano, alto, tenor, and bass recorders, that provide a homogenous sound.

*Context* The social, economic, and political circumstances prevalent in a society that may influence the nature of a creative work.

*Continuo* A technique for providing a harmonic basis in the new homophonic music of the Baroque period. It was a style of accompaniment for a singer or one or two solo instruments. The bass line provided the underlying structure for the harmonies, and it usually was played on a cello. The chords were not completely notated and were improvised on a keyboard instrument, usually a harpsichord. The performer determined what chords to play from the bass line and the figured bass. The figures were numbers below certain notes of the bass line that served as a musical shorthand to indicate the harmonies.

*Contrast* A departure from that which has been presented. A phrase or section that is different from that which preceded it. To achieve contrast, the music will have different tonality, rhythm, melody, tempo, dynamic level, articulation, or mood.

*Cool* An outgrowth of and reaction to the bebop style. Cool jazz arrangers and performers strived to maintain the musical qualities of bebop while making their music more accessible to their audience. They adopted many elements from classical music, including the use of orchestral instruments not commonly used in jazz, such as the flute, oboe, and French horn.

*Counterpoint* The compositional technique of creating polyphonic texture. It is frequently used as a synonym for polyphony. Imitative counterpoint is the creation of two or more independent melodic lines with each entrance beginning with the same melodic shape at the same or a different pitch level.

*Culture* A group of people, a society, characterized by the totality of its arts, beliefs, customs, institutions, and all other products of work and thought.

# D

*Dance suite* A multimovement work for keyboard or orchestra. It includes contrasting, stylized dances popular in the Baroque period. The principal ones are the allemande, courante, sarabande, and gigue.

*Diatonic* The eight tones of a standard major or minor scale. A melody is diatonic if most of its pitches are derived from these eight tones.

*Disjunct* *See* melody.

*Dissonance* An active, unstable sound. *See* consonance.

*Dixieland* The first popular jazz style. It was characterized by group improvisation (clarinet, trumpet, and trombone) supported by a steady ragtime rhythm.

*Dominant* A chord built on the fifth degree of the major or minor scale.

*Duple meter* *See* meter.

*Duration* The length of time a pitch sounds. *See* rhythm.

*Dynamics* The level of loudness. *See* loudness.

# E

*Electrophone* Electronic instruments. The tone is produced, modified, or amplified by electronic circuits. *See* Appendix B, electrophones.

*Ethnic* Pertaining to a group of people recognized as a class on the basis of certain distinctive characteristics, not part of mainstream such as their religion, language, ancestry, culture, or national origin.

*Ethnomusicology* A study of music in culture, considering the context of music in a society, music as it relates to human behavior, and the general attitudes of a people about their music. Ethnomusicologists undertake the research of music in a culture and write and teach others about that culture's music.

# F

*Fasola* A system in which the initial letters of four syllables— fa, sol, la, and mi— are placed on the staff, each representing a different pitch. The fasola system was used in nineteenth-century America to aid in the immediate recognition of scale degrees and in helping people to read musical notation.

*Fiddle tunes* A song from oral tradition used to accompany country dances. The song has a shape and character more appropriate for playing on the fiddle than for singing. Fiddle tunes are frequently played by string bands, bluegrass groups, or solo fiddlers.

*Field recording* A scholarly or professional recording of folk or traditional music made in the environment where the performers typically make music, rather than in a professional recording studio.

*Figured bass* See continuo.

*Fill* Melodic movement and embellishment in jazz while the main melody sustains a tone, such as at the end of a pattern or a phrase.

*Folk music* Usually music of unknown origin, transmitted orally, and enjoyed by the general population. *See* folk art.

*Folk art* Informal, aesthetically and musically unsophisticated music that communicates directly and obviously to large groups within a culture or a subculture, such as a nation or an ethnic minority. It is usually preserved and transmitted by memory (oral tradition).

*Follies* See vaudeville.

*Form* The shape or structure of a piece of music. Form is determined primarily by patterns of contrast and repetition. A two-part form is binary (AB)— no repetition. A three-part form is ternary (ABA)— the first theme or section is repeated after a contrasting phrase or section. A thirty-two-bar song form is aaba, that is, four phrases with the third in contrast to the first two phrases. Other forms include the twelve-bar blues, the verse/chorus or verse/refrain forms, sonata-allegro form, minuet and trio, theme and variations, and rondo.

*Frequency* The rate of speed of sound waves.

*Fuging tune* See psalm singing.

*Fugue* An imitative polyphonic composition that originated as a keyboard genre during the Baroque period. It is, however, a compositional technique used during and since the Baroque in both choral and instrumental music. A fugue is built on a single theme whose entrances appear imitatively in several voices (melodic lines at different pitch levels), usually three or four, and then developed in intricate contrapuntal interplay.

*Fusion* A synthesis of elements of jazz and rock. A style of modern jazz.

# G

*Gagaku* An instrumental music genre of the imperial courts of ancient Japan. It is the oldest documented orchestral music in the world.

*Gamelan* An Indonesian orchestra, particularly from the islands of Bali and Java, that is comprised of various sized drums, metal xylophones, and gongs. Gamelan

music has a long history and has influenced composers of Western classical music as well as jazz and rock performers.

*Genre* A type of music, such as a symphony, hymn, ballad, march, or opera.

*Global perspective* A worldwide point of view, including an awareness of and respect for the life-styles, traditions, values, and arts of nations and cultures.

*Gospel music* Protestant religious music usually associated more with rural, folk roots than with urban, European traditions. American gospel music has evolved in a way that distinct stylistic differences exist between the gospel music of white and black Americans. We now refer to the black gospel and the white gospel styles. White gospel includes camp meeting songs, hymns and songs for revival services, and music from the pentecostal tradition.

*Gregorian chant* See chant.

# H

*Harmony* Pitches heard simultaneously in ways that produce chords and chord progressions.

*Hillbilly* A style of popular song derived from the rural, southern folk tradition and from sentimental songs of the late nineteenth century. It represents a merging of rural and urban influences and a regional, ethnic music made popular nationally and successful commercially.

*Homophony* See texture.

# I

*Idiophone* Percussion instruments that are struck, shaken, plucked, or rubbed. *See* Appendix B, idiophones.

*Impressionism* A style of music, exemplified in the works of Debussy, that avoids explicit statement and literal description, but instead emphasizes suggestion and atmosphere, evokes moods, and conveys impressions of images and feelings.

*Improvisation* The process of simultaneously composing and performing music.

*Intensity* The energy that generates the amplitude or height of sound waves.

*Interval* The difference in pitch between two musical tones.

# J

*Jam session* Where jazz musicians gather, usually "after hours," to improvise and enjoy making music. Because the musicians are not obligated to an employer or a paying audience, they have the freedom to explore and share their musical ideas.

# L

**Lead sheet** A notated melody with chord symbols, usually of a popular song or jazz tune, on which a musical performance is based. A means of structuring a performance in lieu of notating all parts for the entire piece.

**Lead** The soloist in a jazz arrangement or performance.

**Libretto** The words to an opera or other musical stage production. The person who writes the story is the librettist.

Lied *(plural, lieder) See* miniature.

**Lining out** A style of hymn singing whereby a minister or song leader sings one line at a time followed by the congregation singing it back, usually by adding its own individual or collective embellishments and often at a much slower tempo. Lining out is derived from rural, folk traditions and was brought to the United States from the British Isles.

**Loudness** The degree of intensity or energy producing a sound. The loudness or softness of a tone.

**Lyrics** The words to a popular song. The person who writes the lyrics is a lyricist.

# M

**Madrigal** A Renaissance secular contrapuntal work for several voices that originated in Italy and later flourished in England.

**Mainstream** The prevailing characteristics of a society.

**Mariachi** A type of popular Mexican folk music ensemble that includes a harp, violins, various sizes of guitars, and sometimes trumpets.

**Mass** The Roman Catholic worship service. It may be a High Mass or a Low Mass. The High Mass is composed of the Proper and the Ordinary. The Proper varies from Sunday to Sunday throughout the church year. The Ordinary remains the same and is comprised of the Kyrie, Gloria, Credo, Sanctus and Benedictus, and Agnus Dei. Much choral literature has been derived from polyphonic settings of various parts of the Ordinary.

**Melisma** A setting of a text to music wherein one syllable of text is given a series of notes of music. A syllabic setting is one in which one syllable of text is given one note of music.

**Melody** A succession of musical tones usually of varying pitch and rhythm that has identifiable shape and meaning. A melody may be characterized by its smooth, conjunct shape that moves mostly stepwise or its disjunct, angular shape resulting from frequent use of wide intervals (skips). It may be comprised of a wide or a narrow range of pitches.

**Membranophone** A percussion instrument whose sound is produced by the vibration of a stretched membrane, either skin or plastic. *See* Appendix B, membranophones.

**Mestizo** Natives of Mexico and Latin America having mixed Indian and Spanish blood.

**Meter** The organization of rhythm into patterns of strong and weak beats. A pattern in which alternate beats are stressed (strong-weak-strong-weak) is duple meter. A pattern in which every fourth beat is stressed (strong-weak-weak-strong-weak-weak) is triple meter. Each pattern comprises a bar (a measure in notated music). Each strong beat is the downbeat of the bar. Groups of patterns can comprise a phrase (an eight-bar phrase). Combinations of duple and triple (shifting strong beats) is mixed meter. Music is nonmetric if no regular pattern can be perceived.

**MIDI** (Musical Instrument Digital Interface). MIDI is a means for providing electronic communication between synthesizers and computers or other synthesizers. It enables sounds to be stored in memory until needed.

**Miniature** A small-scale composition that became popular in the Romantic era, perhaps as an alternative to the massive size and sounds of the symphony orchestra. It includes the art song (a solo song with piano accompaniment) and the character piece (a one-movement work for solo piano). The art song (commonly known by the German word, lied, or its plural, lieder) is exemplified by the songs of Schubert that he set to German poetry. The character piece is exemplified by the works of Chopin, such as his impromptus, nocturnes, mazurkas, études, polonaises, and preludes.

**Minimalism** A style of composition whose creator attempts to achieve the greatest effect from the least amount of material. It is typically based on many repetitions of simple patterns, creating slow, subtle changes in rhythm, chord movement, or other musical elements. Phillip Glass, a contemporary American composer, is considered the leading exponent of minimalist music.

**Minstrel** A variety show, popular in the nineteenth century, that included songs, dances, and comical skits. Lively, syncopated minstrel songs formed the nucleus of the minstrel show. A product of the merging of rural American folk traditions with urban, composed music, the minstrel song can be considered the first distinctively American musical genre.

**Minuet and trio** A stately dance in triple meter in ABA form. It is found most often as the third movement of a symphony, sonata, or string quartet. A scherzo and trio form is similar, but it has a faster tempo and increased rhythmic energy. The form and function are the same as the minuet and trio.

**Mixed meter** *See* meter.

**Modulation** To change from one tonality to another, frequently by harmonic progression.

**Monophony** *See* texture.

*Motet* A sacred, polyphonic composition with a nonliturgical text. It flourished during the Renaissance and was sung without accompaniment (a cappella) in Latin by trained choirs, typically, in four or five parts. Polychoral motets were written for multiple choirs or choirs divided into two or three distinct groups performing singly (in alternation) and jointly in the full ensemble.

*Motive* A short melodic pattern or phrase that is used for further development and sometimes as the basis of a section of music or a complete composition.

*Motown sound* A style of black popular music derived more from black gospel than blues or jazz traditions. It featured a studio-controlled sound (Motown Records) designed to make black music widely popular and profitable.

*Musical energy* The tendency in some music to have momentum, that is, to move from one point to the next, such as from the beginning of a phrase to its conclusion.

Musique concrète The compositional technique of manipulating tape recorded sounds of existing natural resources. The sounds of recorded instruments, voices, or other sound sources are altered by changing tape speed or direction and by cutting and splicing the tape. These altered sounds, perhaps combined with original sounds, serve as the sound source for an electronic music composition. Edgar Varèse pioneered musique concrète which predated electronically generated or synthesized sounds.

# N

*Nagauta* An ensemble that provides the basic accompaniment on stage in Kabuki theatre, a highly stylized Japanese form of music drama. The ensemble includes perhaps a dozen musicians, including three drums, a flute, several shamisen players, and singers.

*Nashville sound* The sound of hillbilly music produced by sophisticated recording techniques and arrangements controlled by the recording studios to assure the popularity and commercial success of their songs. It minimized the country twang of the singers, reduced the emphasis on fiddle and steel guitar, and included background singers.

*Nationalism* Concert art music that reflects national or regional rather than universal characteristics. The music may describe something derived from the folk or popular traditions of a nation; its history, tales, or legends; its cultural characteristics; or a place that is important to the nation or region. Americanist music or American nationalism refers to composers who sought to develop a distinctively American musical style. They frequently would incorporate familiar patriotic, folk, or religious tunes, or at least fragments of these tunes, in their classical compositions.

*Neoclassicism* A style of modern composition that is based on established forms and structures of the past and particularly on the aesthetics and musical values of the Classic era.

*Nonmetric See* meter.

*Notation* The use of written or printed symbols to represent musical sounds. The notated tradition provides for the preservation and dissemination of music by means of notated music, rather than by memory as in the oral tradition.

# O

*Octave See* interval.

*Opera* A dramatic stage production that involves soloists who sing arias and recitatives, solo ensembles, choruses, dancing, dramatic action, costumes, staging, and orchestral accompaniment. It began at the beginning of the Baroque era and evolved into a genre that continues in popularity throughout the Western world, particularly in Italy.

*Oral tradition* Music learned and passed down by word of mouth as opposed to that which is conveyed in writing.

*Oratorio* An extended, sacred choral work intended for concert performance. It emerged during the Baroque era and has been a common genre since. It is of large proportions, lengthy (many lasting up to three hours), and dramatic in nature, sometimes including the character of a narrator as a soloist. Polyphonic choruses, arias, recitatives, solo ensembles, and orchestral accompaniment are common components of oratorios.

*Ostinato* A rhythmic and/or melodic pattern repeated many times.

*Overture* A festive opening to an opera or other musical stage production. It sets the tone, sometimes identifies principal themes and characters, and prepares an audience for the opening scene. Overtures have become popular concert pieces, sometimes achieving popularity and subsequent performances where the stage production did not. Because of this popularity, many composers have composed overtures as independent concert pieces. In the Baroque era, the French overture was a popular instrumental genre, and in the Romantic period, the concert overture assumed even greater popularity.

# P

*Patterns* Groupings of notes having an identifiable character that, when used repeatedly, help to give form and style to a musical work.

*Pentatonic scale* A five-tone scale that serves as the basis of much music throughout the world.

*Perceptive listening* Listening to music attentively and analytically in an attempt to understand the musical processes and structure that give the music its characteristic qualities.

*Phrase* A section of music with a recognizable beginning and ending. A complete musical thought.

*Pitch* The highness or lowness of a tone produced by a single frequency. Clusters of frequencies produce sounds perceived as registers: high, middle, or low. A melody will have a range of pitches: the lowest pitch to the highest.

*Polychoral motets* See motet.

*Polyphony* See texture.

*Program music* See absolute music.

*Psalm singing* Rhymed, metrical settings of the psalms to hymn tunes suitable for congregational singing. Psalm singing was prevalent in early America. Psalters were the hymn books in which the settings were published with words only or with hymn tunes. A fuging tune was a form of psalm singing popular throughout the eighteenth century. A typical fuging tune was a four-part hymn with a short middle, fugal section where each voice enters at a different time.

*Pulse* The recurring beat of the music.

# R

*Rāga* The basic means by which the melodic or pitch aspects of the classical music of India are determined. Rāgas convey not only melodic shape but mood and aesthetic character, and they provide the basis for extended improvisations. The moods they represent usually are related to temporal elements, such as seasons of the year or times of day (morning or evening rāgas).

*Ragtime* A style of music first popular in the first two decades of the twentieth century. It is characterized by a strongly pulsated, nonsyncopated bass line that supports a highly syncopated right-hand melody. Ragtime remains popular today.

*Range* See pitch.

*Recitative* A vocal solo in opera, cantatas, and oratorios that declaims the text in a sung-speech manner, in free rhythm with minimal accompaniment, so that all listeners can understand the words. It frequently introduces an aria.

*Register* See pitch.

*Repetition* A return to previously stated material. A pattern, phrase, or section that is presented again either exactly or modified but retaining basic characteristics.

*Resolution* See tension.

*Revues* See vaudeville.

*Rhythm* The organization of time in music, creating patterns of long and short durations of pitches to achieve desired degrees of rhythmic energy—the rhythmic impulse.

*Rhythm and blues (R & B)* A style of black popular music that originally featured a boogie woogie-style piano accompaniment in blues form, a blues singer, and electric guitar. Later, R & B symbolized any blues-based black popular music.

*Riff* Short, syncopated patterns usually written for specific groups of instruments in a big band jazz arrangement. Riffs provide punctuated background material while another section or soloist is playing the melody or improvising. Occasionally an entire chorus will be comprised of riffs without a recognizable melody.

*Rock and Roll* An underground, antiestablishment, and protest music that emerged in the 1950s and evolved into a phenomenally successful commercial product. It was derived primarily from a merging of black and white traditions (rhythm and blues and hillbilly) and was a music that appealed mostly to teenagers for both listening and dancing. Influenced by the Beatles, Rolling Stones, Pink Floyd, and other British groups, rock and roll assumed a new character (now known as rock) that featured advanced electronic technology, sophisticated arrangements, and extreme visual impact and on-stage behavior. Rock transformed American popular music and created the study of popular culture.

*Rockabilly* The form of popular music in the 1950s that resulted from the influence of hillbilly singers on the new rock and roll music.

*Rondo* Based on two or more contrasting theme areas, each followed by a return of the opening theme. Common forms of the rondo may be depicted as abaca or abacaba. It is commonly used as the spirited final movement of a Classic era sonata, symphony, or string quartet.

# S

*Salon music* A type of piano music popular throughout the Western Hemisphere during the nineteenth century. Reflecting European practices, salon music was comprised of short, simple pieces published as sheet music and often were created in the style of marches or dances, such as the tango, habanera, conga, polka, bolero, or waltz.

*Sampler* Using MIDI technology, samples of sounds can be recorded and stored in memory to be recalled and performed. The sampled sound is expanded for performance to include the entire range of the keyboard.

*Scale* An ascending or descending series of tones organized according to a specified pattern of intervals.

*Scat singing* Improvised jazz singing using a variety of vocal sounds rather than lyrics. Its purpose is to improvise a vocal solo line in the manner of a lead instrumentalist.

*Score* A printed version of a piece of music. Often refers to the version used by a conductor that depicts the music to be played by all performers—the full score.

*Sections* See big band jazz.

*Sequence* A melodic pattern repeated several times either a step lower or a step higher than the preceding statement.

*Serial composition (twelve-tone technique)*
A set of nonrepeated pitches—a tone row—used as the basis for organizing the vertical and horizontal arrangement of pitches throughout a composition. A system created and refined by Schoenberg, rows originally were comprised of all twelve tones of the chromatic scale. Serialism was created as an alternative to the major/minor tonal system, and it was a means for organizing the chaotic chromaticism prevalent in late nineteenth-century German romantic music and early twentieth-century atonal music. An extension of the twelve-tone technique includes the serialization of note values, timbres, or dynamics. Music in which all these aspects are serialized, including pitch, is known as totally controlled music.

*Shaped-note system* An aid in learning to read music popular in nineteenth-century America. Each pitch of a hymn tune was represented on the staff by a note whose head had a distinctive shape. Each shape represented a specific pitch of the scale.

*Singing schools* Established to introduce and teach singing from musical notation. Their primary purpose was to improve the state of hymn singing in America, that is, to elevate the rural, folk-based hymn derived from oral tradition to the urban, European, notation-based hymn sung in a refined style.

*Sonata* Since the Classic era, a multimovement work for piano or for a solo instrument with piano. The typical order of movements is fast, slow, dance, fast. In the Baroque period, the sonata was a multimovement work written for a solo instrument and continuo, and the trio sonata was written for two solo instruments and continuo.

*Sonata-allegro form* (also sonata form) A structure that composers from the Classic era and since have commonly used for the first movement of a sonata, symphony, concerto, or string quartet (or other similar chamber music work). It includes three main sections: the exposition, development, and recapitulation and often begins with an introduction and ends with a coda. The exposition has two theme areas in contrasting keys. The development is based on material from the exposition. The recapitulation is a return to previous material stated in the exposition.

*Song form* A thirty-two bar aaba chorus (verse). *See* form.

*Soul* An extension of rhythm and blues that has come to symbolize any popular music performed by blacks for black audiences. It combines elements of R & B, jazz, and black gospel.

*Sound source* Any elastic substance capable of generating sound waves that can be perceived as music, such as any conventional band or orchestral instrument, any instrument identified in Appendix B, or any material in the environment used to generate sounds to be incorporated in a piece of music. This material may include pots and pans; taped sounds of water, fire, birds, or whales; or things that people become aware of in a classroom that can be used in an original piece of music.

*Standard* A song that has sustained popularity through decades and generations, transcending changing styles and tastes.

*Strophic* A musical structure in which the same music is used for each stanza of a ballad, song, or hymn.

*Structure* The way in which parts are arranged to form a whole. The form of a piece of music.

*Style* External characteristics of music developed through the creative process that distinguish one piece from another, characteristics that are determined by the composer's use of musical elements, formal design, and emotional expression.

*Subdominant* A chord built on the fourth degree of a major or minor scale.

*Swing* A manner of performance that, in part, separates jazz from other styles of music. It is a manner that generates heightened energy and rhythmic vitality.

*Syllabic setting* *See* melisma.

*Symphonic poem* A programmatic, one-movement work for symphony orchestra with contrasting moods. It became popular during the Romantic period.

*Symphony* A multimovement work for symphony orchestra. The typical order of movements is fast-slow-dance-fast. This pattern was standard in the Classic period but less adhered to in the Romantic and Modern eras.

*Syncopation* The occurrence of accents in unexpected places, usually on weak beats or on weak parts of beats.

# T

*Tāla* The basic means for organizing the durational aspects—the rhythm and meter—of the classical music of India. They involve cycles of counts with regular or irregular subdivisions. For example, a sixteen-count cycle may be subdivided 4 + 4 + 4 + 4 or a fourteen-count cycle may be subdivided 5 + 2 + 3 + 4.

*Tempo* The rate of speed at which music is performed.

*Tension* A perception of instability in traditional Western music that suggests the need for release of tension or resolution. It is often marked by increased harmonic or rhythmic complexity, dissonance, modulation away from the tonic, or a rise in pitch or dynamic level. A lessening of complexity or loudness, a lowering of pitch, a decrease in complexity, a return to consonance or tonic can create stability, resolution, or release of tension.

*Ternary* *See* form.

*Texture* The density of sound. The number of simultaneously sounding lines. Music can have a full, thick texture or a thin, transparent texture. Also, the manner in which the horizontal pitch sequences are organized determine musical texture. A single line melody with no accompaniment or other horizontal or vertical sounds has a monophonic texture; two or more independent, simultaneously sounding melodies having equal emphasis is in polyphonic texture; and a melody that is dominant with other lines supporting the main melody is in homophonic texture.

*Theme and variations* An instrumental form based on a stated theme followed by a series of variations on that theme.

*Timbre* The characteristic quality of the sound of a voice or instrument.

*Tin Pan Alley* A period of popular song writing that began in the 1890s and whose most productive years were in the 1920s and 1930s. Many of America's most beloved songs—the standards—are part of the Tin Pan Alley tradition. Also, Tin Pan Alley symbolized that part of the music industry devoted to the sale of popular songs. The name derived from the street in New York City where virtually every publisher of popular music was located in the early part of the twentieth century.

*Tonality* The gravitational pull of the music towards a tonal center. The key of the music.

*Tone quality* *See* timbre.

*Tone clusters* Three or more adjacent tones sounding simultaneously.

*Tone painting* A technique common in the Baroque period of conveying in the music the moods, emotions, images, and meanings suggested by a text, that is, to mirror the text as literally as possible.

*Tonic* The first and most important note of the major or minor scale. The tonal center of a piece of music.

*Totally controlled music* *See* serial composition.

*Trio sonata* *See* sonata.

*Triple meter* *See* meter.

*Twelve-bar blues* A musical phrase of twelve bars, usually divided into three four-bar segments using a specific set of chord progressions. Some blues melodies have eight or sixteen bars.

*Twelve-tone technique* *See* serial composition.

# U

*Unity* Music that does not ramble, is cohesive, and would have variety and contrast along with repetition and returns to previously stated material.

# V

*Variety* *See* unity.

*Vaudeville* A variety show that was comprised of a sequence of unrelated acts by singers, dancers, comedians, jugglers, child performers, trained animals, and actors. It replaced the minstrel show as America's most popular stage show. New York City was the center of vaudeville, with the more sophisticated shows produced on Broadway. These shows were variously known as revues, vanities, scandals, and follies, of which the most famous were the Ziegfeld Follies produced from 1907 through 1932.

*Verse/chorus* A song in which there are different texts to each verse and a return to the chorus after each verse. *See* form.

*Vibrato* An oscillating variation of pitch that enhances a tone, providing a richness and warmth, particularly to sustained pitches or a slow, lyrical melody.

*Vocables* Words in native-American songs having no meaning and intended only as vocal sounds.

# W

*Walking bass* A jazz bass line played on each beat, frequently with some embellishment, and emphasizing the main tones of the underlying chord structure.

*Western swing* A style of country music that became popular as the popularity of hillbilly music moved westward. It featured a larger instrumental ensemble that includes saxes, brass, and a standard jazz rhythm section.

*White gospel* *See* gospel music.

# Bibliography

## General Sources

Baines, Anthony, ed. *Musical Instruments through the Ages*. London: Faber, 1966.

Hitchcock, H. Wiley, and Stanley Sadie, eds. *The New Grove Dictionary of American Music*. 4 vols. London: Macmillan, 1986.

Marcuse, Sybil. *Musical Instruments: A Comprehensive Dictionary*. New York: Norton, 1975.

Randel, Don Michael, ed. *The New Harvard Dictionary of Music*. Cambridge, Mass.: Belknap Press of Harvard University Press, 1986.

## Vernacular Music

Abrahams, Roger D., and George Foss. *Anglo-American Folk Song Style*. Englewood Cliffs, NJ: Prentice-Hall, 1971.

Brown, Charles T. *The Art of Rock and Roll*. Englewood Cliffs, NJ: Prentice-Hall, 1983.

Courlander, Harold. *Negro Folk Music, USA*. New York: Columbia University Press, 1963.

Feather, Leonard G. *The Encyclopedia of Jazz in the Sixties*. New York: Horizon Press, 1966.

Feather, Leonard G. *The Encyclopedia of Jazz in the Seventies*. New York: Horizon Press, 1976.

Ferris, William, and Mary L. Hart, eds. *Folk Music and Modern Sound*. Jackson, Miss.: University Press of Mississippi, 1982.

Gillett, Charlie. *The Sound of the City*. New York: Outerbridge and Dienstfrey, 1970.

Gridley, Mark C. *Jazz Styles: History and Analysis*. 3d ed. Englewood Cliffs, NJ: Prentice-Hall, 1988.

Haywood, Charles. *Folk Songs of the World*. New York: J. Day Co., 1966.

Jackson, George Pullen. *White Spirituals in the Southern Uplands: The Story of the Fasola Folk, Their Songs, Singings, and "Buckwheat Notes."* Hatsboro, Pa: Folklore Assoc., 1964.

Malone, Bill C. *Southern Music, American Music*. Lexington: University Press of Kentucky, 1979.

Nettl, Bruno. *Folk and Traditional Music of the Western Continents*. Englewood Cliffs, NJ: Prentice-Hall, 1965.

Reynolds, William Jensen. *A Survey of Christian Hymnody*. New York: Holt, Reinhart and Winston, 1963.

Schuller, Gunther. *Early Jazz: Its Roots and Musical Development.* New York: Oxford, 1968.

Stambler, Irwin. *Encyclopedia of Folk, Country, and Western Music.* New York: St. Martin's Press, 1969.

Tirro, Frank. *Jazz: A History.* New York: Norton, 1977.

## World Music

Behague, Gerard. *Music in Latin America, An Introduction.* Englewood Cliffs, NJ: Prentice-Hall, 1979.

Hamm, Charles, Bruno Nettl, and Ronald Byrnside. *Contemporary Music and Music Cultures.* Englewood Cliffs, NJ: Prentice-Hall, 1975.

Idelsohn, A. Z. *Jewish Music in its Historical Development.* New York: Schocken Books, 1967.

Malm, William P. *Japanese Music and Musical Instruments.* Tokyo, Rutland, VT: C. E. Tuttle Co., 1959.

Malm, William P. *Music Cultures of the Pacific, the Near East, and Asia.* Englewood Cliffs, NJ: Prentice-Hall, 1967.

May, Elizabeth, ed. *Musics of Many Cultures: An Introduction.* Berkeley, University of California Press, 1980.

McGee, Timothy. *The Music of Canada.* New York: Norton, 1985.

*My Music Reaches to the Sky: Native American Musical Instruments.* New York: Ford Foundation, 1973.

Nettl, Bruno. *Folk and Traditional Music of the Western Continents.* Englewood Cliffs, NJ: Prentice-Hall, 1965.

Nketia, J. H. *The Music of Africa.* New York: Norton, 1974.

O'Brien, James Patrick. *Non-Western Music and the Western Listener.* Dubuque, IA: Kendall/Hunt, 1977.

Titon, Jeff Todd, ed. *Worlds of Music: An Introduction to the Music of the World's Peoples.* New York: Schirmer, 1984.

Wade, Bonnie C. *Music in India: The Classical Traditions.* Englewood Cliffs, NJ: Prentice-Hall, 1979.

## Western European Classical Music

Austin, William. *Music in the Twentieth Century.* New York: Norton, 1966.

Borroff, Edith. *Music in Europe and the United States: A History.* Englewood Cliffs, NJ: Prentice-Hall, 1971.

Cope, David. *New Directions in Music.* Dubuque, Iowa: W.C. Brown Publishers, 1977.

Grout, Donald Jay. *A History of Western Music.,* New York: Norton, 1980.

Kamien, Roger, ed. *The Norton Scores: An Anthology for Listening.* 2 vols. New York: Norton, 1988.

Longyear, Rey M. *Nineteenth-Century Romanticism in Music.* Englewood Cliffs, NJ: Prentice-Hall, 1973.

Pauly, Reinhard. *Music in the Classic Period.* Englewood Cliffs, NJ: Prentice-Hall, 1973.

Salzman, Eric. *Twentieth-Century Music: An Introduction.* Englewood Cliffs, NJ: Prentice-Hall, 1974.

Schrader, Barry. *Introduction to Electro-Acoustic Music.* Englewood Cliffs, NJ: Prentice-Hall, 1982.

Schwartz, Elliott. *Electronic Music: A Listener's Guide.* New York: Praeger, 1975.

Seay, Albert. *Music in the Medieval World.* Englewood Cliffs, NJ: Prentice-Hall, 1975.

## American Music

Ammer, Christine. *Unsung: A History of Women in American Music.* Westport, Conn.: Greenwood Press, 1980.

Baskerville, David. *Music Business Handbook.* Denver: Sherwood, 1985.

Block, Adrienne Fried, and Carol Neuls-Bates. *Women in American Music: a Bibliography of Music and Literature.* Westport, Conn.: Greenwood, 1979.

Borroff, Edith. *Music in Europe and the United States: A History.* Englewood Cliffs, NJ: Prentice-Hall, 1971.

Chase, Gilbert. *America's Music, from the Pilgrims to the Present.* Westport, Conn.: Greenwood, 1981.

David, Elizabeth A. *Index to the New World Recorded Anthology of American Music.* New York: Norton, 1981.

Hamm, Charles, Bruno Nettl, and Ronald Byrnside. *Contemporary Music and Music Cultures.* Englewood Cliffs, NJ: Prentice-Hall, 1975.

Hamm, Charles. *Music in the New World.* New York: Norton, 1983.

Hitchcock, H. Wiley. *Music in the United States: A Historical Introduction.* Englewood Cliffs, NJ: Prentice-Hall, 1974.

Kingman, Daniel. *American Music: A Panorama.* New York: Schirmer Books, 1979.

Mellers, Wilfrid Howard. *Music in a New Found Land: Themes and Developments in the History of American Music.* New York: Hillstone, 1975.

Shemel, Sidney, and M. William Krasilovsky. *This Business of Music.* New York: Billboard, 1977.

Southern, Eileen. *The Music of Black Americans: A History.* New York: Norton, 1971.

# Photographic Credits

## Chapter 1

**Page 7** *top left:* © Peter Simon/Stock, Boston; *Top middle:* © 1988 Jack Vartoogian; *Top right:* © Bob Daemmrich/Stock, Boston; *Bottom left:* © Vicki Lawrence 1975/Stock, Boston; *Bottom right:* The Bettmann News Photos; **Page 9** *top left:* UPI/Bettmann News Photos; *Top right:* AP/Wide World Photos; *Bottom left:* © Dave Schaefer/The Picture Cube; *Bottom right:* © Sarah Putnam/The Picture Cube.

## Chapter 2

**Page 15:** © Jan Young; **Page 19** *left:* © Richard Wood/ The Picture Cube; *Right:* © Jack Vartoogian; **Page 20:** © Richard Megna, 1984/Fundamental Photographs.

## Chapter 3

**Page 44:** courtesy of Wolf Trap Farm; **Page 46:** Historical Pictures Service, Inc., Chicago; **Page 48** *left:* The Bettmann News Photos; *Right:* © Frederick D. Bodin/ Stock, Boston; **Page 49:** © Mark Lennihan/The Picture Cube; **Page 55:** The Bettmann News Photos; **Page 58:** courtesy of Father Michael Pfleger, Pastor of St. Sabina Church, Chicago.

## Chapter 4

**Page 76:** © Richard Hutchings/Photo Researchers, Inc.; **Page 77:** courtesy of Ray Avery; **Page 78:** © Lionel Delevingne/Stock, Boston; **Page 80:** AP/Wide World Photos; **Page 82** *left:* courtesy of Ray Avery; *Right:* AP/ Wide World Photos; **Page 83:** The Bettmann News Photos; **Page 84** *top left:* © Michael Ochs Archives; *Top right:* AP/Wide World Photos; *Bottom left:* © Sherry Suris/Photo Researchers, Inc.; *Bottom right:* AP/Wide World Photos; **Page 85:** © Steve Kagoon/Photo Researchers, Inc.; **Page 87:** © Louis Ouzer; **Page 88** *top:* courtesy of Tom Capi; *bottom left:* © 1984 Jack Vartoogian; *Bottom right:* courtesy of Passport Designs.

## Chapter 5

**Pages 104, 108** *top:* The Bettmann Archives; *Bottom:* © Charles Klamkin/Old Sheet Music/Hawthorn Books, Inc.; **Page 109:** The Bettmann News Photos; **Page 113:** © Cheryl Higgins 1989/The Decisive Moment; **Page 114** *top left:* AP/Wide World Photos; *Top right:* © Anestis Deakopoulos/Stock, Boston; *Bottom both:* AP/Wide World Photos; **Page 116:** © M. E. Warren/Photo Researchers, Inc.; **Page 117:** © Robert Alexander/Photo Researchers, Inc.; **Pages 118,** *both,* **120:** AP/Wide World Photos; **Page 121:** © Chuck Wyrostock/Appalight.

## Chapter 6

**Page 136:** © Bohdan Hrynewyck/Stock, Boston; **Page 138:** © F. B. Guinzweg/Photo Researchers, Inc.; **Page 139:** Courtesy of Historical Pictures Service, Inc., Chicago; **Page 141** *top:* © Jack Vartoogian; *Bottom:* AP/ Wide World Photos; **Page 143** *top:* © Peter Menzel/ Stock, Boston; *Bottom:* Courtesy of Historical Pictures Service, Inc., Chicago; **Page 145:** © Peter Menzel/Stock, Boston.

## Chapter 7

**Pages 158, 159:** © Jack Vartoogian; **Page 160:** © Katrina Thomas/Photo Researchers, Inc.; **Page 165:** AP/Wide World Photos; **Page 166** *top:* Courtesy of Center for World Music, San Francisco; *Bottom:* © Silverstone/

# Index